Out of his definitive six-volume work on Lincoln and his times, Carl Sandburg has written this superb 430,000 word biography. These volumes have sold over 1,200,000 copies in high-priced editions. Now for the first time they are published in an inexpensive three-volume paperback edition. Here is Volume III, *The War Years (1864-1865)*. Volume I contains *The Prairie Years;* Volume II, *The War Years (1861-1864)*.

CARL SANDBURG was born in Galesburg, Illinois, on January 6, 1878. He graduated from Lombard College in Galesburg, and received honorary degrees from Harvard, Yale, New York University, Northwestern, Knox College, Wesleyan University, Syracuse University, Lafayette, Rollins, Augustana and Dartmouth. At thirty he married Lillian Steichen, sister of the great photographer. He was Secretary to the Mayor of Milwaukee, private in the U.S. Army, newspaper correspondent, editorial writer, film writer, folk song recitalist, poet and Lincoln biographer. In addition to the Pulitzer Prize for Poetry (1950) and the gold medal for history given by the American Academy of Arts and Letters (1952), Sandburg won several literary awards. His published works began with CHICAGO POEMS (1915), REMEMBRANCE ROCK, his only novel, appeared in 1948. ABRAHAM LINCOLN: THE PRAIRIE YEARS was first published in 1926, and THE WAR YEARS in 1939. He died in 1967.

VOLUME III

THE WAR YEARS, 1864-1865

CARL SANDBURG

Abraham Lincoln

THE PRAIRIE YEARS *and* THE WAR YEARS

in three volumes

A Laurel Edition

Published by
Dell Publishing Co., Inc.
1 Dag Hammarskjold Plaza
New York, NY 10017
Copyright, 1954, by Carl Sandburg
Copyright, 1925, 1926, by The Pictorial Review Company
Renewed by Carl Sandburg
Copyright, 1926, by Harcourt Brace Jovanovich, Inc.
Renewed by Carl Sandburg
Copyright, 1939, by Harcourt Brace Jovanovich, Inc.
Copyright, 1936, 1937, 1938, 1939, 1964, 1965, 1966, 1967
by Carl Sandburg
Laurel ® TM 674623, Dell Publishing Co., Inc.
All rights reserved
Reprinted by Arrangement with
Harcourt Brace Jovanovich, Inc.
New York, NY 10017
Printed in U.S.A.
Previous Laurel Edition #4832
New Laurel Edition
First Printing—September 1974
Second Printing—December 1974
Third Printing—June 1975
Fourth Printing—September 1975
Fifth Printing—March 1978
Sixth Printing—May 1981

CONTENTS

VOLUME III—THE WAR YEARS, 1864-1865

Chapter 25

Will His Party Renominate Lincoln?

As the ruthless Republican floor leader, Thad Stevens, kept pushing his program of no mercy to the South, press editorials and street talk of citizens over the North mentioned more often the day when Jefferson Davis and secession leaders would be hanged or shot. Wholesale executions of "rebels" were forecast.

The tone of Congress had an assurance as though the United States would stand for a long time, and there would be in the North a growing World Power, gigantic in commerce and industry from coast to coast. In the South was a deepening courage of despair over the terrorizing possibility that the Confederacy might die, the old South vanish, with its ruling class sunk. One hope still held that the peace party at the North might so weaken the Lincoln administration that in time it would give up the war as hopeless.

To combat those Southern hopes and wear them down was Lincoln's set task. As part of that task he could never afford to lose contact with Congress nor let serious cleavage arise. A worse deliberative body might have been wished on him. He sought the brains and ability there. Reasonable advice, discussion and inquiry, and no tone of faultfinding, stood forth in his papers in the *Congressional Globe* pages so often sprinkled with the item, "A message in writing was received from the President of the United States, by Mr. Nicolay, his Private Secretary." He would communicate a report "in obedience to the resolution of the Senate." He would "earnestly recommend" that a law be modified. He would "invite the early attention of Congress" to a subject. Or he would lay before Congress a letter from an important committee representing four large Northern cities not clear on what should be done for their increasing population of free Negroes. "Not having the time to form a mature judgment of my own as to whether the plan they suggest is the best, I submit the whole subject to Congress, deeming that their attention thereto is almost imperatively demanded."

Early in '64 several newspapers agreed with the Detroit *Free Press* man at Washington: "Not a single Senator can be named as favorable to Lincoln's renomination for President." Any Senator who might want Lincoln for a second term was not making himself heard. On this the Republican party organs were mainly silent.

In the House only one Congressman was definitely committed to Lincoln. A Pennsylvania editor visiting Washington said to Thaddeus Stevens, "Introduce me to some member of Congress friendly to Mr. Lincoln's renomination." "Come with me," said Stevens. He took the editor to Isaac N. Arnold and said: "Here is a man who wants to find a Lincoln member of Congress. You are the only one I know, and I have come over to introduce my friend to you." "Thank you," said Arnold. "I know a good many such and I will present your friend to them, and I wish you, Mr. Stevens, were with us." Thus the scrupulous Arnold recorded the incident.

Mixed motives of Stevens and some of his associates could be gathered from part of a letter of Stevens that year to an intimate, J. B. McPherson: "How little of the rights of war and the law of nations our Pres't knows! But what are we to do? Condemn privately and applaud publicly!"

The only remarks then favoring Lincoln's renomination for President delivered in either Senate or House came from Arnold in the first week of the year and in March. ". . . I ask the ardent and impatient friends of freedom to put implicit faith in Abraham Lincoln. If you deem him slow, or if you think he has made mistakes, remember how often time has vindicated his wisdom. The masses of the people everywhere trust and love him . . . You have a Chief Magistrate . . . sagacious, firm, upright, and true. Somewhat rude and rough, it may be, but under this rough exterior you have the real and true hero . . . Taking the last five years, and Mr. Lincoln has exerted a greater influence upon the popular heart and in forming public opinion than any other man."

Thus Isaac N. Arnold, 49 years old, once a country schoolteacher in New York State, city clerk of Chicago in 1837, practicing attorney of Cook County, put into the *Congressional Globe* an estimate of Lincoln as a hero. Not then nor in many months after did any member of the House or Senate stand up and deliver any similar estimate.

Washburne in November '63 wrote to Lincoln for two executive favors and asking whether the party could count on the President to run for a second term. Lincoln replied that he was enclosing a leave of absence for one of Washburne's brothers from army duty, that to another brother he was tendering the customs collectorship of Portland, Maine, giving Washburne all that was asked for. To this Lincoln added thanks for kind words and intentions, and "A second term would be a great honor and a great labor, which, together, perhaps I would not decline if tendered."

Of Owen Lovejoy in early '64 it should be noted that he was a sick man for months. Lincoln had one note from him saying: "I am gaining very slowly. It is hard work drawing the sled uphill." And Lincoln had repeatedly visited Lovejoy's bedside, once telling the veteran abolitionist: "This war is eating my life out. I have a strong impression that I shall not live to see the end."

"The opposition to Mr. Lincoln," wrote the Indiana Republican Congressman George W. Julian, "was secretly cherished by many of the ablest and most patriotic men of the day . . . Of the more earnest and thorough-going Republicans in both Houses of Congress, probably not one in ten really favored it [his renomination]." No writer of the day laid open clearly the springs and motives of this opposition, or the exact extent of it. Of course, Lincoln had gone too far—or not far enough—in his acts and policies; he was the Man Between. Yet this would not explain why Congress was sore, suspicious, jealous, almost completely silent about his hold on the people. For nearly all political forecasters in early '64 saw the deep popular current over the North with the President. The New York *Herald,* the New York *World,* the Detroit *Free Press,* proclaimed it as an unpleasant fact, while the New York *Times* and other newspapers agreed with the Chicago *Tribune:* "So far as can be gathered, the public generally mean to elect Mr. Lincoln, when the time comes for an election . . . God meant him for President, or the nation is deceived."

A friend of Governor John Andrew of Massachusetts noted that Lincoln's offhand behavior at times had so lowered opinion of him that it was a factor in the secrecy that enveloped the choice of a President in '64. This secrecy, also noted Governor Andrew's friend, "is something marvelous; there were so many concerned in it; when it *all* comes out, it will make a curious page in the history of the time." He wrote:

> . . . reports from Washington in 1863 did impute a frivolity of language and demeanor in the President, which could not but offend many earnest men . . . There was a characteristic anecdote related . . . The legislature has been famous for passing resolutions against slavery . . . a committee brought in a resolve in the fewest words possible.
>
> A friend of the Governor, who also held an official position, desired to present it personally to the President. It was accordingly written on parchment, with the great seal annexed, and plenty of red tape. Arrived in Washington, the messenger by appointment met the President at eleven o'clock the next day, to present this resolve of the Commonwealth of Massachusetts.
>
> The Chief Magistrate of the nation sat in an armchair, with one leg over the elbow, while the emissary of Massachusetts presented the parchment with a little speech.
>
> The President took the document, slowly unrolled it, and remarked in a quaint way, "Well, it isn't long enough to scare a fellow!" It is not remarkable that the Massachusetts official said as he left the room, "That

is certainly an extraordinary person to be President of the United States!"

Thus one incident drawing Andrew toward the anti-Lincoln movement. It was ominous. For Andrew rated as no mere ordinary politician riding the antislavery bandwagon. He had raised troops and funds with a loyalty hardly equaled by any other state governor. He was spoken of by friends as a hope for the Presidency because of clean, rugged manhood he carried. Located in the antislavery crusade's most active center, surrounded by good men impatient with the President's slowness on that issue, Governor Andrew was looking elsewhere than to Lincoln for a Chief Magistrate. He wrote just after the President issued the Emancipation Proclamation, "It is a poor document, but a mighty act, slow, somewhat halting, wrong in its delay until January, but grand and sublime after all." Andrew sat on Beacon Hill now, a square-built, deep-chested man, curly hair topping his round head, a face smooth with kindliness, almost boyishly cherubic, his eyes peering from behind spectacles, wanting results out of his loyal toiling, decisions quicker than Lincoln could give them.

In early February Lyman Trumbull wrote to H. G. McPike of Alton, Illinois: "The feeling for Mr. Lincoln's reelection *seems* to be very general, but much of it I discover is only on the surface. You would be surprised, in talking with public men we meet here, to find how few, when you come to get at their real sentiment, are for Mr. Lincoln's reëlection. There is a distrust and fear that he is too undecided and inefficient to put down the rebellion. You need not be surprised if a reaction sets in before the nomination, in favor of some man supposed to possess more energy and less inclination to trust our brave boys in the hands and under the leadership of generals who have no heart in the war. The opposition to Mr. L. may not show itself at all, but if it ever breaks out there will be more of it than now appears."

The warm kindliness of the New York *Evening Post* had veered into a slight chill: "We deprecate the agitation of a

Presidential nomination as premature . . . a great and important work is yet to be done before we can distinguish the man likely to be approved by the people or who is most worthy to be intrusted with the administration of the government during the next four years."

In a one-column editorial in mid-February '64 Greeley sounded a Joshua ram's horn blast that he hoped would send Lincoln's Jericho walls toppling. Did Mr. Lincoln so overtop all other candidates that no others should be considered? "We answer in the negative," wrote Greeley. "Heartily agreeing that Mr. Lincoln has done well, we do not regard it as at all demonstrated that Gov. Chase, Gen. Frémont, Gen. Butler, or Gen Grant, cannot do *as* well." In reprinting this one-column blast of Greeley, the Chicago *Tribune* credited "its preliminary remarks" as of no account, "being merely the flourish of Greeley's knife before he stabs," editorially estimating Lincoln's ability "at least equal, if not superior to that of any man likely to be elected."

The Republicans had five candidates for President whom the New York *World* set down "in the order of their availability and probable chances": Abraham Lincoln, Salmon P. Chase, John C. Frémont, Nathaniel P. Banks, Benjamin F. Butler. To defeat Lincoln would be simply to nominate Chase, deduced the *World*. "Only the adherents of Chase have any interest in thwarting Lincoln."

Ben Butler hovered available. Chase men offered him second place with their guiding star, Butler smiling that he might yet take Richmond and come thundering home in first place on the Union ticket. Sumner's availability was hinted at slightly. And Sumner's secretary, the studious and scrupulous Edward L. Pierce, recorded Sumner's "distrust of Mr. Lincoln's fitness for his place."

Senators and Congressmen joining in this anti-Lincoln movement had nearly all been handed their share of patronage by the President. He had met them more than halfway in policies of emancipation and arming the Negro. This worried Thurlow Weed in New York, who once wrote to Judge David Davis, "They will all be against him in

1864, why does he persist in giving them weapons to defeat his renomination?"

With a touch of dawn maroon and a faint odor of forget-me-nots, Miss Anna Elizabeth Dickinson flitted into the Washington scene pro-Lincoln and faded out anti-Lincoln. She had won name as a Girl Orator, had developed gifts of swift and withering sarcasm, had nursed and brought along an eloquence that made her a torch of promise to thousands who had heard her on the platform. Her chestnut curls cut close to her clean-shapen head, her virginal beauty, her symmetrical figure, her complete self-possession, her contralto fullness of voice, her discussions of momentous issues beginning gravely and flowing into sudden passionate appeals for the redemption of mankind and the holiness of human freedom—these had brought comparisons of her with the Maid of Orleans who saved France when all others despaired.

She was just past 21 when on January 16, 1864, she spoke in the hall of the House of Representatives, Speaker Colfax sitting on her right hand, Vice-President Hamlin on her left, the President on a bench farther in the foreground, the affair bringing $1,031 for the Freedmen's Relief Association. "How, to such youthful lips, flowed so easily such stately language!" wrote N. P. Willis. Others called it just another stump speech. She referred to the President as though he should be renominated and re-elected. Said the Detroit *Free Press* one day, "The strong-minded Anna Dickinson has renominated the weak-minded Abraham Lincoln."

Two months later Miss Dickinson, in Metropolitan Hall in Chicago, ran on to say that the President's Amnesty Proclamation was a piece of Northern meanness and a usurpation of the functions of Congress: "The President is a lawyer, and a Western one at that; it is a wonder he does not know that the oaths of such men [reconstructed rebels] are but as idle wind . . . These men must be punished. South Carolina should be cut up into twenty acre lots, and as many negroes settled on them as can be got there."

A month later Miss Dickinson called at the White House,

interviewed the President, then went to Boston and in a public lecture satirized the administration and caricatured Lincoln, his twang and his clothes, as she reported her interview. He had said to her: "They tell me you are on my side. I want to know how it is." She told him his emancipation policy was not moving fast enough and pleaded for justice to the Negro.

The President answered, "That reminds me of a story." She had to reply: "I did not come here to hear stories. I can read better ones in the papers any day than you can tell me." He showed her his correspondence with officials in Louisiana and asked her what she thought of his plan of reconstruction there. She replied, "Sir, I think it all wrong; as radically bad as can be." The President then "sugar-plummed" her, as Miss Dickinson phrased it. He told her she could talk better than he, and so forth. Ending their conversation, he remarked, "All I can say is, if the radicals want me to lead, let them get out of the way and let me lead." And, said Miss Dickinson to her Boston audience, "When he said that, I came out and remarked to a friend, 'I have spoken my last word to President Lincoln.'"

From speech to speech Wendell Phillips went on, graphic and simple, and however mistaken and however heady, with a peculiar joy in being temperamentally stubborn. He debonairly justified himself: "Mr. Lincoln is a growing man. And why does he grow? Because we water him."

The bland, bald, large-mouthed William Lloyd Garrison stood up. He had helped nurse the abolition movement, had gone to jail for it, had in one hour stood with a rope around his neck while a mob howled around him—all before young Phillips had enlisted in the cause. "Has not the President," asked the old war horse, "gone as fast and as far as the people would sustain him? ('No, no.') Mr. Lincoln has travelled as fast toward the negro as popular sentiment would warrant him. Butler and Grant have sustained the President's policy. ('No, no, no.') And what about Frémont? Events have occurred within a year greatly to diminish my faith in Frémont. Not a word from him in reference to the President's proclamation of amnesty. What a glorious opportunity was there lost! Then we have had the arming of one hundred thousand blacks, and still not one word of encouragement from Frémont."

Plainly, to the upper circles of Plymouth Church, Brooklyn, the answer was Frémont and nobody else. And it was nothing to talk about in Plymouth Church circles that a son of Henry Ward Beecher, not yet of age, had been commissioned an officer in the Army of the Potomac and, caught in conduct unbecoming to an officer, had been forced to resign. In anxiety and shame Beecher had gone to his handsome young friend, Theodore Tilton, who in turn went straight to the then Secretary of War Cameron and begged for a commission in the Regular Army for young Beecher. From Cameron, Tilton went to the White House and Lincoln signed the appointment of young Harry Beecher, lieutenant of artillery, Regulars.

Wrote Beecher to Chase of the President: "His mind works in the right *directions*, but seldom works clearly and cleanly. His bread is of unbolted flour, & much straw, too, mixes in the bran, & sometimes gravel stones." Beecher had written in the *Independent:* "The President seems to be a man without any sense of the value of time . . . Our armies have been managed as if they were a body of nurses in a foundling hospital."

Early in '64 the New York *World* presented General McClellan as the one man of worth, dignity and patriotism for nomination by the Democratic party to overwhelm Lincoln. In this effort the *World* served financial, industrial and transportation interests represented in politics by Erastus Corning and Dean Richmond of the New York Central Railroad; by William Henry Aspinwall of the New York-to-San Francisco steamship lines and the Panama Isthmus 49-mile railway which up to 1859 had netted him a fortune of $6,000,000; and more directly and dominantly by August Belmont, politically and financially the most eminent Jew in America.

Born in a rich landholding family in Rhenish Prussia in 1816, Belmont at 14 had worked without pay as office boy, swept and dusted the rooms of the powerful banking firm of Rothschild Brothers in Frankfort while learning finance. In the panic year 1837 he set up in New York his own banking house of August Belmont & Company, his great asset being the agency for the Rothschilds in America. Becoming a U.S. citizen, Belmont served on foreign missions, was U.S. Minister to Holland, championed Stephen A. Douglas at the 1860 Baltimore convention, saw himself chosen chairman of the national Democratic committee. He wore side whiskers, owned ponies and enjoyed horse races, collected rare porcelains and masterpieces of painting. And Belmont had anger and courage, for in 1841 he had fought, because of a woman, a duel at Elkton, Indiana, with William Hayward of South Carolina, took a bullet wound and thereafter walked through life with a limp. After an interview with Lincoln and Seward, Belmont had gone to Europe and quietly warned financial circles that the Southern Confederacy was not a good business risk, wreaking practical damage to the South under cover. From England he transmitted to Lincoln a short message he had from an interview with Palmerston: "We do not like slavery, but we need cotton, and hate your Morrill protective tariff."

Belmont had helped raise and equip the first regiment of German troops enlisted in New York City. As a Union man through the war he had run somewhat the course of Governor Seymour. He had sent on to Washington an extract from a letter written at New Orleans, expecting it would be shown to Lincoln. "The time has arrived when Mr. Lincoln must take a decisive course," it read. "Trying to please everybody, he will satisfy nobody." And Lincoln in a long letter to Belmont had urged that his reconstruction policy was clear for those who would read and understand rather than write complaining letters northward. "Broken eggs cannot be mended; but Louisiana has nothing to do now but to take her place in the Union as it was, barring the already broken eggs. The sooner she does so, the smaller will be the amount . . . past mending."

Belmont joined with Aspinwall in belief that McClellan was a "genius" and, as President, would manage to save the

Union without entanglement on the slavery issue. With Seymour he stood for a party policy of unmistakable opposition to the Republicans in power; otherwise the Democratic party would be swallowed and cease to exist in a proposed new National Union party foreshadowed by Lincoln and Weed.

Manton Marble, publisher of the New York *World,* was ably meeting the wishes of Belmont, who was credited with financially backing the newspaper. No other newspaper, not even the New York *Herald,* so incessantly cried down Chase and Federal money affairs on its financial page. They directly insinuated that by advance knowledge of money measures Chase and others were piling up fortunes for themselves. That Chase was in debt, and had to manage carefully to pay small loans from time to time, could never be known to those who believed half they read in the *World*'s financial page.

The President had ended free speech and a free press in America, the *World* said in April, being itself free to say: "In the knots of two or three which sometimes gather, Mr. Lincoln's stories quite as often occupy the time as the momentous interests of a great nation, divided by traitors, ridden by fanatics and cursed with an imbecility in administration only less criminal than treason."

The *World* made public, now nearly two years after its writing, McClellan's letter handed to Lincoln at Harrison's Landing, Virginia, in 1862, in which McClellan unfolded for Lincoln his ideas on how the country ought to be run. On the slavery issue he was not merely reserved but noncommittal: he would not interfere with the institution, it seemed, but he threw no light on what form of compromise could be made with it. Still he held to his declaration: "The Constitution and the Union must be preserved, whatever may be the cost in time, treasure and blood."

Lincoln's darkly solemn letter of April 4 to A. G. Hodges of Kentucky staggered many readers. Hodges with other Border State men had interviewed Lincoln. Lincoln at Hodges' request put into writing, for the country to read, what he had told them face to face in the White House: "I am naturally anti-slavery. If slavery is not wrong, nothing is wrong. I can not remember when I did not so think, and feel." He went on: "I claim not to have controlled events, but confess plainly that events have controlled me." This had the opposition hard put for pertinent comment. Something in it was as basic and strange as the House Divided speech. "Now, at the end of three years struggle the nation's condition is not what either party, or any man devised, or expected. God alone can claim it. Whither it is tending seems plain. If God now wills the removal of a great wrong, and wills also that we of the North as well as you of the South, shall pay fairly for our complicity in that wrong, impartial history will find therein new cause to attest and revere the justice and goodness of God."

An old question bothered Senators and Congressmen and found its way into editorials. The *World* on February 11, 1864, headed one: "Ought a President to Re-elect Himself?" In a sentence in Lincoln's '61 inaugural address, said the one-term advocates who were becoming vocal, it could be seen that the President had pledged himself to one term and no more. That sentence ran, "I now enter upon the same task [as fifteen previous Executives] for the brief constitutional term of four years, under great and peculiar difficulty." Entirely aside from this point, Chase held it had now become an American tradition that the President should not serve a second term; for 30 years no President had served two terms, and the custom was established. Chase wrote this in many letters.

Those favoring the one-term tradition from week to week could glean no satisfaction from Lincoln personally. He had nothing, not even an anecdote, about a second term. Until he should say he was a candidate they were up a row of stumps. He was waiting. What he was waiting for he did not say. Swett noted, "Lincoln kept an eye out for the spot where the lightning was going to strike and tried to be on that spot." Lincoln's belief in lightning was allied to his belief in luck, to his sleep-visioned nature, to the superstitious element, the will of Providence, the dreaming bones that swayed him in vaster matters.

The grinding drama of drums and blood and agony went on. Three years of these rocking lines of destroyers seeking each other and unable to destroy to an end. Three years of it and no foreteller had foretold it as it happened. "God alone can claim it." Inexorable laws and deep-running forces of human society and national life had operated. Any one man in their midst had better count himself of small moment in the blood and slime of the hour. Could it be an hour to step out and form combinations and huckster a candidacy with an eye on November next? Before November would come terrific decisions of men with snarling guns and plunging bayonets. Beyond and out there where men lay rolled in their gray blankets by the bivouac fire under frost or falling rain or white moon—out there lay the dictates of the November election, the action that would sway the November voters.

When Lincoln was actually in a political campaign, as Swett saw him, he never believed in going out to line up factions and interests in his favor. He kept hands off. "I believe he earnestly desired that nomination. He was much more eager for it than he was for the first, and yet from the beginning he discouraged all efforts on the part of his friends to obtain it."

Swett, who had performed confidential errands too delicate to record in telegrams or letters, in Washington in the early months of '64 noted that for a year and more the adversaries of Lincoln had been at work for themselves. "Chase had three or four secret societies and an immense patronage extending all over the country. Frémont was constantly at work, yet Lincoln would never do anything either to hinder them or to help himself." Swett threw his light on how Lincoln managed campaigns by ignoring men and by ignoring all small causes, but by closely calculating the tendencies of events and the great forces which were producing logical results.

The hard-drinking Governor Dick Yates of Illinois early in '64 saw that he belonged politically in the deeper-running Lincoln current, saying in Bryan Hall, Chicago: "It is no use, as I heard a friend of mine say today; the politicians may try to fix it up, but the people will have Old Abe and nobody else. (Applause.) I must confess I am for him first, last and all the time. (Applause.) It is no time to change fronts when you are in the presence of the enemy . . . I stand up here to say that from long acquaintance with him, he is not only one of the honestest men that God ever made, but in clear, cool, statesmanlike judgment, he is without a peer in the history of the world."

Lincoln held no mood fixed and frozen. His eye caught light and shadow, color and mass, in the flow and heave of a reality he termed Public Opinion. His moods ranged with those of the People in a democracy that in spite of war kept a wide measure of freedom in personal expression.

Conscience and expediency told him, rightly or wrongly, for weal or woe, that he himself in justice should continue to be the instrument of the American people to finish the war, and if it might be, to bind up the wounds and heal the scars without malice. Anxiety weighed him down in these moods. Deep gongs rang. He referred to himself as well as Chase, Frémont and Butler in the remark that J. Russell Jones, Provost Marshal General James Fry and Congressman John Kasson said they heard from him as to the desire to be President: "No man knows what that gnawing is till he has had it."

Without a doubt, too, Lincoln felt a loyalty due from him to the people who trusted him, who saw logic and sense in what he was doing, who were afraid to try some other man as President. It was to them Lincoln's Government and Lincoln's Army that held the boys and men from so many homes. Father Abraham was not merely a nickname. He cared. They trusted him as he trusted them. There was this kinship between him and a certain legion of loyalists. He seemed to reason that if they wanted him to go on as President they would have their way—and if they didn't want him, he could stand that if they could.

He heard from his legion often, once in March '64 when the Chicago *Tribune* carried an editorial paragraph: "A sturdy farmer from Oskaloosa, Iowa, one of the bone and sinew class, called upon us yesterday in relation to business matters. Before leaving, we asked him how Mr. Lincoln stood in Iowa. 'Stands?' said the old farmer, with glistening eyes and raising his brawny fist, 'Old Abe stands seventeen feet higher in Iowa than any other man in the United States!' "

A like enthusiasm was found by a Cincinnati *Gazette* writer who in February interviewed John Bright. He quoted this leading English liberal as saying that the re-election of Lincoln would be the hardest blow the North could inflict on the South that year. Bright refused to worry over what he heard of Lincoln as too slow, though he believed a change of Cabinet should be demanded, adding, "Mr. Lincoln is like a waiter in a large eating house where all the bells are ringing at once; he cannot serve them all at once, and so some grumblers are to be expected."

In February '64 the New York *Herald*'s satirically excessive compliments meant to carry barbs: "As a joker Mr. Lincoln is unique. With the caustic wit of Diogenes he combines the best qualities of all the other celebrated jokers of the world. He is more poetical than Horace, more spicy than Juvenal, more anecdotal than Aesop, more juicy than Boccaccio, more mellow than rollicking Rabelais, and more often quoted than the veteran Joe Miller." The idea was that a clown ran the Government. To seven sarcastic reasons why Lincoln should be a candidate again the New York *World* added, "He writes worse English than any President we ever had," and he surpassed in stories "from the broad smutty to the diluted Joe Miller."

The New York *Evening Post* served Lincoln in April by printing on page one a column and more of Lincoln stories and anecdotes. They rendered none of Lincoln's ease in dialect and of course could not carry his personal mimicry and facial mobility.

Not yet was there a photograph of a smiling Lincoln. A face "woebegone" the Quaker boy, Sergeant Spradling, saw at the White House and saw again in waking moments between sleeps at night for days afterward.

While the army had its quota always of deserters, stragglers and malingerers, the mass of sentiment there plainly favored "Old Abe." Thousands of soldier letters written home told this. Letters of protest and murmuring were few in comparison. A veteran on furlough spoke in Chicago on whether the soldiers wanted Lincoln re-elected. He cocked his eyes with a reckless glint: "Why, of course they do. We all re-enlisted to see this thing through, and Old Abe must re-enlist too. He mustered us in and we'll be damned if he shan't stay where he is until he has mustered us out. We'll never give up till every rebel acknowledges he is the Constitutional President . . . I don't give a cuss for this country if the beaten side has a right to bolt after an election; it would not be fit to live in."

Harriet Beecher Stowe having words for what moved her, wrote for the January number of the *Watchman and Reflector* of Boston, with flow and stride:

> The world has seen and wondered at the greatest sign and marvel of our day, to-wit, a plain working man of the people, with no more culture, instruction or education than any such workingman may obtain for himself, called on to conduct the passage of a great people through a crisis involving the destinies of the whole world . . .
>
> Lincoln's strength is of a peculiar kind; it is not aggressive so much as passive, and among passive things it is like the strength not so much of a stone buttress, as of a wire cable. It is strength swaying to every influence, yielding on this side and on that to popular needs, yet tenaciously and inflexibly bound to carry its great end; and probably by no other kind of strength could our national ship have been drawn safely thus far during the tossings and tempests which beset her way.
>
> Surrounded by all sorts of conflicting claims, by traitors, by half-hearted, timid men, by Border State men and free State men, by radical Abolitionists and Conservatives, he has listened to all, weighed the words of all, waited, observed, yielded now here and now there, but in the main kept one inflexible, honest purpose, and drawn the national ship through.

Justice David Davis, his ear to the winds of gossip and change, wrote to a brother-in-law: "The politicians in and out of Congress, it is the current belief, would put Mr. Lincoln aside if they dared. They know their constituents don't back them, and hence they gamble rather than make open war." Seeing itself in a losing contest to nominate General Grant, the New York *Herald* crawfished. "Mr. Lincoln will be the regular nominee of his party. He is in the field and has the reins of the party in his hand. He will enter the canvass as the embodiment of all the blunders, follies, and corruptions of his administration."

Henry C. Work of Chicago added another song to his "Kingdom Coming" and "Wake, Nicodemus"—titled "Washington and Lincoln." One gave the country independence, the other saved the Union and set a people free, said the song. The lines were flamboyant. The cohorts of August Belmont and the New York *World* frowned at it. To them it was flapdoodle. Yet the song strode. As poetry it was so-so. As the offering of Henry C. Work, among greatests of popular song writers, it had import.

Francis Bicknell Carpenter, portrait painter, wished to give his public a momentous historic setting for Lincoln. A rich lawyer friend assured Carpenter six months' income for work on his vision, and Speaker Colfax and Congressman Lovejoy recommended him to the President. Carpenter at a White House reception heard Lincoln with a twinkle of the eye, playfully, "Do you think, Mr. Carpenter, that you can make a handsome picture of *me?*" In his office he said, "Well, Mr. Carpenter, we will turn you loose in here, and try to give you a good chance to work out your idea." In the painting the Cabinet members were to be seated and standing around the President seated at a table, in their midst at the exact center of the design that world-famous parchment, the Emancipation Proclamation. This was the idea Carpenter outlined.

The 37-year-old painter was given the run of the White House, assigned the state dining room with its big chandeliers for lighting his night work, which sometimes lasted till daylight. Carpenter sat with his sketchbook in the President's office, worried visitors hearing from the President, "He is but a painter." At Cabinet meetings Carpenter sketched, the President having explained, "He has an idea of painting a picture of us all together."

More than once Carpenter walked the streets of Washington late at night with Lincoln, no escort or guard. In the temporary studio of sculptor Swayne in the Treasury Building, Lincoln sat for a bust, replying to a query from Swayne that he did not write the verses "Why Should the Spirit of Mortal Be Proud?" though they were often signed with his name. When Carpenter asked for it Lincoln recited the poem.

Carpenter told the President of a New York *Tribune* account, from a correspondent within the Confederate lines, of an elaborate conspiracy worked out in Richmond to kidnap the President, or if kidnaping failed to assassinate him. Lincoln asked for the details, which Carpenter gave him. He smiled as though he could not believe it, "Well, even if true, I do not see what the Rebels would gain by killing or getting possession of me. I am but a single individual, and it would not help their cause or make the least difference in the progress of the war. Everything would go right on just the same." Ever since his nomination at Chicago the regular installment of threats came in the week's mail, and they no longer bothered him, he informed Carpenter. This surprised him, said the young painter. "Oh," said Lincoln, "there is nothing like getting *used* to things!"

On the evening of the day Lincoln reviewed Burnside's corps, Governor Curtin came with a friend to the President's office. And in their talk Curtin referred to the volunteer citizen soldier as "worthy of profound respect." Lincoln gave quiet assent, Carpenter noting a "peculiar dreaminess" creep over his face, as if he could not find words should he try to speak his heart about volunteers his heart knew.

Carpenter made himself at home in the White House, kept busy on his big painting, saw the President and Cabinet on and off parade. He told Lincoln of odd happenings and Lincoln replied with stories, none of which offended him, said the conventional Carpenter. Carpenter repeated Lincoln stories, correcting vocabulary at times, making the words nicer. Where Lincoln said "skunks" or "polecats" in a story, Carpenter, in retelling it, said "those little black and white spotted animals which it is not necessary to name."

While Carpenter wrestled with his work of art the New York *Herald* and other newspapers printed a story that Mrs. Lincoln came in one day to watch him with his paints and brushes and saluted him, "Well, Mr. Carpenter, how are you getting along with your happy family?"

Carpenter in February called on Lovejoy, saw him sit up and take nourishment, saying he was better, not knowing he had only three months to live. On his death Lincoln said to Carpenter, "Lovejoy was the best friend I had in Congress."

Several Copperhead editors made peculiar comment when Lovejoy died. They saluted him as a true man holding mistaken ideas. Underlying these salutations it could be seen that these Copperhead editors divided antislavery men into genuine heroes and counterfeit, true crusaders and bogus.

And to the end Lovejoy, his once magnificent physical frame nearly used up, burned with a loyalty to the President. According to Carpenter, his words ran: "I tell you, Mr. Lincoln is at heart as strong an antislavery man as any of them, but he is compelled to *feel* his way . . . His mind acts slowly, but when he moves, it is *forward*. You will never find him receding from a position once taken. It is of no use talking, or getting up conventions against him. He is going to be the candidate and is sure to be reëlected. 'It was foreordained from the foundation of the world.' "

The dying Lovejoy was writing in a letter to Garrison February 22, 1864, "I write you, although ill-health compels me to do it by the hand of another, to express to you my gratification at the position you have taken in reference to Mr. Lincoln. I am satisfied, as the old theologians used to say in reference to the world, that if he is not the best conceivable President he is the best possible."

Chapter 26

Jay Cooke — Cash for War..—
Hard Times and Flush

The Union Government was spending easily more than $2,000,000 a day for the war. Chase had reason to say that while the other departments stood at the spigots he had to worry about the barrel. Lincoln met the wishes of Chase in many delicate particulars of appointments, arrangements, measures, that would bring in the cash to keep the war going.

In offices across the street from the Treasury Building Jay Cooke & Company hung up their sign. In January '64 this company finished the selling of $513,000,000 worth of U.S. bonds, the issue being oversubscribed, so that Congress had to act in order to legalize the millions over the half-billion. The commission of Jay Cooke on these immense sales was ¼ of 1 per cent, out of which he paid the costs of a large sales force and advertising space in hundreds of newspapers. He had persistently refused offers of Chase to appoint him an Assistant Secretary of the Treasury, his title being merely U.S. Subscription Agent.

The bond-selling campaigns of Cooke under Chase's authority satisfied Lincoln to the extent that he kept his hands off, seeing Cooke only two or three times during many months. Once Cooke had finished breakfast with Chase when a servant announced the President at the door in a carriage with Attorney General Bates. The Secretary went out to the carriage and learned that Cabinet members and their ladies were going that day to a drill review of 10,000 men seven miles beyond Georgetown. Chase begged to be excused. Lincoln insisted on Chase's going and told him to bring Cooke along. As they rode across the country Cooke noticed the President enjoying the holiday. Cooke got to looking at Bates' head of black hair with white whiskers and mustache and said to Bates that his own father had been just like that, not a gray hair in his head but when he grew a beard it always came out white. Cooke said he wondered what was the philosophical and scientific explanation. And according to Cooke, Lincoln gave a quizzical look at Bates and said, "Oh, Mr. Cooke, that is easily accounted for." "I shall be glad to know the reason." "Well, it could hardly be otherwise. The cause is that he uses his jaws more than he does his brain."

Also, Cooke noted, "We all laughed heartily at this impromptu and original joke at Mr. Bates' expense and, as I gave the substance of it to some newspaper men the next day it was published far and wide as one of Lincoln's original sayings."

Jay Cooke's father, Eleutheros Cooke, had built the first stone house in the new town of Sandusky, Ohio, and practicing law, launching a railroad with horse-drawn cars, sitting in Congress at Washington, never lacked fluency of speech. Young Jay read his father's speeches in the *Congressional Globe*, built a 16-inch-long steamboat propelled by power from an old clock spring, took a hand in defending a Negro bootblack from the attacks of other debating-society members who said they could not allow a Negro to listen to their discussions. Jay had clerked in a store, studied bookkeeping, traveled to St. Louis where he again clerked in a store, practiced penmanship in a night school. In Philadelphia, again a clerk, he rose to be at 21 a partner and active manager of E. W. Clark & Company, the largest private banking house in the United States. He married Dorothea Elizabeth Allen, the daughter of a Maryland planter and slaveowner, and she bore him two sons and two daughters.

When the house of E. W. Clark & Company crashed in the 1857 panic, Jay Cooke went in for railroad reorganization, joined the best canals of Pennsylvania into one system. In 1861 he had his own banking house in Philadelphia and introduced himself to the U.S. Treasury officials by sending on Federal loan subscriptions without compensation. Early that year he won national reputation and the gratitude of Governor Curtin by selling at par $3,000,000 in bonds issued by Pennsylvania, which was almost bankrupt.

Both Lincoln and Chase were responsive to the advice of Jay Cooke transmitted through his brother Henry: "I would advise Gov. Chase . . . to keep on the right side of those capitalists who are disposed to dabble in the loans, etc., of the government, and if they do make sometimes a handsome margin it is no more than they are entitled to in such times as these. They can be very useful to the government. I repeat that the Governor should keep on the right side of the capitalists till he gets into smoother water."

The New York *Herald* soon was saying that a delegation of the bankers had appeared in Washington making no secret of their errand of notifying the President that his management of the war had incurred their displeasure, and as they were paying the costs of it, they had come to recommend to him changes in his policy.

Congressman Kellogg stood up to say: "We have summoned the youth; they have come. I would summon the capital; and if it does not come voluntarily, before this republic shall go down or one star be lost I would take every cent from the treasury of the states, from the treasury of capitalists, from the treasury of individuals and press it into the use of the government."

Jay Cooke's plan was to go over the heads of the bankers and reach the small investors, the masses of people who could buy a $100 bond or more, the very ranks from which the bankers got their depositors. His drive got under way in the spring of '63 to sell $500,000,000 of five-twenties, bonds paying 6 per cent interest for 20 years or redeemable in government gold within five years. The newspaper campaign of direct advertising, informative news accounts and editorial comment on the five-twenty bonds that Jay Cooke set going was the most far-reaching, deliberately organized affair of the sort that America had ever seen. At one time 1,800 daily and weekly journals were printing paid advertising. Disloyal sheets that hated the Lincoln administration and all its works could not bring themselves to hate Jay Cooke's cash to the extent of not printing live news, which he sent them fresh from the hands of his large staff of skilled writers.

The telegraph bill ran over $40 a day. From the first weeks, when subscriptions varied from less to more than $1,000,000 a day, on into later weeks when the daily totals were from $2,000,000 to $6,000,000, the drive of Jay Cooke's vision and bustling energy spread out and animated the philosophy of the North. Foreign-language newspapers were brought in. They too published in German, Italian, Yiddish, Polish, advertisements explaining the five-twenty bonds.

Thus Jay Cooke—with Chase backing him and Lincoln backing Chase—put the impress of his personality on the country, outranking Greeley, Beecher and Barnum in his ability to get action from masses of people. His news writers were quick to relay the information to editors that in the week after the Army of the Potomac took its heavy slaughter at Chancellorsville no less than $8,000,000 in bonds were bought.

The tumbling river of cash flowing in to Jay Cooke, and from him to the Lincoln Government,—for men, guns, horses, mules, hardtack and beans to carry on the war, was possible partly because of the breezy, valiant, inextinguishable optimism of Jay Cooke as to his country. Behind a thousand phrasings that came from him lay his theory that the war was an incident, a minor circumstance, in a deep stream of economic events crowding the United States forward into a future of dizzy figures in railroad, steamship, mill, mine and oil financing. Steamers from Europe in 1863 had brought to America 182,808 new laborers and home-steaders, the port of New York doubling its arrivals over the previous year, with 92,000 from Ireland, 35,000 from Germany, 18,000 from England, 11,000 from other countries.

Lincoln's friends Swett and Lamon gambled in oil and quicksilver stocks and went flat broke. The New York merchant A. T. Stewart paid a tax on $4,000,000 of income;

William B. Astor's income was $1,300,000; Cornelius Vanderbilt's $576,000; J. P. Morgan's $53,000. Joshua Bates of Boston, American partner of the Barings of London, died leaving an estate of $8,000,000.

California had dug out $70,000,000 in gold and silver the previous year, and other states $30,000,000. Four out of five white men in California were bachelors, and every steamship from the port of New York for the West Coast held scores of marriageable women sailing to where they would try their luck. In the rush for copper and iron lands in the Lake Superior region entries for 26,000 acres were made in the one month of February '64. The *Tribune* of St. Joseph, Missouri, noted on March 10, 1864, that since February 1, 400 teams and wagons had crossed the Missouri River headed for Western mining regions. East and west were fortune seekers who with Jay Cooke could see a future worth gambling on.

Small, comfortable fortunes had sprung up by thousands across the Northern and Border States, not to mention the Gulf State of Louisiana. Snug accumulations of wartime profits came out of selling wooden and metal legs and arms to men mutilated in battle, and out of providing substitutes to go forth to battle. Hundreds of neat bank deposits traced back to blockade-running and to forbidden traffic in liquor, medical supplies and scarce ingredients of war munitions.

Good to look at and all too rare was the instance cited by a son of George Luther Stearns, the Boston merchant and Negro recruiting officer: "A Boston firm for whom Mr. Stearns had obtained a lucrative government contract, from which they probably had derived a larger profit than they deserved, sent him a cheque for two thousand dollars, which he returned with a note saying as politely as possible that to partake in such transactions was as culpable as theft."

General Sherman cursed the merchants of Cincinnati for readiness to trade the enemy anything for a profit. Grant cursed Lincoln's friend Swett for trying to trade in hay at exceptional profits, and when Swett told Lincoln that Grant had threatened to shoot him if he went into hay deals, Lincoln told Swett to beware, for Grant generally kept his word. Yet the ordinarily scrupulous though occasionally obtuse Grant did not see anything wrong in his giving a kinsman by marriage an inside track on cotton-trading profits, until Rawlins exploded and shamed him about it. To a request of Ohio's first war governor, William Dennison, that Lincoln give a letter of recommendation to military and naval authorities in behalf of a cotton trader, Nicolay wired, "The President thinks he cannot safely write that class of letters."

Personal success in business, a stake that would assure a man comfort for life, was a motive so tangibly in the air that Lincoln, according to Whitney, advised his old law associate that Western land deals could bring him $50,000 in not so long a time. Letters of David Davis, Swett, Lamon, Orme and the Eighth Circuit "orgmathorial" lawyers were touched with hopes and groans related to whether this one or that among them would come through with a stake to give financial security for life. Secretary Welles made the mistake of letting a kinsman by marriage have a rather large-sized fortune as a commission on the negotiation of vessel sales to the Navy; he was fiercely satirized in *Leslie's Weekly*, the New York *World* and the New York *Herald*. But because huge amounts were involved it was generally accepted that Welles took a proper course in letting it be handled at a rather low percentage by a man he considered responsible. Repeatedly in his diary Welles bemoaned the palpable rascals who came trying to sell him worn-out ships at fancy prices.

From Dana and Grant to Stanton and then Lincoln went the cases of several cotton speculators trying to snake out profit-yielding bales of fiber for textile mills. Stanton organized a secret-service force that uncovered corrupt practices and frauds. Dana as Stanton's assistant carried this further and broke down the game of many a thieving quartermaster and contractor.

General James Grant Wilson noted one difficulty was that some of the most competent and most energetic contractors were the most dishonest, could not be content with a fair profit. "In tents, a lighter cloth or a few inches off the size;

in harness, split leather; in saddles, inferior materials and workmanship; in shoes, paper soles; in clothes, shoddy; in mixed horse feed, chaff and a larger proportion of the cheaper grain . . . Every contractor had to be watched." As if this merely was a repetition of European experience, *Blackwood's Magazine* in England commented, "A great war always creates more scoundrels than it kills."

The higher up the hypocrite and thief uncovered by Stanton's secret service, the louder the howling from some newspapers and the heavier the pressure from politicians to let him go. Wilson noted that governors, Congressmen, Senators and even the President himself were pressed into the service of the "best citizens" who had been caught cheating the Government. In the winter of 1863-64 Dana helped supervise the buying of 3,000,000 pairs of trousers, 5,000,000 flannel shirts and drawers, 7,000,000 pairs of socks, 325,000 mess pans, 207,000 camp kettles, 13,000 drums, 14,830 fifes. The War Department paid out from June '63 to June '64 more than $250,000,000.

A procession of mouthpieces and fixers twined in and out of Lincoln's office from week to week, and he had to sit not merely as judge and jury passing on their guilt or innocence and the punishment due; beyond that he had to ask whether the Union cause at the military front, and at the political and economic rear, would be served by his judgment. When a large share of a swindler's stealings had been returned and a Senator of considerable influence interceded for a thief of highly respectable position, Lincoln leaned to what Dana called "moderation," though privately exclaiming to John Eaton that the Senator was "too crooked to lie still." In dealing with various stripes of fox, wolf and hog caught with a smear of guilt on their snouts, Lincoln was more often blamed for "sympathy and clemency" than for vindictiveness. Heavy files of evidence and many intricate considerations stood in the backgrounds of an item in *Leslie's* in June: "The *New York Tribune* says that Capt. Sam Black, U.S. Quartermaster, who was recently convicted at Louisville of perpetrating enormous frauds on the Government, has been pardoned; and that Hall & Smith, Western horse contractors, who had likewise been found guilty of the same offence, have had their sentence suspended."

A tangled affair moved from May 8, 1863, when Lincoln signed the writ his old friend Swett wanted, to August 19, 1863, when the New Almaden gold mine in California at a ridiculously low price passed into the hands of a corporation in which Swett was a stockholder and for which he was a paid attorney. For Swett, Lincoln had no reproaches. In a way he knew Swett better than Swett knew himself. Swett was not so bad, only too anxious about getting a stake for life—too easily played on by sharpers, who paid Swett not as a lawyer but as one who had access to the President.

Lincoln would probably not have disagreed with Bates' diary entry of March 9: "The demoralising effect of this civil war is plainly visible in every department of life. The abuse of official powers and the thirst for dishonest gain are now so common that they cease to shock."

Oliver Wendell Holmes wrote: "Multitudes have grown rich and for what? To put gilt bands on coachmen's hats? To sweep the sidewalks with the heaviest silks the toiling French can send us? To float through life the passive shuttlecocks of fashion, from the avenue to the beaches and back again from the beaches to the avenue?"

New York hotels, theaters, jewelers' retail stores and women's wear establishments were surpassing all former sales records. The shopping crowds and what they were doing was an endless topic in the newspapers. A class of reckless war-profit spenders were named the "Shoddy," a word from the textile trade where a compound of refuse and sweepings pounded, rolled, glued and smoothed into the external form and gloss of cloth was known as shoddy. *Harper's Monthly* of July '64 in a scornful commentary told of soldiers on the first day's march or in their first storm finding their jackets and trousers, overcoats and blankets, scattering to the winds in rags or breaking into scraps and dust under a driving rain. "Shoddy has ever since become a word to represent the fraudulent contractor who makes a display of his ill-gotten gains."

Leslie's Weekly believed it significant that $2,000,000 in diamonds had been imported the previous year. "No wonder Shoddy glitters in the sunlight of Central Park or the gaslight of its own palatial residence; no wonder the jeweler's hands are full, setting gems, while the soldier's feet blister in his paper-soled shoes, and his bare elbows emerge from his worn jacket sleeves." The same editor complained of New York given up to the leg drama, "legs, physical and of unpadded proportions, female pedals as necessary to dramatic success as is a prima donna in an opera." The man who buttoned his vest with diamonds, accompanied by the woman whose hair shook with the glitter of gold dust, went shopping, saying, "We don't feel this war."

When in a slum hut of Columbus, Ohio, the widow of a soldier killed at Chicamauga died lacking food and the decencies of life, the Mahoning *Sentinel* threw a diatribe: "Wealth revels in luxury and worth starves in poverty— shoddy swells in bogus jewelry and like a rotten mackerel emits a dazzling glow from its vulgar splendor—in this paradise of parasites and patriots." This was not a Copperhead political outpouring. It was a cry of the same human pitch as the lamentations of the pro-Lincoln *Harper's Monthly*.

While winter snow blew along the city streets, it troubled Oliver Wendell Holmes that fresh peaches at $24 a basket should be offered in show windows to buyers who had money to throw at the birds. The customers of luxury-dealers made merry over the war. It was a pretty little war and had been good to them, in their slang a "High Daddy."

Prices of food and clothing soared upward while wages stood still or rose slowly. The very process that brought fortunes to speculators and sure-thing gamblers cut the wages and buying power of the workman. As if by instinct and with no traditions or practice for guidance, the working class began using the weapon termed the strike. The very word "strike" was so novel that some newspapers put it in quotes as though it were slang or colloquial, not yet fully accepted in good language. The year 1864 saw more strikes than all previous years in American history. In March the engineers on all railroads entering Chicago were on strike. On the Galena & Chicago Union Railroad the cry was that the company was not meeting an alleged January agreement to pay wages of $3 a day; the strike was broken in two days by engineers who went back to work reinforced by engineers brought on from New York and other eastern cities. The Brotherhood of the Foot-Board, born in Detroit in '63, grew into the reorganized Grand International Brotherhood of Locomotive Engineers in '64.

Payday dollars would buy so little in May '64 that the Chicago newspapers told their readers one day that in desperation the common laborers on every railroad running out of Chicago, except one, were on strike for a wage raise from $1.50 a day to $1.75. The printers in New York, Chicago and other cities formed their Typographical Union, the bakers, the tailors, the ironworkers, the coopers, the journeymen cordwainers, the seamen, each in their own craft, organized a union or "protective association" or "benevolent society," usually meeting behind closed doors. In some cases the labor union was recognized and took permanent form. More often there was a confused development out of which came somewhat better conditions for the workers.

The only strike where Lincoln seemed to have stepped in with his influence as President was but partly told of in his letter of December 21, 1863, to the Secretary of War: "Sending a note to the Secretary of the Navy as I promised, he called over and said that the strikes in the Ship-yards had thrown the completion of vessels back so much, that he thought Gen. Gilmores proposition entirely proper. He only wishes (and in which I concur) that Gen. Gilmore will courteously confer with and explain to Admiral Dahlgren." General Gillmore had a proposition for meeting the demands of the strikers. Admiral Dahlgren did not agree with Gillmore. Lincoln in effect ordered the two of them to get together and settle the strike, Lincoln concurring with Gillmore.

In St. Louis when newspaper printers went on strike General Rosecrans detailed soldiers to take the places of strikers. The union printers sent in a report to Lincoln on their side of the case. And it became a tradition of the labor movement that the President sent word that servants of the Federal Government should not interfere with legitimate demands of labor—and the strikebreaking soldiers were withdrawn.

In the textile trades, in the factories and the homework system, the hours were inhumanly long and the wages so low that respectable newspapers frequently published the figures as though for the amazement of readers that human beings could subsist on so few dollars a week. A strike of factory girls in Paterson, New Jersey, was for higher wages through cutting the workday from 12 and 16 to 10 hours a day.

The necessities of poor and pretty women were made the means of their debauchery by high Government officials, so believed the sober Springfield *Republican*. An editorial summarized Washington scandals which flashed working-girl melodramas of fact through many newspaper columns, all soberly and sadly confirmed as to fact in House reports of May and June. "A bureau of the Treasury Department made a house of seduction and prostitution. Members of Congress putting their mistresses into clerkships. An honorable Senator knocked down in the street by a woman he had outraged. Whisky drinking ad libitum. The government cheated in contracts and openly robbed by its employés. Writes our most careful correspondent, a long resident at the capital, 'Washington was never quite so villainously corrupt as at the present time . . .'"

In the brighter view $5,000,000 of privately raised funds was given to the Sanitary Commission for its many-sided help to soldiers in camp, on battlefield and in hospital. Bedding, clothing, vegetables, supplies, upwards of $15,000,000 worth, went from the people back home to the boys at the front. Endowment funds to colleges ran into millions of dollars.

Of all classes the war was falling most heavily on the soldier, Lincoln remarked in closing a Sanitary Fair in Washington. To the soldier, staking his life and often giving it, went the highest merit. Next perhaps would come the women of America, who had been the chief agents in these fairs for the relief of suffering soldiers and their families.

Said the President, "I have never studied the art of paying compliments to women; but I must say that if all that has been said by orators and poets since the creation of the world in praise of women were applied to the women of America, it would not do them justice for their conduct during this war. I will close by saying God bless the women of America!"

So ran intersecting human streaks across America while Jay Cooke carried on his drive that brought a Niagara of money into the U.S. Treasury, raising in less than 11 months over $500,000,000, a financial feat that to cold European observers indicated some peculiar unity of purpose in the North, and resources that might yet surpass Great Britain's.

Through the advertising and circular literature of the campaign had run a quiet promotion of the idea that Secretary Chase was the most prominent executive at Washington and would make an able President of the United States. Lincoln's estimates of Chase always included high appraisal of heavy labor in a difficult field.

George William Curtis, lavish and loyal friend of Lincoln in his *Harper's Weekly* editorials, wrote to a friend the first week in April, "I have seen Lincoln tête-à-tête since I saw you, and my personal impression of him confirmed my previous feeling." Curtis was 15 years younger than Lincoln, remembered that Lincoln shook hands with him in the manner of a father as they parted, and said: "Don't be troubled. I guess we shall come through."

Two sentences from Lincoln in early '64 had been picked up and in private conversations and public prints threshed out as significant texts or as silly excuses. One was spoken at the Philadelphia Sanitary Fair: "It is difficult to say a sensible thing nowadays." The other was from the Hodges letter: "I claim not to have controlled events, but confess plainly that events have controlled me." Though spacious and simple as sky and air, these two sentences were like the kaleidoscopic American scene. They could be read as having any shade or tint chosen to suit the views of any interpreter.

What was dying might be a little better known than two or three years before. What was being born was more of an enigma than ever.

Chapter 27

Chase Thirsts to Run for President

Three California Congressmen on request called on Secretary Chase in his private office. He had resolved to remove all of the leading Federal appointees of his department at San Francisco. He read to the seated and interested Congressmen a list of the new appointees. The Congressmen had nothing to say, Chase having told them his decision in the matter was irrevocable. They took their hats and walked over to the White House and paid their respects to the President without saying anything about what had just happened. Then they went to New York to take steamships for San Francisco. While they lingered in New York, Noah Brooks was summoned to the White House. There Brooks learned that the President had just heard of the wholesale removals and appointments determined by Secretary Chase.

The President tramped up and down the long room swinging his arms. "Tell me," he demanded of Brooks, "are those California Congressmen angry because the San Francisco mint and custom-house appointments were agreed on without their consent?" It seemed so, replied Brooks. "But the appointments are not agreed on," continued Lincoln. "Nothing is agreed on. I got the impression the California Congressmen were consulted and were satisfied . . . Were they very mad?" Not very, said Brooks. Still they were sore. "The President then angrily asked why I had not told him this before," ran Brooks' account. "I replied that it was not my affair . . . The President expressed his astonishment that he had been kept in the dark about so grave a matter as the emptying and filling of the most important federal offices on the Pacific coast. Then he anxiously asked if there was any way by which the California Congressmen could be reached and brought back."

One had sailed and was now on the high seas, Brooks answered, but two of them were still in New York. Lincoln handed a telegraph blank to Brooks and told him to wire the two Congressmen asking them to return to Washington to see the President, Brooks to sign the telegram.

The two Congressmen came and Lincoln slowly and carefully broke down the list of appointments fixed by Secretary Chase. He told Brooks that Chase was "exceedingly hurt" by the interference with his plans. In the shift of affairs Chase offered to appoint one of the two California Congressmen who had returned to Washington as collector of the port at San Francisco. The President suggested that all three California Congressmen should get together in San Francisco, agree on a list of appointments, and send it to him for approval. This was not agreed on. However, when the two California Congressmen finally took steamer from New York for the West Coast, one of them, Frederick Low, carried with him his commission as collector of the port at San Francisco.

About the same time the Senate threw out an appointment made by Chase to the office of internal revenue collector at Hartford, Connecticut. Chase sent Lincoln a long letter insisting that the President again send the name of Mark Howard, Chase's man, to the Senate, and if the Senate again threw out the Howard appointment, to let Chase then give the President another name to offer the balky Senate. Equally insistent but much shorter was Lincoln's reply to Chase saying that Senator Dixon of Connecticut and Congressman Loomis, both of Hartford, joined in recommending Edward Goodman for the appointment. "I will thank you therefore to send me a nomination, at once, for Mr. Goodman."

Next day Chase again wrote those words which became familiar to Lincoln: "I respectfully resign"—whatever the "respectfully" might mean. But this resignation Chase did

not send to Lincoln, partly because, as Chase explained in
a note to Lincoln, Senator Dixon sent him a note "of great
personal respect and kindness" and he, Chase, had replied
to Senator Dixon also with great personal respect and kindness, upon which Senator Dixon had called on Chase, and
the entire matter was to go over for further consideration
of the President. However, Chase made it clear that his purpose was "to secure fit men for responsible places" without
control of appointments by Senators or Representatives.
Otherwise "I feel that I can not be useful to you or the
country in my present position." From month to month
these summary notices were served on the President that
any moment his Treasury head was ready to quit.

Letters of protest came to Lincoln from Puget Sound citizens who wanted Victor Smith thrown out of the collector's
office in that district. Smith had been an Ohio man, a personal and political friend of Chase, an abolitionist, a spiritualist who believed in rappings, spouted his pet "isms,"
and was an "eccentric functionary." While collector of customs at Port Townsend, Washington Territory, Smith managed to induce the Government to move the customhouse
to another place named Port Angelos, which, combined
with Smith's arrogant personal manners, raised an outcry
from businessmen, politicians and ordinary citizens that he
was a nuisance and an evil to the West Coast.

Joining in the demands on Lincoln for Smith's removal
and the return of the customhouse to its first point were,
according to Brooks, every other Federal officer and nearly
every prominent citizen in the Puget Sound district. Among
the prominent citizens seeking Smith's official scalp was
Anson G. Henry, formerly of Springfield, Illinois, and personal physician years back to a sufferer from hypochondria
named Abraham Lincoln, who as President had appointed
Henry surveyor general of the Territory of Washington.
Henry was among those who gave their word to the President that Smith was a worthless vagabond and an audit
might show him a defaulter.

A delegation that seemed to include everybody then in
Washington, official and unofficial, from the Pacific Coast,

came and filed with the President formal charges against Victor Smith and called for his removal. Lincoln sent Chase a note to "please send me, at once, an appointment of Henry Clay Wilson" to replace Victor Smith. He explained to Chase that his mind was made up to remove Smith, yet in so doing he had not decided that the charges against Smith were true but had only decided that the dissatisfaction with Smith was too great. "But I believe he is your personal acquaintance & friend; and if you shall desire it, I will try to find some other place for him."

Chase on a Monday wrote to Lincoln, "This information surprised and greatly pained me; for I had not thought it possible that you would remove an officer of my department without awaiting the result." Also on this Monday Chase read a note from Lincoln saying he had learned that the man, Henry Clay Wilson, he had appointed Friday to replace Victor Smith was dead, and therefore Lincoln would appoint one Frederick A. Wilson.

Two days later Lincoln sent Chase a letter giving his approval to several matters and closing, *"Please send me over the commission for Lewis C. Gunn, as you recommend, for collector of customs at Puget Sound."* Smith besought Chase to have himself reappointed and Chase replied that Smith was mistaken as to the influence of words from Chase to the administration. "If any word of mine would make you collector again you would be reappointed."

In one phase the Victor Smith affair was a duel of political strength as between Smith and Dr. Henry. Though both were followers of the spiritualist cult and believed they could talk with the dead and departed of another realm, the two men loathed each other and never spoke as they passed by. On the steamer *Brother Jonathan*, bound from San Francisco to Portland, Mr. Smith and Dr. Henry were both drowned when that vessel struck a reef and sank.

In Chase's department were more than 10,000 jobholders high and low, and according to Nicolay and Hay, the President let Chase have his way as to all of these except in rare cases, seldom interfering. The two secretaries saw Chase trying to undermine Lincoln. "He regarded himself as the friend of Mr. Lincoln; to him and to others he made strong protestations of friendly feeling, which he undoubtedly thought were sincere; but he held so poor an opinion of the President's intellect and character in comparison with his own, that he could not believe the people so blind as deliberately to prefer the President to himself."

Still later the secretaries agreed as to Chase, "There never was a man who found it so easy to delude himself." This may have been the key to the wormings and gyrations of Chase. Under the portentous exterior of the handsomest man in the Cabinet was an oversized marionette borne down by delusions of grandeur. Two sorry points Nicolay and Hay recorded of Chase. He had what they called, for want of a better word, "self-love." And he had no sense of humor to tell him when others might be hiding laughter at him.

"Chase looks and acts as if he meant to be the next President," Richard Henry Dana had written from Washington to Charles Francis Adams at London in March '63. A few days after a visit with Lincoln in December, Thurlow Weed wrote from Albany to John Bigelow in Paris: "Mr. Chase's report is very able, and his huge banking machine will make him strong. But how pitiable it is to know that his eye is single—not to the welfare of his country but to the presidency! Mr. Lincoln says he is 'trying to keep that maggot out of his head,' but he cannot."

In scores of letters written to politicians, editors, ministers, Chase over a two-year period sought to spread the impression that in the midst of incompetents he was the one man who would know how if given the power. "Had there been here an administration in the true sense of the word," he wrote to the Reverend Dr. J. Leavitt, January 24, 1864, "—a President conferring with his Cabinet and taking their united judgments . . . we could have spoken boldly and defied the world." To Wayne MacVeagh, Republican state committee chairman of Pennsylvania, two days later: "Oh, for a vigorous, earnest, thorough prosecution of this war!" To Judge Thomas F. Key of Cincinnati the same day: "Some friends are sanguine that my name will receive favorable consideration from the people in connection with the Presidency. I tell them that I can take no part in anything they may propose to do, except by trying to merit confidence where I am." To Thomas Heaton, a Treasury Department agent at Cincinnati: "So far as the Presidency is concerned, I must leave that wholly to the people . . . Whatever disposition they make of it I shall be content."

Perhaps no one else wrote more shifting and contradictory opinions than did Chase of Lincoln. To the wealthiest man in the Senate, his son-in-law, Chase wrote November 26, 1863, that he could never be driven into any hostile or unfriendly position as to Mr. Lincoln. "His course toward me has always been so fair and kind." He dwelt at length on his "respect and affection" for Mr. Lincoln. Yet in the same letter he made the point that no President should have a second term, and "I think a man of different qualities from those of the President will be needed for the next four years."

From his desk Chase sent out dozens of curiously stilted self-portraits of the noble and worthy citizen, the man of grasp, dignity and patience, who against his deeper inclinations would serve his country as Chief Magistrate if called on. He evolved forty ways of saying what he wrote a Wisconsin man in December '63, "There is certainly a purpose to use my name, and I do not feel bound to object to it." Over and again Welles' diary entries had one tone: Chase "lamented the President's want of energy and force, which he said paralyzed everything. His weakness was crushing us. I did not respond to this distinct feeler, and the conversation changed."

From the number of long letters Chase wrote in fixing his political fences, and from the number of interviews and conferences he held toward the same end, it could be estimated that he was giving perhaps half of his time to nursing along his high political hope.

While Carpenter from day to day painted, Lincoln often brought visitors down to see the work of art and, said Carpenter, he came by himself sometimes three and four times in a single day. In his many remarks, seldom did Lincoln indulge in any personal comments on his Cabinet members. However, one day, Carpenter noted, "with a sly twinkle of the eye, he turned to a senatorial friend and said: 'Mrs. Lincoln calls Mr. Carpenter's group *The Happy Family.*' "

A short, thickset man wearing side whiskers and the latest cut of clothes, carrying a monocle in the English manner and sporting a gold-headed walking stick, came to see Lincoln while the Chase movement was under way. And Lincoln gave this man plenty of time and talked much with him. He was Henry Jarvis Raymond, editor and owner of the most distinctly pro-Lincoln daily organ in New York City, the *Times,* the one morning newspaper that tried to hurl back the daily javelins of Greeley, Bennett, Brooks, Fernando Wood. A Congressman-elect from New York State had pressed Lincoln for official action in an important matter, according to Carpenter, and the answer from Lincoln was: "You must see Raymond about this. He is my *Lieutenant-General* in politics. Whatever he says is right in the premises, shall be done."

Raymond was 44 years old. Born in Lima, New York, a University of Vermont graduate, teacher in a young ladies' seminary, he was once editor of a literary weekly. He founded the New York *Times* in 1851 and edited it for a public that wanted more trustworthy reporting of the day's news than was to be had in the brilliant and slimy *Herald* or in the quirks and shifts of the *Tribune.*

A delegate to the Whig national convention of 1850, later lieutenant governor of New York, Raymond had helped organize the Republican party in 1856, stumped for Frémont, in 1858 independently swung away to support of Stephen A. Douglas for President, but in 1860 swung back to Lincoln. He was close to Weed and Seward; the triumvirate of Seward-Weed-Raymond was often satirized and excoriated. And now Raymond worked on the most comprehensive and formidable biography of Lincoln that had ever been attempted, to be published late in the spring. That Raymond in '61 was so hopeless of the Lincoln administration that he urged in his newspaper a provisional government and a dictator [George Law] to replace Lincoln would not be told in the biography. That a movement to nominate Chase for President was supported by scores of Republican leaders in Washington early in '64 would not be told. Except for political family secrets not worth telling in a campaign year, it would be a first-rate campaign biography.

"The most violent opposition to Mr. Lincoln," wrote Raymond, "came from those most persistent and most clamorous in their exactions." In so terrible a crisis, it was unavoidable that "vast multitudes of active and ambitious men should be disappointed in their expectations of position and personal gain," this resulting in powerful and organized efforts against the renomination of Lincoln. "The President has achieved a wonderful success" in maintaining through terrible trials "a reputation with the great body of the people, for unsullied integrity, of purpose and of conduct, which even Washington did not surpass, and which no other President since Washington has equalled." Raymond elaborated this "unspotted character" as a key point in the national situation, as also Lincoln's remarkable faculty of "putting things" in simple language that carried precise ideas. "It gives to his public papers a weight and influence with the mass of the people, which no public man of this country has ever attained. And this is heightened by the atmosphere of humor which seems to pervade his mind, and which is just as natural to it and as attractive and softening a portion of it, as the smoky hues of Indian summer are of the charming season to which they belong."

As to the candidacy of Chase, Lincoln gave an anecdote that Raymond passed on to Carpenter: " 'R[aymond], you were brought up on a farm, were you not? Then you know what a *chin fly* is. My brother and I . . . were once ploughing corn on a Kentucky farm, I driving the horse, and he holding the plough. The horse was lazy; but on one occasion rushed across the field so that I, with my long legs, could scarcely keep pace with him. On reaching the end of the furrow, I found an enormous *chin fly* fastened upon him, and knocked him off. My brother asked me what I did that for. I told him I didn't want the old horse bitten in that way. "Why," said my brother, "that's all that made him go!" Now,' added Lincoln, 'if Mr. C[hase] has a presidential *chin fly* biting him, I'm not going to knock him off, if it will only make his department go.' "

Lincoln possibly told the story much as they gave it. Others heard the story and it was widely published as from Lincoln.

A story was printed about Chase one day giving Lincoln a gloomy recital of the financial situation, gold going higher and greenbacks sinking, and "What can be done about it?" Lincoln: "Well, Mr. Secretary, I don't know unless you give your paper mill another turn." At which Chase almost swore as he flustered out.

Republican and Democratic papers enjoyed reprinting facetious charges of the New York *Herald* that Mr. Chase was "putting his own portrait upon the greenbacks of *small* denominations, which everybody sees, while he sticks Mr. Lincoln's comical phiz upon the *large* bills, in order that he may make himself generally known to the public."

John Hay wrote one day: "I do not know whether the nation is worthy of the President for another term, I know the people want him . . . But politicians are strong yet and he is not 'their kind of a cat.' "

In the fall of '63 Hay had spoken to Lincoln of Chase's "trying to cut under" the administration, the President saying, "Whenever he sees that an important matter is troubling me, if I am compelled to decide it in a way to give offense to some man of influence he always ranges himself in opposition to me and persuades the victim that he would have arranged it differently. It was so with Gen. Frémont— Gen¹ Hunter when I annulled his hasty proclamation—with Gen. Butler when he was recalled from New Orleans—with these Missouri people when they called . . . I am entirely indifferent as to his success or failure in these schemes, so long as he does his duty as the head of the Treasury Department."

On Rosecrans' removal from command after Chickamauga and before his appointment to the Department of

Missouri, Hay told the President that Chase would try to make capital of it. The President laughed. "I suppose he will, like the bluebottle fly, lay his eggs in every rotten spot he can find." In measuring men and reading their hearts Lincoln had the advantage that Chase seldom if ever laughed at himself. To Chase a fool was a dunce and every day in the week a dunce. For Lincoln any dunce might have off days and even the wicked were not wicked all the time.

Chase could only be mystified by a story the New York *Evening Post* laid to Lincoln about a general who hinted to Lincoln that many people took it as settled that he would accept a renomination for President. Lincoln was reminded of an Illinois State official when an itinerant preacher asked for a permit to lecture in the State House. "On what subject?" was asked, and the reply, "On the second coming of our Saviour." "Oh, bosh," said the official, "if our Saviour had ever been to Springfield and got away with his life, he'd be too smart to think of coming back again." This, related the New York *Evening Post*, Mr. Lincoln said was very much his case about the renomination.

That Chase—like Lincoln—wanted to keep clear of anything about which bothersome questions could be asked was seen in his returning to Jay Cooke a $4,200 profit that Cooke had earned for him in a railway stock deal, explaining to Cooke that he must "avoid every act which could give occasion to any suspicion," and "In order to be able to render the most efficient service to our country, it is essential for me to *be* right as well as to *seem* right, and to *seem* right as well as to *be* right."

Theodore Tilton in the *Independent* stressed the fact that Lincoln in writing the Emancipation Proclamation forgot to mention God and it was Chase who suggested the closing phrase which invoked "the gracious favor of Almighty God." A friend said to Lincoln he felt it was improper of Tilton to publish such matters at such a time and Chase had probably seen Tilton and was responsible. Lincoln: "Oh, Mr. Chase had nothing to do with it; I think *I* mentioned the circumstance to Mr. Tilton myself." Thus the man who had it from Lincoln told it to Carpenter.

The Union League Club of Philadelphia came out strong for Lincoln's renomination, the National Union Club of Philadelphia chiming in. In New York City the National Conference Committee of the Union Lincoln Association issued an address "To the Loyal Citizens of the United States" declaring that in electing an "occupant for the presidential chair" the people should choose "a true leader," one "tried and not found wanting," naming Abraham Lincoln. When some postmasters over the country who favored Lincoln's renomination posted this imposing New York declaration where any and all purchasers of postage stamps could see it, the New York *World* howled that the administration had issued an order coercing the postal service into peanut politics.

Horace Greeley a month earlier at an antislavery meeting came forward to say he thought about the largest man in this Government was Governor Chase, a statesman who had been fighting on the hardest ground of all to manage and whose battles had all been victorious. As usual, Greeley wrote and printed a long cool editorial to buttress his short impetuous speech. Hay noted of this: "The Pres^t was greatly amused at Greeley's hasty Chase explosion and its elaborate explanation in the *Tribune*."

While Greeley grumbled and sputtered, some of the most cunning and ruthless political manipulators in the country began working on an upshoot of expression that would cry the mass sentiment favoring Lincoln. Simon Cameron and John W. Forney, practiced professional politicians of the Keystone State, at one extreme, and swaggering gun-fighting Jim Lane of Kansas at another end, saw work ahead they could do. So did the Blair boys and Old Man Blair, besides many political workers who knew left hand from right.

Among Union members of the Pennsylvania Legislature early in January a paper was passed around. An address to the President, it was, saying that the voters of Pennsylvania had endorsed his policies generously at the recent election and "We are only responding to their demand when we thus publicly announce our unshaken preference for your reëlection to the Presidency in 1864." Signed by every Union member of senate and assembly, his paper was sent to Lincoln January 14 by Simon Cameron with the message, "You are now fairly launched on our second voyage . . . Providence has decreed your reëlection, and no combination of the wicked can prevent it."

A New Hampshire State convention of the Union party had already met January 6 to nominate a state ticket, and before the chairman knew exactly what he was doing with so many Treasury Department employees present, the delegates had sent up rockets and declared for Lincoln's renomination. The Union Central Committee of New York unanimously took like action, and in sending the news to Lincoln, Senator Morgan said, "It is going to be difficult to restrain the boys, and there is not much use in trying to do so." With only one dissenting voice both houses of the Kansas Legislature endorsed renomination of the President. The Union members of the legislature of New Jersey joined in saying, without disparagement of other true men, "You are the choice of the people."

California legislators, almost unanimously, declared, "While we revere and honor other noble patriots who have performed their parts, the people will look to Abraham Lincoln as the instrument selected by Providence to lead their country in safety through its perils." In much the same tone the legislatures of Maryland, Michigan, Wisconsin, Rhode Island, declared themselves, as also state conventions in Minnesota, Iowa, Indiana, New Hampshire, Connecticut. When February '64 ended, 14 states had by official action gone on record speaking their preference for Lincoln for a second term.

During the first two months of '64 money was spent, political workers hired, and literature, open and secret, was spread by the quietly working Chase organization. The Washington branch of Jay Cooke & Company, through Henry D. Cooke, was involved in expenditures estimated at $20,000, while Senator Sprague's payments were put at $10,000. The Cooke firm made an outright gift of $5,000 to the Chase committee, of which Senator Samuel C. Pomeroy of Kansas was chairman, and gave a check for $2,000 for the writing and placing of an article about Chase in the *Atlantic Monthly*. And working modestly, quiet as a church mouse, yet fertile of resource and quick of wit, was Kate Chase Sprague, swept and driven by ambition.

While the Chase band wagon was trying at once to make a noise and be quiet, the mass sentiment favoring Lincoln was exploded and reverberated through the state legislatures. Pomeroy and his committee decided in February on a bold play. A circular was prepared—for private and confidential distribution. It was said to be a joint product of Sumner, Stevens, Henry Winter Davis and Wade, though signed by Pomeroy only. Printed copies were mailed over the country and marked "private and confidential." From men inside the President's own party went this appeal to Union men that they must counteract the President's attempt to re-elect himself through using the official machinery of the Government: (1) His re-election was impossible because of the combinations that would be against him; (2) on the face of the President's record his second term would be worse than his first; (3) a second term would give the President more power than was safe for republican institutions; (4) Chase on the other hand would guarantee economy and purity in the Government; (5) the unorganized Chase strength needed only systematic effort to win. Each of these points was made in elaborate and unmistakable language running nearly 600 words.

The *National Intelligencer* at Washington spread this document in full over its pages, for newspapers everywhere to reprint. And the Chase workers, who had counted on secrecy till they had a strength worth bringing into the open, were all surprised, some shocked, Chase himself aghast. Clear and plain to all who read the text of the circular was the shame that the "Committee of Prominent Senators, Representatives and Citizens" who issued the document were so afraid of being caught doing it that they did not sign. In so bold and raw a piece of work it was best to be anonymous. But their work was dragged into the daylight. And they scurried from newspapermen asking, "Who

wrote it?" The Democratic press jibed at the Republicans
in the words of the New York *World*, "Go on, gentlemen!
wash your dirty linen in public." The document which became notorious as "The Pomeroy Secret Circular" had odd
declarations:

> . . . even were the reëlection of Mr. Lincoln desir-
> able, it is practically impossble against the union of
> influences which will oppose him.
> . . . we find united in Hon. Salmon P. Chase more
> of the qualities needed in a President during the next
> four years than are combined in any other available
> candidate . . .
> . . . the discussion of the Presidential question . . .
> has developed a popularity and strength in Mr. Chase
> unexpected even to his warmest admirers . . .
> A central organization has been effected, which al-
> ready has its connections in all the States, and the ob-
> ject of which is to enable his friends everywhere most
> effectually to promote his elevation to the Presi-
> dency . . .

While the circular was still being mailed out, and read as
strictly private and confidential, many copies fell into the
hands of Lincoln workers and soon began coming to the
White House. The President, according to Nicolay, was
absolutely without curiosity in regard to attacks on himself,
refused to look at the circulars; they piled up "unread" on
Nicolay's desk.

On the day the *National Intelligencer* burst into print
with the circular, Chase wrote a sick-at-heart letter to Lincoln saying it was probable he had already seen a letter
printed in the *Intelligencer*. Until he saw it in print, "I had
no knowledge of the existence of this letter." Several gentlemen had called on him some weeks before and urged him
to allow his name to be used toward election as Chief Magistrate. They said their views were shared by many earnest
friends. He had replied that his usefulness as head of the
Treasury Department might be impaired. They had come

again. "We had several interviews." They gave their judgment that he could still be useful while his name was used. "I accepted their judgment as decisive." Chase then wrote more warmly toned feelings than had ever before shown in his letters to Lincoln. "For yourself I cherish sincere respect and esteem; and, permit me to add, affection. Differences of opinion as to administrative action have not changed these sentiments; nor have they been changed by assaults upon me by persons who profess themselves the special representatives of your views and policy . . ."

Lincoln studied this letter with its careful excuses, its blurred justifications, its embarrassed self-portraiture. Next day, February 23, he wrote a one-sentence note to Chase: "Yours of yesterday in relation to the paper issued by Senator Pomeroy was duly received; and I write this note merely to say I will answer a little more fully when I can find the leisure to do so." Lincoln waited six more days. Robert Lincoln on this sixth day was home from Harvard on vacation, strolled into his father's room; his father showed him a long reply to Chase. The son was surprised that his father had not read the Pomeroy Circular and said so. The father stopped the son sternly, saying that a good many others had tried to tell him something it did not suit him to hear, and he asked Robert to call a messenger to take the letter to Chase.

Chase could study the letter, a self-portrait in exchange for the one received from Chase: "I would have taken time to answers yours of the 22nd sooner, only that I did not suppose any evil could result from the delay . . . on consideration, I find there is really very little to say. My knowledge of Mr. Pomeroy's letter having been made *public* came to me only the day you wrote; but I had, in spite of myself, known of it's *existence* several days before. I have not yet read it, and I think I shall not. I was not shocked, or surprised by the appearance of the letter, because I had had knowledge of Mr. Pomeroy's Committee, and of secret issues which I supposed came from it, and of secret agents who I supposed were sent out by it, for several weeks. I have known just as little of these things as my own friends have allowed me to know. They bring the documents to me but I do not read them—they tell me what they think fit to tell me, but I do not inquire for more . . . Whether you shall remain at the head of the Treasury Department is a question which I will not allow myself to consider from any stand-point other than my judgment of the public service; and, in that view, I do not perceive occasion for a change."

Three days later Chase was worried lest Lincoln might give out for publication the interesting letters that had passed between them. He wrote a note for Henry Villard, now of the New York *Tribune,* to carry to the President, who wrote to Chase: "In consequence of a call Mr. Villard makes on me, having a note from you to him, I am induced to say I have no wish for the publication of the correspondence between yourself and me in relation to the Pomeroy Circular—in fact, rather prefer to avoid an unnecessary exhibition—yet you are at liberty, without in the least offending me, to allow the publication, if you choose."

As Chase reread the letters between him and Lincoln he knew he would be the worse damaged by publication. When one of Chase's most loyal friends, Robert B. Warden, read the letters later he wrote that he, Warden, nearly lost his head and was tempted to agree with Tom Corwin's having told Lincoln that Chase was "embodied perfidy."

Thaddeus Stevens as a Chase worker in Pennsylvania had been powerless against Cameron and Forney. Jim Lane in Kansas had overridden the Pomeroy forces. The son-in-law Sprague in Rhode Island had not been able to swing that tiny bailiwick. The Blair family, old Frank and young Frank and Postmaster General Montgomery, had put their influence and advice where it counted.

Still Chase hoped on. Ohio might come his way. His home state might say Yes. Surely the Buckeyes would want their old governor for a White House figure. But the Ohio legislative members plopped one and all for Lincoln. And Chase wrote to the former Ohio Congressman A. G. Riddle, early in March: "I am trying to keep all Presidential aspirations out of my head. I fancy that as President I could take care of the Treasury better with the help of a Secretary than I can as Secretary without the help of a President. But our Ohio folks don't want me enough." He wrote James C. Hall of Toledo that under circumstances that might arise, or that could be arranged, he would lead the Democratic party for the sake of Union, Freedom and Justice. Compared with the cause for which he stood, he wrote, "persons and even parties are nothing."

In such peculiar twilights had Chase run his candidacy that when he requested by letter "no further considerations be given" to his name, it was not taken that he strictly meant what he said. As the Chase boom wavered and sank early in March, Henry Ward Beecher in a Philadelphia speech came forward with flowers of approval for Lincoln as always a man of honest principles rather than tricky expedients, the homely President of a homely people, faithful to the great political truths of the American system. "He has shown the world that successful government is not the mystery that only a privileged few can enact."

As weeks passed Chase continued writing the same sort of letters as before about the waste and bungling of the administration, the President's lacking a firm mind and a strong hand to guide the nation. "It seems as if there were no limit to expense . . . The spigot in Uncle Abe's barrel is made twice as big as the bung-hole."

The National Union party convention which would renominate Lincoln—or not—was to meet in Baltimore June 7, according to a call of its national committee in February. This would be too soon, said Greeley, Bryant and others. Raymond, *Harper's Weekly* and others asked, "Why not?" The ground swell of mass sentiment was for Lincoln, and an early convention would be good strategy. One or two inexplicable disasters might send the mass sentiment dwindling.

A restless but uncrystallized labor movement over the country would cast its ballots in the coming campaign. Lincoln met a small section of it when a committee from the New York Workingmen's Democratic Republican Association called to inform him their association had elected him an honorary member. They had organized the year before and favored trade-unions and bargaining of employees with employers. "The honorary membership in your Association," said the President, ". . . is gratefully accepted. You comprehend, as your address shows, that the existing rebellion, means more, and tends to more, than the perpetuation of African Slavery—that it is, in fact, a war upon the rights of all working people."

He touched on the New York draft riots of the year before: "The most notable feature of a disturbance in your city last summer, was the hanging of some working people by other working people. It should never be so. The strongest bond of human sympathy, outside of the family relation, should be one uniting all working people, of all nations, and tongues, and kindreds. Nor should this lead to a war upon property, or the owners of property. Property is the fruit of labor—property is desirable—is a positive good in the world. That some should be rich, shows that others may become rich, and hence is just encouragement to industry and enterprise. Let not him who is houseless pull down the house of another; but let him labor diligently and build one for himself, thus by example assuring that his own shall be safe from violence when built."

In an autograph album for a Sanitary Fair next day Lincoln wrote: "I never knew a man who wished to be himself a slave. Consider if you know any *good* thing, that no man desires for himself."

In the autograph, in the address to the workingmen's committee, he knew he was helping create opinion, and the mass of his personal contacts and their impression were a part of the political campaign of the year.

A pleasant and idle tale spread in talk and print. Lincoln had gone to a black prophetess in Georgetown. Like King Saul in the Bible, he asked about his future. The voodoo woman went into a dark room to raise up mystic spirits and speak with them, returning to the consultation parlor to tell Lincoln, "General Grant will capture Richmond, you will be the next President—but beware of Chase."

Chapter 28

Spring of '64 — Blood and Anger

Nevada's miners, prospectors, gamblers, gold- and silver-hunters, with 26,000 voters, wanted to have a state and be in the Union. She liked the idea of her little desert population sending a Congressman and two Senators to Washington. Two out of three voters were Republican.

The President called on Assistant Secretary of War Charles A. Dana, who wrote of what followed. Lincoln told Dana the administration had decided the Constitution should be amended to prohibit slavery; this was not only a change in national policy but a most important military measure equivalent to new armies in the field, worth at least a million men, tending to paralyze and break the continuity of enemy ideas. To pass such an amendment would require approval by three-fourths of the states. Nevada might be of critical importance as a state. Dana quoted Lincoln, "It is easier to admit Nevada than to raise another million soldiers."

The Senate bill of February 24, 1864, authorized a Nevada convention the first Monday in July, to declare on behalf of the people that they adopt the Constitution of the United States and to frame a state government. In the House through March this bill was held up by lack of votes. Stevens, the floor leader, simply couldn't line up a majority for it.

Lincoln walked over to Dana's office, said: "Dana, I am very anxious about this vote. It has got to be taken next week. The time is very short. It is going to be a great deal closer than I wish it was . . . There are three [members of Congress] that you can deal with better than anybody else, perhaps, as you know them all. I wish you would send for them." Lincoln told Dana who they were. Dana considered it unnecessary to tell their names to anyone not immediately concerned. One was from New Jersey and two from New York. "What will they be likely to want?" asked Dana. The President said, ". . . It makes no difference what they want. Here is the alternative: that we carry this vote, or be compelled to raise another million, and I don't know how many more, men, and fight no one knows how long. It is a question of three votes or new armies." "Well, sir, what shall I say to these gentlemen?" "I don't know, but whatever promise you make to them I will perform."

Dana sent for the men and saw them one by one. Two wanted each an internal-revenue collector's appointment. "You shall have it," said Dana. The third wanted a customhouse appointment in New York at about $20,000 a year. The Congressman, a Democrat, wanted a Republican appointed. When the Congressman had stated his case, Dana asked, "Do you want that?" "Yes." "Well, you shall have it." "I understand, of course, that you are not saying this on your own authority?" "No. I am saying it on the authority of the President." So the extra votes needed to pass the Nevada bill through the House were gotten. And the Yeas and Nays on the vote in Senate and House were not indexed or recorded in the *Congressional Globe*, whether through clerical inattention or by official arrangement.

Dana believed he and Lincoln knew precisely the fine, thin lines of right, wrong and expediency that wove through this piece of politics. Lincoln had chosen for an intermediary in an intricate operation, a man of delicate methods who had been a terror to fraudulent contractors and get-rich-quick cotton traders, and whose faith in Lincoln had depths. "Lincoln was a supreme politician," wrote Dana. "He understood politics because he understood human nature."

Hay had talked with the President in December about reconstruction in Florida, the possibility of getting one-tenth of the voters in the state to swear Union allegiance and be recorded as U.S. citizens in an oath book. To General Q.

A. Gillmore, in whose department Florida lay, Lincoln wrote January 13 that he had commissioned Hay a major in the army and Hay with oath books and blank certificates would arrive and explain to General Gillmore the President's general views on the subject of reconstructing a loyal state government in Florida. "It is desirable for all to co-operate; but if irreconcileable differences of opinion shall arise, you are master. I wish the thing done in the most speedy way possible, so that, when done, it lie within the range of the late proclamation on the subject . . ."

Hay sailed to Gillmore's headquarters on the South Carolina coast, assured the General it was not the President's intention to do anything to embarrass his military operations. At Jacksonville, Florida, Hay read the President's proclamation of amnesty to a line-up of prisoners, explained that if they signed the oath book, certificates to that effect would be issued to them and they would be allowed to go home. Otherwise they would be sent North as prisoners of war for exchange. "There is to be neither force nor persuasion used in the matter. You decide for yʳselves." They signed, nearly half making their mark. They were tired of the war.

Then came shocking news. General Truman Seymour, a Regular Army officer in charge of some 5,500 men, sought out a Confederate force of about the same size at Olustee River in a picked position, welcoming battle. The Union loss was 1,800, the Confederate half that. Seymour's orders from Gillmore had been to wait. But he had plunged and his army was routed.

With Union bayonets in disgrace for the moment, Hay had a harder time enrolling loyal Unionists. He went to Fernandina, where he got a few more names, noted: "Some refused to sign, on the ground that they were not repentant rebels." On March 3 he wrote, "I am sure that we cannot now get the President's 10ᵗʰ." His hopes vanished that the required 10 per cent of voters to form a state government could be enrolled.

Sailing back to Washington, Hay could read in the New York *Herald* or *World* that the President would not hesitate at murder to win political ends, that Hay had joined with the President in a reckless conspiracy to overawe Florida with military power, to elect himself as a Congressman, to deliver a set of Florida delegates for the President at the nominating convention in June. "Price of Three Votes for the Presidency! One Thousand Lives!" trumpeted the New York *Herald,* while the *World* day after day rehearsed the allegations in new phrases.

The written instructions of Lincoln to Hay and to Gillmore, along with Gillmore's explicit orders to General Seymour, were made public, and it was seen that a brave general in Florida had taken a chance, risked a battle and lost. This amid the hullabaloo of passing weeks came to be regarded as the central fact.

In many forms ran accusations that the President had an eye on Southern delegates to help renominate him. The accusers hoped he would wait until after the November elections before taking a hand in reconstruction, out of fear that anything he did might look as though he were hunting delegates. Sardonic and miserable contradictions were beginning to whirl around the very word "reconstruction." Out of so much death, ashes and devastation, what could in the end be reconstructed? In its beginning it was to rest on a 10 per cent of oath-bound voters regarded as betrayers and outcasts by those whose bayonets and taxes were still keeping the Confederacy alive. The oath itself had lost sanctity in the story of the soldiers who caught a rattlesnake, took it to camp, administered the oath, and let it go.

That wholesale and regimented oath-taking might easily become ridiculous was in Lincoln's mind when he issued the Amnesty Proclamation in December; he had warned that it was only a method, a mode, for re-establishing national authority. He heard in January '64 from General Banks, commanding the Department of the Gulf, that there were loyal Union people in Louisiana who wished to avoid taking the oath prescribed. The President replied: ". . . it is not even a modification of anything I have heretofore said when I tell you that you are at liberty to adopt any rule which shall admit to vote any unquestionably loyal free-state men and none others. And yet I do wish they would all take the oath."

Far down in that changing patchwork of military and civil governments, Louisiana, Lincoln tried to guide General Nathaniel Prentiss Banks, a Democrat, three times governor of Massachusetts. Amid clashing authorities Lincoln wrote him assurance. "I deeply regret to have said or done anything which could give you pain, or uneasiness. I have all the while intended you to be *master . . .*" While fortunes large and small were being harvested in a thousand shady Gulf Coast traffickings, Banks kept an instinct for what Nicolay and Hay named "honorable poverty" rather than such cash winnings as Ben Butler's brother took out of the Crescent City.

Lincoln tried to steer Banks in the governing of some 17 of the 48 parishes of Louisiana controlled by Union armies, an area holding a fourth of the slaves of Louisiana. He would like to see the state recognize the Emancipation Proclamation. "And while she is at it, I think it would not be objectionable for her to adopt some practical system by which the two races could gradually live themselves out of their old relation to each other, and both come out better prepared for the new. Education for young blacks should be included in the plan."

Banks on January 11 proclaimed an election to be held February 22. Free white male voters who had taken the oath of allegiance cast over 11,000 ballots, of which the Banks candidate Michael Hahn received 6,183, J. Q. A. Fellows, a proslavery conservative, 2,996, and B. F. Flanders, 2,232.

In his Louisiana domain Governor Michael Hahn estimated that in three-fourths of the state allegiance lay mainly with the Confederate governor and the legislature in session at the capitol in Shreveport. Hahn was 34 years old. Born in Bavaria, he was as a baby carried by his parents to a ship for New York; he moved with them to New Orleans, where he graduated from the law department of the University of Louisiana, became president of the school board in New Orleans, clung fast to Douglas in politics, though an outspoken antislavery man.

To Hahn, Lincoln wrote a letter marked "Private": "I congratulate you on having fixed your name in history as the first-free-state Governor of Louisiana. Now you are about to have a Convention which, among other things, will probably define the elective franchise. I barely suggest for your private consideration, whether some of the colored people may not be let in—as, for instance, the very intelligent, and especially those who have fought gallantly in our ranks. They would probably help, in some trying time to come, to keep the jewel of liberty within the family of freedom."

With this the President included a one-sentence letter, perhaps equally important, notifying Hahn that until further orders he would be military governor of Louisiana. Thus if his civil authority given him by election was questioned, he could call out the troops and riot squads.

Banks headed in March the Red River expedition of some 40,000 men. And the forces mishandled by Banks were beaten and sent reeling so that Banks was glad to get his army safe in Alexandria, 80 miles back eastward from the town where 20 days earlier he had written John Hay he was anxious lest the enemy might not give him battle.

Lincoln, Seward, Halleck, Grant, Sherman, newspaper correspondents and the cotton traders had, affirmatively or negatively, shared in getting the expedition started and in direction of it after it got going. Banks was pleased to get back with it to the Mississippi and disperse it into various commands. Charges arose that the collapsed Red River expedition had as its main objective capture of immense supplies of cotton to be sold by the Union Government to relieve the textile-mill famine and to put millions of dollars into the U.S. Treasury.

Two men had turned up at Alexandria on the Red River with cotton trading permits in the President's handwriting, William Butler and Thomas L. Casey of Springfield, Illinois, old personal friends of Lincoln. What little cotton they collected was taken away from them by the army and put to military use. But their appearance at the Red River camp with presidential permits set many tongues going. "Much odium was excited by the circumstance," wrote Greeley.

"Reflections more or less severe were cast upon the President," wrote Nicolay and Hay. The secretaries pointed to a pressure "almost incredible" on the President to grant such permits, "and he sometimes, though very seldom, gave way." The letter of the President to Congressman Kellogg audibly groaning his refusal to give a trading permit, was quoted. "I think you do not know how embarrassing your request is," he wrote. Few things were so troublesome to the Government as the fierceness with which the profits in cotton trading were sought. "The temptation is so great that nearly everybody wishes to be in it; and, when in, the question of profit controls all, regardless of whether the cotton-seller is loyal or rebel, or whether he is paid in cornmeal or gunpowder . . . The officers of the army, in numerous instances, are believed to connive and share the profits, and thus the army itself is diverted from fighting the rebels to speculating in cotton . . ."

Kellogg had urged that the President could let him have one or two trading permits and the public need know nothing of it. That had been done. The President noted: "One case cannot be kept a secret. The authority given would be utterly ineffectual until it is shown, and when shown, everybody knows of it."

In May, Banks was relieved of his command and resigned his army commission. "The President gave me too much to do—more than any other major-general in the army," he wrote, as fact and not complaint. Sherman had written Lincoln and Halleck that he deemed it "very unwise at this time or for years to come, to revive the State governments of Louisiana, etc., or to institute in this quarter any civil government in which the local people have much to say." This, however, was precisely what Banks under Lincoln's guidance was trying to do with one hand while with the other he was to slay Confederate armies.

Lincoln and Banks agreed that, if only for its effect on politics and war morale in the North, the ballot should be given to at least a part of the free Negro population. Governor Hahn hoped to work out Lincoln's suggestion that Negroes who had fought for the Union, and possibly those who could read and write, should be the first Negro voters.

Grant suggested General E. R. S. Canby to supersede Banks and it was so ordered. But Lincoln and Banks remained friends and Banks was staying on in New Orleans advising with the Louisiana constitutional convention and reporting to Lincoln.

After General Frederick Steele's column of 13,000 Union troops had marched into Little Rock, the capital of Arkansas, September 13, 1863, a large part of the state came under Union control. Eight regiments of Arkansas citizens had been enlisted under the Union flag. And early in January the President sent oath books and blank certificates to General Steele, for use in reorganizing a state government. Word came to Lincoln of a series of Union meetings with speeches and resolutions and election of delegates to a convention of 44 members who claimed to represent 22 of the 54 counties of the State of Arkansas.

This convention on January 22, 1864, declared secession null and void, slavery abolished immediately and unconditionally, and the Confederate debt repudiated. An address to the voters of Arkansas adopted January 23 frankly acknowledged "that while we could not properly claim to be the people of Arkansas in convention assembled," yet as representatives of a considerable portion of the state, and understanding the sentiment of citizens desiring a government under U.S. authority, they had determined to present a state constitution for the voters to ballot on. They appointed and inaugurated for provisional governor one Isaac Murphy, 62 years old, born near Pittsburgh, Pennsylvania, schoolteacher, lawyer, California gold-hunter, civil engineer and public-land surveyor. As a member in May '61 of the state convention which decided that Arkansas would secede, Murphy was the one delegate voting against secession. He became a staff officer of General Steele and his son Frank a major in the 1st Arkansas U.S. Infantry.

General Steele proclaimed an election for March 14 as scheduled by the convention, the polls to be kept open three days. The returns gave 12,179 votes for the new constitution and 226 against it; for Isaac Murphy, with no opposition candidate for governor, 12,430 ballots were cast by oath-of-allegiance voters in 40 counties. With brass bands, flags and formalities the new state government was sworn in and took office April 11. Its two U.S. Senators-elect and its three Congressmen-elect went to Washington, presented their credentials, heard the wrangling and the squabbling in Senate and House over how the occupied Southern States should be reconstructed, and came back home to tell their people that not yet, though maybe after a while, they might be admitted to seats.

Bushwhackers had sprung up around Little Rock in such force that it was not safe to go a mile out of the capital. Brigadier General C. C. Andrews wrote to Lincoln: "A large majority of planters have taken the oath, pretend to acquiesce in the proclamation setting their slaves free, and still cling to their slaves and to the hope that they will sometime again hold them as slaves." To Lincoln as well as to Rosecrans came Missouri reports of vagabonds, thieves, marauders, bushwhackers, guerrillas, incendiaries, by tens, twenties, hundreds, often wearing the Federal uniform.

A dramatic history-making figure rose out of Missouri affairs, ready to embroil Lincoln in a fiery episode. Born in Lexington, Kentucky, a Princeton graduate who studied law in Washington, Frank Blair, Jr., now 43 years old, was admitted to the bar in Kentucky, practiced in St. Louis, trapped bear and wolf in the Rocky Mountains, fought in the Mexican War, again practiced law in St. Louis, edited the *Missouri Democrat*, went to the legislature, helped found the Republican party in 1856. One of the first Republicans in Congress, in 1857 he advocated compensated emancipation and colonization of the Negroes five years before Lincoln brought those issues to Congress.

Blair had been commissioned general of a brigade he raised himself, and ordered to join Grant at Milliken's Bend in Mississippi. "I dreaded his coming," said Grant, who had known Blair in St. Louis and voted against him for Congress in 1858. To Grant, Blair seemed one more political general, one more politician with unearned stars on the shoulder straps. Then at Chickasaw Bluffs, Arkansas Post, at Hard Times Landing and Champion's Hill, on the Big Black and the Yazoo, Blair had fought in muddy bayous and across cornfields, sending lines of skirmishers or storming columns against the enemy. Grant said he was disappointed, agreeably so, in Frank Blair, "no man braver than he, nor . . . any who obeyed all orders . . . with more unquestioning alacrity." Therefore Grant deduced that Blair was "one man as a soldier, another as a politician." The Senate approved Lincoln's commissioning him major general.

Then Stanton out of suspicion and dislike of the Blair tribe issued an order relieving General Blair of command, having, the Blairs and their friends said, "the effrontery to declare that he did so by order of the President." Sherman still wanted Blair in the saddle with the 15th corps. So did Grant. And Lincoln called on Stanton to revoke the order relieving Blair.

Blair asked his brother Montgomery in the Cabinet to find out the wishes of the President. He would be guided by those wishes. Lincoln wrote to Montgomery Blair:

> Some days ago I understood you to say that your brother, Gen. Frank Blair, desires to be guided by my wishes as to whether he will occupy his seat in congress or remain in the field. My wish, then, is compounded of what I believe will be best for the country, and best for him. And it is, that he will come here, put his military commission in my hands, take his seat, go into caucus with our friends, abide the nominations, help elect the nominees, and thus aid to organize a House of Representatives which will really support the government in the war. If the result shall be the election of himself as Speaker, let him serve in that position; if not, let him re-take his commission, and

return to the Army. For the country this will heal a
dangerous schism . . . He is rising in military skill and
usefulness. His recent appointment to the command of
a corps, by one so competent to judge as Gen. Sherman, proves this. In that line he can serve both the
country and himself more profitably than he could as
a member of congress on the floor. The foregoing is
what I would say, if Frank Blair were my brother instead of yours.

Frank Blair was still in rain and sleet among Union fighters in Tennessee while Congress organized and elected Colfax Speaker of the House. On January 12, 1864, however,
Frank Blair took his seat in Congress. Those who had hated
the sight of him the last time they saw him now hated him
all the more. Stanton's relieving him from command was
considered personal animus. They were uneasy; Blair out-
classed them in the point that he could sit a horse and keep
a cool head while handling a corps of 30,000 troops in a
style up to the requirements of the terrible Sherman.

Blair defended the President's Amnesty Proclamation as
wise statesmanship. He challenged a provision for the lands,
estates and properties of the South to be seized and parti-
tioned among freed slaves and Union soldiers. Blair would
recall Senator Benton's aphorism, "Our troubles come
from the uneasy politicians and our safety from the tranquil masses."

With praise for the President, Blair mingled his plea for
slaveholders loyal to the Union to be paid for their slaves
made free. In this speech of February 5, 1864, Blair put
himself on record with the few Lincoln men in Congress.
In doing so he set himself up as an interpreter of the President's mind and took on the tone of a spokesman and a de-
fender, so that those who heard or read his speech might
believe that the Blair family and the President were in perfect accord. It was a habit and a method that both Montgomery and Frank Blair had. And Lincoln knew its political
folly when he wrote to Montgomery that Frank was "in
danger of being permanently separated from those with

whom only he can ever have a real sympathy—the sincere opponents of slavery." Lincoln saw Blair tearing wider the split between radicals and moderates in Congress, and therefore was making arrangements with Grant and Sherman for Blair to take again his corps command.

Blair struck at Chase in a resolution calling for a committee of five from Congress to investigate acts of the Treasury Department, "to report whether any frauds have been practiced on the Government," whether any favoritism had been shown, and whether the enemy had been helped. The Chase men struck back.

Blair had bought brandy to the amount of 225 gallons and a scandalously large amount of whisky, claret, Catawba wine, besides 25 half-barrels of ale and 225 boxes of canned fruit, while he was at Vicksburg in June '63, according to photographic copies of an order signed by Major General Blair and eight staff officers. This order was published in newspapers and photographic copies of it were circulated among members of Congress. The permit of the customs collector at St. Louis invoiced the purchase at $8,651. The inference of the Chase men and the Missouri radicals seeking Blair's scalp was that Blair and his staff men on duty at Vicksburg could not possibly drink 225 gallons of brandy and a larger amount of other liquors during the war, and the goods had been ordered for speculation and profits. Blair had told the House that the liquor order was a forgery and B. R. Bonner, assistant special treasury agent in St. Louis, would substantiate the fact.

Blair took the floor and requested the House to appoint a committee of three to investigate. A coast-to-coast committee of William Higby of California, Brutus J. Clay of Kentucky and John V. S. L. Pruyn of New York was appointed and reported a month later, April 23, that it appeared satisfactorily in evidence before them that "one Michael Powers, representing himself to be an agent of the Treasury Department . . . had offered his services" to procure a moderate amount of liquor, tobacco and cigars for General Blair and his staff, to cost not more than $175. Since Blair and his officers had signed the order, it had been altered. An order for goods to cost less than $175 had been item by item changed to cost $8,651.

"I am . . . loth . . . to consume the time," began Blair in a speech that ran ten columns in the *Congressional Globe*. When the atrocious slander against him had first been published he was commanding the 15th army corps on its march from Memphis to Chattanooga to drive Bragg from Lookout Mountain and Missionary Ridge. Following publication of the slander, he had been superseded in command. Not satisfied with having thus humiliated him, the originators of the calumny had reiterated it on his return to the House. He spoke regrets at having employed the language ("liar, falsifier, scoundrel") which he did in the House, though making it clear he was still using that same language outside the House. He would not go extensively into the matter of the "forgery perpetrated by a person in the employ of the Treasury Department, uttered and put into circulation by a special agent of the Treasury Department, and printed in a newspaper pensioned by the Secretary of the Treasury." These guilty men he would not follow longer. "These dogs have been set on me by their master, and since I have whipped them back into their kennel I mean to hold their master responsible for this outrage and not the curs who have been set upon me." The liquor order had been made public by a Treasury agent who knew it was a forgery, after the goods it called for had been seized as contraband, after he, Blair, had been assailed in newspapers as a whisky speculator, and "because I had attacked Mr. Chase in a speech in St. Louis and assailed his trade regulations."

Everything true or false that Blair could think of that might possibly blacken or smear Chase was hurled out before a gaping, amazed Congress and press gallery. The same Chase who had opposed the President on the reinforcement of Fort Sumter and would have abandoned the war at the start now favored a war to annihilate the loyal state governments of the South. One letter from the head of a large financial institution in New York City mentioned rumors afloat there: the Secretary of the Treasury had "given to his son-in-law, Governor Sprague, a permit to buy cotton at the South, by which he will probably make . . . $2,000,000." When a congressional committee should make the inquiry that he, Blair, had called for, they would find plenty. "And Mr. Chase cannot escape . . . However deeply the committee may lay the whitewash on, it cannot conceal the dark background."

And though Mr. Chase had written a letter saying he had retired from the canvass for the presidential nomination, that letter was written because the "strictly private" Pomeroy Circular, being made public, had cut the ground from under him. "He wanted to get down under the ground and work there in the dark as he is now doing, running the Pomeroy machine on the public money as vigorously as ever."

When Blair had finished, he had only come short of openly saying he believed Chase to be a respectable masquerading scoundrel, a whited sepulcher, coward, liar, hypocrite, thief and snake in the grass. The leader of one factional clan in politics had been hit below the belt and had hit back—below the belt. It was a double foul, and not easy for Lincoln to referee.

The House two days later asked the President to tell them whether Blair was a Congressman or a general. The President three days later sent the House an explanation:

> . . . when Gen. Grant was made Lieut. General, producing some change of commanders, Gen. Blair sought to be assigned to the command of a corps. This was made known to Generals Grant and Sherman and assented to by them, and the particular corps for him designated. This was all arranged and understood, as now remembered, so much as a month ago; but the formal withdrawal of Gen. Blair's resignation, and making the order assigning him to the command of the corps, were not consummated at the War Department until last week—perhaps on the 23rd of April, Inst. As a summary of the whole it may be stated that Gen. Blair holds no military commission or appointment,

other than as herein stated; and that it is believed he is now acting as a Major General upon the assumed validity of the commission herein stated . . .

The House next day by a vote of 84 to 28 requested the President to send over copies of all documents concerned in the matter. He did so, and Senate and House threshed over the question of whether the President had authority thus to hold resignations. Again the President was overstepping the Constitution and taking powers that belonged to Congress, said several earnest, worthy statesmen, besides several windy blatherskites. The matter finally was referred to a committee, where it lingered and was not brought up.

Late in the day of Blair's speech burning up Chase, Albert Gallatin Riddle, an Ohio friend of Chase, was shown into the railroad car on which Chase was soon starting for Baltimore. "He [Chase] was alone, and in a frightful rage, and controlled himself with difficulty while he explained the cause," noted Riddle. "The recital in a hoarse, constrained voice, seemed to rekindle his anger . . . Mr. Chase thought of remaining in the city, and at once tendering his resignation to the President."

Riddle called on the President with another Ohio Congressman, Rufus Paine Spalding. "The jealous and exacting abolitionists," said the standing Riddle to the seated Lincoln, "forgetting how impossible it is that you can be guilty of an attack upon your Secretary . . . believe that Blair must have had at least your countenance in this wretched business." The President rose from his chair, came around the table, took each man by the hand, then went to the table, took up some papers, and, standing, addressed the two Congressmen for half an hour.

Long before Frank's speech denouncing Chase, he had sent, on Frank's request, an order to the War Department to have him restored as a major general. He heard no more of it till about the noon of the day of Frank's last speech, when Frank had called and said the all-important order had not been made. The President then sent a messenger to the Adjutant General, who replied that Mr. Blair was not known in the department as an officer, whereupon the President ordered his resignation as major general to be canceled, which was done. "Within three hours," said Lincoln, as Riddle noted it, "I heard that this speech had been made, when I knew *that another beehive was kicked over*. My first thought was to have cancelled the orders restoring him to the army. Perhaps this would have been best. On such reflection as I was able to give to the matter, however, I concluded to let them stand. If I was wrong in this, the injury to the service can be set right. And thus you see how far I am responsible for Frank Blair's assaults on Mr. Chase."

The visit of Riddle and Spalding with the President lasted two hours, and they were pleased to go away with their message for Chase and the abolitionists. As matters stood, Chase did not insist on the President's making the public disavowal which at first he had said must be conceded.

Meanwhile in this April of 1864, came news of an affair, the central figure of which was Confederate Major Nathan Bedford Forrest, born for war. Fifteen horses had been killed under him. At Murfreesboro, Shiloh, Chickamaugua, he was in the vortex. No other commanding officer North or South, it was believed, had sat his horse and personally sabered to death so many of the enemy. A log-cabin boy from middle Tennessee, Forrest had never seen West Point nor read a book on military tactics. In Memphis as a real-estate dealer and slave trader he had made a fortune, bought cotton plantations, and when the war started had an income of $30,000 a year. He had raised several regiments, sometimes outfitting them with horses, equipment and rations by raids on Union supply centers. His record for swift movement and fast fighting was compared to that of Stonewall Jackson. His answer to a woman who asked him the secret of his success was, "Ma'am, I got thar fust with the most men." One of his written orders read, "Tell Bell to move up and fetch all he's got." He took whisky only when wounded, spoke prayers in his tent every night, and before wading into the enemy, if there were time, he had a chaplain ask God's blessing on ranks of men with hats off. He had sent pistol balls into more than one runaway trooper of his command.

As a slave trader he had the faint enigmatic odor that traditionally excluded slave traders from exclusive social circles of the South. When it was urged that the war was for Southern independence and not slavery, Forrest replied, "If we aint fightin' fer slavery then I'd like to know what we are fightin' fer." With some 4,000 men Forrest moved up from Mississippi into Tennessee, struck at Sherman's supply connections, enlarged and strengthened his army.

At Fort Pillow, on the Mississippi 40 miles north of Memphis, Forrest with 6,000 troops drove the 600 defenders from outworks into the fort. While his white flags of truce were in the air he served notice that he would storm the fort. The Union commanders claimed that while thus negotiating under flags of truce Forrest moved his troops into better positions, violating the laws of civilized warfare. Forrest's regiments rushed the fort, took it, and put to death over half the garrison, Forrest claiming the fort flag had not been hauled down in token of surrender and in accord with civilized military law. Of the 262 Negro soldiers in the garrison nearly all were killed, wounded in escape, or buried alive.

The news shocked the North. Press, pulpit and politicians of antislavery trend cried the affair as a fiendish atrocity demanding retaliation. Ben Wade for the Senate and Daniel W. Gooch of Massachusetts for the House were appointed a committee to find the facts. They reported "at least 300 were murdered in cold blood after the post was in possession of the rebels and our men had thrown down their arms and ceased to offer resistance . . . Men, women, even children, were shot down, beaten, hacked with sabres; children not more than ten years old were forced to stand up and face their murderers while being shot; sick and wounded were butchered without mercy . . ."

Whether one side tricked the other under a flag of truce

was left in doubt; perhaps neither side could have cleared up the point. But a historian would have to record that a certain moment arrived when Forrest's men were no longer fighting a battle in a war between civilized nations; they were sharing in a race riot, a mass lynching, and the event became an orgy of unleashed primitive human animals riding a storm of anger and vengeance. "Kill the God damned nigger!" ran the recurring line of the published testimony. "Kill all the niggers!" shouted one Confederate officer. General Forrest, riding among scattered wounded Negroes, called out that he knew some of them. "They've been in my nigger-yard in Memphis."

Perhaps half or more of Forrest's men were horrified at what was happening. What they saw was not war but mass murder out of race hatred. They tried to stop it. But it was a cyclone. According to a Negro private of the 6th U.S. Artillery one Confederate officer shouted to his men, "Boys, I will have you arrested if you don't stop killing them boys," another Confederate officer yelling the answer, "Damn it, let them go on; it isn't our law to take any negro prisoners; kill every one of them." Repeatedly the witnesses told of Southern officers ordering men not to shoot, or of Confederate men in the ranks pleading mercy for enemy Negroes and whites. But discipline was gone. What began as a battle ended as a race riot with wholesale murder.

A telegram of Forrest to Richmond reported driving the enemy into Fort Pillow and demanding surrender, "which was declined." Then: "I stormed the fort, and after a contest of thirty minutes captured the entire garrison, killing 500 and taking 100 prisoners . . . I sustained a loss of 20 killed and 60 wounded." Forrest at Paducah and at Columbus in weeks immediately preceding had indicated that if he must storm the works "no quarter" would be shown the Negro troops His view was made clearer a few weeks later when he wrote to a Union general, "I regard captured negroes as I do other captured property, and not as captured soldiers."

Six days after the Fort Pillow massacre Lincoln spoke at

a Sanitary Fair, reminded his Baltimore audience that in looking out on so many people assembled to serve the Union soldiers, the fact was that three years earlier the same soldiers could not so much as pass through Baltimore. "We all declare for liberty; but in using the same *word* we do not all mean the same *thing*. With some the word liberty may mean for each man to do as he pleases with himself, and the product of his labor; while with others the same word may mean for some men to do as they please with other men, and the product of other men's labor . . . The shepherd drives the wolf from the sheep's throat, for which the sheep thanks the shepherd as a *liberator,* while the wolf denounces him for the same act as the destroyer of liberty, especially as the sheep was a black one. Plainly the sheep and the wolf are not agreed upon a definition of the word liberty; and precisely the same difference prevails to-day among us human creatures, even in the North, and all professing to love liberty . . ."

On another subject he felt he ought to say a word: "A painful rumor, true, I fear, has reached us of the massacre, by the rebel forces, at Fort Pillow . . . of some three hundred colored soldiers and white officers . . . There seems to be some anxiety in the public mind whether the government is doing it's duty to the colored soldier, and to the service, at this point . . . We are having the Fort-Pillow affair thoroughly investigated; and such investigation will probably show conclusively how the truth is. If, after all that has been said, it shall turn out that there has been no massacre . . . it will be almost safe to say there has been none, and will be none elsewhere. If there has been the massacre of three hundred there, or even the tenth part of three hundred, it will be conclusively proved; and being so proved, the retribution shall as surely come. It will be matter of grave consideration in what exact course to apply the retribution; but in the supposed case, it must come."

In the storm of guns and blood and death soon to be let loose by Grant and Sherman against Lee and Johnston, in the reddening streams and the shouting and the crying with black silence after, and then the renewal of crimson explosions and the gray monotonous weariness—in this terrific grapple of guns and living wills and dying testaments the Fort Pillow affair was to sink to a lesser significance.

Chapter 29

*Grant's Offensive, '64 — Free Press —
Lincoln Visits the Army*

Across the Rapidan River and into the Wilderness of Spotsylvania, Grant with some 120,000 men had vanished at midnight May 4. On a piece of ground ranging 10 to 12 miles across in any direction Grant was to meet Lee's army. Grant had two men to Lee's one. Lee, as Grant came on, could choose where he wanted to fight Grant. For Grant's men, crossing a river, seeking their opponent and going to him, it would be at times a groping in the dark.

Lincoln sat scanning flimsies in the telegraph room, and during Thursday, May 5, and past midnight of Friday, May 6, had no news of Grant. A locomotive ordered by Lincoln brought a cub reporter, Henry E. Wing, from 30 miles away for a two-o'clock-in-the-morning interview. As Wing told it to Lincoln, Grant had given orders for a daybreak offensive against the enemy and had said to him on leaving, "If you do see the President, see him alone and tell him that General Grant says there will be no turning back." Until four that Saturday morning the man and the youth talked, Lincoln squeezing from Wing every last point as to what he had seen and heard.

While Lincoln tried to sleep, Grant sat by a campfire, his hat slouched low, the collar of his blue overcoat hiding most of his face. He smoked a cigar, slowly chewed it, sat motionless except for an occasional shift of one leg over the other. Grant had lost 14,000 men, killed, wounded or missing, in 48 hours of fighting. Ambulances streaming north choked the roadways. Lee had lost more than he could spare as Grant hour on hour ordered up assaulting columns. After such desperate fighting it was customary to rest an army. Grant could decide to hold back—or go on.

As hours passed after midnight, slouched and grizzled, outwardly calm as bronze and steel but underneath shaken in turmoil, Grant did his thinking and made his decision. He would move on. His reasoning included his proposition, "Accident often decides the fate of battle." He could name the simple accidents that had operated against him and against Lee that day. He reasoned too that there would be an advantage in doing what the other fellow did not want him to do. He would move on, toward Richmond, by the left, toward Spotsylvania Court House. And Lee was at Spotsylvania, again in Grant's path. Till dawn of May 13 the combat went on at Spotsylvania. For ten days the Army of the Potomac had marched and fought continuously, losing 26,815 killed and wounded, 4,183 missing. The Confederates gave out no records of losses, though on the basis of prisoners taken by Grant, it was plain that Lee's army was being mercilessly slashed of irreplaceable manpower.

In the evening Lincoln spoke to serenaders of "our commanders . . . following up their victories resolutely and successfully," and "Gen. Grant has not been jostled in his purposes . . . he has made all his points, and to-day he is on his line as he purposed before he moved his armies . . . I commend you to keep yourselves in the same tranquil mood that is characteristic of that brave and loyal man."

During this week Carpenter in the White House studied every shade of expression in the exterior Lincoln. "Absorbed in his papers, he would become unconscious of my presence . . . In repose, it was the saddest face I ever knew. There were days when I could scarcely look into it without crying. The first week of the battles of the Wilderness he scarcely slept at all . . . One of these days, I met him, clad in a long morning wrapper, pacing back and forth a narrow passage leading to one of the windows, his hands behind him, great black rings under his eyes, his head bent forward upon his breast." Of this same day John W. Forney wrote that he heard Lincoln cry "My God! my God!" over

20,000 men killed and wounded in a few days' fighting.

Good news from the battle front had to be shared. Lincoln could not lie abed with it. "The President came in last night in his shirt & told us of the retirement of the enemy from his works at Spotsylvania & our pursuit," wrote Hay May 14. Considering the wear and tear of events, Hay estimated that Lincoln was holding his weight well.

Leslie's Weekly recorded a gentleman remarking to Lincoln that nothing could cheat him of election as President again except Grant's capture of Richmond when the Democrats would nominate Grant for President. "Well," said the President, "I feel very much like the man who said he didn't want to die particularly, but if he had got to die that was precisely the disease he would like to die of." Worrying friends suggested more than once that he should beware of General Grant. His usual reply, according to his secretaries: "If he takes Richmond, let him have it."

Now emerged Phil Sheridan. His cavalry swept round the flank of Lee's army, tore up ten miles of railway, released 400 Union prisoners, struck the reserve stores of Lee's supplies, destroyed 504,000 rations of bread and 904,000 of meat, and in combat six miles from Richmond killed the dauntless and priceless cavalry officer, J. E. B. Stuart, 31 years old, Lee's most irreplaceable general officer, "the eyes of the army."

Grant's pride and joy among major generals, the dauntless and priceless John Sedgwick, took a sharpshooter's bullet in his brain one May day as he smiled in jest to his soldiers his last words, "Don't duck; they couldn't hit an elephant at that distance." Once Lincoln had offered him command of the Army of the Potomac and in modesty Sedgwick declined it. He was afraid of nothing except immeasurable personal responsibility.

By the left again Grant moved, to Cold Harbor, almost in sight of the steeples of Richmond. There he ordered a frontal assault that in 22 minutes lost 3,000 men. The night of June 3 saw 7,000 Union soldiers dead or ready for hospitals, as against Confederate losses of 1,200 to 1,500. "I have always regretted that the last assault at Cold Harbor was ever made," wrote Grant later. It was 30 days since he had crossed the Rapidan and forced Lee into a succession of battles. Never before had the Army of Northern Virginia been pressed from point to point and day to day of fighting by an Army of the Potomac that never rested or quit. A new mental and psychic factor was entering the war.

What was this new triple combination of Grant in Virginia, Sherman in Georgia and Lincoln at Washington? Would Lincoln, the recruiting agent and supply man at Washington, and Grant and Sherman with men and bayonets, carry on till they established the authority of the Federal Government at Washington over all the states of the old Union?

No longer could Lee go out in the open and send assaulting columns at the Army of the Potomac. The Richmond Government was near its last line of conscripts. Among Lee's men the question was: Will this battle never end? Why kill and kill only to see that army come further south? Among Grant's men the question was: Why should we over and again lose two and three to one fighting an entrenched enemy who forces us to come to him?

Suddenly Grant made a complete shift in his style of fighting. While Lee waited for direct combat and bloody frontal assaults, Grant moved—by night—in so shrouded a secrecy that only a few high officers knew where the army was going. Lee's skirmishers next day brought him word that the long trenches in front of Cold Harbor were empty. Grant was gone. A long march, and the wide James River crossed, brought Grant's army to the Petersburg defenses of Richmond. In four days of assaults 10,000 Union troops were now lost as against half that number of the enemy. On June 19 Grant sent word to Washington that he would order no more assaults. For a time he would rest his army. From the Wilderness through Cold Harbor he had lost 54,000 men, nearly as many as the entire force under Lee, but reinforcements had brought his army to about the same number he had when he crossed the Rapidan in early May.

While the bloody assaults at Petersburg were under way

Grant had a telegram from Lincoln June 15, 1864: "Have just read your despatch of 1 P.M. yesterday. I begin to see it. You will succeed. God bless you all." This implied salutations on the grand strategy. For Grant was directing several armies. Sigel in the Shenandoah had failed him. Butler on the James River had dallied and lost big chances. But Sheridan had performed, while Sherman was steadily approaching Atlanta. Long toils were ahead. Could Sherman and Grant press through and join their armies? If so, the war would be over. "I begin to see it," Lincoln wired Grant.

Lincoln continued service as Grant's head recruiting officer. "War, at the best, is terrible, and this war of ours, in its magnitude and in its duration, is one of the most terrible," said the President at a Sanitary Fair in Philadelphia. "If I shall discover that General Grant . . . can be greatly facilitated in [his] work by a sudden pouring forward of men and assistance, will you give them to me? [Cries of "yes."] Then, I say, stand ready, for I am watching for the chance."

On May 18 at 4 A.M., the press deadline near, there had come to all New York newspapers a proclamation in which the President fixed May 26 as a day of fasting, humiliation and prayer for the nation, called for 400,000 men to be conscripted, and took on a tone of mourning as though the war was lost. Dated at the Executive Mansion, Washington, it opened: "In all seasons of exigency it becomes a nation carefully to scrutinize its line of conduct, humbly to approach the Throne of Grace, and meekly to implore forgiveness, wisdom, and guidance . . . With a heavy heart, but an undiminished confidence in our cause, I approach the performance of a duty . . . by my sense of weakness before [the] almighty . . ."

The *Herald, Tribune* and *Times* editors had received in their offices the same Associated Press manifold sheets as the *World* and the *Journal of Commerce*. The fishy tone of its opening: "Fellow-Citizens of the United States" made it suspect. The *Herald* printed it, but did not send out the one early edition containing it. The two newspapers foremost in violent opposition to the President, however, printed it as a news follow-up on their repeated items about the President's shattered physical health.

Stanton the next morning, according to Nicolay and Hay, wrote a dispatch, with Lincoln's signature, to Major General John A. Dix, commanding in New York: "Whereas there has been wickedly and traitorously printed and published this morning in the New York 'World' and New York 'Journal of Commerce' . . . a false and spurious proclamation . . . purporting to be signed by the President . . . you are therefore hereby commanded forthwith to arrest and imprison . . . the editors, proprietors, and publishers of the aforesaid newspapers." To Governor Yates at Springfield, Illinois, Lincoln wired: "If any such proclamation has appeared, it is a forgery." Seward issued a statement: "The paper is an absolute forgery." Dix arrested the editors of the *World* and the *Journal of Commerce*, under later orders let them go, but for two days would not let them print and sell their papers.

Dix telegraphed Stanton he was sending to Fort Lafayette one Joseph Howard, found to be the author of the forged proclamation. "He is a newspaper man . . . has been very frank in his confession, says it was a stock-jobbing operation." The President directed that, while the editors had no right to plead ignorance or want of criminal intent, he was not disposed "to visit them with vindictive punishment" and authorized Dix to restore to them their establishments. The editor of the *World*, Manton Marble, signed columns of editorials terming the Chief Magistrate tyrant, usurper and despot who had destroyed "freedom of the press." Marble invited and defied the President to again close down the *World*, which didn't happen.

Stanton had rushed the decision to suppress the two papers without asking the President about it, according to Nicolay and Hay. The case was similar to the arrest of Vallandigham and the suppression of the Chicago *Times;* in both the President indicated afterward that he would have preferred another course of action.

Joe Howard meditated in a cell at Fort Lafayette on the easy money he had expected from the rise of gold resulting from his hoax, on the brokers in cahoots with him who had also lost out, on his former days as secretary to the Reverend Henry Ward Beecher, on newspapers over the country saying: "Howard . . . wrote the hoax story in relation to Mr. Lincoln's escape 'in a Scotch cap and long military cloak.' " After a few weeks in jail, Howard was released by order of the President, on request of Henry Ward Beecher.

Governor Seymour called on District Attorney A. Oakey Hall of New York City to punish those who in the suppression of newspapers had offended the law. General John A. Dix and four other army officers were arrested, though not jailed, the proceedings polite and legal. In the finish, Seymour was baffled by Lincoln's order to Major General Dix that until further orders he must stay in command in New York and, in effect, use the U.S. Army and Navy before he let the likes of Seymour and the New York *World* put him in jail.

Elsewhere over the land mobs of Union men had gone far in the suppression of newspapers. In the three preceding months the *Constitution and Union* at Fairfield, Iowa, was destroyed, as was the *Northumberland Democrat* and the Sunbury *Democrat* in Pennsylvania; the Youngstown *Mahoning Sentinel,* the Dayton *Empire,* the Greenville *Democrat,* the Lancaster *Eagle* and the Wauseon *Democrat* in Ohio; the Laporte *Democrat* in Indiana; the Chester *Picket Guard* and the *Gallatin County Democrat* in Illinois; the Belleville *Volksblatt* and the Louisiana *Union* in Missouri. In these cases the mobs demolished office and plant so they could not get out a paper. In Columbus, Ohio, the editor of the *Crisis* was seized and imprisoned; the editor of the *Mahoning Sentinel* narrowly escaped death. Editors at several points were "seized" and sometimes roughly handled. The two-day suppression of two New York newspapers was in accord with a mass trend of the first half of '64.

On the morning of the bogus proclamation the price of gold made fast upswings and the New York Stock Exchange was feverish. To gold speculators who took it as genuine the proclamation meant that Grant was losing and

gold would go higher. The antics and greed of these gamblers had recently been attacked by Congress in a bill empowering the Secretary of the Treasury to sell surplus gold.
Carpenter heard Governor Curtin remark to Lincoln one
day, "I see by the quotations that Chase's movement has
already knocked gold down several per cent." Lincoln's face
knotted. "Curtin, what do you think of those fellows in
Wall Street, who are gambling in gold at such a time as
this?" "They are a set of sharks." "For my part," bringing
a clenched fist down on a table, "I wish every one of them
had his *devilish* head shot off."

In his own mind the President believed the war would
last a longer time than he dared to tell the public, according
to Noah Brooks. He wrote that on June 14 the President
was impatient with the people who expected Grant would
take Richmond before the autumn leaves began to fall.

Down the Potomac and around to the James River Lincoln and Tad rode on a white river steamer and June 21
Lincoln stepped from upper deck to gangway, wrung the
hand of his General in Chief, spoke appreciation. Lincoln
chatted at Grant's headquarters and rode to the Butler and
Meade commands. Astride a horse he wore a tall black silk
hat, black trousers and frock coat. Wrote Horace Porter,
"By the time he had reached the troops he was completely
covered with dust, and the black color of his clothes had
changed to Confederate gray . . . his trousers gradually
worked up above his ankles, and gave him the appearance
of a country farmer riding into town wearing his Sunday
clothes. However, the troops were so lost in admiration of
the man that the humorous aspect did not seem to strike
them. The soldiers rapidly passed the word along the line
that 'Uncle Abe' had joined them, and cheers broke forth
from all the commands, and enthusiastic shouts and even
words of familiar greeting met him on all sides."

After a while Grant suggested they should ride on and
see the colored troops. Lincoln said, "Oh, yes. I want to
take a look at those boys. I read with the greatest delight
the account in Mr. Dana's despatch of how gallantly they

behaved. He said they took six out of the sixteen guns captured that day. I was opposed on nearly every side when
I first favored the raising of colored regiments; but they
have proved their efficiency, and I am glad they have kept
pace with the white troops in the recent assaults . . ."

At the 18th corps camp Lincoln met a torrent of black
men who circled roundabout him. Tears ran down some
faces. Cheers, laughter, songs, mixed and rang in the air.
"God bless Massa Linkum!" "De Lawd save Fader Abraham!" They waved their hands, brandished their arms,
kissed the hands of their mystic hero, crowded around
fondling his horse, bridle and saddle. "The President," noted
Porter, "rode with bared head; the tears had started to his
eyes and his voice was broken."

Lincoln next morning cruised upriver, amid the gunboats, met Admiral Lee and General Butler, saw breast-
works and parapets and heard army men explain them.
Some particularly strong positions recently seized and fortified were pointed out and brought Lincoln's remark to Butler, "When Grant once gets possession of a place, he holds
on to it as if he had inherited it." He sailed back to Washington with new-made friends in the army, not the least of
them the General in Chief. Their bonds drawing closer
would need yet to be stronger.

The Chicago *Times* quoted a Missouri Frémonter as saying Lincoln's head was "too light for the weight of his
foot," and the war was conducted in the manner of the
man found climbing trees to catch woodpeckers. On being
told he could never catch woodpeckers that way, he hol-
lered back, "Well, if I don't catch any I'll worry them like
hell."

Unionist newspapers dwelt on Libby Prison in Richmond
limiting letters to six lines and one prisoner writing: "My
dear Wife—Yours received—no hope of exchange—send
corn starch—want socks—no money—rheumatism in left
shoulder—pickles very good—send sausages—God bless
you—kiss the baby—Hail Columbia! Your devoted Husband."

In an album that held autographs of all the Presidents

of the United States Lincoln wrote his signature. The actress Fanny Kemble donated it to the New York Sanitary Fair.

Over the land stood houses where the war losses came close home. "My oldest boy, not yet twenty," wrote the poet Longfellow to a friend, "in the last battle on the Rapidan shot through both shoulders with a rifle-ball, is now at home. He comes down into my study every day, and is propped up in a great chair. How brave these boys are! Not a single murmur or complaint, though he has a wound through him a foot long. He pretends it does not hurt him."

Homeward went a musician from the Virginia fighting. When he had arrived in hospital, according to the New York *Tribune*, the surgeon said he must be lashed down while a leg was amputated. "No," said the soldier. "Never! Is there a violin in camp?" They brought one. He put it under his chin, tuned it, laughed. "Now, doctor, begin." And he went on playing the violin "without missing a note or moving a muscle" during 40 minutes while they sawed his leg off.

The Buffalo *Express* hung up a slogan: "God—Grant—Victory."

Chapter 30

The Lincoln-Johnson Ticket of the National Union Party

Justice David Davis and Thurlow Weed as between two practical party managers wanted more action from Lincoln toward clinching the nomination for President. To General Orme, Davis confided in a letter: "Mr. Lincoln seems disposed to let the thing run itself and if the people elect him he will be thankful, but won't use means to secure the thing. Mr. Lincoln annoys me more than I can express, by his persistence in letting things take their course—without effort or organization."

Swett wrote to Orme, "Lincoln out of 150 delegates elected previous to May 25, figures them all up for him." The National Union convention was ten days away. And so far no delegates had been picked for anyone but Lincoln.

John Charles Frémont and followers in Cleveland, Ohio, May 31, 1864, organized a party. They met eight days before the National Union convention at Baltimore in order to notify that convention it must not nominate Lincoln. Their platform: the constitutional prohibition of slavery, free speech and a free press, a one-term Presidency, reconstruction of states to be left entirely with Congress. They nominated for President Major General John C. Frémont and for Vice-President Brigadier General John Cochrane. They named their new party Radical Democracy. Frémont accepted the nomination and announced he had resigned as major general in the U.S. Army. He approved of the platform, except the plank calling for seizure of conquered slave soil and its division among soldiers and sailors of the United States. Mildly he spoke. "Had Mr. Lincoln remained faithful to the principles he was elected to defend, no schism could have been created and no contest would have been possible," declared the man who had been the Republican party candidate for President in 1856.

The morning after the convention, according to Nicolay and Hay, a friend gave Lincoln an account of it, and said that instead of the many thousands expected there were present at no time more than 400. The President reached for the Bible on his desk, searched a moment, then read: "And everyone that was in distress, and everyone that was in debt, and everyone that was discontented, gathered themselves unto him; and he became a captain over them; and there were with him about four hundred men."

On June 4, three days before the Baltimore convention, a mass meeting of 20,000 people in Union Square heard ex-Mayor George Opdyke, Senator Pomeroy, Magnus Gross, Hiram Walbridge, James T. Brady, General T. F. Meagher and other orators pay tribute to General Grant. The announced and express purpose of the meeting was "to honor General Grant." The inference was that Grant should be nominated at Baltimore instead of Lincoln. Grant's name in the air as the man of the hour, the doer of straightaway deeds, might suddenly be plucked for service by the emotional delegates of the Baltimore convention.

As the convention date drew near it was plain to many a radical politician that it would be easier sledding in their home territory if they were for Lincoln. Senator Jim Lane of Kansas, who had once led in taking a committee of Missouri-Kansas radicals to the White House for protest of the President's policy, was now on the band wagon, bringing to Baltimore a set of delegates he said were "all vindictive friends of the President."

Of the many who interviewed the President, his secretaries noted: "They were all welcomed with genial and cordial courtesy, but received not the slightest intimation of what would be agreeable to him. The most powerful politicians from New York and Pennsylvania were listened to with no more confidential consideration than the shy and awkward representatives of the rebellious States, who had elected themselves in sutlers' tents and in the shadow of department headquarters."

Hay wrote June 5 that delegations genuine, bogus and irregular saw the President. C. Bullitt "with Louisiana in his trousers' pocket," somewhat stampeded by political rumors in New York, was feeling "uneasy in his seat." "Florida was sending two delegations," Hay noted. "Neither will get in. Each attacks the other as unprincipled tricksters." Then came an odd paragraph: "The South Carolina delegation came in yesterday. The Pres^t says, 'Let them in.' 'They are a swindle,' I said. 'They won't swindle me,' quoth the Tycoon. They filed in: a few sutlers, cotton-dealers, and negroes presented a petition & retired."

June 7 the Baltimore convention of the National Union party met. The name National Union was adopted as a gesture of respect or even reverence for Democrats fighting in the Union armies and those who had continuously supported the Lincoln administration. June 7 Grant was still burying his dead four days after the bloody repulse at Cold Harbor. June 7 the gold speculators in New York were crazy and wild-eyed over the betting that gold, now higher than ever, would go higher yet. June 7 and potatoes were quoted at $160 a bushel in Richmond, cabbage at $10 a head.

The executive committee chairman, Senator Morgan, called the convention to order at noon in sweltering weather. Morgan then turned the convention over to the Reverend Dr. Robert J. Breckinridge of Kentucky, chosen by the national committee for temporary chairman, though it became a Breckinridge family tradition that Lincoln had asked the national committee to choose Breckinridge. The white-haired, bearded and grizzled preacher took the platform amid cheers for the "Old War Horse of Kentucky." Delegates knew they were gazing on an old man who had a nephew and two sons serving as officers in the Confederate Army.

A whirlwind of applause shook rafters and beams at a sentence from Breckinridge: "Does any man doubt . . . that Abraham Lincoln shall be the nominee?" But other solemn duties lay ahead. They would have to tell the country why they were fighting the war. They would have to beware of party politics and sink all for the Union. "As a Union party, I will follow you to the ends of the earth, and to the gates of death. (Applause.) But as an Abolition party —as a Republican party—as a Whig party—as a Democratic party—as an American party, I will not follow you one foot." As to slavery the venerable Kentuckian was crystalline. "I join myself with those who say, away with it forever; and I fervently pray God that the day may come when throughout the whole land every man may be as free as you are, and as capable of enjoying regulated liberty."

After a prayer, Thad Stevens took the floor and objected to the admission of delegates from states "in secession." He had no doubt "excellent men . . . from such States" were present, but protested against any "recognition of the right of States which now belong to the Southern Confederacy to be represented here."

Then arose Horace Maynard of Tennessee, tall and spare, his long black hair, high brow and strong straight nose having brought him the nickname of the "Narragansett Indian." Maynard's high-pitched voice measured out sentences, punctuated by gestures with a forearm and a quivering index finger; he carried to every seat in the theater. His eyes grew wet with tears and many in the audience sobbed aloud as he pictured the conditions of his people and faltered at voicing their desolation. "For you that drink in the cool breezes of the Northern air, it is easy to rally to the flag . . . But we represent those who have stood in the very furnace of the rebellion, those who have met treason eye to eye, and face to face, and fought from the beginning for the support of the flag and the honor of our country. (Great applause.)" Outnumbered and often outlawed, they had seen their sons conscripted in the Confederate Army, their property confiscated, homes burned, brutal guerrilla raids, imprisonment and execution of leaders, and all the woe of a land where contending armies sweep back and forth. A storm of applause swept the main floor and galleries when Maynard finished.

At the evening session the permanent chairman of the convention, ex-Governor William Dennison of Ohio, alluded to the forthcoming unanimous nomination for the Presidency, of "the wise and good man whose unselfish devotion to the country, in the administration of the Government has secured to him not only the admiration, but the warmest affection of every friend of constitutional liberty. (Applause.)"

Next morning the convention voted 440 to 4 in favor of seating the Missouri radicals who had obstructed and harassed Lincoln and by a series of roll calls sifted what it wanted. Only the delegates from South Carolina were thrown out entirely. The Virginia and Florida delegations were admitted to seats with no right to vote. Arkansas and Louisiana were given seats and the right to vote. By 310 to 151 the convention gave Tennessee delegates seats with the right to vote.

The report of the platform committee, offered by its chairman, Henry J. Raymond, resolved in favor of the war, the Union, the Constitution; pledged itself to everything possible to quell the then raging rebellion; no compromise with rebels; a deathblow at the gigantic evil of slavery through a constitutional prohibition of it; thanks and everlasting gratitude to the soldiers and sailors of the Union cause and promise of "ample and permanent provision for those of their survivors who have received disabling and honorable wounds in the service of the country"; approval and applause of "the practical wisdom, the . . . unswerving fidelity to the Constitution . . . with which Abraham Lincoln has discharged, under circumstances of unparalleled difficulty, the great duties and responsibilities of the Presidential office"; justice and protection to all men employed in the Union armies "without regard to distinction of color"; liberal and just encouragement of foreign immigration to "this nation, the asylum of the oppressed of all nations"; speedy construction of the railroad to the Pacific Coast; inviolate redemption of the public debt, economy and responsibility in public expenditures, vigorous and just taxation.

The radical mood was seen in a pledge of the first plank for "bringing to the punishment due to their crimes the Rebels and traitors arrayed against" the Government. The tone indicated criminal trials and hanging of Confederate leaders if and when the North won the war. This part of the platform Lincoln would have revised or delated.

Nominations were in order. Cameron had sent to the clerk's desk a written resolution with a demand that it be read. The convention heard a call for the unanimous renomination of Abraham Lincoln of Illinois and Hannibal Hamlin of Maine.

"A frightful clamor shook the hall," wrote Brooks. "Almost every delegate was on his feet objecting or hurrahing . . . For a few minutes pandemonium reigned, and in the midst of it Cameron stood with his arms folded, grimly smiling, regarding with composure the storm that he had raised. After the turmoil had spent itself . . . Raymond of New York, in an incisive, clear-cut speech, advocated nomination by a call of States . . ." Raymond's resolution passed.

The roll call began. Maine announced 16 votes for Lincoln. New Hampshire, coming next, tried a little speechmaking but was choked off with cries of "No speeches!" From then on each state announced its vote without oratory. One by one the undivided delegations threw in their ballots for Lincoln. Only one snag broke the smooth and orderly unanimity. The Missouri delegation announced it was under positive instructions to cast its 22 votes for Ulysses S. Grant. "This caused a sensation," wrote Brooks, "and growls of disapproval arose from all parts of the convention." Before the result of the balloting was announced Hume of Missouri moved that the nomination of Lincoln be declared unanimous. This under the rules could not be done until the secretary read the results: 484 votes for Lincoln, 22 for Grant. Missouri then changed its vote, and the secretary gave the grand total of 506 for Lincoln.

A storm of cheers was let loose, lasting many minutes, dying down and then flaring up again. "Men hurrahed, embraced one another," noted Brooks, "threw up their hats, danced in the aisles or on the platform, jumped on the benches, waved flags, yelled, and committed every possible extravagance . . . One of the most comical sights I beheld was that of Horace Maynard and Henry J. Raymond alternately hugging each other and shaking hands."

The hilarity over, they settled down to nominations for Vice-President. Cameron presented, under instructions of his state, he said, the name of Hannibal Hamlin. A New York delegate "in behalf of a portion" of his delegation proposed Daniel S. Dickinson of New York. Indiana, under instructions of its state convention, offered Governor Andrew Johnson of Tennessee. Horace Maynard seconded, saying Johnson "in the furnace of treason" would stand by the convention's declarations "as long as his reason remains unimpaired, and as long as breath is given him by his God."

On roll call Maine was solid for Hamlin. The number

of votes Johnson had picked up in other New England States was surprising. Connecticut plopped solid its 12 for Johnson. Massachusetts split with 17 for Dickinson, 3 for Hamlin, 2 for Butler. The chairman was solemn, the convention too, as the New York tally was read: Johnson 32, Dickinson 28, Hamlin 6. Delegates pondered. Louisiana split evenly between Dickinson and Johnson. Arkansas threw its 10 votes to Johnson and Tennessee its 15. The Missouri radicals gladly pinned a rose on Ben Butler with 20 votes, though 2 put in for Johnson. The final total was shocking and almost unbelievable to the Hamlin men: Johnson 200, Dickinson 108, Hamlin 150.

Kentucky now announced that its complimentary vote of 21 for its General Rousseau and 1 for Tod would be thrown to Johnson. Oregon and Kansas followed for Johnson. A wave of applause came with Cameron handing Pennsylvania's 52 to Johnson. As New Jersey swung into line Senator Morrill of Maine, Hamlin's manager, who the night before had been publicly and privately confident of Hamlin's chances, changed the vote of Maine in favor of the Tennessee tailor. The convention secretary announced: Johnson 494, Dickinson 17, Hamlin 9.

A. K. McClure's judgment ran with Lamon's that "Lincoln was guided in what he did, or what he did not, in planning the great campaign of his life that involved the destiny of the country itself, by the single purpose of making success as nearly certain as possible." McClure saw "not a trace of prejudice or even unfriendliness toward Hamlin" in all that Lincoln said in their second interview.

Two reasons Lincoln gave McClure for Johnson's candidacy. First, he was the ablest of all War Democrats and in a position to draw that element toward the Government; Johnson was then dramatically before the people in his work of restoring his state to the Union. The second reason was with Lincoln stronger and more imperative, according to McClure. "Lincoln was firmly convinced that by no other method could the Union sentiment abroad be so greatly inspired and strengthened as by the nomination and election of a representative Southern man to the Vice-

Presidency from one of the rebellious States in the very heart of the Confederacy."

Nicolay was to say that McClure misstated the facts, that Lincoln had kept his hand out of the nomination of Johnson, that McClure imputed double-dealing to an honest Chief Magistrate. McClure was to reply that he did not at all accuse Lincoln of deceit or insincerity. "It was quite as much a necessity for Lincoln to conceal his movements for the nomination of Johnson as it was, in his judgment, a necessity for him to nominate a Southern man and a War Democrat. He simply acted with rare sagacity and discretion in his movements, and with fidelity to the country."

The ancient factor of effective oratory had swayed the convention toward Johnson, several observers noted. The most memorable voices were those of the Border State men, Breckinridge, Brownlow and Maynard. In two speeches Maynard with fierce and moving phrases named Johnson as someone to think about. There was design wrought from some quarter in the staging of these scarred orators for their early roles at the convention.

"Of Andrew Johnson it is enough to say that there is no man in the country, unless it be Mr. Lincoln himself, whom the rebels more cordially hate," said *Harper's Weekly* in June. "He fought them in the Senate, when they counted upon his aid, and he has fought them steadily ever since." Greeley in the *Tribune* saw as "happy" the nomination of Johnson, who had "never wavered or faltered" in the Union cause, a man who would be hanged at noon on the day the Confederates captured him. From various points now was voiced one thought or instinct that had lain behind the framing of the Lincoln-Johnson ticket: it would nationalize the Republican party; no longer would Lincoln stand as the head of a sectional party.

The plan so odious and stenchladen to the radicals, known as "Lincoln's ten-per-cent plan," had only to be announced for Johnson to leap to embrace it. In a speech six months earlier Johnson had said: "Abraham Lincoln is a honest man and is going to put down this infernal rebellion. He is for a free government and I stand by him . . ."

Of medium height, a little swarthy of skin, with fine shoulders and a deep chest, Johnson carried a massive head. His deep-set and darkly piercing eyes looked at men without fear. Weapons and threats had no effect on him. If an idea or an impulse of depth moved him, he acted on it and stood by it. Physically he trusted the revolver in his right hip pocket and spiritually he had an ego that rested on a bulwark he called his conscience. He wore clean linen, was almost dainty about his collar and his shirt front, had small hands and feet; but the blandishments of the social set couldn't sway him.

From his beginnings in politics Johnson had voiced the poor whites as against the exclusive and propertied aristocracy which for 30 years had ruled the South and unduly controlled at Washington. Sometimes he was brave unto stubborn folly. He could wear his hate of the aristocrats and his passion for democracy till it was a pose and an overdone attitude. He could be so overly zealous to stand square and clear on a human issue that important half-lights of it were lost to him. Perhaps only such a man could have been the first to so manage a seceded state that it could give some color of promise to "Lincoln's ten-per-cent plan."

Many messages of congratulation rolled in to Lincoln on his renomination but none from Johnson. Many telegrams and letters came to Johnson but none from Lincoln. Each said publicly that the ticket was a good one. But neither sent word to the other that it was pleasant they were running mates.

Horace White, from a wire in the convention hall had sent Lincoln the first message of congratulation on renomination. This with the news from Nicolay arrived at the War Department telegraph office. When Major Eckert congratulated him, his face lighted elusively. "What! Am I renominated?" Operator Tinker showed him Nicolay's telegram. "Send it right over to the Madam. She will be more interested than I am."

To a committee the next day notifying him of his nomination, the President answered: "I will neither conceal my

gratification, nor restrain the expression of my gratitude . . ." The same day he said to a National Union
League delegation: "I have not permitted myself, gentlemen, to conclude that I am the best man in the country;
but I am reminded, in this connection, of a story of an old
Dutch farmer, who remarked to a companion once that 'it
was not best to swap horses when crossing streams.' "

The convention platform and the President's public ad-
dresses had projected above all other immediate issues the
need of a Constitutional amendment to prohibit slavery.
But one week after the convention adjourned, when the
House of Representatives took up a joint resolution to that
effect, 64 members voted Nay, and it failed for lack of a
two-thirds majority. The Nay votes were all Democratic
and forecast a campaign issue.

In Middletown, Connecticut, a clergyman lighted his
front door with a transparency quoting from Genesis 22:15:
"The angel of the Lord called unto Abraham out of heaven
a second time." The Troy *Times* was naïve and sweet. "If
Mr. Lincoln has fallen into errors and made mistakes—if
he has done some things that he ought not to have done,
and left undone some things that he ought to have done,
who that was ever called upon to do so much has erred so
little?"

Hannibal Hamlin in Bangor, Maine, three days after the
convention spoke of the President as "a man of eminent
abilities," as one who would "lead the nation out of its present difficulty and plant it on the eternal principle of liberty,"
as one "whom the people loved."

The New York *World* on June 9 spoke for August Belmont and many wealthy and respectable Democrats. "In a
crisis of the most appalling magnitude, requiring statesmanship of the highest order, the country is asked to consider the claims of two ignorant, boorish, third-rate backwoods lawyers, for the highest stations in the government."

"I, A. Lincoln, hereby nominate myself as a candidate
for reëlection," said the Chicago *Times* June 11. Various
anti-Lincoln journals reprinted a long editorial from the
Richmond *Dispatch,* not entirely courteous: "We say of Old

Abe it would be impossible to find such another ass in the United States, and therefore, we say let him stay."

A one-column letter of Wendell Phillips in the *Independent* was reprinted in the New York *Tribune,* the New York *World* and across the country. "The Baltimore Convention was largely a mob of speculators and contractors willing to leave to their friend, Mr. Lincoln, his usurped power of reconstruction." Its "meaningless and hypocritical platform" was "a mixture of claptrap compliments and brave demands forced by the Cleveland movement . . . As long as you keep the present turtle at the head of the Government you make a pit with one hand and fill it with the other." Of the gyrations of Phillips *Harper's* remarked: "Mr. Phillips has no right whatever to call them hypocrites . . . his vast vituperation and bitter assaults . . . are things which make many an admiring friend sad and sorry for him, and will they not one day make him profoundly sorry for himself?"

Party lines were shaken. Two men, one a Republican and the other a Democrat, were heading a National Union ticket. The great American game of politics was in chaos. In Maine and California, in Ohio and Connecticut, the state governors were War Democrats. In the patronage portioned out by the President, the War Democrats got more than a fair share, said organization Republicans.

The supreme American botanist, president of the American Academy of Arts and Sciences, Asa Gray, saw Lincoln at this time as having deep roots in good loam. To his English friend Charles Darwin, Gray wrote, "Homely, honest, ungainly Lincoln is the representative man of the country."

Twice in the week of the Baltimore convention William Lloyd Garrison had interviews with Lincoln. At one interview Theodore Tilton of the *Independent* accompanied Garrison, and it seemed that both hardened abolitionists would swing in for the Lincoln and Johnson ticket. Garrison and Tilton had taken a walk around Baltimore and tried to find the old jail that once held abolitionist Garrison many years back for voicing subversive doctrines. They said they couldn't find the jail and Lincoln laughed. "Well,

Mr. Garrison, when you first went to Baltimore you couldn't get *out;* but the second time you couldn't get *in!*"

From a photograph by Gardner of Lincoln seated, with Nicolay and Hay standing, *Harper's Weekly* made a drawing which it presented to its readers the week after the Baltimore convention. "In this earnest care-worn face," it commented, "saddened by a solemn sense of the great responsibility which in God's providence has devolved upon him, we see the man who said to his neighbors, as he left his home three years ago, that he was called to a graver task than any chief magistrate since Washington. Through an infinite perplexity of events the faith of the President has never faltered . . . Look thoughtfully at this rugged face. In its candor, its sagacity, its calmness, its steadiness and strength, there is especially conspicuous the distinctive American. Turn then to the portrait of General Grant . . . and there you see another purely American face, the same homely honesty, capacity and tenacity. Children of the people both of them . . . these two men illustrate at once the character of American civilization. There is but one prayer in the great multitude of American hearts today, God bless President Lincoln and General Grant!"

In a thin mist of evening air with willows nearby trembling to a low breeze, amid a cool dew flung out by old oaks above them, Lincoln on the Soldiers' Home grounds stood with others silent over a thoughtful twilight. By and by, as a California woman remembered it and soon wrote home to San Francisco, Lincoln said softly:

> " 'How sleep the brave, who sink to rest
> By all their country's wishes blest—' "

She was too "easily melted," wrote the California woman. "It made us cry." And she heard him further in the purpling shadows:

> " 'And women o'er the graves shall weep,
> Where nameless heroes calmly sleep.' "

Chapter 31

Washington on the Defensive — Peace Babblings

The night of June 14, 1864, a man in his room in Hiron's House, Windsor, Canada, stands before a mirror and in an amateur way arranges himself a disguise. On his unshaven upper lip he smooths a large false mustache, over the close-trimmed beard of his chin and jaws a long flowing set of whiskers. He blackens his reddish eyebrows. Under trousers and vest he buttons a bed pillow.

Nobody bothers him as he rides the ferry to Detroit. A customs officer punches him lightly in the stomach and lets it go at that. A policeman in Detroit is suspicious, takes him to a street gaslight, looks him over and lets him go. On a train out of Detroit a passenger bends down to whisper, "I know your voice but you are safe from me." Snuggled in the berth of a sleeping car he rides safely overnight to Hamilton, Ohio.

This is the return of the Honorable Clement L. Vallandigham from alien land to native soil. He spoke to a convention that day: "I return of my own act . . . I was abducted from my home and forced into banishment. The assertion or insinuation of the President, that I was arrested because laboring with some effect to prevent the raising of troops . . . is absolutely false . . ."

Noah Brooks in Lincoln's office referred to Vallandigham in Ohio. The President with a quizzical look: "What! has Vallandigham got back?" Brooks had to say everybody knew it, and heard from the President: "Dear me! I supposed he was in a foreign land. Anyhow, I hope I do not know that he is in the United States; and I shall not, unless he says or does something to draw attention to him."

June 27, 1864, Chase sent the President the nomination of Maunsell B. Field for Assistant Treasurer at New York. Lincoln next day wrote Chase: "I cannot, without much embarrassment, make this appointment, principally because of Senator Morgan's very firm opposition to it," and naming three men Morgan had mentioned to Chase, "It will really oblige me if you will make choice among these three . . ."

Chase wrote asking an interview and the President the same day replied reciting inexorable political considerations, and, "When I received your note this forenoon suggesting a verbal conversation . . . I hesitated, because the difficulty does not, in the main part, lie within the range of a conversation between you and me. As the proverb goes, no man knows so well where the shoe pinches as he who wears it . . ."

The tone of this was a little new to Chase. Once more he resigned. This made four times. And now Lincoln wrote to Chase that his resignation was accepted. "Of all I have said in commendation of your ability and fidelity, I have nothing to unsay; and yet you and I have reached a point of mutual embarrassment in our official relations which it seems cannot be overcome, or longer sustained, consistently with the public service." In his diary Chase wrote: "So my official life closes. I have laid broad foundations . . . I am too earnest, too anti-slavery, and, say, too radical, to make the President willing to have me connected with the Administration, just as my opinion is that he is not earnest enough, not anti-slavery enough, not radical enough."

The summer had brought stench of scandal. The New York *World* and other hostile newspapers day on day aired the matter of women from the Printing Bureau of the Treasury Department dressing in men's attire and attending at the Canterbury Inn in Washington lewd performances to which men only were supposed to have admission. Two newspaper columns of affidavits recited details giving the impression that the Treasury Department offices held a fast and loose set of public servants. This to one as spotless as Chase in relation to women was not to be laughed off.

The New York *Tribune* presented Chase's view that the affair was a conspiracy and dirty politics.

Hay read mixed motives. The resignation came when gold reached a new high point, when despair over government finance was deepest. The political motive, however, outweighed all others, the yearnings of Chase in his remark to the editor of the Indianapolis *Independent*, "After all, I believe that I would rather that the people should wonder why I wasn't President than why I was."

Lincoln named former Governor David Tod of Ohio, an old Douglas Democrat, to replace Chase. The Senate Finance Committee called in a body on Lincoln to protest that Tod hadn't the ability. A telegram from Tod to the President said his health would not permit him to head the Treasury. So Tod was out of the way.

Early next morning the President wrote out a nomination for William Pitt Fessenden, Senator from Maine, to fill the vacancy. The Senate took about one minute to confirm the nomination unanimously.

As chairman of the Senate Finance Committee Fessenden knew the money market was feverish, public confidence wavering; yet his friends were saying a financial crash would follow his refusal. He wrote: "Foreseeing nothing but entire prostration of my physical powers, and feeling that to take the Treasury in its exhausted condition would probably result in destroying what little reputation I had, it was still my duty to hazard both life and reputation if by so doing I could avert a crisis so imminent. I consented, therefore, to make the sacrifice."

Telegrams and letters of approval beyond precedent had poured in on Fessenden. The New York and Boston clearinghouses, bankers and merchants in all quarters, it seemed, urged his acceptance of the President's nomination when it was reported he would refuse. At the first report that Fessenden was to be Secretary of the Treasury, Government bonds advanced, pork declined $10 a barrel, and all provisions went to lower prices.

Fessenden was sworn in. The press held forth in compliments such as never before, except in the case of Grant, over a major Lincoln appointment. Hay quoted the President: "It is very singular, considering that this appointment of F.'s is so popular when made, that no one ever mentioned his name to me for that place . . ."

Fessenden had attacked the administration on the $300 clause of the draft law. He would credit the Government with the best intentions and would sustain it thoroughly, but he was opposed to "the system of high bounties which made people forget that their first duty was to the country."

Three of Fessenden's four sons had gone into the Army. Sam had been killed in battle at Centerville in '62; the others had won advancement by valor and ability to brigadier general and colonel. In '64 Frank was on the Red River in Arkansas, Jim with one leg gone was on Hooker's staff with Sherman trying to take Atlanta.

Starting as a young lawyer in Portland, Maine, Fessenden had become a Whig Congressman, later a Senator, helped found the Republican party, watched the tariff, fisheries and shipping interests of his state, clashed with Welles over Maine's share of favors and patronage, and was now to undergo the trials of an executive. The national debt was $1,700,000,000, the Treasury almost empty, the war costing $2,000,000 a day.

For several weeks it would seem Fessenden held off from making arrangements with Cooke, saying in effect that newspapers and politicians had made out too strong a case against Cooke's garnering a large comfortable fortune for himself in the selling of Government bonds. Out of interviews with Fessenden and Lincoln it followed that Jay Cooke & Company were once more harnessed into Government service.

Seventeen days before Chase resigned Congress had passed the Gold Bill and the President signed it. To buy or sell gold for delivery later than the day of signing the contract was made a crime. To contract to buy or sell gold not in the hands of the seller when selling was made a crime. The purpose was to stop speculation and gambling in gold. In the past six months gold had steadily climbed from 150 to 250. The Gold Bill made the course of gold crazier than before. It cavorted and somersaulted so fast in such a price range that it was the gambler's perfect delight. And actual gold was sent into deeper hiding and became scarcer for its functions of paying interest on Government bonds and foreign exchange.

After the 17 days of gold-price acrobatics Congress repealed the Gold Bill and the President signed the repeal. From then on the gold gamblers were accepted by the Government as an evil beyond control. Nothing came of a Union League meeting in June '64 urging that "Congress at once order the erection of scaffolds for hanging" the gold speculators.

In the deep gloom months of July and August '64, the barometric indicator, gold, was to say that Lincoln and the Union Government were failing. Thirty-nine dollars of gold would buy $100 of greenbacks. This was the bottom gold price of the Union Government's paper promises to pay. One interpretation was that the holders of gold in those months had less hope than ever of the Union Government winning its war.

On July 4 of this gloomy summer Congress adjourned. Among the bills piled on the President's desk for signature was one that would slash the slender supports on which the "Lincoln ten-per-cent plan" rested. Since December '63, when the President had launched his plan, much had happened to it. Then Hay wrote in his diary that all factions in Congress seemed to agree, and on the reading of the President's message, "Men acted as if the millennium had come. Chandler was delighted, Sumner was beaming." Border State men said they were satisfied.

Then slowly had come deepening suspicions of the President's motives, more open claims that the states in secession had committed suicide and that the President was impossible in his plan for a loyal 10 per cent to be authorized to reorganize the governments of those states. Henry Winter Davis led this opposition in the House, and Ben Wade in the Senate. Davis was tall, slender, with wavy hair and a curly mustache, a musical voice, mental caliber, oratorical and theatrical style. Born in a Maryland slave-holding family, he had come to hate slavery as fiercely as any New Englander. In politics first a Whig, then an American or Know-Nothing, he became a Republican. That Monty Blair of Maryland should be named Postmaster General was a stench in his nostrils. He led in Maryland a faction that hated Blair.

Davis brought in a bill intended to block the restoration efforts already started by the President in Louisiana and Tennessee; the measure aimed to stop the spread of the President's policy in other Southern States. In the House Davis was the one radical most often reminded by Thaddeus Stevens that he was going too far and ought to take what he could get now. The one speaker who could draw in more members from the cloakrooms than any other was Davis. He spoke his guess and vision for the Negro with cadence: "The folly of our ancestors and the wisdom of the Almighty, in its inscrutable purpose, having allowed them to come here and planted them here, they have a right to remain here to the latest syllable of recorded time."

The quixotic political artist, Davis, with his ally Ben Wade, saw a wide chasm between them and the President. They nursed suspicions into what they believed were facts. The President was too slow, too hesitant, too loose with expedient, they believed, and Congress would be more firm. New state governments could be referred "to no authority except the judgment and will of the majority of Congress," said Davis in behalf of his bill of February 15, 1864. Under the bill the President with Senate consent would appoint for each state in rebellion a provisional governor to serve until Congress recognized a regular civil government as existing therein, the loyal people of the state entitled to elect delegates to re-establish a state government. "Until therefore," said Davis, "Congress recognize a State government, organized under its auspices, there is no government in the rebel States except the authority of Congress." Davis rejected the President's Amnesty Proclamation and its "ten-per-cent plan" as lacking guarantees.

The debate ran long, a festival of constitutional lawyers. How and when does a state become a state, and under what conditions can it lose its face as a state and again later have its face put back? This question was argued up, down and across. The unconstitutional and despotic acts of the President would be legalized and perpetuated by the proposed bill, declared Representative Charles Denison of Pennsylvania. Perry of New Jersey was positive the Machiavellian hand of the President was behind the bill. Nor was Thaddeus Stevens satisfied with the Davis bill. "It does not, in my judgment, meet the evil." Its acknowledgment that the "rebel States have rights under the Constitution" he would deny. His chief objection was that the bill removed the opportunity of confiscating the property of the disloyal.

By 73 to 59 the Davis bill passed the House May 4, 1864. In the Senate its course had been guided by Wade, who said: "The Executive ought not to be permitted to handle this great question to his own liking." That a state should have self-government originated by one-tenth of the population seemed to Wade absurd, anti-republican, anomalous and entirely subversive.

In what the President had thus far done he was "equally a usurper with Caesar, Cromwell and Bonaparte," said Garrett Davis of Kentucky. In exploiting the Peace Democrat viewpoint Garrett Davis spread over the pages of the *Congressional Globe* a diatribe of several thousand words on Lincoln's ambition, desire for re-election, love of power and money. "He is no statesman, but a mere political charlatan. He has inordinate vanity and conceit. He is a consummate dissembler, and an adroit and sagacious demagogue." The tentative and hazardous state governments set up by the President in Louisiana, Tennessee and Arkansas were denounced by Garrett Davis as "lawless and daring political enterprises" intended to garner electoral votes in the coming November.

The main bill of Wade, which had been on the Senators' desks for five months, passed July 2, 1864, by 26 Yeas to 3 Nays, with no less than 20 Senators absent. The bill went into conference. Wade moved that the Senate agree to the House [Davis] bill. The Senate agreed by 18 Yeas and 14 Nays, no less than 17 Senators being absent.

In the months the bill had been before Congress, "The President declined to exercise any influence on the debate," said his secretaries, meaning that no Senators or Representatives were privately called in by the President to hear a request that they should do the best they could against it.

Into this confusion and perplexity four days after Congress adjourned the President stepped with an amazing document. He issued a proclamation reciting that Congress had passed a bill to guarantee republican form of government to certain states, and "the said bill was presented to the President of the United States for his approval less than one hour before the *sine die* adjournment of said session, and was not signed by him." Never before had an Executive assumed to reject those provisions in a legislative measure he disliked and to adopt those acceptable to him. And he went straight to the people proclaiming what he did. He had neither signed the bill nor vetoed it. "He put it in his pocket." Madison and others had used this pocket veto. He was "fully satisfied" with part of the bill but as to other parts he was "unprepared." The key of the matter was in his saying he could not be "inflexibly committed to any single plan of restoration." Over the heads of Congress and its embittered and warring factions, he put his case to the country and the people.

Ben Wade and Henry Winter Davis raged privately and stormed publicly. In the New York *Tribune* of August 5 they published their joint answer to Lincoln, picked up and reprinted over the country, "The Wade-Davis Manifesto." The language was fierce and polite at once. They hoped to blast the pinions from under the President and blister his name and give him a lesson. Addressing themselves "To the Supporters of the Government," they said they had "read without surprise, but not without indignation" the President's proclamation of July 8. They would maintain it was a right and a duty "to check the encroachments of the Executive on the authority of Congress, and to require it to confine itself to its proper sphere." The President did not sign the bill in question. "The bill did not therefore become a law; and it is therefore nothing. The proclamation is neither an approval nor a veto of the bill; it is therefore a document unknown to the laws and Constitution of the United States . . . The committee sent to ascertain if the President had any further communication for the House of Representatives reported that he had none; and the friends of the bill, who had anxiously waited on him to ascertain its fate, had already been informed that the President had resolved not to sign it. The time of presentation, therefore, had nothing to do with his failure to approve it.

"The President persists in recognizing those shadows of governments in Arkansas and Louisiana, which Congress formally declared should not be recognized—whose representatives and senators were repelled by formal votes of both Houses of Congress . . . They are the mere creatures of his will." The President held "the electoral votes of the rebel states at the dictation of his personal ambition." He had "greatly presumed" and they would give warning. "He must understand . . . that the whole body of the Union men of Congress will not submit to be impeached by him of rash and unconstitutional legislation: and if he wishes our support he must confine himself to his executive duties— to obey and to execute, not make the law."

On hearing the rasp and snarl of this family quarrel in the Republican party the opposition rejoiced. One who was hot under the collar came to Lincoln about it. And according to Carpenter, the President philosophized: "It is not worth fretting about; it reminds me of an old acquaintance, who, having a son of a scientific turn, bought him a microscope. The boy went around experimenting with his glass on everything that came in his way. One day, at the dinnertable, his father took up a piece of cheese. 'Don't eat that, father,' said the boy; 'it is full of *wrigglers.*' 'My son,' replied the old gentleman, taking, at the same time, a huge bite, 'let 'em *wriggle;* I can stand it if they can.' "

Welles wrote: "The President, in a conversation with Blair and myself on the Wade and Davis protest, remarked that he had not, and probably should not read it." And Welles strayed into dejection over the President's having advised only with Seward on his pocket-veto proclamation, having called no Cabinet meeting on it.

The main landscape of the country was too somber for people to care that Wade and Davis had lost their heads or that Davis by his false stride was to fail of nomination and lose his seat in Congress to a Unionist colonel who had come near death from wounds in the Wilderness. One viewpoint was given by *Harper's Weekly*. "We have read with pain the manifesto of Messrs. Wade and Winter Davis, not because of its envenomed hostility to the President, but because of its ill-tempered spirit, which proves conclusively the unfitness of either of the gentlemen for grave counselors in a time of national peril . . . It was the President's constitutional right to let the bill drop and say nothing more about it."

In the three days immediately preceding his proclamation concerning the Wade-Davis bill the President issued, with detailed reasons, a proclamation suspending the writ of habeas corpus in Kentucky, and another proclamation, by direction of Congress, appointing the first Thursday of August as a day of national humiliation and prayer.

Once more General Robert E. Lee played a bold defensive game and struck fear into the heart of the Union cause. He gave Jubal A. Early and John C. Breckinridge an army of 20,000 men. Sheltered by the Blue Ridge Mountains, they marched up the Shenandoah Valley, slipped through a pass, headed for Washington.

Early's men collected $20,000 cash at Hagerstown, tore up 24 miles of Baltimore & Ohio Railroad tracks, wrecked and burned mills, workshops, factories, at Baltimore burned the home of Governor Bradford, reached Silver Spring and in sight of the Capitol dome seized private papers, valuables, whisky, in the home of Postmaster General Blair, and then set the house afire. "Baltimore is in great peril," telegraphed a mayor's committee to Lincoln, asking for troops. Lincoln wired: "I have not a single soldier but whom is being disposed by the Military for the best protection of all. By latest accounts the enemy is moving on Washington. They can not fly to either place. Let us be vigilant but keep cool. I hope neither Baltimore or Washington will be sacked."

Lew Wallace, department commander at Baltimore, had marched troops out to Monocacy, fought a battle and, heavily outnumbered, was routed. His defeat delayed Early's army one day. That one day, it was generally admitted, saved Washington from the shame of capture. Gustavus Vasa Fox, without the President's knowing it, had a steamer ready for him in case the city was taken. In the Gold Room in New York June 11 the wild-eyed gamblers saw gold go to its peak price of 285.

Raw troops and soldiers just out of hospital made up the 20,000 men scraped together for manning the forts around Washington against Early, who had cut all wires north and July 11 marched his men on the Seventh Street Road that would lead him straight to the offices, arsenals, gold and silver, of the U.S. Government. Early halted his men just a little over two miles from Soldiers' Home, where Lincoln the night before had gone to bed when a squad from the War Department arrived with word from Stanton that he must get back to the city in a hurry. The President dressed and rode to the Executive Mansion.

Next day Lincoln saw through a spyglass transport steamers at Alexandria coming to unload two magnificent divisions of veteran troops fresh from Grant at City Point. The President met them at the wharf, touched his hat to them; they cheered and he waved his hand and smiled and they sent up more and more cheers. No mail, no telegrams, arrived from the outer world that day of July 12 in Washington.

From where Lincoln stood on a Fort Stevens rampart that afternoon he could see the swaying skirmish lines and later the marching brigade of General Daniel D. Bidwell, a police justice from Buffalo, New York, who had enlisted in '61 as a private, advanced in rank, and with his men had heard the bullets sing from Antietam through Gettysburg and the Wilderness. Out across parched fields, dust

and a haze of summer heat marched Bidwell's men in perfect order, to drive the enemy from a house and orchard
near the Silver Spring Road. Up a rise of ground in the face
of a withering fire they moved, took their point and pushed
the enemy pickets back for a mile—the cost 280 men killed
and wounded.

While Lincoln stood watching this bloody drama a bullet whizzed five feet from him and struck Surgeon Crawford
of the 102d Pennsylvania in the ankle. Within three feet of
the President an officer fell with a death wound. Those who
were there said he was cool and thoughtful, seemed unconscious of danger, and looked like a Commander in Chief.
"Amid the whizzing bullets," wrote Nicolay and Hay, the
President held to his place "with grave and passive countenance," till finally "General Wright peremptorily represented to him the needless risk he was running." Official
records gave the Union losses at 380 killed and 319
wounded.

Next morning Early's army was gone. Again on July 14
Washington had mail and telegrams. Somewhere toward the
Shenandoah Valley marched Early's army with its plunder-
laden wagons, audacity on its banners, money in its strong-
boxes, shoes on feet that had started north barefoot. Early
got away for the same reason, it was said, that he arrived.
"Nobody stopped him."

And why? The answer would require a diagram of the
overlapping authorities and departments; of many physical
and psychic factors, of slackness, fears, jealousies, rivalries.
Nicolay and Hay recorded: "Everybody was eager for the
pursuit [of Early] to begin; but Grant was too far away to
give the necessary orders; the President, true to the position
he had taken when Grant was made general-in-chief, would
not interfere, though he observed with anguish the undis-
turbed retreat of Early." Halleck assumed that he was in
fact, as he ranked, a chief of staff and not a commander
from whom strategy was required. "Put Halleck in command of 20,000 men," said Ben Wade, "and he would not
scare three sitting geese from their nests." "Today," wrote
Bates in his diary, "I spoke my mind very plainly, to the

Prest. (in presence of Seward, Welles and Usher) about the ignorant imbecility of the late military operations, and my contempt for Genl. Halleck."

On July 25 Grant sent a dynamic constructive proposal to Lincoln on "the necessity of having the four departments of the Susquehanna, the Middle, West Virginia, and Washington, under one head." He had made this proposal before and the War Department had rejected it. Now he was urging it again. And again he was naming General William B. Franklin, one of the abler major generals of distinguished field service, "as a suitable person to command the whole." Two days later the Secretary of War notified not General Franklin, but Halleck, that "the President directs me to instruct you that all the military operations" of the four departments and all the forces in those departments, "are placed under your general command."

It seemed that Grant wanted Franklin, or some other proven field general, at the head of the defense of Washington, while Stanton wanted the desk strategist, Halleck, elevated from staff chief to commander. And as between Stanton and Grant the President was saying Yes to Stanton and No to Grant. On the face of the matter Lincoln was going back on Grant and taking a stand with the established political bureaucrats who muddled instead of performing. Stanton's order accommodating Grant by joining four departments into one, and then giving Grant the last man Grant would have picked to head the new four-in-one department, was dated July 27.

And on that day Grant took to drink. Had Rawlins been there, Rawlins would have cursed him and put up arguments and returned to cursing and Grant would have stayed sober. As it was, Rawlins on July 28 got back from Washington to write his wife: "I find the General in my absence digressed from his true path. The God of Heaven only knows how long I am to serve my country as the guardian of the habits of him whom it has honored."

Whether the death of Major General James B. McPherson could have had anything to do with Grant's drinking on July 27, Rawlins did not write his wife. Five days before,

McPherson, bronzed, tall, tireless, in boots and gauntlets on a beautiful black horse, had ridden away from a talk with Sherman to examine the cause of a new roaring note in the firing on the left of their army near Atlanta. McPherson was only 35, with a future of hope ahead of him and a sweetheart dated to marry him when Atlanta should be taken. And McPherson's black horse had come racing back with saddle empty. Later they found him with a bullet near his heart—a soldier so rare that Grant had him in mind to take Sherman's place if anything happened to Sherman, a friend and comrade so rare that Sherman at the news paced back and forth in a headquarters room barking orders, barking his grief, tears running down his cheeks into the red beard. Grant too at the news had wet eyes, and his voice broke in saying, "The country has lost one of its best soldiers, and I have lost my best friend."

What was the balancing circumstance that made Lincoln say Yes when Stanton brought him the suggestion that Halleck and not Franklin must head the new four-in-one department? Could Stanton have boldly said to Lincoln that he must have this point or he would resign? Would that have been past Stanton? And could Lincoln at this hour have taken on himself the burden of finding a new Secretary of War to replace Stanton? If so, who would make a better one than Stanton? In telegrams they exchanged July 28 and 29 it was evident that Grant and Lincoln each understood delicate and involved matters of administration and personnel they could neither write nor telegraph. Both men were working at a furious pace in the fevered air of decisive events. On July 19 Grant had telegraphed the President a suggestion to call for another draft of 300,000 men and Lincoln had replied: "I suppose you had not seen the call for 500,000 made the day before, and which I suppose covers the case. Always glad to have your suggestions."

In grief over losing his library and many valuable papers when Early's men ransacked, looted and burned his Silver Spring house, Monty Blair said nothing better could be expected while "poltroons and cowards" manned the War Department. Ready tongues carried this to Halleck. At once

Halleck had to write about it to Stanton. "I desire to know whether such wholesale denouncement and accusation by a member of the Cabinet receives the sanction and support of the President of the United States." Stanton chose to pass the letter without comment to the President, who remarked, "Men will speak their minds freely in this country," and wrote to the Secretary of War:

". . . Gen. Halleck's letter . . . in substance demands of me that if I approve the remarks, I shall strike the names of those officers from the rolls; and that if I do not approve them, the Post-Master-General shall be dismissed from the Cabinet. Whether the remarks were really made I do not know; nor do I suppose such knowledge is necessary to a correct response. If they were made, I do *not* approve them; and yet, under the circumstances, I would not dismiss a member of the Cabinet therefor. I do not consider what may have been hastily said in a moment of vexation at so severe a loss, is sufficient ground for so grave a step. Besides this, *truth* is generally the best vindication against slander. I propose continuing to be myself the judge as to when a member of the Cabinet shall be dismissed." Thus Lincoln was peremptory, decisive, perfectly understanding and sweetly courteous, in a single letter.

In the cross play of hates, guesses were made as to whether some of the Federal Government servants hated each other any less than they hated the enemy. A peculiar mental attitude or a hoodoo spell pervaded much of Washington. Lincoln and Grant were aware of it. Grant on August 1 acted to evade it; he notified Halleck that he was sending Sheridan to "expel the enemy from the border " Sheridan's record and status, his complete aloofness from the desk strategists of Washington, were such that there was nothing they could do about it. Lincoln approved the action and August 3 sent Grant a telegram momentous in its confession of a spirit that held powerful sway: "I have seen your despatch in which you say 'I want Sheridan put in command of all the troops in the field, with instructions to put himself South of the enemy, and follow him to the death.

Wherever the enemy goes, let our troops go also.' This, I think, is exactly right, as to how our forces should move. But please look over the despatches you may have receved from here, even since you made that order, and discover, if you can, that there is any idea in the head of anyone here, of 'putting our army *South* of the enemy' or of 'following him to the *death*' in any direction. I repeat to you it will neither be done nor attempted unless you watch it every day, and hour, and force it."

Grant journeyed from south of Richmond to Monocacy north of Washington, August 6, 1864, for personal communication with Sheridan; his telegrams through the War Department were too often translated into something else. Or as he put it later: "I knew it was impossible for me to get orders through Washington to Sheridan to make a move, because they would be stopped there and such orders as Halleck's caution (and that of the Secretary of War) would suggest would be given instead, and would no doubt, be contradictory to mine." The four times' use of "would" had to be read more than once—and then there was no mistaking what Grant meant to say.

Weeks were to pass with Sheridan on trial, with Sherman on trial, one in the Shenandoah, the other in Georgia, two commanders not yet proved as Grant had been proved, both of them held by Grant as unbeatable. And the delays and failure of immediate victory were blamed, by those in black moods for blaming that summer, chiefly on the President, who upheld all three and never let up in his efforts to meet their requirements.

Later in a political matter Sherman refused to correct a policy of Grant when so requested, saying, "Grant stood by me when I was crazy, and I stood by him when he was drunk, and now we stand by each other."

Halleck had written to Sherman that the President wished to give him appointment as a major general in the Regular Army. "I wish you to say to the President," wrote Sherman, "that I would prefer he should not nominate me or anyone." He had all the rank he needed.

With the Armies of the Cumberland, Tennessee and Ohio

joined into a force of 99,000, Sherman began his campaign from Chattanooga aimed at the capture of Atlanta. Between him and Atlanta was a Confederate army of 41,000, soon reinforced to 62,000, commanded by the master strategist General Joseph E. Johnston. Carrying scars of wounds from Florida Indian wars, from Cerro Gordo and Chapultepec in the Mexican War, from Seven Pines in the Peninsular campaign near Richmond, now 57 years old, a West Pointer, a Virginian who had never owned slaves, a clean sportsman of a fighter, a silent, cautious Fabian— little Joe Johnston, familiar with the red hills of Georgia, seemed the one marshal in gray best able to stop or delay Sherman. He led Sherman on. He fought and faded and waited. At Dalton, past Buzzard's Roost, through Snake Creek Gap, back to Resaca and Cassville, across the Etowah, through Allatoona Pass, and after clashes at New Hope Church, not until Kenesaw Mountain did Johnston in his slowly maneuvered retreat lure Sherman into a frontal attack.

Sherman piled in his men on the fortified lines of Johnston hoping to break through and win victory and Atlanta. Sherman lost 3,000 as against the Confederate's 800. "One or two more such assaults would use up this army," said Old Pap Thomas. Not least of Johnston's hopes was the one that he could hold off any Sherman victory until the November elections in the North. He would like to make Sherman's efforts look useless in order to persuade Northern citizens that the Lincoln administration was useless.

Davis and Bragg at Richmond wanted more decisive action. Davis on July 17 replaced Johnston with General John B. Hood, who, they knew, would not wait and fade and hope. In 11 days Hood fought and lost three battles at a cost of 10,841 men to Sherman's 9,719. Sherman had at last reached the Atlanta area. But would he take Atlanta? The North hoped. And the North despaired. Why did it take so long? Why had the whole war gone on so long? From Lincoln the last week of July Sherman had a long telegram which closed: "My profoundest thanks to you and your whole Army for the present campaign so far."

Many were tired of the war, its cost, its betrayals and corruptions. Peace movements gained headway from this feeling in the North and the South. Fernando Wood in seeking to have Congress empower the President to appoint commissioners to discuss peace terms with Southern representatives was playing with this sentiment. To Davis in Richmond and to others Governor Zebulon B. Vance of North Carolina wrote of "discontent" in his state. "I have concluded it will be impossible to remove it except by some effort at negotiation with the enemy." Davis gave Vance three instances wherein he had made "distinct efforts" to communicate with Lincoln, never once connecting, and to send peace proposals was "to invite insult and contumely, and to subject ourselves to indignity without the slightest chance of being listened to."

The New York *World* and its country newspaper following would not let their readers forget that Lincoln's inaugural address carried the portentous words: "Suppose you go to war, you cannot fight always; and when, after much loss on both sides, and no gain on either, you cease fighting, the identical old questions, as to terms of intercourse, are again upon you."

Horace Greeley in July '64 received a letter from a fellow signing himself "William Cornell Jewett of Colorado." Jewett wrote many letters—to Lincoln, to Jeff Davis, to the New York *Herald*. Jewett needed listeners. Now he picked on Greeley, writing, "I am authorized to state to you, for your use only, not the public, that two ambassadors of Davis & Co. are now in Canada, with full and complete powers for a peace." If the President would accord protection for these "ambassadors" they would meet in Niagara Falls whomsoever Lincoln might choose to send for a private interview.

The quavering Greeley again wrote to Lincoln one of his long letters, both pleading and cudgeling. Lincoln discounted Jewett's story but within two days wrote to Greeley: "If you can find, any person anywhere professing to have any proposition of Jefferson Davis in writing, for peace, embracing the restoration of the Union and abandonment of slavery, what ever else it embraces, say to him he may come to me with you, and that if he really brings such proposition, he shall, at the least, have safe conduct, with the paper (and without publicity, if he chooses) to the point where you shall have met him. The same, if there be two or more persons."

On July 13 Greeley again wrote Lincoln; now he had confidential information that the two Confederate ambassadors waiting and ready to cross over from Canada and talk peace terms at Niagara Falls were the Honorable Clement C. Clay of Alabama and the Honorable Jacob Thompson of Mississippi, each an ex-U.S. Senator from his state. Lincoln telegraphed two days later: "I was not expecting you to *send* me a letter, but to *bring* me a man, or men. Mr. Hay goes to you with my answer."

In New York Hay handed Greeley Lincoln's letter which stated his disappointment over Greeley's not having produced the commissioners and "if they would consent to come, on being shown my letter to you of the 9th. Inst. . . . bring them. I not only intend a sincere effort for peace, but I intend that you shall be a personal witness that it is made." Greeley didn't like the letter, noted Hay, said he was the worst man the President could have picked for such a mission. Lincoln, it was evident to Hay, was pressing the matter. Whatever reality or illusion might be hovering on the Canadian border, he was going to smoke it out.

At the town of Niagara Falls Greeley met Jewett and sent by him a letter to Clay, Thompson and a University of Virginia professor, James P. Holcombe, saying he was informed they were accredited from Richmond as bearing propositions looking toward peace, that they desired to visit Washington in their mission, George N. Sanders accompanying them, and "if my information be thus far substantially correct, I am authorized by the President of the United States to tender you his safe conduct on the journey proposed." Greeley heard in reply that Jacob Thompson was not one of them, that none of them had authority to act for the Richmond Government, but they were acquainted with the views of their Government and could easily get credentials, or other agents could be accredited in their place, if they could be sent to Richmond armed with "the circumstances disclosed in this correspondence."

Greeley telegraphed Lincoln the substance of this letter. Lincoln consulted with Seward and gave Hay a paper in his own handwriting to take to Niagara. There on July 20 Hay saw Greeley nettled and perplexed at reading:

> Executive Mansion,
> Washington, July 18, 1864.
>
> To Whom it may concern:
>   Any proposition which embraces the restoration of peace, the integrity of the whole Union, and the abandonment of slavery, and which comes by and with an authority that can control the armies now at war against the United States will be received and considered by the Executive government of the United States, and will be met by liberal terms on other substantial and collateral points; and the bearer, or bearers thereof shall have safe-conduct both ways.
>
> ABRAHAM LINCOLN

Greeley proposed bringing Jewett into conference. Hay declined. Greeley then refused to cross the suspension bridge into Canada unless Hay would go with him and deliver the Lincoln paper into Confederate hands. The two then crossed the bridge, met Holcombe in a hotel room in Clifton, Canada, and handed him the President's letter. Greeley took a train for New York, but before doing so had an interview with Jewett, unknown to Hay. Hay stayed on a day and then wrote Holcombe asking when he might be favored with a reply to the communication addressed "To Whom it may concern." "Mr. Holcombe greatly regrets," was the reply, "if his [Hay's] return to Washington has been delayed by any expectation of an answer." Jewett then wrote the Confederate emissaries that Greeley was gone and he regretted "the sad termination of the initiatory steps taken for peace," placing the blame on "the change made by the President in his instructions"; they could communicate with Greeley through him, Jewett.

The Confederates replied with compliments and a long letter to Greeley, holding the President responsible for the collapse of peace hopes. Without notifying Hay, Jewett gave this letter to the press, letting Hay know afterward that this was a mild form of revenge. The letter made interesting reading for a gloom-struck nation. Those who saw the President as "indecisive" had a new item to contemplate. Others saw the President as more astute, if not wiser, than they had expected.

There was drama bordering on farce in the Confederate diplomats, at the end of the suspension bridge connecting the United States and Canada, accusing Lincoln of high crimes. They assumed people would believe the President's duty was to invite unauthorized Confederate agents to Washington to receive peace terms to carry to Richmond. They had hoped to use Bennett of the New York *Herald* for their game, Sanders remarking to Hay once, "I wanted old Bennett to come up, but he was afraid to come." They had used Jewett to lure Greeley, Jewett having followed his first letter to Greeley with a telegram: "Will you come here? Parties have full power." Greeley had believed the parties had full power; Lincoln hadn't and by a little memorandum addressed to nobody or anybody had thwarted them. Greeley's course in the end brought ridicule on him; Lincoln at a climactic point turned the incident into a dramatic presentation of his Government's viewpoint as to peace proposals.

Another peace mission was undertaken by Colonel James Frazier Jaquess, a Methodist clergyman from Illinois commissioned to raise and lead the 73d Illinois Volunteers, and James R. Gilmore, a newspaperman. Without Government authority from Lincoln, it was permitted by him under pressure. Under flags of truce the two men arrived in Richmond, and in an evening interview with Jefferson Davis, they had from him the declaration: "I worked night and day for twelve years to prevent it [war], but I could not. The North was mad and blind, would not let us govern ourselves, and so the war came; now it must go on until the last man of this generation falls in his tracks and his children seize his musket and fight our battles, *unless you acknowledge our right to self-government.* We are not fighting for slavery. We are fighting for independence, and that, or extermination, we *will* have."

Gilmore published the interview in the *Atlantic Monthly,* and the article, widely reprinted, went to millions of readers. At Niagara, through Greeley, Lincoln had given the world his peace terms; at Richmond, Davis had made himself clear.

Intricate in vast detail, droll, fantastic, comic in various phases, the Greeley and Jaquess-Gilmore peace missions had been affairs of risk. Any slight circumstance could have put Lincoln in a false light. Only a certain procedure of guns, men, blood and iron, could bring peace, it seemed. "Peace," said *Leslie's Weekly* August 6, 1864, "must come through the powerful negotiations of Gens. Grant and Sherman."

Chapter 32

"The Darkest Month of the War" — August '64

Speaking in February '64, Senator Henry S. Lane of Indiana said the operation of the $300 clause in the conscription act had not been in favor of the poor man. "The poor man had to go at all events; he could not raise the $300; but it has operated, perhaps, beneficially upon the middle classes, and has exempted the rich entirely, for they could all pay the $300 exemption." What did it matter that $12,000,000 had been paid into the Government Treasury for draft exemptions? The measure was not intended to raise revenue. "We need men more than money. If we could print soldiers as fast as we print greenbacks, there would be something in this argument; but it cannot be done."

Congress had kept to itself certain strict powers. The President could be a dictator in enforcement of the draft law, but he was limited to *advising* Congress what the draft law should say. And so, June 8, 1864, Executive Document No. 97 went to Congress with the signature of Abraham Lincoln: "I have the honor to submit, for the consideration of Congress, a letter and inclosure from the Secretary of War, with my concurrence in the recommendation therein made." The letter enclosed, signed by Stanton and addressed "To the President," recommended "a repeal of the clause in the enrollment act commonly known as the $300 clause."

Attached to Stanton's recommendation was a report signed by Provost Marshal General Fry on the operation of the enrollment act as amended by Congress February 24, 1864. "I invite your attention," noted Fry, "to the small proportion of soldiers being obtained under the existing law. I see no reason to believe that the Army can be materially strengthened by draft so long as the $300 clause is in force."

Congressman Schenck brought before the House a bill to repeal previous draft laws. It declared "hereafter no payment of money shall be accepted or received by the Government to release any enrolled or drafted man from obligation to perform military duty." One exception was made. Any man could send a substitute for himself if it be his father, brother or son. Schenck mentioned the President as seeing "the necessity for having men and not money only to carry on this war against the rebels, and finding the present existing enrolling act does not produce men by a draft, because of . . . circumstances, such as commutation and substitution, and other things which intervene to prevent the procuring of men." Schenck raised a class issue in his argument, saying the committee proposed such limits in conscription that "no man, whether a man of means or not, whether rich or poor, shall in any case get rid of furnishing a substitute unless he be one of his own blood."

Representative John W. Chandler of New York said that

though the bill masked itself as "a poor man's friend" it was nevertheless drawn from "the horrid example of the European system. The President is given unlimited control over the lives of every family in the land."

James G. Blaine of Maine moved to strike out the first section of the bill, saying it was made to appear "that the *people* need to be goaded and driven"; that a *"compulsory draft"* would require troops to shoot down rioters and demonstrators; that the people were "patriotically willing" and there was no necessity for a conscription "absolutely merciless and sweeping"; that the draft as it was being enforced would bring "a very large amount of money with which to pay bounties to volunteers." His own state was raising its quota, said Blaine; other parts of the Union might be disorderly, but not Maine.

If Blaine's motion should pass, it would kill the bill and defeat Lincoln, Stanton, Schenck and the Military Affairs Committee in their attempt to get universal selective military service, making money payments unlawful. "Do not, I pray you," cried Blaine, "by any action here proclaim to the world that you have no faith in the loyal people of the United States." The debate was brief; the Yeas and Nays were called for. And the President, the War Department and Schenck were beaten by a vote of Yeas 100, Nays 50, not voting 32.

The 50 Congressmen who with Lincoln gambled their political futures (by risking the ill will of all potential drafted men having $300 with which they wished to buy exemption) were Republicans. The 100 who voted to keep the $300 exemption clause were Republicans joined by a minority of Democrats, including George H. Pendleton of Ohio, close political ally of Vallandigham. Congressmen plainly were afraid that the drastic action proposed by Stanton, concurred in by Lincoln, and advocated by Schenck, Frank P. Blair and others on the floor, would offend men of influence and property in their home districts, resulting possibly in upheavals and violence. Mostly these fears were kept under, were left plainly implied.

In the Senate political instinct ran the same as in the

House. The Senators were decisively for bounties and substitutes. Also they were as hazy and groping as House members on the ways and means of getting soldiers. The ballots
ran close, as in the House, and about a proportional number
stayed away and didn't get into the record. Wade, Wilson,
Reverdy Johnson and other Senators spoke fears of giving
the President power to draft men for three years. The result
might be a country ruled by a military despotism working
through a horde of professional soldiers.

Schenck in the House and Sprague in the Senate had
pointed out how clear it was that the President, the Cabinet
and the War Department wanted the $300 commutation
clause absolutely repealed. This was done by such a device
that in the campaign of that year it could be said in speech
and pamphlet and editorial that the commutation clause *was*
absolutely repealed. Yet what was substituted for it was
nearly an equivalent. The President had authority to call
for *volunteers* for one, two or three years, the one-year
men to be paid $100 bounty, the two-year men $200,
the three-year men $300, each receiving the final one-third
installment of his bounty on completion of service.

On a clear-cut issue between Lincoln and Congress he
was refused by overwhelming votes what he asked for in an
essential point for carrying on the war. The refusal of Congress extended to Grant and Sherman, who favored a policy
of no money payments and no substitutes entangling and
retarding the draft. Grant and Sherman stressed the point
that money payments brought a poorer brand of soldiers.
Lincoln was speaking both as an executive in office and as
a political candidate with re-election at stake in four
months. He was willing to take his chances on whatever dis-
order might result from a new principle in the draft. And in
face of political unrest and a vast gloom savage with suspicion and recrimination, Lincoln two weeks after the draft
act was passed by Congress July 4, 1864, proclaimed a call
for a half-million volunteers.

With the $300 clause done away with, any man drafted
must either go into the Army himself or pay someone else
to go for him. Such a substitute had to be either an alien, a

veteran of two years' service, or a boy under 20. Hustlers, in the business of finding substitutes and selling them to those who wished to buy, came forward. "Wanted. Irishmen, Englishmen, Scotchmen, Germans, Frenchmen, to enlist as volunteers." Thus one amid columns of similar ads, paid for at regular rates, in the New York *Herald*. Only four days after the President's proclamation one New York *Herald* ad made the appeal: "It is clearly to the interest of every man liable to military duty to procure an alien substitute at once and save dollars, cents and worry. The price of substitutes will soon reach $1,200, because of the great bounties that will be offered by cities, towns and States."

"Six hundred dollars cash paid for substitutes," ran one ad in newspapers of Cincinnati, where on August 20 prices went to $1,200 and $1,500 for substitutes, for men to replace the fallen or the vanished in the ranks of Grant and Sherman. "A nice farm of eighty acres worth $600" was offered by one lacking cash and seeking a substitute.

Under way in northern New York State was a stampede of men seeking draft evasion, wrote the provost marshal of Albany requesting authority to stop the men at the Canadian border. Thousands of "miserable, cowardly Copperhead scoundrels" were fleeing across Minnesota for the Canadian border, ran a report from Milwaukee. An Ohio writer put the case with more care, observing for *Appleton's Annual Cyclopaedia:* "The voluntary absenteeism from the State of persons liable to military service, on the approach or during the pendency of the draft, was estimated to exceed twenty thousand. A large number left during the ten days allowed by law between draft and notification . . . in some cases, there were not men enough left in the townships to fill the quota. Many men drafted in one section of the State went into other sections."

Amid chaos, gloom, forebodings over the country, amid howlings that they were inhuman monsters and God would bring them retribution, Lincoln and Stanton carried through, with every employable resource at their hands, the procurement of troops to maintain the strength of Grant's and Sherman's armies, to impress the Southern people anew with the man power of the North. "All who will not help should be put in petticoats and deprived of the right to vote in the affairs of the nation," Sherman wrote home. "This army is much reduced in strength by deaths, sickness, and expiration of service. It looks hard to see regiments march away when their time is up."

What Congress did, after many conferences between Senate and House, was to provide that pay equal to that of the white soldiers should be given to all regularly enlisted "persons of color who were free" April 19, 1861. This resulted in an ingenious oath being used in many of the Negro regiments. Drawn up by Colonel E. N. Hallowell of the Massachusetts 54th, it required men to swear that they "owed no man unrequited labor on or before the 19th day of April, 1861." Thus they might be swearing to the truth and the fact, though they would be evading the category in which the U.S. Constitution still held them as chattels and property. Here and there, said Massachusetts colonels, were black men whose pride put them above a trick oath for evading a Constitution which still held them as chattels and property.

The necessity of men killing men, since there was a war on, stood forth in Lincoln's writing to Vice-President Hamlin that on the issuance of the Emancipation Proclamation troops came forward more slowly than ever: "The North responds to the proclamation sufficiently in breath; but breath alone kills no rebels." Killings were wanted. Enough killings would end the war. "I have seen your despatch," he wired Grant one hot August day of '64, "expressing your unwillingness to break your hold where you are. Neither am I willing. Hold on with a bull-dog grip, and chew & choke as much as possible."

From Chicago came a committee of three appointed at a mass meeting to ask the Secretary of War for a new enrollment figure. Their quota had been put too high, they believed. Stanton refused any concession. So they went to Lincoln, who said, "I will go with you to Stanton and hear both sides." Heading the committee was Joseph Medill, editor of the Chicago *Tribune,* who argued before Lincoln,

Stanton and Fry that the Chicago quota should be lowered. Chicago had already sent 22,000 men and was drained. Lincoln heard the argument sitting quietly, and in time lifted his head and spoke.

"Gentlemen," he said, as Medill's memory served, "after Boston, Chicago has been the chief instrument in bringing this war on the country. The Northwest has opposed the South as the Northeast has opposed the South. You called for war until we had it. You called for emancipation and I have given it to you. Whatever you have asked for you have had. Now you come here begging to be let off from the call for men which I have made to carry out the war which you have demanded. You ought to be ashamed of yourselves. I have a right to expect better things of you. Go home and raise your 6,000 extra men. And you, Medill, are acting like a coward. You and your *Tribune* have had more influence than any paper in the Northwest in making this war. You can influence great masses, and yet you cry to be spared at a moment when your cause is suffering. Go home and send us those men."

Some sort of writhing, intense speech like that came from Lincoln, and as Medill confessed: "I couldn't say anything. It was the first time I ever was whipped, and I didn't have an answer. We all got up and went out, and when the door closed, one of my colleagues said, 'Well, gentlemen, the old man is right. We ought to be ashamed of ourselves. Let us never say anything about this, but go home and raise the men.' And we did, 6,000 men, making 28,000 in the war from a city of 156,000."

"I hev lost, sence Stanton's order to draft, the use of wun eye entirely, and hev kronic inflammashen in the other," wrote Petroleum V. Nasby, gloom-chaser for the President. "My teeth is all unsound, my palit ain't eggsactly rite, and I hev hed bronkeetis 31 yeres last Joon. At present I hev a koff, the paroxisms uv wich is friteful 2 behold. I am afflictid with kronic diarrear and kostivness. I am rupcherd in 9 places, and am entirely enveloped with trusses. I hev korns and bunions on both feet, wich wood prevent me from marchin."

Walt Whitman wrote from Washington to his mother that the feeling was "savage & hot" against draft evaders. "I do not feel it in my heart to abuse the poor people, or call for a rope or bullets for them, but that is all the talk here, even in the hospitals." The author of "Blow, Bugles, Blow!" who had welcomed war, like many others who brooded over the balances of justice in it now felt himself blown to and fro in its windy passions. "The deeper they go in with the draft, the more trouble it is likely to make. I have changed my opinions and feelings on the subject. We are in the midst of strange and terrible times. One is pulled a dozen different ways in his mind, & hardly knows what to think or do." And of the President and General Burnside reviewing the 9th corps parade up Pennsylvania Avenue Whitman wrote to "dearest mother": "Five regiments of new black troops looked and marched very well. It looked funny to see the President standing with his hat off to them just the same as the rest as they passed by."

When a man enlisted as a substitute, pocketed the cash bounty, jumped elsewhere to enlist again and pocket another cash bounty, he was known as a "bounty-jumper." Newspapers carried a stream of items about fugitive and captured bounty-jumpers. One sentenced to four years in the Albany penitentiary confessed to having jumped the bounty 32 times.

Those who took flight to evade the draft, known as "skedaddlers," changed their names and sought localities where voters and officials were hostile to the Lincoln administration. They moved to lonely mining camps or settlements unfriendly to provost marshals and reached by hard travel.

A Vermont woman, according to *Leslie's*, having an errand in Canada, was shocked at meeting her husband in Montreal. Had she not received official word from the Government that her husband had died on the field of battle as a hero? Had she not mourned and put on widow's garb, and later married another man? Now she learned from him that he had nursed no wish to fall with honor on the field of glory, and therefore had stuffed her letters to him, her photographs, her locks of shining bronze hair, into the pockets and bosom of a dead soldier, removing from the corpse any contradictory evidence. Then he had deserted and made his way to Canada. He promised her, "I'll never trouble you again," and she warned him not to.

In the war chronicle of the summer of '64, with its plodding in blood and muck, were two bright spots for the Union cause. On a Sunday morning in June, outside the international line off the coast of France at Cherbourg, two ships met and battled. The one flying the Confederate flag had cruised thousands of miles in the South Atlantic and Indian Oceans since August '63, had captured 62 merchantmen, and burned most of them at sea. She was the hated and feared *Alabama*, British-built, her seamen and gunners mainly British.

The *Kearsarge* had long trailed the *Alabama* and at last penned her in Cherbourg Harbor. Three hundred and seventy shells from the *Alabama* left the *Kearsarge* practically undamaged, with only the loss of a smokestack, while nearly every one of the 173 projectiles from the *Kearsarge* found its target and tore open the sides of the *Alabama* till she began sinking. Forty were killed on the *Alabama* under the Confederate flag; on the *Kearsarge* the losses were three men wounded, of whom one died.

In August, the Confederacy lost its most essential port on the Gulf of Mexico. Lashed to a flagship mast and leading his fleet into Mobile Bay, Admiral Farragut prayed, "O God, who created man and gave him reason, direct me what to do. Shall I go on?" His order, "Damn the torpedoes! Full speed ahead!" became a Unionist slogan. His fleet captured the ram *Tennessee*, rated one of the most powerful vessels of war afloat in any waters, and with land forces reduced the three forts guarding Mobile. Lincoln termed it a "brilliant achievement."

Lincoln with Grant believed a strangle hold was being put on the South. But a large number of people, some of them highly vocal in this August of '64, did not so believe or were not particularly interested in believing in anything connected with the continuance of the war.

Near the town of Mount Vernon, Ohio, lived a farmer and his wife who believed that Vallandigham was telling the truth about the war, that Lincoln was a deceiver, a monster and a fiend perpetuating a needless war, the woman saying to her children, "Lincoln! how I loathe that name between my lips!" To her Vallandigham was a hero and brave truth-teller. Nothing Lincoln said reached her. She and her husband worked their farm without help, kept a sober and orderly household, read their Bible and went to a Congregational church on the Sabbath, had no traffic with ill-gotten gains of the war. They were for peace. They saw Lincoln as against peace. And her children, not yet of age to be drafted, heard her with immemorial woe and hate in her voice, "Lincoln! how I loathe that name between my lips!"

Here and there despair over the war became despair over the President and his seeming failures. "The war and its constant expectations and anxieties oppress me," wrote James Russell Lowell. "I cannot think. I hear bad things about Mr. Lincoln and try not to believe them." William Cullen Bryant wrote to John M. Forbes of "the Seward and Weed faction filling all the offices with its creatures," saying further, "I am so disgusted with Lincoln's behavior that I cannot muster respectful terms in which to write him." From Bloomington August 4 David Davis wrote to a brother that while in Chicago he had talked with many people from different parts of the country and found growing uneasiness and distrust. "People are getting tired of the war. Some of them can't see a ray of light. I am speaking of good men. Two years ago I succeeded in raising 1,300 men in this country. It took about ten days. There is no note now of any volunteering . . . There is faith in the administration, and yet you will hear *whispering* inquiries as to whether the plan they are pursuing is the best . . . Keep these views to yourself, and burn this letter."

Former President Millard Fillmore August 10, 1864, was writing to John T. Stuart, urging that "all men who value their own liberty should unite to change the administration . . . for without this all is lost." One other living ex-President, Franklin Pierce, was saying the same where he thought it might help to crush Lincoln.

Across weeks of August '64, a movement, necessarily secret, among Republican party leaders operated with the aim of replacing Lincoln with another nominee for President. The Jonah of the Ship of State was Lincoln. He should be flung overboard. Among Republican conferences in New York City was one at the home of David Dudley Field August 14, with Greeley, Mayor George Opdyke, Parke Godwin of the *Evening Post,* William Curtis Noyes, Henry Winter Davis, Theodore Tilton, Franz Lieber and 20 or more others. It was agreed that a committee should request Lincoln to withdraw as a presidential candidate. The name of Grant was most favored to replace that of Lincoln. A call was prepared for a convention to be held in Cincinnati September 28.

"Mr. Lincoln is already beaten," wrote Greeley to Mayor Opdyke. "We must have another ticket to save us from utter overthrow. If we had such a ticket as could be had by naming Grant, Butler, or Sherman for President, and Farragut as Vice, we could make a fight yet."

The antislavery wheel horse, John Jay, believed a letter might be prepared which would "compel Mr. Lincoln's acquiescence" to another nominating convention. Senator Charles Sumner indicated his wish that Lincoln should withdraw, but in case Lincoln should refuse it would not be so good. "It may be," wrote Sumner, "that Mr. Lincoln will see that we shall all be stronger and more united under another candidate."

Whitelaw Reid of the Cincinnati *Gazette* wrote to the committee's secretary: "That which I could do in the direction you indicate has been done in inducing the *Gazette* to come out for Mr. Lincoln's withdrawal. The article has been telegraphed east, and I hope has done some good." Rugged John Andrew spoke for himself and others of unquestionably clean motives when he wrote to Greeley: "Mr. Lincoln *ought* to lead the country. But he is essentially lacking in the quality of leadership, which is a gift of God and not a device of man."

Carl Schurz rode with Lincoln in a carriage from the White House to Soldiers' Home. Lincoln said he would not complain of the burden of care put on his shoulders. "They urge me with almost violent language to withdraw from the contest, although I have been unanimously nominated . . . God knows, I have at least tried very hard to do my duty, to do right to everybody and wrong to nobody. And now to have it said by men who have been my friends and who ought to know me better, that I have been seduced by what they call the lust of power, and that I have been doing this and that unscrupulous thing hurtful to the common cause, only to keep myself in office! Have they thought of that common cause when trying to break me down? I hope they have." So he went on, as if speaking to himself, noted Schurz, sometimes as if Schurz were not there at all.

"Ten days since, I told Mr. Lincoln that his re-election was an impossibility," wrote Thurlow Weed to Seward August 22. "Mr. Raymond, who has just left me, says that unless some prompt and bold step be now taken all is lost. The people are wild for peace. They are told that the President will only listen to terms of peace on condition slavery be abandoned." Therefore Weed was urging that the President should offer the Richmond Government the conditions of the Crittenden Compromise of the winter of '60-'61, with the Union to be restored and the South writing its own constitutional sanction of slave property.

Events had brought new and definite viewpoints to the President. To Judge Joseph T. Mills and ex-Governor A. W. Randall of Wisconsin at Soldiers' Home Lincoln unburdened himself. "There are now between 1 & 200 thousand black men in the service of the Union . . . There have been men who have proposed to me to return to slavery the black warriors of Port Hudson and Olustee to their masters to conciliate the South. I should be damned in time and eternity for so doing. The world shall know that I will keep my faith to friends and enemies, come what will. My enemies say I am now carrying on this war for the sole purpose of abolition. It is & will be carried on so long as I am President for the sole purpose of restoring the Union. But no human power can subdue this rebellion without using the Emancipation lever as I have done . . . My enemies condemn my emancipation policy. Let them prove by the history of this war, that we can restore the Union without it.

"Freedom has given us the control of 200,000 able bodied men, born & raised on southern soil. It will give us more yet. Just so much it has sub[t]racted from the strength of our enemies, & instead of alienating the south from us, there are evidences of a fraternal feeling growing up between our own & rebel soldiers." This gave him a glow. He seemed to welcome news of fraternal feeling rather than hate, as though should the Union be saved, that fraternal feeling could be built on.

The Badger State visitors saw Lincoln enter the room with shoulders inclined forward, gait rapid "and shuffling, ample understandings with large slippers, and Briarian arms, a face radiant with intelligence and humor." A version of this peculiarly significant interview *Harper's Weekly* of New York reprinted from the *Grant County Herald* of Wisconsin, whereupon scores of newspapers in America and the London *Spectator* and other journals in England gave it to their readers.

Raymond was hearing but one report. "The tide is setting strongly against us." Washburne in Illinois, Cameron in Pennsylvania, were saying their states at the moment were against the administration. Only strenuous efforts could carry Indiana, Governor Morton had written. Two special causes were assigned for this feeling against the administration: want of military success, and "the impression in some minds, the fear and suspicion in others, that we are not to have peace in any event under this Administration until slavery is abandoned." The suspicion seemed widespread that peace with Union was to be had. "It is idle to reason with this belief—still more idle to denounce it." Therefore Raymond would suggest the President appoint a commission to proffer peace to Davis "on the sole condition of acknowledging the supremacy of the Constitution—all other questions to be settled in a convention of the people of all the States."

Raymond waited in New York. From the President came no reply. In Washington the President was viewing the national situation. He was a candidate for re-election with as yet no opponent. It would be a week or more before the Democrats at Chicago would name a man to run against him; yet the signs were that he was already beaten by whoever might be named. In his own later words, "At this period we had no adversary and seemed to have no friends." When his Cabinet met August 23, he handed around a sheet of paper so folded and pasted that what was inside could not be read. He requested each member to sign his name across the back of the sheet. Each one wrote not knowing what he was signing. It was a memorandum for possible future use:

> Executive Mansion,
> Washington, Aug. 23, 1864.
>
> This morning, as for some days past, it seems exceedingly probable that this Administration will not be re-elected. Then it will be my duty to so co-operate with the President elect, as to save the Union between the election and the inauguration; as he will have secured his election on such ground that he can not possibly save it afterwards.
>
> A. LINCOLN

Two days later Raymond and the national executive committee of the Republican party, not having heard from the President that he would publicly proffer peace to the Richmond Government, arrived at the White House. They were, according to Nicolay and Hay, "in obvious depression and panic." Raymond was in a final and confidential session with the President and three Cabinet members when Welles entered. "I went in as usual unannounced," wrote Welles in his diary. "I found Messrs. Seward, Fessenden, and Stanton with Raymond . . . in consultation with the President. The President was making some statement as to a document of his, and said he supposed his style was peculiar and had its earmarks, so that it could not be mistaken. He kept on talking as if there had been no addition

to the company, and as if I had been expected and belonged
there. But the topic was not pursued by the others when the
President ceased. Some inquiry was put to me in regard to
intelligence from the fleet at Mobile . . . Mr. Fessenden rose
and, putting his mouth to the ear of the President, began
to whisper, and as soon as I could answer the brief inquiries,
I left the room. It was easy to perceive that Seward, Stanton, and Raymond were disconcerted by my appearance.
Except the whispering by Fessenden I saw nothing particular on his part."

Nicolay wrote to Hay in Illinois as between two cronies:
"Hell is to pay. The New York politicians have got a stampede on that is about to swamp everything. Raymond and
the National Committee are here to-day. R. thinks a commission to Richmond is about the only salt to save us; while
the Tycoon sees and says it would be utter ruination. The
matter is now undergoing consultation. Weak-kneed
damned fools . . . are in the movement for a new candidate
to supplant the Tycoon. Everything is darkness and doubt
and discouragement."

And what of the document Welles heard the President
say was in his own "peculiar" style, having his personal
"earmarks"? Lincoln had written it to meet squarely the
proposals of Raymond for a peace proffer to Richmond.
Dated August 24, 1864, it was concrete, exact, decisive as
a slide rule measuring in fractions:

> Sir:
> You will proceed forthwith and obtain, if possible, a
> conference for peace with Hon. Jefferson Davis, or
> any person by him authorized for that purpose.
> You will address him in entirely respectful terms, at
> all events, and in any that may be indispensable to se-
> cure the conference.
> At said conference you will propose, on behalf of
> this government, that upon the restoration of the Union
> and the national authority, the war shall cease at once,
> all remaining questions to be left for adjustment by

peaceful modes. If this be accepted hostilities to cease at once.

If it be not accepted, you will then request to be informed what terms, if any embracing the restoration of the Union, would be accepted. If any such be presented you in answer, you will forthwith report the same to this government, and await further instructions.

If the presentation of any terms embracing the restoration of the Union be declined, you will then request to be informed what terms of peace would be accepted; and on receiving any answer, report the same to this government, and await further instructions.

As Nicolay wrote in his private notebook, the President "and the stronger half of the Cabinet, Seward, Stanton, and Fessenden," showed Raymond that they had thoroughly considered and discussed his proposals of a peace proffer. "He very readily concurred with them in the opinion that to follow his plan of sending a commission to Richmond would be worse than losing the Presidential contest—it would be ignominiously surrendering it in advance. Nevertheless the visit of himself and committee here did great good. They found the President and cabinet much better informed than themselves, and went home encouraged and cheered." And into files to which Greeley and Bennett had no access went the unused, unsent peace proffer.

Returning to New York, Raymond threw amazement into the Republican anti-Lincoln ranks with his positive statements in the *Times* that peace negotiation stories had no bottom; "the President stands firm against every solicitation to postpone the draft"; and as to rumors of this and that about the Government, "You may rest assured . . . its sole and undivided purpose is to prosecute the war until the rebellion is quelled."

And perhaps it was the mercurial Bennett himself who in the *Herald,* the day after Raymond's return, mocked and gabbed and jibed: "The Republican leaders may have their personal quarrels, or their shoddy quarrels, or their nigger quarrels with Old Abe; but he has the whiphand of them, and they will soon be bobbing back into the Republican fold, like sheep who have gone astray . . .

"Whatever they say now, we venture to predict that Wade and his tail; and Bryant and his tail; and Wendell Phillips and his tail; and Weed, Barney, Chase and their tails; and Winter Davis, Raymond, Opdyke and Forney who have no tails; will all make tracks for Old Abe's plantation, and soon will be found crowing and blowing, and vowing and writing, and swearing and stumping the state on his side, declaring that he and he alone, is the hope of the nation, the bugaboo of Jeff Davis, the first of Conservatives, the best of Abolitionists, the purest of patriots, the most gullible of mankind, the easiest President to manage, and the person especially predestined and foreordained by Providence to carry on the war, free the niggers, and give all the faithful a fair share of the spoils. The spectacle will be ridiculous; but it is inevitable."

John Eaton, with a pass signed by the President was authorized to "visit Gen. Grant at City Point, Va." Grant held strictly to army matters in the talk of the two men that ran past midnight. Eaton was interested, but was trying to find some entering wedge on political affairs. Finally he mentioned to Grant a conversation on a railroad train with army men who had asked Eaton if he thought Grant could be induced to run as a citizen's candidate for President. "The question is," said Eaton to Grant, "not whether you wish to run, but whether you could be compelled to run in answer to the demand of the people for a candidate who should save the Union."

Grant's instant reply amazed Eaton. The General brought his clenched fists down hard on the strap arms of his camp chair, "They can't do it! They can't compel me to do it." "Have you said this to the President?" "No, I have not thought it worth while to assure the President of my opinion. I consider it as important to the cause that he should be elected as that the army should be successful in the field."

Eaton, back at Washington, entering Lincoln's office heard the eager question, "Well, what did you find?" "You were right." And the President "fairly glowed with satisfaction," noted Eaton, as he heard Lincoln say, "I told you that they could not get him to run until he had closed out the rebellion."

Grant resumed his noncommittal attitude toward Lincoln as a candidate for the Presidency. To the country Grant gave no sign that he was for or against Lincoln. Lincoln may have guessed that Grant had a fear of the Washington hotbed of intrigues and the political guile that had been a curse on the Army of the Potomac. Lincoln may have instigated the mission of Congressman Washburne to Grant asking him to publish a letter in favor of Lincoln's election. If Washburne carried back to Lincoln what Grant had to say, Lincoln might have taken a healthy laugh for himself. Grant told Washburne that "for the President to answer all the charges the opposition would bring against him would be like setting a maiden to work to prove her chastity."

Grant's letter for publication dated at City Point, August 16, 1864, took no sides with any Republican or Democratic party faction, was neither pro- nor anti-Lincoln. And in its closing paragraph it endorsed by inference the President's emancipation policy. The old Steve Douglas Democrat, Grant, was saying by implication that the slavery issue had progressed to where the complications were inexorable: there was nothing else to do but free the slaves and make a peace that kept the slaves free. Regarding the war and the draft he wished to give the impression that the Confederacy was becoming a hollow shell sucked of its vitality.

"I state to all citizens who visit me that all we want now to insure an early restoration of the Union is determined unity of sentiment in the North. The Rebels have now in their ranks their last man . . . They have robbed the cradle and the grave equally to get their present force. Besides what they lose in frequent skirmishes and battles, they are

now losing from desertions and other causes at least one
regiment per day . . . Their only hope now is a divided
North, and this might give them reinforcements from Kentucky, Tennessee, Maryland and Missouri, while it would
weaken us . . . they are exceedingly anxious to hold out
until after the Presidential election; for they have many
hopes upon its result." This letter Stanton withheld for
later publication, probably after conference with Lincoln,
as though written appeals could be of little use in that dark
August.

Editor Sam Bowles of the Springfield *Republican* had to
write in a letter: "Do you notice that the Anti-Slavery
Standard and the Liberator, representatives of the old Abolitionists, are both earnest for Lincoln? Yet a new crop of
radicals have sprung up, who are resisting the President and
making mischief. Chase is going around, peddling his griefs
in private ears, and sowing dissatisfaction about Lincoln."
Chase amid his other doings had opened a correspondence
with August Belmont, chairman of the Democratic national committee, letting Belmont know that if the Democratic party at its Chicago convention would insert a
platform plank declaring for the abolition of slavery, he,
Chase, would then be willing to run as the Democratic
candidate for the Presidency.

Lincoln knew that no words, explanations, persuasions,
letters, speeches, could save his cause. Only bayonets tri-
umphant and red-dripping with Confederate defeat could
bring anything like magic or potency to anything he might
have to say. While decisive events waited he would manage
a course as best he could, saying: "The pilots on our western rivers steer from point to point, as they call it—setting
the course of the boat no farther than they can see. And
that is all I propose to do in the great problems that are set
before us."

A summer for sure it had been of steering from point to
point, from Sherman's drive toward Atlanta and Grant's
lunges at Richmond to the arrival of Early at the gates of
Washington and the sinking of the *Alabama* and the capture

of Mobile; from the smooth unanimous nomination of Lincoln at Baltimore to the clawing scorn of the Wade-Davis Manifesto; from the peace missions of Greeley at Niagara and Jaquess-Gilmore at Richmond to the secret Republican party manipulations hoping to replace Lincoln at the head of the ticket; from draft legislation authorizing conscripts to buy substitutes to the attempt to detach 50,000 men from Grant's army to enforce the draft in Northern cities, oath-bound secret societies threatening to take over the Government at Washington and one committee of Republican party leaders begging the President not to make his call for a draft of a half-million men until after the November election. He had given reply: "What is the Presidency worth to me if I have no country?"

Midsummer, Lincoln had told a Boston *Journal* man: "I have faith in the people. They will not consent to disunion. The danger is, in their being misled. Let them know the truth and the country is safe." He looked haggard and careworn to the correspondent, who said, "You are wearing yourself out with work." "I can't work less. But it isn't that. Work never troubled me. Things look badly, and I can't avoid anxiety . . . I feel a presentiment that I shall not outlast the rebellion. When it is over, my work will be done."

William Bross one August day found Lincoln "cordial but rather melancholy." A brother of Bross had fallen at the head of his regiment in fighting before Petersburg and Bross was on his way to recover the body. Deep-chested, heavily full-bearded with bristling hairs, flashing-eyed, one of the owners and editors of the Chicago *Tribune,* Bross was the Union party candidate for lieutenant governor of Illinois. Lincoln asked Bross anxiously for news from the West. Gloom hung over the West and the entire country, Bross believed. Lincoln agreed that neither of them could shut their eyes to the condition, Bross saying that the people expected a more vigorous prosecution of the war; more troops and appliances would be forthcoming from the people, if called for. And Bross felt assured that Lincoln spoke his "inmost sentiments" in a brief and graphic commentary which Lincoln plainly wished Bross to carry back to the

Union men of Illinois: "I will tell you what the people want. They want and must have, *success*. But whether that come or not, I shall stay *right here* and do my duty. Here I shall be. And they may come and hang me on that tree [pointing out of the window], but, God helping me, I shall never desert my post."

In the progress of the war Lincoln had constantly drawn closer to the churches. He replied to one delegation in May '64: "It is no fault in others that the Methodist Church sends more soldiers to the field, more nurses to the hospital, and more prayers to heaven than any. God bless the Methodist Church. Bless all the churches." And replying to a Baptist delegation later in the same day: "I have had great cause of gratitude for the support so unanimously given by all Christian denominations of the country."

Late in the summer of '64 came a committee of colored people from Baltimore, their spokesman in an elaborate address presenting Lincoln with a richly wrought Bible. He could only now say as so often before, "It has always been a sentiment with me that all mankind should be free . . . To you I return my most sincere thanks for the very elegant copy of the great Book of God which you present."

Writing to the Quaker woman Eliza P. Gurney, Lincoln dwelt on the searchings of conscience that might divide a man in time of war: "I am much indebted to the good christian people of the country for their constant prayers and consolations; and to no one of them, more than to yourself. The purposes of the Almighty are perfect, and must prevail, though we erring mortals may fail to accurately perceive them in advance. We hoped for a happy termination of this terrible war long before this; but God knows best, and has ruled otherwise. We shall yet acknowledge His wisdom and our own error therein. Meanwhile we must work earnestly in the best lights He gives us, trusting that so working still conduces to the great ends He ordains. Surely He intends some great good to follow this mighty convulsion, which no mortal could make, and no mortal could stay."

Chapter 33

The Fierce Fall Campaign of '64

Before leaving for Chicago to report the Democratic national convention, Noah Brooks heard Lincoln: "They must nominate a Peace Democrat on a war platform, or a War Democrat on a peace platform; and I personally can't say that I care much which they do."

In the same Wigwam in Chicago where Lincoln had been nominated in 1860, the convention met August 29, a boiling kettle of partisans that included Peace Democrats, War Democrats, Whigs, Know-Nothings, Conservatives, states' rights extremists who endorsed secession, millionaires in broadcloth, run-down politicians in paper collars, men who had braved mobs and suffered for the rights of free speech and a free press, and a remnant of Confederate loyalists who could not be open about their efforts. The delegates were called to order by August Belmont.

On taking the gavel as permanent chairman, Governor Seymour said the present administration could not now save the Union if it would, but "If the administration cannot save this Union, we can. (Loud applause.) Mr. Lincoln values many things above the Union; we put it first of all." The platform then adopted declared for the Union, the Constitution, civil liberty, and "care, protection, and regard" for the soldiers of the country.

Against persistent opposition Vallandigham in the resolutions committee carried through a straight-out peace plank declaring "that immediate efforts be made for a cessation of hostilities, with a view to an ultimate convention of the States."

The measures of immediate action on taking power, directly pledged in the platform, were: (1) the armies would be ordered to cease hostilities and go home; (2) the Southern States would then be asked to join a convention to restore the Union; (3) free speech and a free press would be allowed and no matter what the opposition to the Government there would be no arbitrary arrests, while habeas corpus and trial by jury would return.

Delegate Stambaugh of Ohio believed "they might search hell over and they could not find a worse candidate than Abraham Lincoln." Delegate Alexander, a circuit court judge from Kentucky, made public, according to the Chicago *Times,* his favorite anecdote "of a Kentucky gentleman who thought that as Mr. Lincoln was so fond of the negro, he should have one of the slain ones skinned and made into a pair of moccasins for his daily wear." The Honorable W. W. O'Brien, a Peoria delegate, was certain that the convention's candidate for President would on the next fourth of March "apply his boot to 'Old Abe's posterior' and kick him out of the Presidential chair."

Vallandigham on the streets was cheered. As a delegate he was a presence. John J. Van Alen of New York early intimated that he and others would not accept the nomination of McClellan for President, nor any candidate "with the smell of war on his garments." These anti-McClellan peace men were given a free hand in writing a peace plank.

On the final showdown George B. McClellan had 202½ votes as against little more than one-tenth of that number for one T. H. Seymour of Connecticut. Vallandigham amid cheers moved that the nomination of McClellan for President be made unanimous, which was done with further cheers. Senator George H. Pendleton of Ohio, on his record entirely satisfactory to the peace men, was named for Vice-President. The politicians went home fairly well satisfied. Was not victory in the air? In that week did not everyone know that the leading prophets and weather vanes of the Republican party were conceding defeat?

Then fate stepped in. Like a moving hour hand on a clock of doom came news flung world wide, news setting crowds of Northern loyalists to dancing with mirth and howling with glee, news centering about one little dispatch from Sherman September 3. Lincoln read a flimsy saying: "So Atlanta is ours and fairly won . . . Since May 5th we have been in one constant battle or skirmish, and need rest."

The dull ache of defeat and failure in many hearts took a change. In all news sheets the first item, the one story overwhelming all others, was around Sherman's words: "Atlanta is ours and fairly won." A strategic crossroads, supply depot and transportation center of a pivotal Cotton State in the Deep South was gone. Vicksburg, New Orleans and the Mississippi River gone, Kentucky, Tennessee and Nashville gone, Mobile gone. Lee and his army penned between Grant and Richmond for how long? Bells rang again, guns boomed.

The President requested thanksgiving to be offered in all places of worship the following Sunday and announced: "The national thanks are herewith tendered by the President to Major General William T. Sherman, and the gallant officers and soldiers of his command before Atlanta . . . The marches, battles, sieges . . . must render it famous in the annals of war . . ."

A few days later the country read McClellan's acceptance of the nomination for President in a letter throwing no light on what he would do about slavery except let it alone. "The Union is the one condition of peace—we ask no more."

As gently as McClellan could put it to those favoring immediate peace on any terms—and they were an influential fraction of his party—he seemed to be saying with a finality, hesitant yet final, that if the states out of the Union refused to come back on his invitation if he were President, then he would fight them. He hoped for peace "without the effusion of another drop of blood" but possibly there might have to be more fighting if the Union were to be saved. The General wrote: "Let me add, what I doubt not was, although unexpressed, the sentiment of the Convention, as it is of the people they represent, that when any one State is willing to return to the Union, it should be received at once, with a full guarantee of all its constitutional rights . . . the Union must be preserved at all hazards. I could not look in the face my gallant comrades of the army and navy who have survived so many bloody battles, and tell them . . . we had abandoned that Union for which we have so often periled our lives. A vast majority of our people, whether in the army and navy or at home, would, as I would, hail with unbounded joy the permanent restoration of peace, on the basis of the Union under the Constitution, without the effusion of another drop of blood. But no peace can be permanent without Union." Having thus deftly and gently thrown out the most labored point of the Chicago platform, McClellan closed in a belief "that the views here expressed are those of the Convention and the people you represent."

Vallandigham for the Peace Democrats scoffed at McClellan's repudiation. "The Chicago platform enunciated its policy and principles by authority and was binding upon every Democrat, and by them the Democratic Administration must and should be governed."

Now in this September of '64 Phil Sheridan was heard from. For the first time in the war the Shenandoah Valley saw a destroyer with a system. Whatever would nourish man or provide fodder for beast was to be taken or burned or spoiled. When Grant's order should be met, then a crow would have to carry its own rations flying over the valley. At Harrisonburg from Gibbs Hill, residents counted 20 barns in the same hour lighting the dark night of the valley as the flames roared upward.

Four days' fighting at Winchester and Fisher's Hill followed Grant's order "Go in!" and Sheridan's telegram to Grant the night of September 19 had first place in all news sheets of the country: "I attacked the forces of General Early . . . completely defeated him, and driving him through Winchester, captured about 2,500 prisoners, 5 pieces of artillery, 9 army flags, and most of their wounded." To his army next day Sheridan read a telegram signed "A. Lincoln": "Have just heard of your great victory. God bless you all, officers and men. Strongly inclined to come up and see you."

A *Harper's Weekly* writer had noticed a man at a news bulletin board reading one of Sheridan's dispatches to Grant and commenting, "A few more such victories and Abe Lincoln will be elected in November." They were what Lincoln had wanted. No campaign speeches could equal them. The least he could do was appoint Sheridan a brigadier general in the Regular Army and place him in permanent command of the Middle Division, which he did.

A committee appointed by the Rockingham County Court later estimated $25,000,000 worth of property had been destroyed by Sheridan's troops, itemizing 50,000 bushels of corn, 100,000 bushels of wheat, 450 barns, one furnace, three factories, 30 dwelling houses, 31 mills, besides livestock. Grant's order had said: "If the war is to last another year we want the Shenandoah Valley to remain a barren waste."

In a Washington dispatch Whitelaw Reid voiced those who had sought to replace Lincoln with another candidate. "The general apathy and discontent and the apparent certainty of Mr. Lincoln's defeat" had all changed. Greeley announced that the *Tribune* would "henceforth fly the banner of Abraham Lincoln for President." Chase spoke likewise and prepared to go on the stump with speeches alongside Ben Wade and Henry Winter Davis. Gloomy August became a September edged with a few splinters of dawn.

On September 22 a letter was published of Frémont dropping his third party and coming out for Lincoln. And next day Lincoln asked Blair to leave the Cabinet and Blair did. Whether Lincoln made a deal for Frémont's return to the fold on condition of Blair's being ushered out of the Cabinet was anybody's guess. It came as a necessary piece of work for Lincoln to write in his letter to Blair: "You very well know that this proceeds from no dissatisfaction of mine with you personally or officially. Your uniform kindness has been unsurpassed by that of any friend . . ."

Welles asked Blair what had led up to it. Blair said he had no doubt he was "a peace-offering to Frémont and his friends." The secretaries Nicolay and Hay would not stress any one factor as bringing the President to oust his Postmaster General. Blair "wearied the President by insisting

upon it that all the leading Republicans were Lincoln's enemies." Lincoln lost the fine edge of his patience, once saying to Blair in the hearing of John Hay, "It is much better
not to be led from the region of reason into that of hot
blood by imputing to public men motives which they do not
avow."

"The union of the Republican party has become a para-
mount necessity," ran Frémont's letter withdrawing his
candidacy in favor of "the Republican candidate pledged to
the reëstablishment of the Union without slavery . . . however hesitating his policy may be." Frémont could have
said too that fate was playing hard with him in his 44,000-
acre Mariposa estate in California, once valued at $10,-
000,000, that debts on it had reached a total of $1,250,000
with interest charges of $13,000 monthly, that one fee of
$200,000 had been charged him by David Dudley Field for
attorney's services, that by frauds not strictly illegal and by
mismanagement and bad turns of luck he was slowly being
eased out of an almost fabulous fortune in land and gold.
His brownstone mansion in New York and his summer
home north of Tarrytown, the big gray-stone house that
commanded a beautiful view of Tappan Zee, were to go in
pawn and then fail to meet the demands.

Some newspapers made much of a remark dropped by
Simon Cameron that in the event of re-election the President would call around him fresh and earnest men. Hay
referred to this. Lincoln said: "They need not be especially
savage about a change. There are now only 3 left of the
original Cabinet."

William Dennison, lawyer, president of the Exchange
Bank of Columbus, governor of Ohio the first two years of
the war, a cordial friend of the Blair family, was in Lincoln's mind to fill the vacant Cabinet office. On September
24 the President telegraphed Dennison: "Mr. Blair has resigned and I appoint you Postmaster-General. Come on
immediately."

For campaign purposes both parties now made use of the
long letter McClellan had handed to Lincoln at Harrison's

Landing more than two years before. The Democrats offered it as a modest self-portrayal of a Christian gentleman, a soldier and a statesman. The Republicans picked at it in editorials and squibs, the more radical editors saying its ego and covert insolence should have brought instant removal of a general stepping so completely out of the military field into politics.

On one point the Republicans and Democrats seemed to agree: that on July 7, 1862, when he dated that letter, and for some time before, McClellan had the definite notion in his head that he might make a good President and had carefully studied what he would announce as his policies if he were a candidate. Whether or not Fernando Wood had seduced McClellan into politics, as some believed, it was now in McClellan's favor that Wood announced in view of McClellan's repudiation of the Chicago platform he, Wood, could not support McClellan for President.

When this September swing into party unity had been accomplished Lincoln was in "a more gleeful humor," according to Lamon, who found him alone one evening and met the greeting, "I am glad you have come in. Lamon, do you know that 'we have met the enemy, and they are *ourn*'? I think the cabal of obstructionists 'am busted'! . . . I now am inspired with the hope that our disturbed country further requires the valuable services of your humble servant. 'Jordan has been a hard road to travel,' but I feel now that, notwithstanding the enemies I have made and the faults I have committed, I'll be *dumped* on the right side of that stream."

Of the few "obstructionists" still unyielding was Wendell Phillips, writing as late as September 27 to Elizabeth Cady Stanton: "I would cut off both hands before doing anything to aid Abraham Lincoln's election . . . Justice is still more to me than Union." This was September. October was to see Phillips on the stump for Lincoln, and Thad Stevens commending "the firm grasp of the pilot at the helm," who had risen above "Border State seductions and Republican cowardice."

Collections for the campaign went on, among government employees and elsewhere. Leonard Swett wrote to his wife that he and Congressman Washburne had managed to get a campaign fund of $100,000, assuring her: "Don't think it is for improper purposes. It is not . . . Innumerable expenses have to be incurred."

John Hay noted September 23: "Senator Harlan thinks that Bennett's support [with the New York *Herald*] is so important, especially considered as to its bearing on the soldier vote, that it would pay to offer him a foreign mission for it." Lincoln, it seemed, definitely promised to appoint James Gordon Bennett U.S. Envoy Extraordinary and Minister Plenipotentiary to France. An associate, confidant and go-between of Bennett's, W. O. Bartlett, wrote to Bennett November 4, 1864:

> I am from Washington, fresh from the bosom of Father Abraham. I had a full conversation with him, alone, on Tuesday evening, at the White House, in regard to yourself, among other things.
>
> I said to him: "There are but few days now before the election. If Mr. Bennett is not *certainly* to have the offer of the French Mission, I want to know it *now*. It is important to me."
>
> We discussed the course which the *Herald* had pursued, at length, and I will tell you, verbally, at your convenience, what he said; but he concluded with the remark that in regard to the understanding between him and me, about Mr. Bennett, he had been a *"shut pan,* to every body"; and that he *expected to do that thing* (appoint you to France) *as much as he expected to live.* He repeated: *"I expect to do it as certainly as I do to be re-elected myself."*

It carried Lincoln's lingo. Bennett and his *Herald* were of moment for the election a week away. And far more in the labors to follow a re-election would it count for Lincoln to have good will and co-operation from that most humanly interesting newspaper in the Western Hemisphere.

Marshaled solidly behind McClellan were powerful forces, the banking and transportation interests linked with August Belmont, Dean Richmond, Aspinwall, the industrialist churchman seen pre-eminently in Cyrus H. McCormick of Chicago, an array of respectably wealthy, intellectual or aristocratic types embodied in Horatio Seymour of New York and Robert C. Winthrop of Boston. Marching along were two-fisted and riotous elements, joined by those to whom the race issue was uppermost, fearful the Emancipation Proclamation might bring political and social equality. The recoil over McClellan's repudiation of the peace platform came in some of the most vocal sections of the party. The *Metropolitan Record* and the *Daily News* in New York announced they could not go along with McClellan. The *Crisis* at Columbus, Ohio, held that "fraudulent sale is not binding in law" and the "sell-out" in Chicago was treachery. With Vallandigham these organs continued their attacks on Lincoln, pouted disapproval of McClellan, and seemed to be saying they hoped McClellan could be elected, after which they could force him into respect for the Chicago demand for peace through "cessation of hostilities." This too seemed to be the position of McClellan's running mate, Senator George H. Pendleton.

A letter of the Reverend Dr. Moncure Conway in the Boston *Commonwealth* reported Conway, with antislavery associates, interviewing the President. And the careful and scrupulous Conway recorded the President as saying: "Gentlemen, it is generally the case that a man who begins a work is not the best man to carry it on to a successful termination. I believe it was so in the case of Moses, wasn't it? He got the children of Israel out of Egypt, but the Lord selected somebody else to bring them to their journey's end. A pioneer has hard work to do, and generally gets so battered and spattered that people prefer another, even though they may accept the principle." Conway commented: "Under him [Lincoln] the war was begun; he had to deal with the disaffected; is it not possible that he has become so *battered and spattered* as to make it well for him to give up the leadership to some Joshua?"

The printing press worked overtime. The electorate saw literature hauled by the ton. Pamphlets, leaflets, brochures, cards, tracts, envelopes colored with party emblems, in quantity lots came to voters. The Republicans seemed to outdo the Democrats in the amount of educational material, but no voter went hungry who wanted reading matter that lambasted Lincoln and sang the praises of McClellan. A list of horrors, including the debauchery of young women and the jailing of boys in foul and dismal cells for two years, filled a fearsome Democratic brochure titled *Mr. Lincoln's Arbitrary Arrests.*

In one leaflet was an anecdote from General Schenck in an Ohio speech. The Chicago peace platform with a war candidate reminded Schenck of an old lady selling apples at the courthouse door in Cincinnati. On a customer asking, "Are they sweet or sour?" she would lead on into finding out what might be wanted by the assurance, "Why, sir, they are rather acid; a sort of low tart, inclined to be very sweet."

A speech of Carl Schurz at Philadelphia, September 16, was an extraordinary effort in persuasion. The Union Congressional Committee circulated it among all groups, with emphasis on the Germans. Schurz had grown restless in command of a corps of instruction at Nashville and had taken to the stump after a conference with Lincoln. Undoubtedly they had one of their long talks again. And probably Lincoln wrote parts of Schurz's speech or Schurz, with his remarkably acute literal memory, incorporated something of the flair and wording of Lincoln's conversation into a speech. "The mouth of the Mississippi in the hands of a foreign power? Let it be so and half our independence is gone . . . The people of the United States have bought the mouth of the Mississippi, once with their money, and twice with their blood. To give it away would be merely to produce the necessity of buying it a fourth time. Can the South yield it? No. Can the North do without it? No. And then?"

The vote for the platform at Chicago was far more unanimous than the vote for the candidate, in which connection Schurz would speak from experience: "There is no American who does not know that a President's policy is not made by him alone, but by those who have made him." In closing Schurz let the American Eagle scream. In 50 years the country would have 100,000,000 people, in another century 500,000,000, and the purpose of the North was a free republic *"so strong that its pleasure will be consulted before any power on earth will undertake to disturb the peace of the world."*

In a Union party pamphlet Professor Edouard Laboulaye spoke for French liberals. "The world is a solidarity, and the cause of America is the cause of liberty." So long as a society of 30,000,000 people across the Atlantic lived "under a government of their choice, with laws made by themselves," Europe could hope. "But should liberty become eclipsed in the New World, it would become night in Europe," and power would go to "the whole school which believes only in violence and in success." Therefore Laboulaye and his associates were "praying God that the name which shall stand on the ballot [of November] shall be that of honest and upright Abraham Lincoln." From the English liberal leader John Bright in a letter to Greeley came the wish that Lincoln be re-elected because it would over Europe "and indeed throughout the world" deepen men's faith in republican institutions.

Three speeches of Lincoln to Ohio regiments, "three months' men" going home, gave his attempt to tell in a few simple words what the shooting and crying, the war, was about. "A free government where every man has a right to be equal with every other man" was endangered. "Nowhere in the world is presented a government of so much liberty and equality. To the humblest and poorest amongst us are held out the highest privileges and positions. The present moment finds me at the White House, yet there is as good a chance for your children as there was for my father's. I happen, temporarily, to occupy this White House. I am a living witness that any one of your children may look to come here as my father's child has."

A committee of McClellan Democrats carrying an elaborate document of protest arrived at the White House and John Lellyet of Nashville read the recital of their wrongs to Lincoln. Lincoln was brusque. "May I inquire how long it took you and the New York politicians to concoct that paper?" Lellyet replied that none but Tennesseans had had a hand in it. Lincoln: "I expect to let the friends of George B. McClellan manage their side of this contest in their own way, and I will manage my side of it in my way." Adding that he might make some further answer in writing, Lincoln closed. They saw he was abrupt and filed out.

Mingled flamboyance and romance of democracy as it moved in Andrew Johnson came to the fore one October night as he rose to address the torchlighted faces of a crowd that included practically the entire Negro population of Nashville. He had a proclamation to make: "Standing here upon the steps of the Capitol, with the past history of the State to witness, the present condition to guide, and its future to encourage me, I, Andrew Johnson, do hereby proclaim freedom, full, broad and unconditional, to every man in Tennessee." A roar of rejoicing and a wild clamor of gladness broke from Negro throats, drums and trumpets added jubilation, and banners waved over circling torches. Johnson's voice rang again. "This damnable aristocracy should be pulled down. No longer should the wives and daughters of the colored men of Tennessee be dragged into a concubinage compared to which polygamy was a virtue." Radicals who had found Lincoln a poor instrument for their measure began saying, "Johnson is our man, one of us."

Singing "Blow ye the trumpet, blow," 144 Negro delegates met in Syracuse, New York, four October days. They spoke for the free Negroes of 18 states, including seven Slave States, and organized the National Equal Rights League, petitioning Congress to remove "invidious distinctions, based upon color, as to pay, labor, and promotion" among Negro troops. Thanks were accorded the President and Congress for opening the way to colored mail carriers, for abolishing slavery in the District of Columbia, for recognition of the Negro republics Liberia and Haiti, for a retaliatory military order invoked because of "barbarous treatment of the colored soldiers of the Union army by the rebels." Further and special thanks were accorded Senator Sumner and General Butler.

On October 11 the stump speakers and the tub thumpers paused slightly, the torchlights and the transparencies halted a moment, and there was less fury in the pamphlets blown loose as wild geese across the autumn sky. The electorate went to the polls that day in Pennsylvania, Ohio and Indiana. At eight o'clock in the evening the President with Hay walked over to the War Department.

The telegraph keys clicked. Governor Morton and the entire Republican ticket in Indiana were elected by 20,000 majority, with a gain of four Congressmen. Pennsylvania's Congressmen, equally divided between two parties, changed to 15 Republicans against 9 Democrats. The Union ticket carried Ohio by 54,000 and the 14 Democrats and 5 Republicans of '62 shifted now to 17 Republicans and 2 Democrats in Congress. The defamatory Peace Democrat "Sunset" Cox lost his seat to Samuel Shellabarger. Not least was the news from Maryland and her adoption of a new state constitution abolishing slavery; the majority was slim, the soldier vote giving emancipation its day.

On October 12 Roger Brooke Taney died and the President must name a new Chief Justice. Spheres of influence formed and sought to have Lincoln name Montgomery Blair, Bates, Fessenden, Salmon P. Chase or some other one. And Lincoln was to hear them and to wait and to consider carefully and hold his patience.

Browning sounded Fessenden on whether he would permit his friends to mention Browning to the President for Chief Justice and heard Fessenden's refusal. To the War, Treasury and State Departments in the morning, to his room in the afternoon, went Mr. Browning, ex-U.S. Senator Browning, holder of the seat vacated by Steve Douglas until Illinois had gone Democratic again. He was the one old-time Illinois lawyer associated with Lincoln who most often was seen at the White House. "At the Departments in the forenoon, and at work at my room in the afternoon" ran the most frequent item of his diary, though the next most frequent seemed to be "At night went to the President's." And unless the President was over at the War Department Browning was let in. The President liked his company, though it seemed that along in the fall of '64 the President came to look at Browning as one of the most peculiarly befuddled individuals that had come out of the war, and he became less free in outpourings of mind and spirit to Browning.

When Smith had retired as Secretary of the Interior, Browning had hoped the President would agree with Mrs. Lincoln that he should have the place. When Browning brought to the President the matter of the vacant Chief Justiceship, he was not without faint hope he might be the man. Known as a familiar of the President, for him doors swung open when he sent his card in at the departments. He rode with the President and navy heads to the navy yards to witness the throwing of rockets and signals from 6- and 12-pound guns. He worked in his office till night "then went and saw the President about fees in the Phillips cases, about Adml Wilke's case, and about appointment of Eben Moore to Montano."

Browning refused the request of Seward and the President that he take the appointment of commissioner for claim adjustments of the Hudson Bay and Puget Sound agricultural companies. "I find the duties will be very arduous, and the compensation $5000 inadequate." When the hay contractors Covert & Farlin had been arrested and put on trial before a court-martial charged with fraud, the hay contractors hired the two lawyers in Washington nearest to the President in confidence and longest in acquaintance, Orville H. Browning and Leonard Swett. To the War Department, to the Quartermaster General, to the Judge Advocate went Browning, sometimes in company with Swett, with the result that the hay contractors got "an extension of 30 days to enable them to fill their contracts— They discharged from arrest and proceedings in Court Martial suspended," according to Browning's diary.

Wearing a serenity bland and colorless, almost empty of

humor, precise in the forms and manners, overly vain about his scruples, Browning went here and there, saw everybody who was anybody, made the entries in his diary, two lines, ten lines, without elation or melancholy, earnest and careful. When a band of serenaders came to his Quincy home the night of McClellan's nomination for President, Browning was earnest and scrupulous enough to tell them he was not a Democrat, yet sufficiently careful to repeat that McClellan was "a great general" and would have his support if elected President. In like manner he would support Frémont or any other administration. The name of Browning's intimate personal friend and political benefactor, then a candidate for re-election, escaped his mention. He may have wished that Lincoln might be President another four years, but the wish did not reach his tongue. It was likewise when Browning spoke before a crowd jubilating over the capture of Atlanta. Then too, as he wrote in his diary, "I carefully avoided subjects of a merely partizan character, and made no allusion to the Presidential candidates." On September 16, 1864, his entire diary entry read: "Honorable C. B. Lawrence dined with me today. Has urged me earnestly to declare myself in favor of the re election of Mr. Lincoln."

The days ran on through the campaign and Browning was to hold back from any word that he would vote for Lincoln. His calls on the President seemed to increase and nearly always the favor he asked was granted. "At night went to the Presidents and got order for release of Capt Saml Black." "At Presidents and got order for Judge Advocate Burnett to examine & report on cases . . . and of Captain Black." Nothing less than "an interview of three hours" with the President was accorded him one evening "in regard to Capt Blacks case." Or again one Sunday: "At night went to the Presidents, and got an order for the release of Ludwell Y. Browning, a rebel prisoner at Camp Douglas."

Only once in his diary did Browning record an open rebuff from the President. Browning possibly omitted some points of circumstance in the entry:

At night went to see the President on behalf of Mrs Fitz, a loyal widow of Mississippi owning a cotton plantation there, and from whom the U S Army had taken all her slaves amounting to 47, and 10,000 bushels of corn—She is now a refugee in St Louis, reduced to indigence She asks no compensation for her slaves, but wishes the government to give her a sufficient number of negroes out of those accumulated upon its hands to work her farm the ensuing season, and enable her to raise a crop of cotton, she to pay them out of the proceeds the same wages which the government pays those it employs. I made the proposition to the President thinking it reasonable and just, and worthy at least of being considered.

He became very much excited, and did not discuss the proposition at all, but said with great vehemence he had rather take a rope and hang himself than to do it. That there were a great many poor women who had never had any property at all who were suffering as much as Mrs Fitz—that her condition was a necessary consequence of the rebellion, and that the government could not make good the losses occasioned by rebels. I reminded him that she was loyal, and that her property had been taken from her by her own government, and was now being used by it, and I thought it a case eminently proper for some sort of remuneration, and her demand reasonable, and certainly entitled to respectful consideration. He replied that she had lost no property—that her slaves were free when they were taken, and that she was entitled to no compensation.

I called his attention to the fact that a portion of her slaves, at least, had been taken in 1862, before his proclamation, and put upon our gun boats, when he replied in a very excited manner that he had rather throw up, than to do what was asked, and would not do anything about it. I left him in no very good humor.

All the numerous past incidents of trust, affection and benefits bestowed on him did not bring out Browning in favor of Lincoln for President. He said nothing for or against a second term for Lincoln. To that extent Browning helped the McClellan ticket and cause.

Unionist serenaders from Baltimore arrived at the White House in late October, and facing them, Lincoln made reference to Democratic newspaper clamor that the Lincoln administration aimed to keep its power whatever the verdict at the polls in November. Lincoln told the serenaders that in contrast "others regard the fact that the Chicago Convention adjourned, not *sine die*, but to meet again, if called to do so by a particular individual, as the intimation of a purpose that if their nominee shall be elected, he will at once seize control of the government." He hoped the people would suffer no uneasiness on either point, delivering himself of momentous words:

"I am struggling to maintain government, not to overthrow it. I am struggling especially to prevent others from overthrowing it. I therefore say, that if I shall live, I shall remain President until the fourth of next March; and that whoever shall be constitutionally elected therefor in November, shall be duly installed as President on the fourth of March; and that in the interval I shall do my utmost that whoever is to hold the helm for the next voyage, shall start with the best possible chance to save the ship. This is due to the people both on principle, and under the constitution . . .

"I may add that in this purpose to save the country and it's liberties, no classes of people seem so nearly unanimous as the soldiers in the field and the seamen afloat. Do they not have the hardest of it? Who should quail while they do not? God bless the soldiers and seamen, with all their brave commanders."

A call signed by eminent and influential Democrats of the past endorsed the Lincoln-Johnson ticket. The call asked what kind of a Democratic party it was that excluded John A. Dix, Alexander T. Stewart, Theodore Roosevelt, Sr., R. B. Roosevelt, Peter Cooper, John A. Logan, John M. Palmer and many others who till now had

had no political home except the Democratic party. "If these men are not Democrats, who are?"

"Should the soldier in the field have the right to vote in elections?" Two Union party pamphlets called the roll on the various states. *Harper's Weekly* summarized the points. In New York the Union men passed a soldier-vote bill by 65 Yeas to 59 Copperhead Nays; Governor Seymour vetoed the bill, but the Unionists went over his head and against prolonged Copperhead opposition procured a soldier-vote amendment to the state constitution. In New Hampshire the law passed the legislature by 175 to 105. In Rhode Island, Connecticut, Maine, Michigan, Ohio and other states the only opposition was from McClellan-for-President men. In New Jersey 31 Copperhead Nays against 19 Union Yeas defeated the soldier vote, and likewise in Delaware. In Michigan the soldiers in the field were accorded the ballot over the opposition of the "Detroit *Free Press* and the entire Copperhead press." In California, Iowa, Minnesota and Missouri it was Union men against Copperheads that won the soldier's right to vote. In Indiana a Copperhead legislature naturally refused it. In Ohio in the October election, out of 55,000 soldier votes a majority of 48,000 were for the Union party candidates.

In more than one case officious army politicians refused a pass, previously promised, to a soldier wearing a McClellan campaign badge. Friends of one such soldier brought his case before Lincoln, who investigated, sent for the soldier, and then handed him a pass in the President's own handwriting along with a handshake and "God bless you, my boy. Show them that. It'll take you home."

The draft meanwhile proceeded. The relentless dragnet moved. Grant and Sherman wanted men. "Leading Republicans all over the country," noted Nicolay and Hay, "fearing the effect of the draft upon the elections, begged the President to withdraw the call or suspend operations under it." Cameron advised against it in Pennsylvania. Chase telegraphed from Ohio urging a three weeks' suspension. To an Ohio committee earnestly requesting suspension until after the November elections, Lincoln quietly answered, "What is the Presidency worth to me if I have no country?"

Twice came Governor Morton of Indiana, whose soldiers could not vote in the field, applying for the return of all Indiana soldiers possible on Election Day. And at Lincoln's refusal to go over the heads of his generals and order the soldiers home to vote, it was suggested that if Indiana went Democratic she could give no more help to the Government. Lincoln met this point: "It is better that we should both be beaten than that the forces in front of the enemy should be weakened and perhaps defeated on account of the absence of these men." Morton suggested that no Indiana troops be kept in hospitals outside his state and that all troops unfit for service be sent home. On these points Lincoln got action. And Stanton had Lincoln's approval in ordering home from Sherman's army for campaigning in Indiana six prominent Hoosier officers, along with Major Generals Logan and Frank Blair to stump Indiana and nearby states. In fact, Logan later wrote to Sherman that "when I left on leave after the Atlanta campaign, to canvass for Mr. Lincoln, I did it at the special and private request of the President. This I kept to myself and never made it public."

"There was a constant succession of telegrams from all parts of the country," wrote Dana of the War Office, "requesting that leave of absence be extended to this or that officer, in order that his district at home might have the benefit of his vote and political influence. Furloughs were asked for private soldiers whose presence in close districts was deemed of especial importance, and there was a widespread demand that men on detached service and convalescents in hospitals be sent home. All the power and influence of the War Department, then something enormous from the vast expenditure and extensive relations of the war, was employed to secure the re-election of Mr. Lincoln. The political struggle was most intense, and the interest taken in it, both in the White House and in the War Department, was almost painful."

Along the Canadian border and the shore lines of the Great Lakes there were in the summer and fall of '64 plots, adventures, explosions, robberies, espionage, propaganda. From the dwindling hoard of Confederate gold, Jacob Thompson of Mississippi, formerly Secretary of the Interior under Buchanan, passed money to Sons of Liberty for armed revolts to be started in various states. "Lincoln had the power and would certainly use it to reëlect himself," wrote Thompson later in a report to Judah P. Benjamin at Richmond, "and there was no hope but in force. The belief was entertained and freely expressed, that by a bold, vigorous and concerted movement . . . Illinois, Indiana, and Ohio could be seized and held." Plans were laid in detail for a general uprising on an appointed day, seizure of arsenals at Indianapolis, Springfield, Chicago and Columbus, release of Confederate prisoners at four camps, arming of prisoners, overthrow of the state governments in Ohio, Indiana, Illinois, Missouri, formation of a Northwestern Confederacy. Then they would dictate peace.

The uprising collapsed. The Confederate operations from Canada annoyed the North but they were more noisy than effective. Thompson, who was Jeff Davis' personal choice for the work of embroiling the Northwestern States in an uprising, lacked the required touch; he moved at cost and found the result was a rubber dagger limp on the hide of a rhinoceros.

Again Sheridan, his men and horses, were heard from. When the hour cried for it Sheridan had the genius of a daredevil who could make other men in the mass want to be daredevils. At ten o'clock the night of October 19 Sheridan telegraphed Grant: "My army at Cedar Creek was attacked this morning before daylight, and . . . in fact, most of the line . . . driven in confusion with the loss of twenty pieces of artillery. I hastened from Winchester, where I was on my return from Washington, and found the armies between Middletown and Newtown, having been driven back about four miles. I here took the affair in hand . . . formed a compact line of battle, just in time to repulse an attack of the enemy, which was handsomely done at about 1 P.M. At 3 P.M., after some changes of the cavalry from the left to the right flank, I attacked, with great vigor, driving and routing the enemy, capturing, according to the last report, forty-three pieces of artillery, and very many prisoners . . . Affairs at times looked badly, but by the gallantry of our brave officers and men disaster has been converted into a splendid victory."

Lincoln telegraphed Sheridan October 22: "With great pleasure I tender to you and your brave army, the thanks of the Nation, and my own personal admiration and gratitude, for the month's operations in the Shenandoah Valley; and especially for the splendid work of October 19, 1864."

Twenty days before the November elections Sheridan gave the North one of the most dramatic victories of the war, following a methodical devastation of the Shenandoah Valley, with the result soon to come that his own army and the shattered forces of Early would be transferred to operations before Richmond. From innumerable platforms of the North were recited the verses of "Sheridan's Ride" by Thomas Buchanan Read. As a campaign tract it was fetching. As he heard this piece many and many a time Sheridan said he believed that what people liked best in the poem was the horse.

Soon now, on November 8, the American electorate would choose between Lincoln and the Baltimore platform and McClellan and the Chicago platform as revised by McClellan. That day of ballots would fix a momentous decision in the life of the American people.

Chapter 34

Lincoln's Laughter — and His Religion

Lincoln was the first true humorist to occupy the White House. No other President of the United States had come to be identified, for good or bad, with a relish for the comic. This had brought him to folk masses as a living man they could feel and picture. The *Saturday Review* of London said: "One advantage which the Americans now have in national joking is the possession of a President who is not only the First Magistrate, but the Chief Joker, of the land. Collections of American jests are advertised as containg 'Mr. Lincoln's latest jokes,' and some of his stories are certainly good . . . The Puritan familiarity without intention of irreverence we have in the camp story of the Colonel (reprinted in all American papers), who, hearing from the Baptist chaplain that there had been ten conversions in a rival regiment, exclaimed, 'Do you say so? Sergeant Jones! detail fifteen men of my regiment for immediate baptism.' "

Before Lincoln's renomination at Baltimore the New York *Herald* did its best to attach infamy to Lincoln as a jester, "a joke incarnated, his election a very sorry joke, and the idea that such a man as he should be the President of such a country as this a very ridiculous joke."

In one little mock biography, originally intended to wrap up Lincoln as entirely ridiculous, a genius of nonsense let himself go: "Mr. Lincoln stands six feet twelve in his socks, which he changes once every ten days. His anatomy is composed mostly of bones, and when walking he resembles the offspring of a happy marriage between a derrick and a windmill. When speaking he reminds one of the old signal-telegraph that used to stand on Staten Island. His head is shaped something like a rutabago, and his complexion is that of a Saratoga trunk. His hands and feet are plenty large enough, and in society he has the air of having too many of them. The glove-makers have not yet had time to construct gloves that will fit him. In his habits he is by no means foppish, though he brushes his hair sometimes, and is said to wash. He swears fluently. A strict temperance man himself, he does not object to another man's being pretty drunk, especially when he is about to make a bargain with him. He is fond of fried liver and onions, and is a member of the church. He can hardly be called handsome, though he is certainly much better looking since he had the small-pox."

An Illinois cavalry colonel, John F. Farnsworth, quoted Lincoln on his storytelling: "Some of the stories are not so nice as they might be, but I tell you the truth when I say that a funny story, if it has the element of genuine wit, has the same effect on me that I suppose a good square drink of whiskey has on an old toper; it puts new life into me." Lamon said the President used stories as a laugh cure for a drooping friend or for his own melancholy, yet also to clinch an argument, to lay bare a fallacy, to disarm an an-

From a campaign comic life of Lincoln. *Upper left:* Telling little stories in camp. *Upper right:* Writing his letter of acceptance. *Lower left:* Assuming command of the Army and Navy. *Lower right:* Splitting rails in Sangamon.

tagonist, but most often the stories were "labor-saving contrivances."

"I am glad to take the hand of the man, who, with the help of Almighty God will put down this rebellion," said an earnest citizen in line at a reception. The answer flashed, "You are more than half right, sir." To one asking whether the town of Lincoln, Illinois, was named after him Lincoln said: "Well, it was named after I was."

Perhaps one-sixth of the stories credited to him were old acquaintances, Lincoln told Noah Brooks. The other five-sixths came from other and better storytellers than himself. "I remember a good story when I hear it, but I never invented anything original. I am only a retail dealer."

Many yarns, anecdotes and puns credited to Lincoln were definitely inventions of others who took Lincoln as a handy peg on which to hang them. His own admitted stories might number a hundred, noted Nicolay. On the flyleaf of a replete book of *Anecdotes of Abraham Lincoln,* Isaac N. Arnold wrote that in his judgment about half were probably stories Lincoln had actually told.

Sometimes, noted Sumner, Lincoln insisted that he had "no invention, only a good memory" for anecdotes. And Sumner, it seemed, cultivated a manner of keeping some actual sense of humor hidden, or he could not have managed one of the best metaphors coined about the way Lincoln used stories to support argument. "His ideas moved," noted Sumner, "as the beasts entered Noah's ark, in pairs."

And of Lincoln's humor operating with iron and without anecdote, Sumner had an instance of the President saying to him of a political antagonist indifferent to slavery: "I suppose the institution of slavery really looks small to him. He is so put up by nature, that a lash upon his back would hurt him, but a lash upon anybody else's back does not hurt him." Fearful lashes on the back had been taken by Sumner, and any study of the relations of Lincoln and Sumner could not leave out Lincoln's awareness of the long-drawnout suffering Sumner had borne. Lincoln possibly even suspected what Sumner's best friend Longfellow had written in a diary, that the spinal lacerations from the cane of Preston Brooks had not left the brain unaffected.

In the telegraph office one evening Lincoln confessed to David Homer Bates that his storytelling was a habit formed

in his younger days and his case was like that of an old
colored man on a plantation, who let his work slide to
preach to the other slaves. His master rebuked him, but
the old man had the spirit of the gospel in him, kept on
preaching, even when he knew the lash might be waiting
for him. At last one day he was ordered to report at the Big
House. There the master scolded, told him he would get
hard punishment next time he was caught preaching. Tears
came to his eyes:

"But, marsa, I jest cain't help it; I allus has to draw in-
frunces from de Bible textes when dey comes into my haid.
Doesn't you, marsa?" "Well, uncle, I suspect I do something of that kind myself at times, but there is one text I
never could understand, and if you can draw the right inference from it, I will cancel my order and let you preach
to your heart's content." "What is de tex, marsa?" " 'The
ass snuffeth up the east wind.' Now, uncle, what inference
do you draw from such a text?" "Well, marsa, I's neber
heerd dat tex' befo', but I 'spect de infrunce is she gotter
snuff a long time befo' she git fat!"

Carpenter after his six months in the White House could
not recollect a Lincoln story "which would have been out
of place uttered in a ladies' drawing-room." Isaac N. Arnold endorsed this as his own observation of Lincoln over
a 20-year period. These friends, however, were neither the
crony familiars nor the bores and nuisances to whom Lincoln told his stories questioned as "not in good taste."

Lincoln's transition from mood to mood impressed Andrew D. White, educator and a member of the New York
State senate. White saw Lincoln in the White House
"dressed in a rather dusty suit of black," resembling "some
rural tourist who had blundered into the place." Lincoln
entered the room and approached White's group. He
seemed, to White, "less at home there than any other person present" as he "looked about for an instant as if in
doubt where he should go." Others had seen and written
of the same thing. And White's impression recorded itself:
"As he came toward us in a sort of awkward, perfunctory
way his face seemed to me one of the saddest I had ever

seen, and when he had reached us he held out his hand to the first stranger, then to the second and so on all with the air of a melancholy automaton. But suddenly someone in the company said something which amused him and instantly there came in his face a most marvelous transformation. I have never seen anything like it in any other human being. His features were lighted, his eyes radiant, he responded to sundry remarks humorously, then dryly, and thenceforward was cordial and hearty."

By mid-1863 several large editions of Lincoln joke books had been printed and sold. *Old Abe's Jokes—Fresh from Abraham's Bosom* ran the title of one and *Old Abe's Joker, or Wit at the White House* another. One page had a bad-tempered old fellow calling to a noisy boy, "What are you hollering for when I'm going by?" The boy: "What are you going by for when I'm hollering?" This had its parallels when one day Lincoln came into the telegraph office, found Major Eckert counting greenbacks, and Lincoln said it seemed the Major never came to the office any more except when he had money to count. Eckert said it was just a coincidence, but it reminded him of Mansfield, Ohio, where a certain tailor was very stylish in dress and airy in manner. A groceryman, seeing the tailor passing one day, puffed himself up and gave a long blow. The tailor snorted, "I'll learn you not to blow when I'm passing," the groceryman answering, "And I'll learn you not to pass when I'm blowing."

Lincoln found this very good—like the man in an open buggy caught at night on a country road in a heavy downpour of rain. He was hurrying to shelter, passing a farmhouse where a man somewhat drunk put his head out of a window and yelled, "Hullo! hullo!" The traveler stopped his buggy in the rain and asked what was wanted. "Nothing of you," came the voice at the window. "Well, what in the damnation do you yell hullo for when people are passing?" "Well, what in the damnation are you passing for when people are yelling hullo?"

Lincoln heard from Alexander Stephens when they were in Congress, and may have retailed, the incident of an undersized lawyer in an acrimonious stump debate with the massive Robert Toombs. Toombs called out, "Why, I could button your ears back and swallow you whole." The little fellow retorted, "And if you did, you would have more brains in your stomach than you ever had in your head."

A current quip was adapted as personal to the President. "I feel patriotic," said an old rowdy. "What do you mean by feeling patriotic?" inquired the President, standing by. "Why, I feel as if I wanted to kill somebody or steal something." Under the heading "Old Abe's Story of New Jersey"—politically more anti-Unionist than any other of the Northern States—was the tale of a shipwrecked-sailor drifting toward land, where friendly hands flung him a rope. He took hold of the rope, asking, "What country is this?" and hearing "New Jersey" let go the rope and moaned, "I guess I'll float a little farther!" A man visiting a hospital in Washington noticed a soldier in one bed "laughing and talking about the President." The visitor was educated, drew fine distinctions, and said to the soldier, "You must be very slightly wounded." "Yes," said the soldier. "Very slightly— I have lost only one leg."

The joke books, with like published material, were giving a large mass of people an impression of a plain, neighborly, somewhat droll man, nobody's fool, at home to common folks. He could refer to a soprano voice so high that it had to be climbed over by a ladder or a German worried because "somebody tied my dog loose." A Boston man wished information. "You never swear, Mr. President, do you?" And Lincoln laughed, not loud but deep, the Bostonian noted. "Oh, I don't have to. You know I have Stanton in my Cabinet."

Grown-up men and women, even nations, at times were like the little girl Lincoln told Gustave Koerner about She asked her mother if she could run out and play. The mother refused, and the girl begged harder, kept teasing till the mother gave her a whipping. When that was over the girl said, "Now, ma, I can surely run out and play."

A newly elected Congressman came in, Lincoln knowing

him to have a sense of humor, for the gay greeting was: "Come in here and tell me what you know. It won't take long."

To illustrate a shifting political policy, Lincoln told of a farm boy whose father instructed him in plowing a new furrow. "Steer for that yoke of oxen standing at the further end of the field." The father went away. The boy followed instructions. But the oxen began moving. The boy followed them around the field, furrowed a circle instead of a line!

An ex-governor brought up the case of a woman named Betsy Ann Dougherty. "She did my washing for a long time. Her husband went off and joined the rebel army, and I wish you would give her a protection paper." Lamon was looking on, noted the President masked his humor and with inimitable gravity inquired, "Is Betsy Ann a good washer-woman?" She was indeed, said the ex-governor. "Is your Betsy Ann an obliging woman?" She was certainly very kind, the ex-governor responded soberly. "Could she do other things than wash?" the President asked without batting an eyelash. Oh, yes, she was very kind—very. "Where is Betsy Ann?" It came out she was in New York, wanted to come back to Missouri, but was afraid of banishment. "Is anybody meddling with her?" "No; but she is afraid to come back unless you give her a protection paper." Thereupon, noted Lamon, Lincoln turned to his desk and wrote on a card, which he signed: "Let Betsy Ann Dougherty alone as long as she behaves herself." Handing over the card, he said it should be given to Betsy Ann. "But, Mr. President, couldn't you write a few words to the officers that would insure her protection?" "No, officers have no time now to read letters. Tell Betsy Ann to put a string to this card and hang it around her neck. When the officers see this, they will keep their hands off your Betsy Ann."

Lamon gave this as an instance of Lincoln using "mirth-provoking trifles" out of the day's routine for relaxation. When the ex-governor, accompanied by a committee from Missouri, had left with his card for Betsy Ann, Lincoln had a laugh about it, and then, said Lamon, "relapsed into his accustomed melancholy, contemplative mood, as if looking for something else—looking for the end." He sat in thought for a time at the desk and turned to Lamon. "This case of our old friend, the governor and his Betsy Ann, is a fair sample of the trifles I am constantly asked to give my attention to. I wish I had no more serious questions to deal with. If there were more Betsy Anns and fewer fellows like her husband, we should be better off. She seems to have laundered the governor to his full satisfaction, but I am sorry she didn't keep her husband washed cleaner."

During the Trent Affair Lincoln urged, "The less risk we run the better," and mentioned a recent battle where amid furious fire of shot and shell an officer drew his revolver and ordered a running soldier: "Go to the front with your regiment or I'll shoot you." The private yelled, "Shoot and be damned—what's one bullet to a whole hatful?!" Once when the interference of foreign nations with American affairs was under discussion, the President was quoted in a reminiscence of early Indiana days when he had called at a farmhouse overrun with children managed by a redheaded mother who kept a whip and made everyone come to time at her orders. "There's trouble here, and lots of it," she blurted, "but I kin manage my own affairs without the help of outsiders. This is jest a family row, but I'll teach these brats their places ef I have to lick the hide off every one of them. I don't do much talkin', but I run this house, an' I don't want no one sneakin' round tryin' to find out how I do it, either." Lincoln ended: "That's the case with us. We must let the other nations know that we propose to settle our family row in our own way."

At a mention of some persons' not capitalizing the name of the Deity, the President was reminded of a Confederate soldier's letter saying the Yankees would be licked in the next battle "if goddlemity spares our lives."

Brigadier General John Gross Barnard, chief engineer to the Army of the Potomac in the Peninsula campaign, told of the President asking General McClellan why such heavy embankments and gun emplacements had been located to the north of Washington. McClellan replied: "Why, Mr. President, if under any circumstances, however fortuitous, the enemy, by any chance or freak, should in a last resort get in behind Washington in his efforts to capture the city, why, there is the fort to defend it." The precaution, said the President, reminded him of a lyceum in Springfield. "The question was, 'Why does man have breasts?' and after long debate was submitted to the presiding judge who wisely decided 'that if under any circumstances, however fortuitous, or by any chance or freak, no matter what the nature or by what cause, a man should have a baby, there would be the breasts to nurse it.'"

One anecdote Nicolay heard in use by Lincoln was of a backwoods housewife in her messed-up log cabin, many ragtag children running around. A wandering Methodist preacher tried to sell her a Bible and she didn't like the way he pushed some questions. Shouldn't every home have a Bible? Did they have a Bible in this home? Her sharp answer came that of course they owned a Bible. If so, where was it? the man asked. She began a hunt, finding no Bible. She called the children and they joined in the hunt. At last one of them dug up from some corner and held up in triumph a few torn and ragged pages of Holy Writ. The man tried to argue this was no Bible, and how could they pretend it was? The woman stuck to her claims. Of course they had a Bible in the house. "But I had no idea we were so nearly out!"

The seizure early in the war of all copies of dispatches in the major telegraph offices of the country uncovered names, individuals, disloyalties, to an extent shocking. Lincoln told of an Illinois farmer who for years had prized and loved a soaring elm tree that spread its branches near his house. One day, the farmer saw a squirrel scurry up the giant elm's trunk and suddenly disappear in a hole. Looking farther, he found the great tree hollow, the whole inside rotten and ready to fall. The farmer moaned to his wife, "My God! I wish I had never seen that squirrel!" Lincoln pointed to the piles of telltale dispatches: "And I wish we had never seen what we have seen today."

Hay heard Lincoln tell of a conscript recruit unable to name his father, explaining, "Captain, sir, I guess I'm just a camp-meetin' baby." More longspun was one Lincoln told Lamon, in connection with current turmoil between North and South. A man chased around a tree by a bull gained on the bull and got it by the tail. The bull pawed, snorted, broke into a run, the man after it still holding to the tail and bawling, "Darn you, who commenced this fuss?"

Governor Yates gave to the 10th Illinois Cavalry, according to the Chicago *Tribune* of February 4, 1864, a message brought by "my friend Bill Green of Menard County." Green before leaving Washington had asked, "Mr. Lincoln, what shall I say to the people of Illinois?" "Say to them," replied the President, "that I have Jeff Davis by the throat." And from the 10th Illinois Cavalry applause and cheers roared.

A California Republican, Cornelius Cole, called on business so tangled that it reminded Lincoln of a young Universalist preacher who came to Springfield. Three ministers of orthodox churches agreed "to take turns and preach this young fellow down." A Methodist preached the first sermon. "He commenced by telling his large congregation how happily they were all situated in Springfield. Launching into his sermon the Methodist shouted, 'And now comes a preacher preaching a doctrine that all men shall be saved. But, my brethren, let us hope for better things.'" This one Seward too had heard, repeating it as a sample of Lincoln humor.

Another caller told about a friend, early in the war, ordered out of New Orleans as a Unionist. He asked to see the writ by which he was expelled, and the Confederate committee told him their government was issuing no illegal writs, and he would have to get out of his own free will. Lincoln then told of a St. Louis hotelkeeper who claimed a record no one had ever died in his hotel. "Whenever a guest was dying in his house, he carried him out to die in the street."

A general was being outmaneuvered in West Virginia. At the high danger point Lincoln said the general was like a man out west who put his boy inside a barrel to hold up the head while the father pounded down the hoops. When the job was done the father saw he hadn't figured on how to get the boy out again. "Some people can succeed better in getting themselves and others corked up than in getting uncorked."

Of a Union and a Confederate army maneuvering as if they might soon be fighting, though not reaching the combat stage, Welles noted the President's remark they were like "two dogs that get less eager to fight the nearer they come to each other." Fears were telegraphed by Burnside's command, lost down in Tennessee and not heard of for some time. Lincoln told of Sally Ward on an Illinois farm with 14 children. Sometimes one of them got hurt and let out a loud cry somewhere in the cornfield or the timber. Then Sally Ward would sing out, "Thank Heaven there's one of my children that ain't dead yet."

Signing a brigadier general's commission for Napoleon Jackson Tecumseh Dana, Lincoln pronounced the name; it would "certainly frighten the enemy." Wishing to check a newspaper Biblical reference, Lincoln asked for a copy of the Bible. A polite offer to get a Bible came from Albert Johnson, Stanton's secretary, described by David Homer Bates as "a very obsequious, dapper little man." Johnson soon brought in and laid before the President a Bible. Lincoln looked up the reference he wanted. Johnson meantime had left the room. Then, according to Bates, Lincoln arose with a smile. "I am always interested in the movements of Johnson. Now let me show you how he did that." Then in mimicry, Lincoln took the Bible in his hands, presented it in a very obsequious style to Major Eckert and said, "That is the way Johnson did that." This, noted Bates, created a laugh among those looking on. An odd little functionary, a curious and incessant yes-man to Stanton, Lincoln impersonated in a funny little errand with a Bible.

Lincoln's tough hide, or lack of fine sensibilities, in Donn Piatt's view, was traced tersely by the Wendell Phillips expression that Lincoln was "the white trash of the South spawned on Illinois." Educated men troubled themselves with attempts to reduce to simple points the shifting lights and glooms of the Lincoln personality.

Galusha Grow told of his taking a Pennsylvania infantry company to see the President, who stepped out of the White House, looked around, put his hand behind him. "When I get this handkerchief out of this coat-tail pocket I intend to shake hands with you boys!"

To illustrate the petty jealousies and bickerings among Congressmen and army generals, James M. Scovel said Lincoln told the story of two Illinois men, one Farmer Jones, a churchman gifted in prayer, the other Fiddler Simpkins, welcome at every country merry-making. At one prayer meeting Brother Jones made a wonderful prayer which touched the hearts of all. And Brother Simpkins felt called on to rise and say, "Brethring and sistring, I know that I can't make half as good a prayer as Brother Jones, but by the grace of God I *can* fiddle the shirt off of him."

"Can this man Lincoln *ever* be serious?" wrote Richard Henry Dana in a letter. For the President would tell, in the midst of tremendous efforts to draft a new army, of the boy under fire whose commanding officer called, "You are crying like a baby," getting the answer, "I knows it, Ginral. I wish I was a baby, and a gal-baby, too, and then I wouldn't have been conscripted."

The telegrapher Bates heard of Lincoln telling about a man going into an asylum and meeting a little old fellow who demanded a salute. "I am Julius Caesar." The salute was given, the man went on his errand, returned soon, and again the little fellow demanded a salute. "I am Napoleon Bonaparte." "Yes, Napoleon, but a while ago you told me you were Julius Caesar." "Yes, but that was by another mother!" And there was the man who asked a friend to lend him a clean boiled shirt, getting the answer, "I have only two shirts, the one I have just taken off, and the one I have just put on—which will you have?"

Lincoln heard the telegrapher Bates tell of a man who enters a theater just as the curtain goes up. So interested is the man in looking at what is happening on the stage that he puts his tall silk hat, open side up, on the seat next to him, without noticing a very stout woman who is near-sighted. She sits down. There is a crunching noise. The owner of the flattened hat reaches out for it as the stout woman rises. He looks at his hat, looks at her: "Madam, I could have told you my hat wouldn't fit you before you tried it on." Dozens of such stories in the repetitions came to be told as though these things had happened to Lincoln.

On the day after Fredericksburg the staunch old friend, Isaac N. Arnold, entered Lincoln's office, was asked to sit down. Lincoln then read from Artemus Ward. One spring he got "swampt in the exterior of New York State, one dark and stormy night, when the winds Blue pityusly, and I was forced to tie up with the Shakers." He knocked at a door. "A solum female, looking sumwhat like a last year's bean-pole stuck into a long meal bag, axed me was I athurst and did I hunger? to which I urbanely ansered 'a few.' " That Lincoln should wish to read this nonsense while the ambulances were yet hauling thousands of wounded from the frozen mud flats of the Rappahannock River was amazing to Congressman Arnold. As he said afterward he was "shocked." He inquired, "Mr. President, is it possible that with the whole land bowed in sorrow and covered with a pall in the presence of yesterday's fearful reverse, you can indulge in such levity?" Then, Arnold said, the President threw down the Artemus Ward book, tears streamed down his cheeks, his physical frame quivered as he burst forth, "Mr. Arnold, if I could not get momentary respite from the crushing burden I am constantly carrying, my heart would break!" And with that pent-up cry let out, it came over Arnold that the laughter of Lincoln at times was a mask.

Possibly only a crony from the old Eighth Circuit could have called out the peculiar humor Leonard Swett met one gloomy day of the summer of '64. Grant was pounding to-ward Richmond, the ambulances groaned with their loads, hospitals filled beyond capacity. Men should be rushed to the front. This and much else Swett poured out to Lincoln, with a flood of suggestions on what should be done and immediately. "The President was sitting by an open window," noted Swett. "And as I paused, a bird lit upon a branch just outside and was twittering and singing joyously. Mr. Lincoln, imitating the bird, said: '*tweet, tweet, tweet;* isn't he singing sweetly?' I felt as if my legs had been cut from under me. I rose, took my hat, and said, 'I see the country is safer than I thought.' As I moved toward the door, Mr. Lincoln called out in his hearty, familiar way, 'Here, Swett, come back and sit down.' Then he went on: 'It is impossible for a man in my position not to have thought of all those things. Weeks ago every man capable of bearing arms was ordered to the front, and everything you suggested has been done.' "

Far and wide through newspaper reprints went an eye-witness account of Lincoln's pertinence, bordering on horse-play, during a spiritualist séance in the White House arranged by Mrs. Lincoln. Curiously enough there was little or no hostile comment on this procedure. It was one of a series of odd incidents that built up a portrait of an American in the White House who could be keen, possibly wise, amid the ludicrous, the shallow, the bottomless.

Though paper was costly in '64 and its newspaper size diminished, the Charleston *Mercury* went on reprinting occasional Lincoln wit from Northern newspapers, one incident going far. A minister in a delegation meeting the President "hoped the Lord is on our side." The President: "I don't agree with you." There was amazement. The President continued: "I am not at all concerned about that, for we know that the Lord is always on the side of the right. But it is my constant anxiety and prayer that I and this nation should be on the Lord's side."

"Lincoln is called the American Aesop," said the New York *Herald,* November 21, 1863, a week later taking the liberty of inventing a comic insidious anecdote as from the President's mouth.

To run down all the suspicions, insinuations, inveracities, innuendoes, uttered against a man in his place, said Lincoln, "would be a perpetual flea hunt."

The foremost funnymen of the age, the leading American comics, understood Lincoln. They shaded their foolery and colored their jests as if in the White House was one of their own. Artemus Ward, Petroleum Vesuvius Nasby, Orpheus C. Kerr, Miles O'Reilly, the young burblers of the satirical weekly *Vanity Fair*, all wrote with a gay though covert affection for the President. And it came to them that the President was one of their faithful readers, seemed to believe they were important voices of democracy in a living republic.

Forty thousand copies had been sold of *Artemus Ward: His Book* published in May '62. The author, Charles Farrar Browne, was only 28 years old. Born in Waterford, Maine, his father was a justice of the peace, his mother of Puritan stock, the son writing, "I think we came from Jerusalem, for my mother's name was Levi, and we had a Moses and a Nathan in the family, but my poor brother's name was Cyrus so, perhaps, that makes us Persians." He learned typesetting on the Skowhegan *Clarion*. Drifting west as a tramp printer, Browne finally took a $12-a-week job as reporter on the Cleveland *Plain-Dealer*, going then to the staff of *Vanity Fair* in New York.

One Ward sketch "In Washington" had a mock interview with Lincoln:

> I called on Abe. He received me kindly. I handed him my umbreller, and told him I'd have a check for it if he pleased. "That," sed he, "puts me in mind of a little story. There was a man out in our parts who was so mean that he took his wife's coffin out of the back winder for fear he would rub the paint off the doorway Wall, about this time there was a man in a adjacent town who had a green cotton umbreller."
>
> "Did it fit him well? Was it custom made? Was he measured for it?"
>
> "Measured for what?" said Abe.
>
> "The umbreller?"
>
> "Wall, as I was sayin," continnerd the President, treatin the interruption with apparent contempt, "this

man sed he'd known that there umbreller ever since it was a parasol. Ha, ha, ha!"

"Yes," sed I, larfin in a respectful manner, "but what has this man with the umbreller to do with the man who took his wife's coffin out of the back winder?"

"To be sure," said Abe—"what was it? I must have got two stories mixed together, which puts me in mind of another lit—"

"Never mind, Your Excellency. I called to congratulate you on your career, which has been a honest and a good one—unscared and unmoved by Secesh in front of you and Abbolish at the back of you—each one of which is a little wuss than the other if possible!

"Tell E. Stanton that his boldness, honesty, and vigger merits all prase, but to keep his under-garmints on. E. Stanton has appeerently only one weakness, which it is, he can't allus keep his under-garmints from flyin up over his hed. I mean that he occasionally dances in a peck-measure, and he don't look graceful at it."

I took my departer. "Good bye, old sweetness!" sed Abe, shakin me cordgully by the hand.

"Adoo, my Prahayrie flower!" I replied, and made my exit. "Twenty-five thousand dollars a year and found," I soliloquised, as I walked down the street, "is putty good wages for a man with a modist appytite, but I reckon that it is wurth it to run the White House."

David R. Locke's letter dated at "Confederate X Roads which is in the State of Kentucky," had their signer, the Reverend Petroleum Vesuvius Nasby, set up as pastor of a church and a seeker of office. Lincoln kept a pamphlet of these Nasby letters in a desk drawer. Locke was a year older than Ward, and like Ward had been a tramp printer, learning to set type on the Cortland, New York, *Democrat,* serving on the Pittsburgh *Chronicle,* having a hand in running newspapers in Plymouth, Mansfield, Bucyrus and Bellefontaine, Ohio. In April '62, in a Findlay, Ohio, newspaper he ran the first of the Nasby letters, dating it at Wingert's Corners, a village in Crawford County where the citizens almost to a man were secessionists.

Fifteen Negroes had arrived at the place, "yisterday another arrove," and P. V. Nasby, alarmed, prepared resolutions: "Wareas, we vew with alarm the ackshun uv the President uv the U. S., in recommendin the immejit emansipashun uv the slaves uv our misgided Suthern brethrin, and his evident intenshun uv kolonizin on em in the North, and the heft on em in Wingert's Corners; and Wareas, Eny man hevin the intellect uv a brass-mounted jackass kin easily see that the 2 races want never intendid to live together; and Wareas, Bein in the magority, we kin do as we please and ez the nigger haint no vote he kant help hisself; therefore be it Resolved, That the crude, undeodorized Afrikin is a disgustin obgik. Resolved, That this Convenshun, when it hez its feet washed, smells sweeter nor the Afrikin in his normal condishun, and is there4 his sooperior."

One Nasby piece Lincoln carried a clipping of in his vest pocket and memorized. And Noah Brooks told of an evening at Soldiers' Home when visitors came and talk fell on freed slaves in the Border States. Lincoln stood before the fireplace and recited from the Wingert's Corners piece: "Arouse to wunst! Rally agin Conway! Rally agin Sweet! Rally agin Hegler's family! Rally agin the porter at the Reed House! Rally agin the cook at the Crook House! Rally agin the nigger widder in Vance's Addishun! Rally agin Missis Umstid! Rally agin Missis Umstid's children by her first husband! Rally agin Missis Umstid's children by her sekkund husband! Rally agin all the rest uv Missis Umstid's children! Rally agin the nigger that cum yisterday! Rally agin the saddle-culurd girl that yoost 2 be hear! Ameriky for white men!" Lincoln at intervals used to quote these mock rallying cries, said Brooks, long after other men had read and forgotten them.

Sometimes before reading aloud from the pamphlet of Nasby papers taken from his desk drawer, Lincoln made such remarks as one to Sumner, "For the genius to write these things, I would gladly give up my office," or as he told several officials and private citizens one evening, "I am going to write Petroleum to come down here, and I intend to tell him if he will communicate his talent to me, I will swap places with him." These javelins of horselaugh journalism Lincoln welcomed. They fought for his cause. It was not strange he got out of bed and paraded around the White House past midnight to find someone else awake to share his reading of Nasby.

Robert H. Newell, creator of Orpheus C. Kerr (Office Seeker), was under 30, of Scotch-Welsh stock, a New York City boy; his father was the inventor of a sewing machine that had won gold medals at the London and Vienna world expositions. While young Newell served as assistant editor of the New York *Sunday Mercury,* he wrote letters dated at Washington or in the field with the army of the Potomac. He opened one with "not wishing to expire prematurely of inanity." On the face of them his sketches were an escape from inanity. Of the national capital he alleged: "The most interesting natural curiosity here, next to Secretary Welles' beard, is the office of the Secretary of the Interior. Covered with spider-webs, and clothed in the dust of ages, sit the Secretary and his clerks, like so many respectable mummies in a neglected pyramid."

While this humorist steadily upheld Lincoln and the Union cause, and directed ridicule at the South and the Copperheads, he also kept on with sarcasm and irony aimed at the pretenses and pomps of war, at showy military heroes, at loud-mouthed statesmen. Kerr burlesqued McClellan's careful instructions for the return of slaves to their owners, with the order: "If any nigger comes within the lines of the United States Army to give information, whatsomever, of the movements of the enemy, the aforesaid shall have his head knocked off, and be returned to his lawful owner, according to the groceries and provisions of the Fugitive Slave Ack."

In the month that Lincoln finally removed McClellan, Kerr argued that as the army had marched 15 miles in six weeks, they were going up steep hills and Lincoln had a choice of removing either the Blue Ridge or McClellan.

To have removed the Blue Ridge would have been "construed into proof that the Honest Abe had yielded to the fiendish clamor of the crazy Abolitionists." Also it would occasion heartburnings among the Democrats. "Hence our Honest Abe has concluded to leave the Blue Ridge where it is, and remove the idolized General."

A letter of Kerr published in early '63 led off with a deep-toned psalm of praise to Lincoln: "Standing a head and shoulders above the other men in power, he is the object at which the capricious lightnings of the storm first strike; and were he a man of wax, instead of the grand old rock he is, there would be nothing left of him but a shapeless and inert mass of pliable material by this time. There are deep traces of the storm upon his countenance, but they are the sculpture of the tempest on a natural block of granite . . . Abused and misrepresented by his political foes, alternately cajoled and reproached by his other foes,— his political friends,—he still pursues the honest tenor of the obvious Right, and smiles at calumny. His good-nature is a lamp that never goes out, but burns, with a steady light, in the temple of his mortality . . ."

Hours of easy reading for two years prepared Lincoln's reply to General Meigs' query who this person Orpheus C. Kerr might be. "Why, have you not read those papers? They are in two volumes; any one who has not read them is a heathen." The Kerr papers were uneven and sporadic in production as compared with those of Nasby and Ward, this possibly resulting from his adventures in search of a wife. He married in September '61 the actress-poet Adah Isaacs Menken, who had divorced Alexander Isaacs Menken, a wealthy Cincinnati dry-goods merchant, her first husband, and John C. Heenan, a famous prize fighter, her second husband. Dazzling stage success in Baltimore after her marriage to Kerr brought her a gift of diamonds worth $1,500; she announced herself a secessionist, was arrested and released on parole, while her husband went merrily along writing for the Union. He sailed with her in July '63 to San Francisco, where she won the plaudits of a group including Mark Twain, Bret Harte, Artemus Ward, Joaquin

Miller and others. Kerr in April '64 sailed with her from San Francisco down to the Isthmus. There she embarked for London, where her poetry and acting met higher praise than ever before—and her husband in New York never saw her again. While his beautiful and insatiably ambitious wife pursued her career, Kerr followed his bent toward nothing in particular. He would have been heartbroken except for the balance wheel that once enabled him to write, "Our President, my boy, has a tail for every emergency, as a rat-trap has an emergency for every tail."

Thus the three most eminent American comic writers favored Lincoln and generated good will and affection for him and his cause.

Two Quakeresses in a railway coach were overheard in a conversation: "I think Jefferson will succeed." "Why does thee think so?" "Because Jefferson is a praying man." "And so is Abraham a praying man." "Yes, but the Lord will think Abraham is joking."

This in newspapers added the information that Lincoln said it was the best story about himself he had "ever read in the papers." Lincoln let this story spread. Nevertheless his most deliberate public appearances and utterances encouraged no one to take him for a trifler. The series of photographs by Brady, Gardner and others without exception portrayed a man sober, solemn, grim.

Continuously Lincoln gave no definite impression that he belonged to any particular church or endorsed any special faith or doctrine. That he was a man of piety and of deep religious belief was conveyed to large numbers of people by unmistakable expressions in his speeches and messages. The President and his wife usually drove to the New York Avenue Presbyterian Church but sometimes walked, accompanied by a guard, arriving punctually and never delaying Dr. Gurley's opening of the services, wrote the guard Crook. The President and his wife would walk down the center aisle, and on the right take the eighth pew from the pulpit. During this proceeding, wrote Crook, "out of respect for the great office he occupied, those in the church when the President arrived would rise from their seats and remain standing."

The good, upright, usually well-tempered Fessenden, it was told over Washington, in a rage over some unjust distribution of patronage turned loose a flow of "intemperate language" on Lincoln one morning. Lincoln kept cool. The fury of his Maine friend spent itself. Lincoln inquired gently, "You are an Episcopalian, aren't you, Senator?" "Yes, sir. I belong to that church." "I thought so. You Episcopalians all swear alike. Seward is an Episcopalian. But Stanton is a Presbyterian. You ought to hear him swear." Then Lincoln went on telling about several varieties of profanity, and he and Fessenden settled down to an even-toned conversation.

The press in October '63 reported a call paid Lincoln by members of the Baltimore (Old School) Presbyterian Synod. The Moderator, the Reverend Dr. Septimus Tustin, said the synod wished as a body to pay their respects, and that each member "belonged to the Kingdom of God, and each was loyal to the Government." The President's reply, in the Associated Press report, read in part: "I have often wished that I was a more devout man than I am. Nevertheless, amid the greatest difficulties of my Administration, when I could not see any other resort, I would place my whole reliance in God, knowing that all would go well, and that He would decide for the right. I thank you, gentlemen, in the name of the religious bodies which you represent, and in the name of the Common Father, for this expression of your respect. I cannot say more."

To Methodist and Baptist delegations of ministers the President had spoken with rich praise. His speech one May day in '62 began: "I welcome here the representatives of the Evangelical Lutherans of the United States. I accept with gratitude their assurances of . . . sympathy and support . . . in an important crisis which involves, in my judgment, not only the civil and religious liberties of our own dear land, but in a large degree the civil and religious liberties of mankind in many countries and through many ages." That he had a creed of some religious faith, which he might be able to amplify *in extenso* if required, he would have them know by his closing statement to them: "I now humbly and reverently, in your presence, reiterate the acknowledgment of that dependence, not doubting that, if it shall please the Divine Being who determines the destinies of nations that this shall remain a united people, they will, humbly seeking the Divine guidance, make their prolonged national existence a source of new benefits to themselves and their successors, and to all classes and conditions of mankind."

Bishop Ames as chairman headed a large Methodist delegation that came to the White House in May '64 to present an address. The President read to them his reply:

> In response to your address, allow me to attest the accuracy of it's historical statements; indorse the sentiments it expresses; and thank you, in the nation's name, for the sure promise it gives.
>
> Nobly sustained as the government has been by all the churches, I would utter nothing which might, in the least, appear invidious against any. Yet, without this, it may fairly be said that the Methodist Episcopal Church, not less devoted than the best, is, by it's greater numbers, the most important of all. It is no fault in others that the Methodist Church sends more soldiers to the field, more nurses to the hospital, and more prayers to Heaven than any. God bless the Methodist Church—bless all the churches—and blessed be God, Who, in this our great trial, giveth us the churches.

After handshaking, the delegates took leave amid a general smile over one saying, "Mr. President, we all hope the country will rest in Abraham's bosom for the next four years."

In proclamations, in recommendations of thanksgiving or of fasting and prayer, in numerous references to God, Providence, the Almighty, the Common Father, sometimes having their meaning colored by special events or conditions, Lincoln had given the impression to a multitude that he might have a creed. At a later time a clergyman sought to formulate such a creed from Lincoln's own words, changing the text merely to the extent of transposing pronouns from plural to singular, making other slight modifications, and prefixing the words "I believe." These were parts of such a creed:

> I believe in national humiliation, fasting, and prayer, in keeping a day holy to the Lord, devoted to the humble discharge of the religious duties proper to such a solemn occasion.
> . . . I believe in Him whose will, not ours, should be done.
> I believe the people of the United States, in the forms approved by their own consciences, should render the homage due to the Divine Majesty for the wonderful things He has done in the nation's behalf, and invoke the influence of His Holy Spirit to subdue anger.
> . . . I believe in His eternal truth and justice.
> I believe the will of God prevails; without Him all human reliance is vain; without the assistance of that Divine Being I cannot succeed; with that assistance I cannot fail.
> I believe I am a humble instrument in the hands of our Heavenly Father; I desire that all my works and acts may be according to His will; and that it may be so, I give thanks to the Almighty and seek his Aid.
> I believe in praise to Almighty God, the beneficent Creator and Ruler of the Universe.

Among steadfast loyal friends of Lincoln, keenly attuned to the Lincoln personality, was Jesse Fell who wrote it was a "well-known fact" that on religion "Mr. Lincoln seldom communicated to anyone his views." After free and familiar talks on religion, Fell had presented to Lincoln Channing's sermons, printed entire, and Fell wrote that Lincoln's beliefs were "derived from conversations with him at different times during a considerable period." Of those beliefs the scrupulous recorder, Jesse Fell, wrote:

> On the innate depravity of man, the character and office of the great head of the Church, the Atonement, the infallibility of the written revelation, the performance of miracles, the nature and design of present and future rewards and punishments (as they are popularly called) and many other subjects, he held opinions utterly at variance with what are usually taught in the Church. I should say that his expressed views on these and kindred subjects were such as, in the estimation of most believers, would place him entirely outside the Christian pale. Yet to my mind, such was not the true position, since his principles and practices and the spirit of his whole life were of the very kind we universally agree to call Christian; and I think this conclusion is in no wise affected by the circumstance that he never attached himself to any religious society whatever.
>
> His religious views were eminently practical and are summed up, as I think, in these two propositions: "the fatherhood of God, and the brotherhood of man." He fully believed in a superintending and overruling Providence that guides and controls the operations of the world, but maintained that law and order, not their violation or suspension, are the appointed means by which this Providence is exercised.

Noah Brooks, out of his close and continuous friendship with the President, wrote of "something touching in his childlike and simple reliance upon Divine aid," especially in extremities of fateful events. Then, "though prayer and reading of the Scriptures was his constant habit, he more earnestly than ever sought that strength which is promised when mortal help faileth." Brooks said Lincoln could quote whole chapters of Isaiah, and the New Testament and the Psalms were fixed in his memory. He would sometimes correct a misquotation of Scripture and give chapter and verse where it could be found. Once in regard to his own age and strength he quoted, "His eye was not dim, nor his natural force abated." He found meaning in the Scriptural phrase, "the stars in their courses fought against Sisera."

To Joshua Speed's mother the President sent a photograph of himself inscribed: "For Mrs. Lucy G. Speed, from whose pious hand I accepted the present of an Oxford Bible twenty years ago."

Months after the Battle of Fredericksburg came word of the Massachusetts soldier who had carried over his heart a pocket Bible that stopped and held a rifle ball. The President sent the boy another Bible, with a personal inscription.

Out of the Cold Harbor slaughter emerged Carter E. Prince of the 4th Maine Volunteers. A bullet hit his suspender buckle and carried it through the New Testament in the pocket of his blouse. Pushed by the bullet, the buckle went through all the chapters between Revelation and St. Mark and came to rest at Mark 12:36, where is recorded the saying of the Lord: "Sit thou on my right hand, till I make thine enemies thy footstool."

With such incidents, and with men who could speak at firsthand of them, Lincoln became familiar.

A distinct trend toward a deeper religious note, a piety more assured of itself because more definitely derived from inner and private growths of Lincoln himself, this could be seen as the President from year to year fitted himself more deeply and awarely into the mantle and authorities of Chief Magistrate.

To others besides Alexander H. Stephens, Lincoln had a "mystic" zeal for the Union cause. In one sense Lincoln saw himself as a crusader and a holiness preacher for an indissoluble unity of one common country. To the sacred devotions of his own cause he would join any others of capacity for sacred devotions.

He could not be impervious to the Reformed Presbyterian Church ("Scotch Covenanters"), through a committee in dark months of 1863, "by every consideration drawn from the Word of God" enjoining him "not to be moved from the path of duty on which you have so auspiciously entered, either by the threats or blandishments of the enemies of human progress." Nor could he have been unmoved by the New School Presbyterians in 1862 through their General Assembly sending word: "Since the day of your inauguration, the thousands of our membership have followed you with unceasing prayer, besieging the throne of Heaven in your behalf."

The German Reformed Synod, the Lutheran General Synod, the Moravian Synod, had passed resolutions of varied texts declaring themselves in favor of the war. In the autumn of '64 the Congregational churches of New York, New Jersey and Pennsylvania placed themselves squarely in favor of Lincoln's re-election through the declarations of their General Association: "Make the decision of the people on the 8th of November final and fatal to the hopes of traitors in arms and conspirators in political councils."

The Roman Catholic church was less demonstrative and vocal than the Protestants. But it was a Roman Catholic, General William S. Rosecrans, who had resisted the pressure of Greeley to place him at the head of the Union ticket instead of Lincoln. And General Rosecrans' brother, a Catholic bishop in Cincinnati, had continuously approved of Lincoln's progressive antislavery policy. Archbishop John Hughes, despite his tardiness of action during his illness while the New York antidraft riots raged, had kept in close touch with Secretary Seward and rendered important loyalist service. In the ranks and among the shoulder straps of the Union armies Catholics of several nationalities, and particularly the Irish, had records for gallant and distinguished service.

As a Chief Magistrate having a common bond with all of these faiths and churches that moved toward a national unity beyond any future breaking, Lincoln's piety was manifest. A blood fellowship of death and suffering moved him.

Answering a kindly letter from Rhode Island Quakers, Lincoln acknowledged that he expected no reputation as a peace man while up to his armpits in war blood. "Engaged as I am, in a great war, I fear it will be difficult for the world to understand how fully I appreciate the principles of peace inculcated in this letter and everywhere by the Society of Friends." That such true and perfect lovers of peace as the Quakers could send him from their Iowa organization, through Senator Harlan, an address voicing accord with him, was deeply moving.

According to an interview reported by the Iowa Congressman, James F. Wilson, in June '62, when Jeb Stuart had taken his gray horsemen in a circle around McClellan's army and cut the communications, Lincoln had remarked there was no news: "Not one word . . . I don't know that we have an army." One member of the delegation with which Wilson called urged a more resolute policy on slavery. "Slavery must be stricken down wherever it exists," this radical emphasized. "If we do not do right I believe God will let us go our own way to our ruin. But if we do right, I believe He will lead us safely out of this wilderness, crown our arms with victory, and restore our now dissevered Union."

Wilson saw that this trend of speech affected the President deeply, and expected "from the play of his features and the sparkle of his eyes" there would be a response. The listless Lincoln slowly arose to full height, "his right arm outstretched towards the gentleman who had just ceased speaking, his face aglow like the face of a prophet," saying to his admonisher, "My faith is greater than yours," agreeing fully with what had been said of the role of God and Providence. Then he proceeded: "But I also believe He will compel us to do right in order that He may do these things, not so much because we desire them as that they accord with His plans of dealing with this nation, in the midst of which He means to establish justice. I think He means that we shall do more than we have yet done in furtherance of His plans, and He will open the way for our doing it. I have felt His hand upon me in great trials and submitted to His guidance, and I trust that as He shall further open the way I will be ready to walk therein, relying on His help and trusting in His goodness and wisdom."

Wilson added that Lincoln, with his dejection gone, resumed his seat and in a reassured tone continued. "Sometimes it seems necessary that we should be confronted with perils which threaten us with disaster in order that we may not get puffed up and forget Him who has much work for us yet to do."

John W. Widney of Piqua, Ohio, a sergeant wounded at the Wilderness, starting a furlough home for complete recovery before return to duty, saw Lincoln on the White House walk from the War Office, "dressed in black, with frock coat, stove-pipe hat, walking slowly, shoulders bent forward, hands folded behind his back." Lincoln asked the Sergeant, "What State and regiment?" Widney answered, and Lincoln, with a "God bless you and I hope you will get home safe," passed into the White House while Widney stood gazing and feeling a "burden of sorrow" on the shoulders under the stovepipe hat. Widney was a churchman who favored his Bible and said that no other words fitted the moment for him like those of (to use his words) an old prophet: "O Jerusalem, Jerusalem, how often would I have gathered thee beneath my wings, as a hen gathers her chicks, but ye would not."

Chapter 35

The Pardoner

In, through and around the city of Washington moved the signs of human storm. Out of the storm and into the White House over its heavy carpets and past the tall mirrors came the spick-and-span, the dustily ragged and worn. Before Lincoln's eyes the drama surged in lines and waves, and his mood varied from telling a man, "The only thing to do is to keep pegging away," and once murmuring halfdreamily to a Michigan woman: "I'm a tired man. Sometimes I'm the tiredest man on earth."

The city and suburbs, all the main streets, in latter '64 swarmed with soldiers, "more than ever before," wrote Walt Whitman in his journal. Blue pants and coats were everywhere. "The clump of crutches is heard up the stairs of the paymasters' offices, groups often waiting long and wearily in the cold. Furloughed men, singly, in small squads, make their way to the Baltimore depot. Patrol detachments move around, examining passes, arresting all soldiers without them. They do not question the one-legged, or men badly disabled or maimed, but all others are stopt." Of a large brick mansion on the banks of the Rappahannock, used as a hospital during a battle, Whitman had noted, "Out doors, at the foot of a tree, within ten yards of the front of the house, I notice a heap of amputated feet, legs, arms, hands, &tc., a full load for a one-horse cart."

The city of Washington seemed to be one immense hospital. The inadequate and cruder equipment of the earlier war years had grown into a vast establishment, much of it still temporary and improvised. Churches, private homes and government buildings were commandeered. Board barracks and white army tents met the eyes of the President on almost any walk or ride around the city.

Late in October '64 Whitman wrote of seeing squads of Union Army deserters, over 300 of them, marching between armed guards along Pennsylvania Avenue, "all sorts of rigs, all sorts of hats and caps, many fine-looking young fellows, some shame-faced, some sickly, most of them dirty, shirts very dirty and long worn, &c . . . (I hear that desertions from the army now in the field have often averaged 10,000 a month)."

The timebeat of the war went on, bluecoat streams pouring south, miles of men and boots, leather, hardtack, tents, steel, lead, powder, guns. As miles of wagon supplies, mountains of hardtack, were used up, more and more poured south. And moving north, flung back out of the muddy and bloody recoils, came stragglers, deserters, bounty-jumpers, the furloughed, the sick and wounded— while beyond the battle fronts toward the south, living skeletons in prison offered prayers that the timebeat of the war would end, that the sad music of rifle volleys and cannonading guns would close over in some sweet silence.

At one crowded White House reception, when so many people pressed into the room that handshaking had to be dispensed with, Lincoln stood bowing acknowledgments. Then his eyes fell on a soldier, pale, crippled, moving through with a plainly dressed mother. Before they could get to the door Lincoln made his way to them, took each by the hand, told them he was interested they had come, and he could not let them go without his welcome. He said to young Henry E. Wing, the New York *Tribune* cub who scouted among many regiments and reported to the President on the rank-and-file feeling in the armies, "I would rather be defeated with the soldier vote behind me than to be elected without it."

The number of soldiers who felt they had met Lincoln personally, now in latter '64 ran into many thousands. At reviews he had dismounted from his horse, walked along the company lines, shaken hands with soldiers in the front rank and reaching through to the rear file, and spoken such words as, "Glad to see you looking so well, boys, glad to meet you."

The flimsy excuses some brought him, hoping for a furlough, the good and valid reasons others had—these too he knew. Out of the hospitals from fevers and amputations they came to the White House, some shaken, palsied, dumb, blind.

Widows and mothers who had lost husbands and sons in the war numbered more than 150,000 in February '64, according to claims filed in the Pension Office. Not often was the President troubled by claimants in connection with the dead. But those with petitions in behalf of the living came every hour of the day. And many of the living were young. The war was being fought by the young. Not yet voters, all of them under 21, were some 30 per cent of the troops in the U.S. armies. Another 30 per cent were 21 to

24. Still another 30 per cent were from 25 to 30, leaving only 10 per cent over 30.

A cadaverous young man, white of face, his clothes hanging loose, was given a chair. He talked for half an hour about himself and army conditions, under Lincoln's questioning. The 40 pieces of bone that had oozed out from his shoulder wound, were laid out on a desk and examined. On his original commission as lieutenant the President wrote an endorsement. When this was presented next morning to the officer having power to act, the officer looked disturbed, finally said, "This seems peremptory in its terms," and issued an order for back pay due and too long refused. After a furlough the young lieutenant returned to service and within a year stepped in to say thanks for a commission as captain, and to show Lincoln he was now plump, erect and hoping he looked every inch a soldier, even though 40 pieces of bone were lacking from one shoulder.

Major C. J. Stohlbrand walked in one day and handed Lincoln "important dispatches" from General Sherman. A Swedish-blooded citizen from the West, he had volunteered at Lincoln's first call in '61 and served continuously, at times in field emergencies acting as colonel or brigadier general. No promotions coming, he was leaving the service. Sherman didn't want to lose his Major Stohlbrand, asked him to go home by way of Washington and hand some "important dispatches" to the President. Lincoln opened the sealed papers, read them and put out his hand. "How do you do, General?" Stohlbrand corrected, "I am no general; I am only a major." Laughed Lincoln: "You are mistaken. You are a general." And in a few hours, with his commission signed by Lincoln, Stohlbrand was on his way back to Sherman's army.

Old Jim Conner of Miami County, Indiana, arrived home from a long trip to tell what had happened to him. His four sons and some neighbor boys were with the Army of the Potomac and he had gone with his Congressman to ask Stanton for a pass to see the boys. Stanton said No, and soon Old Jim and the Congressman were seeing Lincoln, Conner crying, "My God! I'll never go back home to face those women." The President thought it over, and then: "Conner, I can't overrule Stanton, but I need a special commissioner to go among the rank and file of the army to find out what the soldiers of this country think of the government in its greatest crisis. Conner, will you be a special commissioner?"

In a voice of high rage a crippled private near the War Office was cursing out the Government from the President down, just as Lincoln happened along and asked what was the matter. "I want my money. I've been discharged here and can't get my pay." Lincoln told the private he used to practice law and maybe could help. Lincoln sat down at the foot of the tree, ran over the papers handed him, wrote a notation on the back of one and told the private to take them to Chief Clerk Potts of the War Department. Lincoln walked on, and A. W. Swann of Albuquerque, New Mexico, who had been looking on, asked the private if he knew who he had been talking with. "Some ugly old fellow who pretends to be a lawyer," was the guess. Then Swann went with the private, saw him get the money due him, saw him stand sort of puzzled as to whether he ought to be glad or sorry he had cursed the President to his face.

An earnest Republican of proved deeds asked that his son be appointed an army paymaster. How old was the son? "He is twenty—well, nearly twenty-one." "Nearly twenty-one! I wouldn't appoint the angel Gabriel a paymaster if he wasn't twenty-one!"

A 14-year-old who had run away from his Kansas home and enlisted began crying as he heard a note Lincoln wrote for him to carry to Stanton. The boy had expected he would be shot at sunrise. But instead he read words to this effect: "Hadn't we better spank this drummer boy and send him back home to Leavenworth?" Lincoln sent the lad to a hotel and arranged for his ticket home.

"The boy is not going to be *shot*," Congressman Kellogg cried at a refusal from Stanton, near midnight, the execution set for sunrise. Kellogg went to the White House, broke down the refusals of the guards, reached the room where the President lay in bed, and cried: "This man must not be shot. I can't help what he may have done. Why, he is an old neighbor of mine; I can't allow him to be shot!" Lincoln stayed in bed, listened quietly to the pleas of a man he had known many years, then slowly: "Well, I don't believe *shooting* will do him any good. Give me that pen."

To his desk, to the tents of his generals in the field, came the appeals of valorous fighters found guilty of drunkenness, looting, of being absent without leave, of many varieties of insolence or disobedience. Lincoln's view joined that of Sherman regarding some of his 8th Missouri lawbreakers. "Their conduct for courage under my own eye was such that I would have pardoned them for anything short of high treason."

Press accounts told of an army surgeon court-martialed and his attorney bringing the papers to Lincoln, who read the indictment of "drunkenness," commenting, "That's bad, very bad," and further along as to "insulting a lady": "That's bad, too. An officer shouldn't insult a lady, by any means."

Lincoln read further the specifications regarding an attempt to kiss a lady, scratched his head, looked up to the attorney. "Really, I don't know about this. There are exceptions to every rule but as a general thing it's very hard to insult a lady by kissing her. But it seems the doctor only *attempted* to kiss her—perhaps the insult consisted in his not fully succeeding. I don't know as I ought to interfere in behalf of a man who attempts to kiss a lady and doesn't do it."

The attorney urged that a third party had made the complaint, with no evidence that the lady herself felt insulted. "That's a fact," said the President. "We can easily dispose of the kissing part. But I must look into the drunkenness a little. I can't overlook that. I'll have to get good evidence that it was strictly a New Year's offence, and is not a common occurrence with the doctor." He took the case under advisement.

Lincoln took a deep interest in James Madison Cutts, a brother of the second wife of Senator Douglas and secretary to Douglas through all the hard campaigning of 1860. After graduation at 24 from Harvard Law School, Cutts had gone west, stood at the bedside of the dying Douglas, then enlisted as a private in the Union Army. In May '61, Cutts had presented to Lincoln a letter of recommendation from Douglas and Lincoln had appointed him a captain in the Regular Army. While a staff officer under Burnside, Cutts wrote two letters to the President pouring out hate of Burnside's highhanded methods. For this and another offense a court-martial had found Cutts guilty of conduct unbecoming to an officer and gentleman. He had been caught in a hotel hallway standing on a valise looking through a transom at a woman undressing. The President had approved the findings of the court-martial but changed the sentence of dismissal from the Army to a reprimand. Lincoln wrote that he would not "add a pang to what you have already suffered," and then as father to son:

> You were convicted of two offences. One of them, not of great enormity, and yet greatly to be avoided [the hotel hallway affair], I feel sure you are in no danger of repeating. The other [insubordination] you are not so well assured against . . . No man resolved to make the most of himself, can spare time for personal contention. Still less can he afford to take all the consequences, including the vitiating of his temper, and the loss of self-control. Yield larger things to which you can show no more than equal right; and yield lesser ones, though clearly your own. Better give your path to a dog, than be bitten by him in contesting for the right. Even killing the dog would not cure the bite.
>
> In the mood indicated deal henceforth with your fellow men, and especially with your brother officers; and even the unpleasant events you are passing from will not have been profitless to you.

In a sense the reprimand was a quiet portrait of Lincoln himself. Captain Cutts took it and in the forefront as a field officer under Grant earned an award, the "Medal of Honor of the United States." For three distinct acts of extraordinary bravery, his triple medal read: "For gallantry at Wilderness, Spotsylvania, and Petersburg, 1864." Among those proud of it was the widowed sister, Adèle Cutts Douglas.

In April '64 came a letter from a Quaker girl in Washington County, Pennsylvania, giving "a brief history connected with myself and would be husband." They had been engaged for some years. In August '62 he enlisted for three years. In October '63 he was furloughed to go home and vote. "It was our design to marry while he was at home and under those determinations we very foolishly indulged too freely in matrimonial affairs . . ." She named the father of her unborn child, a private in the 140th Pennsylvania Volunteers with the Army of the Potomac. Word had come from him that army orders forbade soldiers writing furlough-begging letters to those higher up. Therefore she wrote to the President. On the back of her letter Lincoln wrote April 14, 1864, to the Secretary of War: "Send him to her by all means."

David R. Locke, on the second of the only two calls he paid Lincoln in Washington, asked a pardon for an Ohio deserter who had enlisted and kissed good-by to a girl he was engaged to marry. She would be true to her hero who had marched away to war. So he believed. Then rumors came to him. A rival she had rejected, a rival he hated, was keeping company with her. She was pretty. She liked company. What was happening? While he was at the battle fronts perhaps the hated rival would win her. He applied for a furlough. It was refused him. Reckless and half-crazy, he deserted, went home, found the rumors partly true, but he had come in time. He married the girl. Then came his arrest, trial and sentence to be shot. "I stated the circumstances, giving the young fellow a good character," wrote the creator of Petroleum V. Nasby, "and the President at once signed a pardon."

With the pardon went Lincoln's comment to Locke: "I want to punish the young man—probably in less than a year he will wish I had withheld the pardon. We can't tell, though. I suppose when I was a young man I should have done the same fool thing."

The same Duff or William Armstrong that Lincoln had helped clear of a murder charge, the son of Hannah and Jack Armstrong, himself explained his case: "The four brothers of us enlisted. Jim was wounded at Belmont. Pleasant died. I served on. Mother took a notion she wanted me. People laughed at her when she said she would write to the President, but she said, 'Please goodness, I am a-going to try it.' She got Squire Garber of Petersburg to write to 'Uncle Abe,' and in a few days mother got a telegram signed 'A. Lincoln,' telling her I had been honorably discharged. I was at Elmira, New York, helping pick up deserters, and a discharge was the last thing I dreamed of."

In the chronicle of Confederate spies saved from death by Lincoln was Lieutenant Samuel B. Davis of Delaware, son of a Presbyterian minister, 24 years old, tall, slender, handsome, dauntless, distant kin to Jefferson Davis, who sent him on a secret mission to Ohio. His hair dyed, traveling on a British passport with a false name, he was recognized by two Union soldiers who got on at Newark, Ohio, as an officer on duty when they were Confederate prisoners. In the main room of the Newark jail young Davis was seen to remove his coat, rip open the lining, take out dispatches and drawings penciled on white silk. These he burned at a stove around which other prisoners were gathered.

On trial, Davis pleaded "not guilty of being a spy" but "guilty of being a bearer of dispatches." The judge advocate argued that he had been found within the Union lines in disguise and under a false name at places where he could have obtained valuable information, whether he did or not. Lieutenant Davis proposed to show by testimony of President Davis and Secretary of State Judah P. Benjamin that he was sent as a bearer of dispatches. The court-martial refused a continuance of the trial for the purpose of getting such testimony. Young Davis made a speech. He faced, as he spoke, several haggard and battered Union veterans, some with empty sleeves. They were cold as he began. When he finished his short speech they were not so cold.

The day was set for his hanging on Johnson's Island near Sandusky, Ohio. Among those who asked Lincoln for suspension of sentence were William T. McClintick, president of the Cincinnati & Marietta Railroad, and Senator Saulsbury of Delaware, one of the most violent of Senate critics of Lincoln. Saulsbury wrote to Lincoln: "You know I am neither your personal nor political friend, but Senator Douglas once told me you were a kind-hearted man. Read the inclosed speech of this young officer condemned as a spy. There is nothing like it in history save Robert Emmet's. I ask you to act in this matter as the President of the United States should act."

How could Saulsbury, reputed the hardest drinker in the Senate, sometimes attending public sessions drunk, have guessed that such a note would hit where Lincoln was weak? Lincoln undoubtedly read more than once the little gem of a note from Saulsbury with its wonderfully sober dignity. Then he must have read more than once the little speech of Lieutenant Samuel B. Davis facing haggard and battered Union veterans: "I fear nothing on this earth. I do not fear to die. I am young and I would like to live, but I deem him unworthy who should ask pity of his foemen. Some of you have wounds and scars. I can show them, too. You are serving your country as best you may. I have done the same. I can look to God with a clear conscience, and whenever the Chief Magistrate of this nation shall say 'Go,' whether upon the scaffold or by the bullets of your soldiery, I will show you how to die."

The day set for the hanging drew near. Lieutenant Davis wrote to Major Lewis H. Bond: "The court of which you are the judge-advocate having sentenced me to be hung, at least grant the request of one whose days are numbered. I desire that, if possible, one or more members of the court will come and witness my execution. Take this as the request of one who is about to be launched into eternity. Come and see it done, and you shall at least have the satisfaction of knowing that you hung a brave man. Be kind enough to answer this hasty note. It is not written through disrespect, but for the reason I have already assigned." Judge Advocate Bond wrote that he would be there with regret and sadness, that "by your manly conduct and heroic bearing under the most trying circumstances, you have won the respect and excited the admiration of your foemen."

The evening before the hanging date the scaffold lumber, the rope, had been tested, and the headquarters commandant at Johnson's Island had gone to bed expecting first thing in the morning to witness the neck of young Davis broken in due process of law. A pounding at the door woke the commandant from his sleep. A messenger handed him an order from the President directing that the execution be suspended and the prisoner sent to Fort Warren. The grounds in international law for a death sentence were clear. But Lincoln held international law not always applicable to a civil war where hope was nursed of reconciliations to come.

Dr. David M. Wright, a reputable citizen of Norfolk, Virginia, tried by a military commission, was sentenced to be hanged for murder. Judge Advocate General Holt, on Lincoln's request, sent a transcript of the trial to the President, with an opinion that the deed was "undefended assassination." Petitioners surpassing in number those of any other pardon appeal during the war, it seemed, protested to Lincoln from the North, the South and Canada, with letters, telegrams, personal calls. "Do not let execution be done until my further order," Lincoln telegraphed Fortress Monroe.

A crying issue stood out. Up one of the main streets of Norfolk July 11, 1863, had marched a company of Negro troops. At their head was Anson L. Sanborn, a second lieutenant of the 1st U.S. Colored Troops. From the sidewalks came taunts and hoots. Among onlookers was Dr. Wright, a man of exceptional works and good character, widely known. He was suddenly in a clash with Lieutenant Sanborn, drew a revolver, shot the 20-year-old officer dead.

War Secretary Seddon at Richmond endorsed one petition with sympathy over the "natural indignation of Dr. Wright at the shameful spectacle [of Negro troops], and his prompt vindication of his honor." The daughter of Dr. Wright was permitted an extended visit alone with him in his prison cell. He walked out of the prison—in her clothes —beginning his escape. A Union officer in the street noticed his walk as "a masculine stride" and took Dr. Wright back to his cell.

On October 7 Lincoln had delayed execution nearly three months and wrote that no proper question remained open except as to the alleged insanity of the accused. On that point, including all evidence from counsel of the accused, a noted alienist wrote findings that Wright was not insane prior to the killing, "that he has not been insane since, and is not insane now." Therefore the President was directing that the sentence of death be carried into execution October 16. On pleas of one of Wright's attorneys Lincoln postponed execution to October 23, adding, "This is intended for his preparation and is final."

On October 17 the Fortress Monroe commandant telegraphed Lincoln that Dr. Wright's wife desired to visit Washington to intercede with the President for her husband's life. He replied: "It would be useless for Mrs. Dr. Wright to come here. The subject is a very painful one, but the case is settled."

The day before October 23, according to David Homer Bates, his office associate Richard O'Brien, "was approached by a man who said that if he would anticipate a telegram which was hourly expected from President Lincoln granting a reprieve, he would be paid $20,000 in gold, and would be given free passage to England on a blockade runner. O'Brien indignantly refused the bribe."

October 23 dawned. Hope had not died in some quarters that in the last hour a telegram from Lincoln might arrive. Hours passed. No Executive Mansion telegram came. At 11:20 in the morning word was put on the wires: "Dr. Wright was executed this morning." On the scaffold his last words came from tremulous lips: "Gentlemen, the act which I committed was done without the slightest malice."

A young Virginia woman whose family had long been familiars of the Blairs was brought to Lincoln by Old Man Blair. He had warned her beforehand; she was impulsive and must be careful not by any word to betray her Confederate sympathies. She wished a pass to visit her brother, a Confederate soldier and a prisoner in the Union lines. Her eyes flashed. She was a vivid presence. The President bent toward her, searched her face, and, "You are of course, loyal?"

She hesitated a moment, met his gaze frankly, then, "Yes, loyal to the heart's core—to Virginia!" He kept his eyes on her face a moment longer, went to a desk, wrote a line or two and handed her a folded paper. She bowed herself out with Mr. Blair, who was saying: "Didn't I warn you to be very. careful? You have only yourself to blame." She unfolded the paper and read words to this effect signed by the President: "Pass Miss ——— ———; she is an honest girl and can be trusted."

Mrs. Thomas Theophilus Brown, her baby in her arms, came to the President September 7, 1863; she had been to the War Department and elsewhere, in fear and anxiety over her husband and his brother, taken prisoners at Gettysburg. Their home was in Alexandria, Virginia. Though they had fought with the Confederate Army, they were not spies. Yet they had been held for weeks in Old Capitol Prison and it was whispered would be shot as spies. Lincoln heard her through. She was crying when she finished. Her baby, however, was smiling and making eyes at Lincoln. Lincoln added to the confusion. He lifted the baby up in his arms and held her to his cheeks. The baby burbled, "Papa." Lincoln laughed, put the baby back in the mother's arms, walked to and fro a few times, then wrote a paper for Mrs. Brown to take to Stanton. At the door he said, "Mrs. Brown, you are a brave little woman." The paper she carried read in part: "This lady says . . . they were conscripted into the rebel army, and were never for the rebel cause, and are now willing to do anything reasonable to be at liberty. This may be true, and if true they should be liberated. Please take hold of the case, and do what may seem proper in it."

Official action for this woman was rapid. Having taken the oath of Union allegiance, three days later at the prison gates the two brothers walked out free men. And Mrs. Thomas Theophilus Brown kissed her ragged, shaggy husband, trembling with fever and nerves, his feet torn and scarred. She took him home to Alexandria and nursed him back to health, waiting till he was strong again before she dared to tell him of the man farther up the river, in the White House, who understood her language and heard their baby call him "Papa."

With the North squeezing the South toward its last loaf of bread and final bullet, Lincoln looked to the day when it would be an advantage to have a political record free from vengeance, with no avowals of punishment and retribution to come.

A pitiless logic at times led men from bad to worse, with no going back. In more than one case Stanton and other Cabinet members strictly were on the side of right and abstract justice with Lincoln ordering a course for the sake of political considerations not to be laughed off lightly in a republic at war with itself.

The President once dropped a few kind words about the enemy. They were human beings—were they not? One could not be completely remorseless, even in war. The line must be drawn somewhere. An elderly woman in the reception room flashed a question; how could he speak kindly of his enemies when he should rather destroy them. "What, madam?" slowly as he gazed into her face, "do I not destroy them when I make them my friends?" This type of anecdote gained circulation, in both England and America.

Once Thad Stevens asked a pardon for a young constituent who had gone to sleep on picket duty. Lincoln handed Stevens a telegraph blank, Stevens wrote a reprieve, signed "A. Lincoln" to the dispatch, and sent a messenger on the run to a telegraph office. This happened soon after an informal agreement between Lincoln and Stanton that the President would consult the War Secretary on reprieves in capital cases.

"I see, Mr. President," huffed Stanton on his early entry into Lincoln's office, "you have signed another reprieve contrary to your agreement not to do so without first consulting the War Department." "No. I have signed no reprieve. I have kept my word." "But I just saw one going over the wires. And your name is signed to it." "But I did not write it." "Did not write it! Who did write it?" "Your friend, Thad Stevens." Stanton took his hat and left.

A sobbing old man told the President his son with Butler's army had been convicted of a crime and sentenced by court-martial to be shot. The President read a telegram from General Butler protesting against executive interference with army courts-martial. The dazed old man shook with a desperate grief, Lincoln watching a minute, and "By jings, Butler or no Butler, here goes," wrote a few words. He showed them to the old man, a presidential signed order that the son was "not to be shot until further orders from me."

The old man was still in grief. "I thought it was to be a pardon. But you say 'not to be shot till further orders,' and you may order him shot next week." Lincoln smiled. "Well, my old friend, I see you are not very well acquainted with me. If your son never looks on death till further orders come from me to shoot him, he will live to be a great deal older than Methuselah."

A young woman in neat and plain dress was heard with respect and frank speech. "My poor girl, you have come with no governor, or senator, or member of Congress, to plead your cause. You seem honest and truthful, and *you don't wear hoops;* and I'll be whipped but I'll pardon your brother!"

An ancient rule of law held that pirates should be hanged. Nevertheless Lincoln pardoned a pirate, Alfred Rubery, captured in San Francisco in March '63 and held in jail for months till released on order of the President. Two reasons were given the public. The pirate was a British subject. And

John Bright had written to the President asking the pardon as a favor. "In consideration of Mr. Bright's eminent services, the President at once acceded to his request," said *Leslie's Weekly,* January 2, 1864. "Mr. Bright has some strange friends." The comment was too easy. Lincoln saw little to be gained in that hour by hanging a British subject. And he believed John Bright was entitled to one pardon and no questions asked.

In the case of Louis A. Welton, sentenced to prison, Senator Morgan, Thurlow Weed and Raymond of the *Times,* were asking Lincoln to pardon him. Lincoln plainly believed the man to be a liar and a scoundrel taking profits out of trading with the enemy. Yet Lincoln pardoned Welton. It was the last week in August '64. The three men asking Welton's pardon were not to be thrust away with abrupt refusals. Lincoln wrote a statement giving his belief that Welton was a falsifier and a species of traitor intent on money-making from treason, and his further belief that Welton ought not to be pardoned. However if Messrs. Morgan, Weed and Raymond would on the same sheet with his statement of the case write their requests for Welton's pardon it would be done in deference to their wishes. Two of the three petitioners did so. Welton was saved from prison. Lincoln held in his possession a paper which the opposition would have seized on as luridly scandalous had it been made public:

> Mr. Louis A. Welton came from the rebel lines into our lines with a written contract to furnish large supplies to the rebels, was arrested with the contract in his possession, and has been sentenced to imprisonment for it. He, and his friends complain of this, on no substantial evidence whatever, but simply because his word, only given after his arrest, that he only took the contract as a means of escaping from the rebel lines, was not accepted as a full defence. He perceives that if this had been true he would have destroyed the contract so soon as it had served his purpose in getting him across the lines; but not having done this, and being

caught with the paper on him, he tells this other absurd story that he kept the paper in the belief that our government would join him in taking the profit of fulfiling the contract.

This is my understanding of the case; and I can not conceive of a case of a man found in possession of a contract to furnish rebel supplies, who can not escape, if this be held a sufficient ground of escape. It is simply for the accused to escape by telling a very absurd and improbable story. Now, if Senator Morgan, and Mr. Weed, and Mr. Raymond, will not argue with me that I *ought* to discharge this man, but will, in writing on this sheet, simply request me me to do it, I will do it solely in deference to their wishes.

A. LINCOLN

Then appearing on the same sheet of paper were the endorsements:

We respectfully request the President to pardon the within named Louis A. Welton, now at Fort Delaware.

THURLOW WEED.

I have read Mr. Welton's statement and if it is true, (and I know no reason for distrusting it,) his pardon would be an act of *justice*. I concur in Mr. Weed's request.

H. J. RAYMOND.

Lincoln's hands-off attitude in some cases may have meant he had heard enough of the case to believe the court-martial findings were probably true and correct. Or it may have been that, much as he would have liked to take a day or two for the study of the extended evidence in a case, he had no such day or two to spare.

Congressman Kellogg brought in the affair of a helter-skelter lad who before the war served six months in the Regular Army, deserted, came home, told his father nothing about it, sobered up and settled down. Later the boy volunteered at the beginning of the war, helped raise a regiment, was elected one of its officers, and in a charge across a bridge during one battle saw his colonel at his side killed and took wounds himself. Then an old-timer of the Regular Army recognized him, and let him know he would be exposed as a deserter. He managed to get furloughed home, told his father he would "die first" rather than be arrested as a deserter. Lincoln wasn't interested until the charge across the bridge. "Do you say the young man was wounded?" "Yes, badly." "Then," musingly, "then he has shed his blood for his country." And with a brightening, "Kellogg, isn't there something in Scripture about the 'shedding of blood' being the 'remission of sins'?" "Guess you're about right there." "It is a good point, and there is no going behind it." The President took a pen, wrote a pardon without condition or reservation.

An anxious old woman came with Congressman Charles Denison of Pennsylvania. Her son, John Russell, a private soldier, was under sentence to be shot in 48 hours. Lincoln heard them and sent for the papers in the case. It seemed that in a recent bloody battle Russell's captain had run away and after the battle found half of his command lost. Russell, meeting his captain, walked toward him, rifle in hand, and burst out, "Captain, you're a damned coward and ought to be shot for cowardice." The captain pulled his revolver; others came between them. The captain then charged insubordination, got a court-martial to give the lad a death sentence. Lincoln revoked the court-martial findings and ordered Private Russell restored to his command in good standing.

Joseph Holt, Judge Advocate General, laid before the President a flagrant case of a soldier in the heat of battle, affecting others by his cowardice, throwing down his gun and hiding behind a tree stump. The court-martial found he had neither father nor mother living, nor wife nor child; he was a thief, stealing from comrades on duty, by all standards unfit to wear the uniform. "Here is a case," said Judge Holt to the President, "exactly within your requirements; he does not deny his guilt; he will serve his country better dead than living . . . no relations to mourn for him . . . not fit to be in the ranks of patriots."

The President ran his long fingers through his hair: "Well, after all, Judge, I think I must put this with my leg cases." Judge Holt frowned. Was this a humorous matter? "What do you mean by leg cases, sir?" "Why, why, do you see those papers crowded into those pigeonholes? They are the cases that you call by that long title 'cowardice in the face of the enemy,' but I call them, for short, my 'leg cases.' But I put it to you, and I leave it for you to decide for yourself: if Almighty God gives a man a cowardly pair of legs how can he help their running away with him?"

On several bounty-jumpers Lincoln let the firing squads do their work. He refused mercy to bounty-jumpers—or again he intervened. The eccentric versatility of Robert Lane appealed to him. Lane enlisted first in Loomis' battery, left the service on a physical-disability discharge, stayed in Detroit, bobbed up in Nashville with a sutler, clowned with a circus, performed as a sword-swallower, rode a horse in a Kentucky cavalry regiment, was next heard of as a sergeant in one Indiana infantry company, leaving that for another. While held in an Indiana penitentiary Robert Lane was by court-martial ordered to be shot. Lincoln for reasons known to himself commuted the sentence of this flagrant bounty-jumper and scalawag to one year's hard labor with chain and ball. Possibly he saw genius and wit allied to madness in the case of Robert Lane.

A newspaperman and an Ohio colonel, after an interview on Great Lakes commerce, requested Lincoln to hear an old man waiting outside whose boy was to be shot. They waited. Nicolay came in with the old man's card, leaned over Lincoln's chair and whispered. Lincoln spoke, harassed yet decisive: "Tell him I will not see him. I cannot. Don't ask me again. Tell him I have read the papers in the case, all of them, fully, word for word. The boy deserted three times, the last time when on guard at Washington, and he cannot be pardoned. I will not interfere. He must be shot."

One guerrilla failing of mercy at Lincoln's hands was a

Missouri leader named Nichols. Judge Holt gave Carpenter details about Nichols. "He was in the habit of filling the ears of Unionists who fell into his hands with gunpowder, setting fire to it, and blowing their heads to pieces. When captured, a number of human *ears* were found on his person."

The guard Crook took note of a woman intercepting Tad in a corridor, telling Tad her boys and girls were cold and starving because their father was shut up in prison and couldn't work for them. Tad ran to his father with the story. The father sat at a desk with papers, an absent look on his face, said he would look into the case as soon as he had time. Tad clung to his father's knees and begged till his father listened. And Tad ran back and told the woman her husband would be set free. The woman blessed him and cried, and Tad cried, and Crook said he had to cry too.

A rough rider of the Confederate Mosby's raiders awaited the firing squad while his wife came to Lincoln with her story. The President, knowing how fierce Mosby's men were in the field, asked her what kind of a husband her man was. Did he get drunk? Did he beat her and the children? "No, no," said the wife. "He is a good man, a good husband. He loves me. He loves the children. And we can't live without him. The only trouble is that he is a fool about politics. I live in the North, born there, and if I can get him home he will do no more fighting for the South." "Well," said Lincoln as he thumbed through the papers, "I will pardon your husband and turn him over to you for safe keeping." Here the woman broke into tears, into a sobbing beyond control. "My dear woman, if I had known how badly it was going to make you feel, I never would have pardoned him." "You don't understand me," she cried between sobs, in a fresh flow of tears. "Yes, yes, I do. And if you don't go away at once I shall be crying with you."

A woman knelt to give thanks for the release of her husband. "Don't kneel to me but thank God and go" was the President's dismissal of her.

There were tender scenes with no overplaying of them. A woman with tears filling her eyes tried to speak gratitude for a "suspension of execution" granted her husband. "Good-by, Mr. Lincoln. I shall probably never see you again till we meet in heaven." She had taken one of his hands. He took her right hand in both of his. They walked to the door as he spoke softly: "I am afraid with all my troubles I shall never get to the resting-place you speak of. But if I do, I am sure I shall find you. That you wish me to get there is, I believe, the best wish you could make for me. Good-by."

"If he has no friend I'll be his friend," was Lincoln's remark as he penned a reprieve for one unbespoken. Once he sat up in his nightshirt, just awakened from sleep, heard the story of a 19-year-old boy having fallen asleep on picket duty, wrote a reprieve in bed, then worried that the order might go wrong, dressed himself and went over to the War Department to make sure the order was understood. This was one story and a likely one. Another ran that in fear a similar pardon order might go astray he sent telegrams to four different authorities. Of one of these pardons saving the life of a sleeping picket, he remarked to a Congressman as he read an order he had written: "I could not think of going into eternity with the blood of that poor young man on my skirts. It is not to be wondered at that a boy, raised on the farm, probably in the habit of going to bed at dark, should, when required to watch, fall asleep; and I cannot consent to shooting him for such an act."

On Monday morning, September 9, 1861, the 3rd Vermont Volunteers regiment was drawn up to hear the reading of General Order No. 8, issued by General McClellan. It began with reciting William Scott's trial and sentence, the appeals of brigade, regiment and company officers, together with privates, that Scott's life be spared. "And," it continued, "the President of the United States had expressed a wish that, as this is the first condemnation to death in the army for this crime, mercy may be extended to the criminal. This fact, viewed in connection with the inexperience of the condemned as a soldier, his previous good conduct and general good character, and the urgent entreaties made in his behalf, have determined the Major General to grant the pardon so earnestly prayed for." Then came a warning that pardons might not always be given to boys who slept on sentinel duty, as it was an offense to which "all nations affix the penalty of death." Then came the order releasing Scott for duty with his regiment.

This same William Scott seven months later among the fresh growths and blooms of Virginia springtime at Lee's Mill took the burning messages of six bullets into his body. All he could give Lincoln or his country or his God was now given.

Pardon appeals where an executive Yes or No must decide whether a soldier face the firing squad—these troubled from several approaches. From a cold practical viewpoint it was good politics to have a reputation as a pardoner, softhearted rather than hardhearted, even though it affected army behavior. Mothers and sisters wept as the President one day signed a reprieve. "Well, I have made one family happy, but I don't know about the discipline of the army!"

In the seven days between December 26, 1863, and January 3, 1864, six soldiers received pardons or stays of death sentences from the President. "Do not execute him till further order" or "Suspend execution of sentence and forward record of trial for examination" was the repeated essential of the telegrams. The most sweeping order of this class ever sent by the President was on December 10, 1863, to Major General Butler at Fortress Monroe: "Please suspend execution in any and all sentences of death in your Department until further orders." To the army of no other general than Butler did it seem that Lincoln issued so inclusive an order regarding stays of execution. Butler seemed to be the one major general who openly and directly blamed his military losses on the President's lack of severity. Butler gave his answer why the war was lasting so long: "Pusillanimity and want of executive force of the government."

Donn Piatt wrote of how he heard Brigadier General Daniel Tyler of Connecticut in an antechamber of the War Department tell the President that reverses in Kentucky and Tennessee were due to the one condition that Bragg, the

Confederate commander, had shot his deserters, but "if we attempt to shoot a deserter, you pardon him and our army is without discipline." Tyler went on: "Why do you interfere? Congress has taken from you all responsibility." The President, swiftly and impatiently: "Yes, Congress has taken the responsibility and left the women to howl about me." And he strode away.

Many opponents and critics of Lincoln believed that realistic political and military purposes moved him entirely in his pardons. The popular belief in Lincoln's mercy was "erroneous," Donn Piatt would say. "His good-natured manner misled the common mind." Piatt doubted whether Lincoln "had at all a kind, forgiving nature," pointing to history and successful leaders of men as "round, oily, elastic" on the outside, giving way in trifles, while "angular, hard," on the inner purposes. In his guess at this phase of Lincoln, Piatt was half-correct at least. Lincoln had disciplined himself to hide his deeper purposes under the spoken immediate ones. He could be smooth toward rough ends when he considered it necessary. "I heard Secretary Seward say," wrote Piatt, "that President Lincoln 'had a cunning that was genius.'" Coming from Seward that was some manner of tribute.

The sound of musketry fire blew from Virginia camps into the White House one afternoon as Lincoln sat with John Eaton. He stepped to an open window and looked to the Virginia shore. "When he turned again, the tears were running down his cheeks," wrote the responsible Eaton, who heard him say, "This is the day when they shoot deserters." Nevertheless it was not so easy as that. By his pardons he had lowered army morale. "Some of our officers feel that," he said to Eaton. "Our" officers had that feeling. After all it was "our" army and he too was part of "they" who were shooting deserters.

To what extent did the President's frequent pardons interfere with army discipline? Chauncey M. Depew was to answer by quoting General Sherman. "How did you carry out the sentences of your court-martials and escape Lincoln's pardons?" Depew asked. Sherman answered, "I shot them first!" Whatever the irregular or illegal device used by Sherman in this respect, it was probably also used by Grant, Thomas, Sheridan and every other commander who won campaigns and battles.

Well enough was it known in the army that being saved from a firing squad by a President's pardon often meant iron bars, prison fare, close confinement, hard labor, the ball and chain. Far and wide went the press item in 1864: "President Lincoln directed that the sentences of all deserters who had been condemned to death by court-martial, and that had not been otherwise acted upon by him, be mitigated to imprisonment during the war at the Dry Tortugas, Florida, where they would be sent under guard." In a tropical climate, cut off by the sea, with war-torn states and the Atlantic Ocean between them and the Northern home states, some of the deserters, thieves, cowards, "leg cases," mutineers, malingerers, bounty-jumpers, doing the lock step in the Dry Tortugas Islands wrote home that it was a hard life.

In a single year the army courts-martial were handling 30,000 cases of offenders against military law. Many capital cases eventually drifted to Lincoln's desk. Of one hot summer afternoon John Hay wrote in his diary that the President spent six hours on court-martial transcripts, catching at any fact that would justify saving a life. In one case he doubted "it would make any man better to shoot him," urging that if the Government kept him alive it could at least get some work out of him. One endorsement read, "Let him fight instead of shooting him."

The young Indiana Democratic Congressman Daniel W. Voorhees heard from Lincoln the confession: "No one need ever expect me to sanction the shooting of a man for running away in battle. I won't do it. A man can't help being a coward any more than he could help being a humpback." It was on another White House call, according to Voorhees, that Lincoln, with a pathetic look of anxious pain, made the little inquiry, "Voorhees, don't it seem strange to you that I who could never so much as cut off the head of a chicken, should be elected, or selected, into the midst of all this blood?"

Chapter 36

The Man Who Had Become the Issue

The Man Lincoln, his person and mind, had come to be the pivotal issue of the 1864 campaign. Some would vote for him with no particular faith, others in a loyalty that had seldom or never swerved. In the chaos of the times he was to these folk a beacon light that in moments almost flickered out into a black despair, yet returned to shine without wavering. His life in the White House, his decisions, speeches and messages issued from there, went out over the country for interpretations, for thanks, curses, doubts. Those interpretations would be told of in the November 8 ballot boxes.

"The great West is with you," Ralph Emerson of Rockford, Illinois, assured him. "Yes—but I am sometimes reminded of Old Mother Partington on the sea beach. A big storm came up and the waves began to rise till the water came in under her cabin door. She got a broom and went to sweeping it out. But the water rose higher and higher, to her knees, to her waist, at last to her chin. But she kept on sweeping and exclaiming, 'I'll keep on sweeping as long as the broom lasts, and we will see whether the storm or the broom will last the longest.' " At the final words, according to Emerson, Lincoln's jaws came together, his face grim rather than funny.

In Illinois, Dick Oglesby, recovered from bullet wounds, was running for governor on the Union ticket and saying that in 1858 at Urbana in a walk with Lincoln—he distinctly recalled it—Lincoln told him, "Remember, Dick, to keep close to the people—they are always right and will mislead no one."

Nathaniel Hawthorne nursed his complex grief over the awful war game and died in '64, mostly of heartbreak, from looking too close and too long at the riddle Lincoln had formulated in the Gettysburg speech. Mrs. Hawthorne had once written her husband of "a paragraph in the paper about your being at Washington, and that the President received you with especial graciousness . . . I suspect the President is a jewel. I like him very well." She loved her husband and wrote as a lover. "If it were not such a bore, I could wish thou mightest be President through this crisis . . . I should not wonder if thy great presence in Washington might affect the moral air and work good. If you like the President, then give him my love and blessing."

Of Lincoln's plea for gradual compensated emancipation, she wrote, "The President's immortal special message fills me with unbounded satisfaction. It is so almost superhumanly wise, moderate, fitting that I am ready to believe an angel came straight from heaven to him with it. He must be honest and true, or an angel would not come to him. Mary Mann says she thinks the message feeble, and not to the point. But I think a man shows strength when he can be moderate at such a moment as this. Thou hadst better give my regards to the President."

The lights of such spirits as hers did reach Lincoln. Precious affection came his way. Motives beyond price were unbosomed to him. They lighted, changed and deepened him, perhaps saddened him. He had hours when, like Hawthorne, he hardly knew what took his strength away. Of one vicious personal criticism of him, he said mildly that it wasn't well timed; and of one bitter political enemy, "I've been told that insanity is hereditary in his family, and I think we will admit the plea in his case."

Events moved him to change his policies. Some were baffled by his transitions. Congressman John B. Alley suddenly found the President differed with him on a matter where they had been agreed. "Mr. President, you have changed your mind entirely within a short time." "Yes, I have. And I don't think much of a man who is not wiser today than he was yesterday."

Every phase of the war lived and rang in the rooms of the White House, where, according to Crook, "As he went upstairs and entered his own room, Lincoln's last act was to turn to the guard on duty in the corridor and wish him good-night. Then he would enter his room, and close the door, and I—if it were my turn to stand guard—would settle down for eight hours of duty." In the silence of the night was despair—and hope. Though torn with intestinal violence, the Government of the United States was still a vast going concern, having immense transactions in land, money, shipbuilding, the first tentative projections of the Union Pacific Railway under way, an around-the-earth international telegraph system being wrought toward reality, mails being carried, pensions paid to widows and orphans, river and harbor works in process, emigrants thronging U.S. consulates in Europe with anxiety to go to "the free country" overseas. And the question running over the world: Would the Union Government be able to hammer out an indissoluble unity of its states? Alongside this world of red war and this other world of constructive realities in which Lincoln had to immerse himself daily, there was the formal realm of conventions, of "society," of ordained contacts necessary to the role of being President. The night of the weekly reception—more often termed a levee—"was always a trying one to the President," wrote Carpenter.

Seven biographies published in '64 presented Lincoln favorably for various audiences of readers. Several small paper-covered books issued by the opposition were chiefly humorous and satirical. Immense editions were sold of an issue of the monthly *Beadle Dime Library* by O. J. Victor and another "popular life" by the Reverend William M. Thayer of Boston. Each emphasized the opportunity before any American poor boy who wished "to climb the heights."

Leslie's Weekly enumerated "sweet scented compliments" paid by the opposition press to the President of the United States, namely: ape, gorilla, fool, filthy storyteller, despot, liar, thief, braggart, buffoon, usurper, monster, tortoise, ignoramus, old scoundrel, perjurer, robber, swindler, tyrant, fiend, butcher, land pirate.

The effect of this savage verbal warfare? In October '64 *Harper's Weekly* appraised it: "The personal character of the President is the rock upon which the Opposition is wrecked. It dashes against him and his administration, hissing and venomous, but falls back again baffled . . . the popular confidence in the unswerving fidelity and purity of purpose of the President has smiled the storm to scorn." *Harper's Weekly, Harper's Monthly,* the *Atlantic Monthly, Leslie's Weekly, Godey's Lady's Book,* the larger part of the more formidable and solid periodicals, either in quiet and reserved tones or with direct and sonorous declarations, favored Lincoln and the National Union ticket during the campaign.

Lamon and Piatt accepted with full credence an account by the economist and financier Amasa Walker of an interview he and Chase had with Lincoln about a proposed greenback issue Chase feared was unconstitutional. Piatt wrote:

> Mr. Chase made a long and elaborate constitutional argument against the proposed measure . . . said Mr. Lincoln . . . "This thing reminds me of a story I read in a newspaper the other day. It was of an Italian captain, who ran his vessel on a rock and knocked a hole in her bottom. He set his men to pumping and he went to prayers before a figure of the Virgin in the bow of the ship. The leak gained on them. It looked at last as if the vessel would go down with all on board. The captain, at length, in a fit of rage at not having his prayers answered, seized the figure of the Virgin and threw it overboard. Suddenly the leak stopped, the water was pumped out, and the vessel got safely into port. When docked for repairs, the statue of the Virgin Mary was found stuck headforemost in the hole."
>
> "I don't see, Mr. President, the precise application of your story," said Mr. Chase.
>
> "Why . . . I don't intend precisely to throw the Virgin Mary overboard, and by that I mean the Constitution, but I will stick it in the hole if I can. These rebels

are violating the Constitution to destroy the Union. I
will violate the Constitution, if necessary, to save the
Union, and I suspect . . . that our Constitution is going
to have a rough time of it before we get done with this
row. Now, what I want to know is whether, Constitution aside, this project of issuing interest-bearing notes
is a good one."

"I must say," responded Mr. Chase, "that with the
exception you make, it is not only a good one, but the
only way open to us to raise money. If you say so, I
will do my best to put it into immediate and practical
operation, and you will never hear from me any opposition on this subject."

One October evening in '64 a torchlight procession of
hundreds of Negroes marched to the White House lawn,
carrying banners and transparencies, a brass band blaring,
loud and repeated cheers bringing the President. He looked
out from the portico on jubilant black faces, heard in the
half-lighted darkness their moving hoarse voices, and began,
"I have to guess, my friends, the object of this call which
has taken me quite by surprise this evening." Then according to Noah Brooks' news report, a spokesman shouted,
"The emancipator of Maryland, sah!" The newly adopted
constitution of that state was in their favor. The President
proceeded: "It is no secret that I have wished, and still do
wish, mankind everywhere to be free." (Great cheering and
cries of "God bless Abraham Lincoln.")

The tall, gaunt, slave-born black woman Sojourner Truth
arrived at the Executive Mansion from Battle Creek, Michigan, "a long and halting journey," she said. The President
gave Sojourner his hand, bowed. "I am pleased to see you."
Then Sojourner released her speech poem: "Mr. President,
when you first took your seat I feared you would be torn to
pieces, for I likened you unto Daniel, who was thrown into
the lions' den; and if the lions did not tear you to pieces, I
knew that it would be God that had saved you; and I said
if He spared me I would see you before the four years ex-

pired, and He has done so, and now I am here to see you for myself." He took the little book she brought out, and as Sojourner phrased it, "The same hand that signed the death-warrant of slavery wrote as follows":

For Aunty Sojourner Truth,
Oct. 29, 1864.   A. Lincoln

Lincoln wrote checks payable to "Mr. Johns, a sick man," "Lucy (colored woman)," and a wanderer on the White House lawn, "Colored Man, with one Leg." And how and why he endorsed notes for other Negroes was not a matter of publicity and news. To the ears of Nicolay it came, however, that a cashier of one of the Washington banks, meeting an old friend of Lincoln on the street one morning, had to say: "That President of yours is the oddest man alive. Why, he endorses notes for niggers!"

In the Executive Mansion for the first two years no colored persons were employed. "But," wrote Brooks, "the President has succeeded in getting about him a corps of attachés of Hibernian descent." Brooks wrote that the Irish coachman "did not consider it his business to run errands. This coming to the President's ears he ordered up the carriage next morning at six o'clock and sent a member of his household in the equipage to the Avenue where he bought a paper and rode back, with the mortified coachee on the box."

To the White House often had come the master photographer Mathew B. Brady. Since February '60, at the time of the Cooper Union speech, Brady had by autumn of '64 photographed Lincoln more than 30 times. From his profitable portrait gallery on Broadway and Tenth, New York, Brady had come to the war with his camera. Out in the camps, on the march and on battlefields Brady and his assistants made both single and stereoscopic wet-plate exposures and were achieving a camera record comprising thousands of convincing likenesses of scenes and people. Lincoln wrote and signed a heavy card with the large scrawl "Pass Brady," which took Brady nearly everywhere he cared to go.

Collections of *cartes de visite,* photographs of fine clarity and definition of line, mounted on small cards usually 2¼ by 3½ inches, were in many thousands of homes. Brady and Gardner photographs of Lincoln were often on show there. Frequently the illustrated weeklies, *Harper's* and *Leslie's,* and occasionally the daily newspapers, published large drawings from photographs, so that Lincoln's face and figure had become familiar to those who read, and of course to some who enjoyed pictures though they couldn't read.

A Connecticut painter's portrait of Lincoln, done for Secretary Welles, hung for a time in Lincoln's office. Welles, turning toward it one afternoon, said it was a successful likeness. From Lincoln came a hesitant "Yes," noted Carpenter, and then a story of a Western man who had himself painted secretly, giving his wife the picture for a birthday present. "Horridly like," she pronounced it. "And that," said Lincoln, "seems to me a just criticism of *this!*"

Carpenter's painting, "The First Reading of the Emancipation Proclamation by President Lincoln to His Cabinet" was nearly finished. In his six months' stay he and Lincoln had passed many pleasant hours. Thirty-four years old, slender and delicate, with bushy black hair, devout in religion and strict in manners, Carpenter had a loyalty to the President and a belief that his painting would be a help. "I must go in and take one more look at the picture before you leave us," said Lincoln one July day. Carpenter spoke of the unvarying kindness the President had always shown him. Lincoln listened, kept gazing on the picture, and turned to say, "Carpenter, I believe I am about as glad over the success of this work as you are." By permission of the President the painting, when finished, was placed in the East Room, open to the public for two days, and was viewed by several thousand visitors.

At 11 o'clock one night Carpenter found Lincoln alone signing military commissions. He went on signing, presently remarking, "I do not, as you see, pretend to read over these documents. I see that Stanton has signed them, so I conclude they are all right." He chatted and wrote, finished the lot, rose, stretched, "Well, I have got that job *husked out,* now I guess I will go over to the War Department before I go to bed, and see if there is any news."

Readers saw with interest press items of Mrs. Lincoln paying a complimentary visit to General Scott at West Point and receiving a salute of 15 guns; of her going to Harvard in June to attend the graduation of Robert; of her buying a set of earrings and a pin for $3,000 and a shawl for $5,000 on successive shopping trips to New York City; of her sister Martha Todd White of Selma, Alabama, receiving a pass signed by the President giving her passage, with baggage, through the Union Army lines, resulting in rumors and accusations that she had been accorded special privileges and had smuggled contraband goods, including, *Leslie's Weekly* alleged mistakenly, "a rebel uniform, the buttons of which were gold, worth $40,000."

Cases of assorted wines and liquors piled high in the White House cellar. Arrivals of whisky, brandy, rum were acknowledged with thanks and word that they were to be distributed among hospitals.

Blue Room, East Room, Red Room, Green Room, long and stately with lofty ceilings, with gas chandeliers spreading like huge jungle flowers of glass further decked with glittering balloons of whitened glass—these on the downstairs floor of the White House overlooked much small talk and idle chatter. Seven o'clock strictly was the hour for state dinners, according to the Department of State. On request it furnished the White House with elaborate details on tradition and accepted form. At times the stairways leading up to the offices were blocked with callers and curiosity seekers.

Somehow the tale went forth and became published as fact that Senator Sumner strolled in to find the President polishing his own boots. "Why, Mr. President, do you black your own boots?" "Whose boots did you think I blacked?"

Congressman Alley's version ran that Chase found Lincoln rubbing his leather footwear with a brush. Remarks were exchanged. "Mr. Lincoln, gentlemen don't black their own boots." "Whose boots do they black?"

A dusty and worn dispatch-bearer with secret papers of importance handed them to the President seated alone in his office. And young Major Gerrard Whitehead of the Philadelphia City Troop took a seat where the President motioned him and watched the President fall into a deep study, lost entirely in the revelations of the dispatches.

"The one window of the room was open," Whitehead wrote. "Across the sultry sky came up heavy thunder clouds. The storm broke and rain began to pour into the room. The officer did not think of moving while the Commander in Chief of the Army was so engrossed. So he sat and watched the rain form a pool on the floor and slowly trickle across it, almost to the feet of the President, absorbed and unconscious. At last Mr. Lincoln made his decision, seemed to rouse from his deep reflections and becoming conscious of the young despatch bearer, told him to return in an hour, when the answering despatch would be ready for him."

On occasion Lincoln kept a weather eye on his caller, as when in April '64 press items told of "the lunatic who harangued the President, claiming to have been elected President in 1856." And again when an incoherent individual styling himself "Major General of the Anti-Renters," babbled that he had been imprisoned in "Castle Thunder" in Richmond, raved over vast schemes to end the war, was led away and adjudged insane.

That the President's earlier suspicions of Count Adam Gurowski were partly justified was seen in August '64 when that neurotic growler was locked up in a police station and after a hearing before a magistrate was fined $5. Witnesses testified that Gurowski had "attempted to discipline" the Washington Fire Department. Yelling that they were moving too slow toward the conflagration, "he drew a pistol on the firemen to make them run faster."

One evening Robert W. McBride, serving as corporal of the guard, picketed his horse in the rear of the White House and was standing in the driveway of the front portico. As he stood there he saw the President come out alone and walk to the edge of the portico where the steps began. There under a lighted gas jet the President stood, alone. His hands behind him, he stood there in a reverie. A few feet away, across the driveway, Corporal McBride had drawn his saber and stood at attention. As a corporal it was his duty to stand at attention and salute any officer, and particularly the Commander in Chief of the armies of the United States.

"Just how long he stood there I do not know," said McBride. "I know he stood there so long I became very tired." It was to McBride as though, were some marksman hidden anywhere, the President wished to make himself a perfect target by standing alone in the full light of the gas jet. But after a time, possibly several minutes, he came down the steps, and hardly seeming to notice the corporal, nevertheless gravely lifted his hat as a return salute and walked toward the War Department, alone. In about a half-hour he came back, alone.

Stanton's anxiety over the President's safety continued. He gave one standing order. Although the President might come to the War Office at midnight alone, as happened often, he should never be permitted to return alone, but must be escorted by a file of four soldiers and a noncommissioned officer.

During the autumn of '64 the cavalry guard at Soldiers' Home was cautioned repeatedly to be "extremely vigilant," and according to its lieutenant, George C. Ashmun, "the whole company was kept under arms with horses saddled," ready for any night disturbance. The President was leaving the house late at night, taking solitary walks. Of one Lincoln ramble alone under the stars Ashmun noted: "One beautiful Indian Summer night, about 12 o'clock, as I was returning across the grounds from a visit to one of our pickets who had fired at something, I saw a man walking leisurely and alone across the path I was taking. As I came nearer I saw it was Mr. Lincoln. At an earlier hour I would have kept from speaking, but, prompted by anxiety, I said, 'Mr. President, isn't it rather risky to be out here at this hour?' He answered, 'Oh, I guess not—I couldn't rest and thought I'd take a walk.' He was quite a distance outside the line of infantry guards about the house where the family was staying. He turned back after I spoke to him, and I passed on to where the escort was camped."

Four police officers in November '64 were detailed by the chief of police of the District of Columbia, to serve as special guards for the President. They were John F. Parker, Alfonso Dunn, Alexander Smith and Thomas Pendel. On Pendel's later being appointed doorkeeper, that vacancy was filled by William H. Crook. Noted Crook, "The night guards were expected to protect the President on his expeditions to and from the War Department, or while he was at any place of amusement, and to patrol the corridor outside his room while he slept."

In March and April of '64 the New York *Tribune* gave the country several news letters from a Washington correspondent who named one Colonel Margrave as having submitted to the Confederate War Department plans to kidnap Lincoln and carry him to Richmond, "or if it should be found impossible to escape with him to the rebel lines, to assassinate him." The story did not quite stand up, yet was taken in some circles friendly to Lincoln as perhaps having a slight basis—"Where there is so much smoke there must be some fire." The New York *World* said: "This ridiculous canard was telegraphed all over the country, and has found its way into nearly every journal in the land. It is absurd on its face. Mr. Lincoln is of much more service to the rebels where he is than if they had him in Richmond."

Of an odd affair about mid-August '64, nothing should be said, ran Lincoln's advice to John W. Nichols, a guard since the summer of '62. Nichols, on duty at the large gate entrance to the Soldiers' Home grounds, one night about eleven heard a rifle shot in the direction of the city and soon after heard the hoofbeats of a horse coming nearer and nearer. In two or three minutes a horse came dashing up. On it Nichols saw the President, bareheaded, and Nichols helped to quiet a favorite saddle horse. The President was now saying: "He came pretty near getting away with me, didn't he? He got the bit in his teeth before I could draw rein." To Nichols' query about his hat the President answered that somebody had fired a gun off down at the foot of the hill, and that his horse had become scared and had jerked his hat off.

Nichols led the horse to the executive cottage, held it while the President dismounted and went into the house, then saw the horse to the stables. Nichols with a corporal began a search for the hat. At a point where the sound of the shot had come from, a driveway intersection with the main road, they found the President's hat, the familiar plain silk stovepipe. "Upon examination," proceeded Nichols' story, "we discovered a *bullet-hole* through the crown. We searched the locality thoroughly, but without avail. Next day I gave Mr. Lincoln his hat, and called his attention to the bullet-hole. He made some humorous remark, to the effect that it was made by some foolish marksman and was not intended for him; but added that he wished nothing said about the matter. We all felt confident it was an attempt to kill the President, and after that he never rode alone."

This made twice that Lincoln lost his hat while riding at night, the first time telling Lamon about it as a comic affair worth a laugh.

To the theater Lincoln continued to go, though warned that he was an easy target. He heard of clergymen murmuring about his moral support of the playhouse. One Hay diary entry read: "Spent the evening at the theatre with President, Mrs. L., Mrs. Hunter, Cameron and Nicolay. J. Wilkes Booth in the 'Marble Heart.' Rather tame than otherwise."

Alone often, yet again with varied companions, Tad or Mrs. Lincoln, or Hay, Brooks, Sumner and others, the President went to the drama, visiting Grover's Theatre perhaps a hundred times since coming to Washington. When there was opera at Grover's, Mrs. Lincoln invariably attended with the President. "Mr. Grover, I really enjoy a minstrel show," Lincoln suggested once. And when Grover later announced Hooley's Minstrels soon to come Lincoln laughed. "Well, that was thoughtful of you."

Once in '64 Tad quietly slipped away from a box at Grover's. And soon the father saw his boy on stage with a chorus singing "The Battle Cry of Freedom," Tad half lost in a Union Army blue uniform blouse.

To Grover's one night came Mr. and Mrs. Lincoln with Speaker Colfax, and no guard or other company. Grover met them at the curb, conducted them from their carriage, through a private passage to their box. After the play he took them by the same passage to the street, where they found a crowd of more than a hundred jeering and laughing around the President's carriage. Grover opened the carriage door, handed his guests in and watched a scene grotesque and sad.

On the carriage box holding the reins of two lively horses sat a boy who had been a drummer, had lost an arm in battle, had then been given a place at the White House. The regular coachman, a young man clumsy from drink, jabbering in Irish brogue, was trying to climb onto the box. Three hours earlier, invited for a few drinks, he had left his horses in charge of the one-armed boy. The crowd saw him slump to the street cobblestones and slowly get to his feet. "He staggered slightly," wrote Grover, "and then with a supreme effort, clambered over the wheel, landed on the box, seized the reins from the hand of the drummer-boy, and turning to take his seat—fell sprawling his full length on the sidewalk. The jeering shout which followed had a threatening tone. Any overt act, the throwing of a stone, might have resulted in catastrophe."

Grover took the reins, sprang to the box, started the span of horses, asked the President where to drive, took Speaker Colfax home first, then delivered the White House folks to their home where Lincoln spoke grateful words. Leonard Grover wrote with a modest accuracy: "Some people went so far as to say that I had saved Mr. Lincoln's life. I knew that I had extricated him from a very annoying situation." The drunken coachman and the one-armed drummer-boy were lost in a confusion of chronicles.

Lincoln had seen for the first time a performance of *Hamlet,* with Edwin Booth in the leading role. It had "at all times a peculiar charm for Mr. Lincoln's mind," noted Carpenter, who quoted Lincoln: "There is one passage very apt to be slurred over by the actor . . . It is the soliloquy of the king, after the murder . . ." He took up the words:

> "O! my offence is rank, it smells to heaven;
> It hath the primal eldest curse upon 't . . ."

The entire passage of 37 lines moved from him smoothly, with feeling and shadings; Carpenter rated it "unsurpassed by anything I ever witnessed upon the stage." With a natural ease Lincoln then stepped into the character of Richard and gave the famous soliloquy with a power that to Carpenter "made it seem like a new creation." Carpenter laid down palette and brushes, gave a burst of handclapping applause.

To Carpenter he once read aloud his letter to the Owen Lovejoy Monument Association, as though the lines were worth his intoning: "Let him have the marble monument along with the well-assured and more enduring one in the hearts of those who love liberty unselfishly for all men."

In April '61 Lincoln had appointed Mark Delahay to be surveyor general for Kansas and Nebraska. In October '63 Delahay resigned and Lincoln named him U.S. District Judge for Kansas. Letters and speeches against Delahay had to do mainly with his being "so ignorant as a lawyer that no one would employ him," and with his itch for unearned money and his heavy drinking. Yet Lincoln over a powerful opposition drove through the nomination. And the friend to whom Lincoln had shown so unfailing a loyalty began a course of conduct on the Federal bench that resulted eventually in his being impeached on charges of incompetency, corruption, drunkenness on and off the bench, Delahay resigning while the impeachment committee was taking testimony.

Thus ran in brief essentials the course of the only man it was ever known to whom Lincoln promised and paid money for personal political promotion. Whatever the underlying facts, they were probably more essential than any that came to light. One consideration operated. As far back as 1846

Delahay as a Whig party man had worked loyally and actively to nominate and elect Lincoln to Congress. He had come from Kansas to be part of the White House guard in the spring of '61 when mail, telegraph and railroad communication with the outside world were cut off. This loyal activity Lincoln couldn't forget—and there was the vague factor that Delahay's wife was distant kin of Lincoln's beloved stepmother.

Often in subdued corners was talk of Colonel La Fayette C. Baker, chief of the Detective Bureau, a czar of various underworlds. He had 1,000 to 2,000 men operating under his orders, their webs and tentacles flung out among the just and the unjust, his bureau under Stanton. Baker's grandfather, named Remember Baker, was a Revolutionary War captain under Ethan Allen, and his father, named Green Mountain Boy Baker, was a Michigan farmer whose boy went east, then west, to become one of the most active members of the Vigilante Committee that overrode the openly lawless of San Francisco.

Early in the war La Fayette Baker had gone afoot, so he said, to Richmond, and returned with a detailed story of being arrested, jailed and having several interviews with Jefferson Davis during his three-week trip. It became definitely known that he could tell a story to his own advantage, that he could be careless with facts. He was often clever— or again merely glib and loose. Stanton believed him useful in tracing conspiracies and thwarting Confederate spies. His work was naturally such that he made enemies and roused ill will. Welles wrote that from what he had heard and seen Colonel Baker was "wholly unreliable, regardless of character and the rights of persons, incapable of discrimination, and zealous to do something sensational."

Register of the Treasury Lucius E. Chittenden pictured Baker as "cruel and rapacious"; his detectives were put on the rolls "without recommendation, investigation, or any inquiry." Usually the suspect arrested was handcuffed, and brought to Baker's office, then in the basement of the Treasury building. There the suspect was "subjected to a brow-beating examination, in which Baker was said to rival in impudence some heads of the criminal bar," this examination being repeated as often as he, Baker, chose. "Men were kept in his rooms for weeks, without warrant, affidavit, or other semblance of authority. If the accused took any measures for his own protection, he was hurried to the Old Capitol Prison, where he was beyond the reach of the civil authorities.

"Corruption spread like a contagious disease, wherever the operations of these detectives extended . . . Honest manufacturers and dealers, who paid their taxes, were pursued without mercy for the most technical breaches of the law, and were quickly driven out of business. The dishonest rapidly accumulated wealth, which they could well afford to share with their protectors." Turning to a concrete instance, Chittenden wrote of catching Colonel Baker in the act of forgery and "Perfectly unabashed, without a blush, the fellow smiled as he looked me in the face and said, 'That game didn't work, did it?' " This secret-service head once said he had 2,000 men inside and outside Washington, reporting to him their findings, and he at the central controls. Others than Chittenden felt Baker was an ever-lurking evil shadow over the administration.

Baker had a way of talking and writing as though he were a confidant and a trusted operative of the President. "I was sent for by Mr. Lincoln," or "I was summoned to report in person to Mr. Lincoln." Yet there seemed to be no record of the President writing any communication to Baker or to anyone else about Baker, and none of Lincoln's closer associates recorded that he had any intimacy with Baker.

Senator Wilkinson of Minnesota heard presentations to Lincoln by Senators Sumner, Wade and others, hotly urging removal of a prominent official. "The President listened with his head down," noted Wilkinson. "At the conclusion he looked up with a sorrowful face and said, 'Well, gentlemen, it does seem to me that whenever I have a particular friend in office, everybody is down on him.' This ended the matter, and the official was not removed."

Among odd political fish with whom Lincoln dealt was one he named in a note to Stanton in November '63: "I personally wish Jacob R. Freese, of New-Jersey, to be appointed a Colonel for a colored regiment—and this regardless of whether he can tell the exact shade of Julius Caesar's hair." Nothing seemed to come of this. Freese the next year while editing a newspaper in New Jersey wrote to Secretary Chase proposing that he be made collector of revenue in that state. This could be done through Chase removing the man holding the office, who was "a warm Lincoln supporter." Once in office as collector, Freese explained, he could make certain that all Treasury officials would be Chase-for-President workers at the proper time. Furthermore, the office would furnish an excuse for Freese visiting all parts of the state and building a Chase-for-President movement. This didn't seem to interest Chase, possibly because Freese's newspaper never had any real Chase-for-President editorials or news items. In September '64 Lincoln wrote the New Jersey Senator John C. Ten Eyck: "Dr. J. R. Freese, now editor of a leading Union Journal in New-Jersey, resided, for a time, in Illinois, where & when I made his acquaintance, and since when I have enjoyed much of his friendship. He is somewhat wounded with me now, that I do not recognize him as he thinks I ought. I wish to appoint him a Provost-Marshal in your State. May I have your approval?" In the moving stream of politics Lincoln accommodated himself to changing events regardless of the exact shade of Julius Caesar's hair.

Well enough Lincoln knew that two men he had just appointed to nice offices had talked mean about him. On Lamon asking why he should put them in office, he answered that Lamon couldn't *think* one of them to be half as mean as he *knew* him to be. "But I can't run this thing on the theory that every officeholder must think I am the greatest man in the nation."

Several delegations had presented claims, each for his own man to get a forthcoming appointment. And Lincoln one day refused to receive as a caller an old and dear personal friend, because the friend was one of the candidates for the appointment. Carpenter heard his regrets: "If I was less *thin-skinned* about such things, I should get along much better." Another time he had to refuse a sutlership to a soldier who had served three years with an honorable record, because of Stanton saying the place should go to a soldier who had lost an arm or a leg. "I have thousands of applications like this every day," the President was quoted, "but we cannot satisfy all for this reason, that these positions are like office-seekers—there are too many pigs for the tits."

Whitney noted his repeated refusals to a man who wanted appointment as an inspector of army horses, and the final outburst, "I hain't got anything to give you!" In one state two party factions were each pushing for their own man to fill a high position. The President passed by both factions, made an appointment neither faction could criticize, an able army officer who in valiant service had lost a leg.

The phrase "lame duck" entered political lingo. A Western Senator on introducing his successor to Lincoln put in his request for himself to be Commissioner of Indian Affairs. Lincoln cut him short, it was said, and later explained: "I hate to have old friends like the Senator go away. And another thing I usually find out is that a Senator or Representative out of business is a sort of *lame duck*. He has to be provided for."

A Methodist minister, claiming relation to the inventor of ironclad gunboats, wished to be a hospital chaplain. The President could do nothing and said so curtly. The place seeker had heard that such appointments were made by the President. The President made clear: "When there are vacancies I appoint, not without."

Into the hands of Josiah Gilbert Holland, special writer for and one-fourth owner of the Springfield *Republican*, came a letter written by an extraordinary woman who had several interviews with President Lincoln on successive days. Her account of these days achieved a vivid word portrait of a man writhing, elusive, tormented, lighted with awkward humors, using words sometimes to mask his thought. Her account was put in print by Holland.

She was Mrs. Louis Powell Harvey, wife of the Governor of Wisconsin elected in 1861. Her husband was drowned while moving supplies for soldiers wounded in the Battle of Shiloh. She asked Governor Edward Salomon of Wisconsin for permission to visit hospitals in the Western military depot as an agent of the state. Southward along the Mississippi River she visited many general hospitals. She saw Northern boys wasting away in the heat of semitropical summers, noxious and contagious diseases bringing the mortality too high, taking many who might under different climatic and sanitary conditions have lived. She met surgeons appalled at conditions.

She entered alone to find the President alone "in a folded-up sort of way, in his arm-chair." He held her letter, made a feint at rising, looked from under his eyebrows. "Mrs. Harvey?" He took her hand, "hoped she was well," gave no smile of welcome. She read his face, deep-lined, almost stern. He motioned her to a chair. He finished her letter, looked up, ran his fingers through his slightly silvered dark-brown hair. "Madam, this matter of northern hospitals has been talked of a great deal, and I thought it was settled; but it seems this is not the case. What have you got to say about it?"

"Simply this," she replied, "that many soldiers, sick in our western army on the Mississippi, must have northern air, or die. There are thousands of graves along the Mississippi and Yazoo, for which the government is responsible—ignorantly, undoubtedly; but this ignorance must not continue. If you will permit these men to come North, you will have ten men in one year where you have got one now."

Shrugging his shoulders, smiling: "If your reasoning were correct, your argument would be a good one. I don't see how sending one sick man North is going to give us ten well ones." The lady: "You understand me, I think." "Yes, yes," said he, "I understand you; but if they go North they will desert, and where is the difference?" Her reply: "Dead men cannot fight, and they may not desert." "A fine way to decimate the army!" exclaimed the President. "We should never get a man back—not one—not one." "Pardon me," responded the lady, "but I believe you are mistaken. You do not understand our people. They are as true and as loyal to the government as yourself. The loyalty is among the common soldiers, and they are the chief sufferers." Almost with contempt Lincoln replied, "This is your opinion!"

In this exhibition of petulance, were there signs the President saw he was being undermined? "Mrs. Harvey," said he earnestly, "how many men of the Army of the Potomac do you suppose the government was paying at the battle of Antietam? . . ." He threw himself awkwardly around in his chair, with one leg over the arm, and spoke slowly: "This war might have been finished at that time, if every man had been in his place who was able to be there . . . The consequences, you know, proved nearly disastrous." The President paused.

Her response came: "It was very sad; but the delinquents were certainly not in northern hospitals . . ." The President: "Well, well; you go and call on the Secretary of War and see what he says." He then took her letter, and wrote on the back: "Admit Mrs. Harvey at once . . . She is a lady of intelligence, and talks sense. A. Lincoln." "May I return to you, Mr. Lincoln?" she inquired. "Certainly," said he, gently. Then Mrs. Harvey in Mr. Stanton's office was treated with great kindness, but he had to be guided by the medical authorities.

She returned to the President. No one was waiting. She passed directly into the President's room. Mr. Lincoln motioned her to a chair, inquired what the Secretary of War had said to her. She gave him a full account, and added, "I have nowhere to go but to you." He replied: "I will see the Secretary of War myself, to-night; and you may come again in the morning." He then dismissed her, she noted, "in the kindest manner and with the kindest words."

Had he from this moment determined to grant the woman her request? In these interviews he seemed to be arguing against and opposing his own decisions.

In the morning, she returned. The President said good morning, pointed to a chair, seemed annoyed at something, and waited for her to speak. She waited for him. "Well?"

said he, after a minute of delay. "Well?" replied his visitor.

He looked up under his eyebrows, a little startled, and inquired, "Have you nothing to say?" "Nothing," she replied, "until I hear your decision. Have you decided? You know you bade me come this morning." "No, I have not decided; and I believe this idea of northern hospitals is a great humbug, and I am tired of hearing about it."

The woman pitied him in his weak and irritable mood. "I regret to add a feather's weight to your already overwhelming care and responsibility. I would rather have stayed at home." With a feeble smile, he responded, "I wish you had."

She was earnest, and replied: "Nothing would have given me greater pleasure, sir; but a keen sense of duty to this government, justice and mercy to its most loyal supporters, and regard for your honor and position, made me come . . . Mr. Lincoln, I do believe you will yet be grateful for my coming . . . I plead for the lives of those who were the first to hasten to the support of this government, who helped to place you where you are—for men who have done all they could; and now, when flesh and nerve and muscle are gone, who still pray for your life, and the life of the republic. They scarcely ask for that for which I plead. They expect to sacrifice their lives for their country. I know that, if they could come North, they could live, and be well, strong men again—at least many of them. I say I know, because I was sick among them last spring, surrounded by every comfort, with the best of care, and determined to get well. I grew weaker and weaker, day by day, until, not being under military law, my friends brought me North. I recovered entirely by breathing northern air."

Mr. Lincoln's expression of face changed often, but he did not take his eyes from her. He seemed distressed at being convinced she was speaking the truth. His face contracted almost painfully. "You assume to know more than I do." The tears almost came in the woman's eyes. "Pardon me, Mr. Lincoln, I intend no disrespect; but it is because of this knowledge, and because I do know what you do not know, that I come to you. If you had known what I know, and had not already ordered what I ask, I should know that an appeal to you would be in vain; but I believe in you. I believe the people have not trusted you in vain. The question only is—do you believe me, or not? If you believe in me, you will give us hospitals; if not—well."

"You assume to know more than surgeons do," said Lincoln, sharply. "Oh no," she replied: "I could not perform an amputation nearly so well as some of them do! But this is true: I do not come here for your favor. I am no aspirant for military favor or promotion . . . For eight long months —from early morning until late at night, sometimes—I have visited the regimental and general hospitals on the Mississippi, from Quincy to Vicksburg; and I come to you from the cots of men who have died, and who might have lived if you had permitted it. This is hard to say, but it is true."

While she was speaking the last sentences, Lincoln's brow set with hard furrows; a look of pain gathered on his whole face. Then he sharply asked her how many men her state had sent to the field. She replied, "About fifty thousand." "That means," he responded, "that she has about twenty thousand now." With an unpleasant voice and manner he continued. "You need not look so sober; they are not all dead." The veins filled in his face painfully; one across his forehead was fearfully large and blue. Then, with an impatient movement of his whole frame: "I have a good mind to dismiss them all from the service, and have no more trouble with them."

Mrs. Harvey was astonished. She knew he was not in earnest. They sat looking at one another in silence. He had become very pale. At last she broke the silence. "They have been faithful to the government; they have been faithful to you; they will still be loyal to the government, do what you will with them. But, if you will grant my petition, you will be glad as long as you live. The prayers of grateful hearts will give you strength in the hour of trial, and strong and willing arms will return to fight your battles."

The President bowed his head and, with a look of sadness she thought impossible for language to describe, said, *"I shall never be glad any more.*" All severity had passed away from his face, and he seemed looking inward and backward, unconscious that he was not alone. Great burdens he had borne, terrible anxieties that had poisoned his life at the fountain, peaceful scenes he had forever left behind—did these sweep across his memory? And then the added thought that perhaps his mistaken judgment had done injustice to the men who had fought the nation's battles.

The woman said, "Oh! do not say so, Mr. Lincoln, for who will have so much reason to rejoice as yourself, when the government shall be restored—as it will be?" "I know—I know," he said, pressing a hand on either side, "but the springs of life are wearing away, and I shall not last." She asked him if he felt that his great cares were injuring his health. "No," he replied; "not directly, perhaps." She asked him if he slept well. He never was "a good sleeper," he replied, and of course slept now less than ever before.

The woman, feeling that she had occupied too much of his time, rose to take her leave. "Have you decided upon your answer to me?" "No," he replied, "come to-morrow morning:—stop, it is cabinet-meeting to-morrow. Yes, come at twelve o'clock; there is not much for the cabinet to do to-morrow."

The next morning Mrs. Harvey found that her interview had prostrated her, but at twelve o'clock she was at the White House. The President sent her word that the Cabinet would adjourn soon, and that she must wait. For three long hours she waited, receiving occasional messages to the effect that the Cabinet would soon adjourn, and he would then see her.

She was in distress, expecting defeat. She walked the room, and gazed at the maps, and at last she heard the sound of feet. The Cabinet had adjourned. The President did not send for her, but came shuffling into the room, rubbing his hands, and saying, "My dear madam, I am sorry I have kept you waiting so long, but we have this moment adjourned." "My waiting is no matter," she replied, "but you must be very tired, and we will not talk to-night."

Bidding her to a seat, she having risen as he entered, he

sat down at her side, and quietly remarked, "I only wish to say to you that an order which is equivalent to the granting of a hospital in your state, has been issued from the War Department, nearly twenty-four hours."

The woman could make no reply, except through the tears that sprang at once. Lincoln looked on, and enjoyed it. When at last she could command her voice, she said: "God bless you!" Then, as doubts came as to the order, she said earnestly, "Do you mean, really and truly, that we are going to have a hospital now?" With a look full of benevolence and tenderness—such a look, the woman wrote, "as rarely illuminates any face"—he said, "I do most certainly hope so." Then he told her to come on the following morning, and he would give her a copy of the order.

But she was too much affected to talk; and noticing this, he changed the subject, asking her to look at a map which hung in the room, representing the great battlegrounds of Europe. ". . . a great work, whoever executed it. Who was it, Mr. President?" "McClellan," he answered, and added: "He certainly did do this well. He did it while he was at West Point."

Next morning, sick with the excitement through which she had passed, Mrs. Harvey was at the White House again. She found more than 50 persons waiting for an audience; so she sent in her name, and said she would call again. The messenger said he thought the President would see her, and she had better be seated. Soon afterward he informed her that the President would see her. As she passed in, she heard the words from one of the waiting throng: "She has been here six days; and, what is more, she is going to win."

As she entered, the President smiled pleasantly, drew a chair to his side, and said, "Come here, and sit down." As she did so, he handed her a copy of the coveted order. She thanked him, and apologized for not being more promptly at the house; she had been sick all night. "Did joy make you sick?" he inquired. "I suppose," he added, "you would have been mad if I had said 'no.'" She replied, "No, Mr. Lincoln, I should have been neither angry nor sick." "What would you have done?" "I should have been here at nine o'clock this morning." "Well," said he, laughing, "I think I have acted wisely then."

Then he turned suddenly and looked into her face as he said, "Don't you ever get angry?" She replied that she never did when she had an important object to attain. There was more conversation on the naming of the hospital. The woman rose, and said, "You will not wish to see me again." "I did not say that, and I shall not say it," said the President. "You have been very kind to me, and I am very grateful for it."

He looked up at her from under his eyebrows, in his peculiar way, and said, "You almost think I am handsome, don't you?" His face was full of benevolence, and his countenance lighted by a cordial smile; and it was not strange that Mrs. Harvey exclaimed, "You are perfectly lovely to me *now*, Mr. Lincoln." The President colored a little, and laughed a good deal at the impulsive response, and reached out his hand to bid her farewell. She took it reverently, bowed her head upon it, and, bowing, prayed: "God bless you, Abraham Lincoln." Then she turned, heard his good-by and was gone.

Thus ran one transcript, more scrupulously complete and accurate, without a doubt, than perhaps half the accounts of what Lincoln said and did within eyesight and earshot of those who gave the accounts. Her return from the Secretary of War to say "I have nowhere to go but to you" struck him with its simplicity. Her waiting for him to speak was proper. Her "Well?" to his "Well?" could not have been better. To his startled "Have you nothing to say?" came her "Nothing until I hear your decision," the perfect essence of truth. To her abrupt point that she would "rather have stayed at home" than add "a feather's weight" to his overwhelming care, his "I wish you had" was probably with design, as again his later "You assume to know more than I do."

During this third interview in which he told her that he believed her project "a great humbug," everything she asked for had already been granted, an order issued, as he told her the next day, "issued from the War Department, nearly

twenty-four hours." Then in the last one of their interviews
he had been luminous with humor, shining with a benevolent wit, sharing with her the gladness that came through
her tears, refuting his own cry that he would never be glad
again—naïve and bubbling his query "You almost think I
am handsome, don't you?"

Mrs. Harvey went away to be a witness of the building
of the Harvey Hospital at Madison, Wisconsin, named for
her husband, another general hospital at Prairie du Chien,
and still another in Milwaukee—three hospitals resulting
from her interviews with her President.

Had the people and events of those tornado years shaped
Lincoln more and more into a man paradoxically harder
than ever, yet also more delicate and tenuous in human
judgments and affairs? Was there more often a phantom
touch in what he did? Did certain men and women who
studied him either close up or from far away feel that a
strange shade and a ghost, having often a healing power,
moving toward wider and surer human solidarity, lived and
spoke in the White House? For such as there were of these,
who knew an intimacy with Lincoln even when he was at
his loneliest, who were ready to uphold him when they had
no inkling of where his next decision might bring the country—for these one writer tried in *Harper's Weekly* of September 24, 1864, to voice a faith and offer a parable bearing on the election to come in November. This was George
William Curtis, signing his paragraphs with his initials.

He could see a ship torn and worn with a long voyage,
met by head winds and baffling currents. "A feeling of disappointment and despondency takes possession of the pas-
sengers and the crew, and each one attributes to the officer
of the ship the inevitable and necessary delays and discour-
agements . . ." Then the long-wished-for land heaves into
view. "Certainty takes the place of disappointed hopes, and
they feel with mortification and regret how unjust they have
been to the officer whose every hour and thought has been
devoted to their welfare, and who has at length brought

them with safety, and with a prosperous voyage, to the end of their journey."

Beyond parties or partisan success were other motives to which G.W.C. would appeal in this popular pictorial weekly magazine going to nearly all towns of the North and camps of the Union Army. Though no loyal heart could envision Mr. Lincoln replaced "by some other, any other, man," his influence could not end with his discontinuance of power. "There is a fame which no station or absence of station can add to or diminish. His work, like that of the most obscure soldier who lies buried under the sod of Gettysburg or Antietam, has been done . . . Faithful and consecrated to the service of his country, his memory, though it were nameless as that of any private in our armies or any nurse in our hospitals, will, like theirs, be sweet in the heart of every true American . . ."

A San Francisco woman wrote for a home newspaper of how she quoted for Lincoln a line from Starr King's burial speech for Ned Baker—"Hither in future ages they shall bring . . . the sacred ashes of the advocate and soldier of liberty"—and of how in evening mist among the Soldiers' Home trees Lincoln kindled to the picture of a grand procession in solemn hush winding its way through street crowds of San Francisco on up the heights to the open grave on Lone Mountain. "It seemed to rise before them out of the quiet sea, a vast mausoleum from the hand of God, wherein to lay the dead."

There amid grasses where sea wind and land wind met they had laid for his long sleep the old and treasured friend whose death at Ball's Bluff had meant tears and grief to Lincoln. Now, thought the woman, this weary though lighted and strange man, Lincoln, seemed almost to be dreaming of rest for himself sometime, perhaps in envy of the rest that had come to the bright and daring Ned Baker. He gave a eulogy of his old friend "in a few deep-toned words."

Chapter 37

Election Day, November 8, 1864

Of November 8, 1864, the day of the national election, John Hay wrote that the White House was "still and almost deserted." The sky hung gray. Rain fell. About noon Brooks called on the President "and to my surprise found him entirely alone, as if by common consent everybody had avoided the White House." Lincoln had no ease, saying to Brooks: "I am just enough of a politician to know that there was not much doubt about the result of the Baltimore convention; but about this thing I am very far from being certain. I wish I were certain."

At seven o'clock that evening Lincoln with Hay stepped out of the White House into a night of wild rain and storm. They splashed across the grounds to the War Department telegraph office. At a side door a wet and steaming sentinel huddled in a rubber coat. As Lincoln entered the second-floor telegraph office a dispatch was put in his hands from Forney at Philadelphia claiming 10,000 majority there. "Forney," said Lincoln, "is a little excitable." To Mrs. Lincoln he sent over early reports, saying, "She is more anxious than I."

In Stanton's office later Lincoln saw Gustavus Vasa Fox in glee over two hated opponents beaten. "You have more of that feeling of personal resentment than I," said Lincoln, Hay noted. "Perhaps I may have too little of it, but I never thought it paid. A man has not time to spend half his life in quarrels. If any man ceases to attack me, I never remember the past against him."

The wires worked badly because of the rain-and-wind storm. In a long lull about ten, wrote Brooks, "The President amused the little company in the War Office with entertaining reminiscences and anecdotes." In and out moved Eckert, handing telegrams to Stanton, the President then studying them and commenting. "Presently there came a lull in the returns," wrote Charles A. Dana of the evening, "and Mr. Lincoln called me to a place by his side.

" 'Dana,' said he, 'have you ever read any of the writings of Petroleum V. Nasby?' 'No, sir,' I said: 'I have only looked at some of them, and they seemed to be quite funny.' 'Well,' said he, 'let me read you a specimen'; and, pulling out a thin yellow-covered pamphlet from his breast pocket, he began to read aloud. Mr. Stanton viewed these proceedings with great impatience, as I could see, but Mr. Lincoln paid no attention to that. He would read a page or a story, pause to consider a new election telegram, and then open the book again and go ahead with a new passage . . .

"Mr. Stanton went to the door and beckoned me into the next room. I shall never forget the fire of his indignation . . . that when the safety of the republic was thus at issue . . . the leader, the man most deeply concerned . . . could turn aside to read such balderdash and to laugh at such frivolous jests was, to his mind, repugnant, even damnable. He could not understand, apparently, that . . . this was Mr. Lincoln's prevailing characteristic—that the safety and sanity of his intelligence were maintained and preserved."

As the evening wore on the wires worked badly from Illinois and from states west of the Mississippi. The returns in, however, were running close to the tabulation Lincoln had made weeks before of his own estimates. Toward midnight, noted Brooks, "It was certain that Lincoln had been re-elected, and the few gentlemen left in the office congratulated him very warmly on the result. Lincoln took the matter very calmly, showing not the least elation or excitement, but said that he would admit that he was glad to be relieved of all suspense, grateful that the verdict of the people was likely to be so full, clear, and unmistakable that there could be no dispute." At a midnight supper, Hay noted, "The President went awkwardly and hospitably to work shovelling out the fried oysters." It was two in the morning when he started to leave the War Office, at the door meeting serenaders with a brass band, with cheers calling for a speech. The rain, the storm, was over.

The President told them, "I earnestly believe that the consequences of this day's work, if it be as you assure me and as now seems probable, will be to the lasting advantage, if not to the very salvation, of the country . . . I do not impugn the motives of any one opposed to me. It is no pleasure to me to triumph over any one; but I give thanks to the Almighty for this evidence of the people's resolution to stand by free government and the rights of humanity."

A day of great fate was over. There was no going behind the returns. Complete tabulations yet to come were a mere formality. At thousands of polling places some 4,000,000 men had marked ballots. A nation had made a decision.

Chaos, hate, suspicion, mistrust, vengeance, dark doubts, were in the air. But the marking, handling, counting, of the ballots went on in quiet and good order, fraud or violence showing only in minor incidents. The miscounts and repeaters were only ordinary. Free speech and license to print were so operating that either side would have flared forth about any flagrant departure from the customary election methods.

The American electorate, "the People," spoke on whether a colossal, heavy, weary war should go on, under the same leadership as it had begun, on whether the same guiding mind and personality should keep the central control and power. On a day of rain and wind that wrecked telegraph systems, the people said Yes to Lincoln.

Brooks directly quoted Lincoln as saying the day after: "I should be the veriest shallow and self-conceited blockhead upon this footstool if, in my discharge of the duties which are put upon me in this place, I should hope to get along without the wisdom which comes from God and not from men."

The election returns when analyzed admonished humility. In the Electoral College vote, all the Northern States except Kentucky, Delaware and New Jersey went to Lincoln. But it was not so sweeping a triumph in the total of popular ballots. They gave Lincoln a majority of slightly more than

400,000. The votes for Lincoln from coast to coast, 2,203,-831, represented 55.09 per cent of all that were cast, said *Appleton's Annual Cyclopaedia* for 1864. McClellan had 44.91 per cent of the total: between New York and San Francisco were 1,797,019 male voters opposed to Lincoln, his administration and his policies. In New York City McClellan carried by 78,746 against Lincoln's 36,673; in the Empire State Lincoln won with 50.47 per cent of the vote as against McClellan's 49.53 per cent. It was formidable that 212 of the Electoral College votes should go to Lincoln, with McClellan getting only 21. But a study of three states with the largest electoral votes, New York, Pennsylvania and Ohio, showed Lincoln receiving 930,269 to 843,862 for McClellan, a difference of only 86,407 votes, but giving Lincoln 80 in the Electoral College. Had these three key states by their narrow margin gone for McClellan and been joined by two or three other states, McClellan would have been elected.

Humility was counseled even in the one little news bulletin: "The official majority of votes cast for General McClellan in Mr. Lincoln's own county of Sangamon, Illinois, is 376." Also a study of Illinois returns showed that every county bounding Sangamon had gone for McClellan and against Lincoln. But in the one spot in the returns where Lincoln's heart would have been sore had not the ballots thundered and roared high for him—the soldier vote—he won home big, the forecast being fulfilled that they would vote as they shot.

Grant wired from City Point, "The victory is worth more to the country than a battle won." General Frank Blair wrote to Hay from Georgia, where he headed an army corps under Sherman, "The vote in this army today is almost unanimous for Lincoln. Give Uncle Abe my compliments."

And highlighted in the background of Lincoln's victory was the fact that hundreds of thousands of soldiers whose ballots would have been given to the President had no chance to vote, either because of required marching and fighting, or because their home-state legislatures had refused them the right of voting in the field. And in the foul rooms of Libby Prison at Richmond the votes were 276 for Lincoln, 95 for McClellan.

On the night of November 10 a procession with banners, lanterns, transparencies marched to the White House, surged around the main entrance and filled the front grounds. The newly elected President stepped out of a window opening on the north portico and the crowd uproar was many minutes going down. Lincoln made ready to read his script to the people. Hay stood alongside with a candle to light the written page. "Not very graceful," he smiled to Hay, "but I am growing old enough not to care much for the manner of doing things."

"It has long been a grave question," Lincoln began, under the night stars, "whether any government, not *too* strong for the liberties of its people, can be strong *enough* to maintain its own existence, in great emergencies. On this point the present rebellion brought our republic to a severe test . . . the election was a necessity. We can not have free government without elections; and if the rebellion could force us to forego, or postpone a national election, it might fairly claim to have already conquered and ruined us . . . Human-nature will not change. In any future great national trial, compared with the men of this, we shall have as weak, and as strong; as silly and as wise; as bad and good . . . Gold is good in its place; but living, brave, patriotic men, are better than gold."

He voiced the human spirit he would prefer to have breathing across the future. "So long as I have been here I have not willingly planted a thorn in any man's bosom. While I am deeply sensible to the high compliment of a re-election; and duly grateful, as I trust, to Almighty God for having directed my countrymen to a right conclusion, as I think, for their own good, it adds nothing to my satisfaction that any other man may be disappointed or pained by the result . . . And now, let me close by asking three hearty cheers for our brave soldiers and seamen and their gallant and skilfull commanders." The applause and cheers roared. Then slowly the faces, lights and voices dwindled. The

White House lawn took on its accustomed night shadows of trees, fences, buildings, and silence.

The outlook Lincoln had voiced was toward conciliation —no retaliation, no reprisals, no thorns knowingly planted in the bosoms of others. On November 11 at the Cabinet meeting the President took from his desk the folded and pasted memorandum that Cabinet members had signed August 23 without knowing what it said. He read it with its now odd-sounding statement of probability "that this Administration will not be re-elected."

On Election Day McClellan resigned as a major general in the Regular Army. To fill this vacancy Lincoln signed a commission for General Philip H. Sheridan. McClellan began on his plans for a trip to Europe, which would keep him away from the American scene and its war for many months.

The Charleston *Mercury* on November 22 printed Lincoln's speech of November 10, in full. The news item preceding the speech read: "The Abolition Clubs of Washington went to Lincoln's White House on Thursday evening, and, after firing off a cannon, proceeded to hurrah, etc., until the Gorilla came out and made the following speech." Confederate newspapers in the main interpreted for their readers the election of Lincoln as an advantage to their cause. A Richmond *Sentinel* commentary held: "There are some names more odious among us even than that of Abraham Lincoln. We know Seward as a snake, a cunning plotter of mischief and contriver of frauds wherever his faith is pledged. We know Sumner as a mouthing thunderer of great words, but of weak spine and trembling knees. We know Butler as a beast. Compared with these detestable qualities Mr. Lincoln's joking propensities appear, if puerile, yet harmless. If they excite our contempt, they yet appeal to our good nature."

A cartoon in *Harper's Weekly,* titled "Long ABRAHAM LINCOLN a little Longer," stretched Lincoln's length of form till he soared to an impossible height.

Overseas that political fraction known as liberals had

relief and joy over Lincoln's re-election. In France, said the *Journal des débats*, "It is the first time that a people in possession of universal suffrage has been called to pronounce directly and finally for or against the continuation of a painful war." Never in any other land, it seemed, had a people in the waste and anguish of war voted Yes or No, freely and without hindrance, whether a war should go on.

The *Spectator* of London, November 26, saw the North had pronounced by a majority that "though its land be covered with hospitals and its cities filled with bankrupts, though every family weep for its sons and the course of material civilization be thrown back centuries, it is ready to fight manfully on rather than freedom should be proved a chimera . . . Had the North shrunk, or even faltered, had she refused the necessary sacrifices or accepted the evil compromise, the cause of liberty would have received a heavy, perhaps a deadly wound." New England, the West, the great States of New York and Pennsylvania, had declared that Mr. Lincoln, "this shrewd peasant with his noble purpose and his deadly tenacity, expresses their resolve; that despite endless charges of oppression and occasional realities of failure, despite uncouthness and occasional want of tact, he is the fitting mouth-piece of the nation in its struggle for life or death." The *Spectator* writer from his long-distance view listed the mighty factors of advantage that lay with Lincoln. "He is securely President until March, 1869." Victory now needed only persistence. "And persistence is the one quality Mr. Lincoln is certain not to lack."

Consul Bigelow in Paris wrote November 22 of Lincoln's election as ". . . more significant than is realized even in America . . . more worthy of a National thanksgiving than any event, humanly speaking, which has occurred since the Revolution."

Grant's telegram to Lincoln held true. The November election counted for more than a great battle won. It answered many questions. Would the war go on? Yes, more brutally than before. Would conscription go on? Yes, and with less outspoken opposition. Those claiming free speech and a free press? They would be less noisy and foul, though not giving up old habits. Some were a little stunned and helpless.

"Our people are excited," read a telegram November 25 from Governor Curtin, "by a rumor that three States have offered to return to their allegiance. Is it true?" Lincoln's instant and positive reply: "I have no knowledge, information, or belief, that three States, or any state, offer to resume allegiance."

The morning after Election Day Hay's diary recorded: "W. H. L. [Ward Hill Lamon] came to my room to talk over the Chief Justiceship . . . He took a glass of whiskey and then, refusing my offer of a bed, went out &, rolling himself up in his cloak, lay down at the President's door; passing the night in that attitude of touching and dumb fidelity, with a small arsenal of pistols & bowie knives around him. In the morning he went away leaving my blankets at my door, before I or the President were awake."

Chapter 38

Lincoln Names a Chief Justice

Who would be named as Chief Justice? In the press, in political circles, across tea cups and over whisky toddies, there was guess and gossip. Of the eminent New York attorney William M. Evarts, Justice Swayne, Justice David Davis, there was public mention. Attorney General Bates modestly and privately mentioned in his diary that his appointment would be a fitting close to his career. Fessenden said for himself he could not consent. Browning wrote: "Called on the President and urged on him the appointment of Mr. Stanton as chief Justice. He said nothing in reply to what I urged except to admit Mr. Stantons ability, and fine qualifications."

Formidable pressure arose for Montgomery Blair. James Gordon Bennett and Thurlow Weed, an odd team of editors, went to Washington and held a conference with Blair on how to stop Chase, whom everyone considered in the lead.

Across November the President heard a series of delegations and individual callers and gave them no committals. Union League Club men from Philadelphia spoke for Chase, and read a signed memorial. The President replied: "Will you do me the favor to leave that paper with me? I want it in order that, if I appoint Mr. Chase, I may show the friends of the other persons for whom the office is solicited by how powerful an influence and by what strong personal recommendations the claims of Mr. Chase were supported." The Union Leaguers, pleased and satisfied at this, then noticed the President had not finished. He had merely paused. Now he went on. "And I want the paper also in order that, if I should appoint any other person, I may show his friends how powerful an influence and what strong personal recommendations I was obliged to disregard in appointing him." The Philadelphians walked out knowing no more than when they came.

Richard Henry Dana and Judge E. R. Hoar called together and told Lincoln that if, as rumor had it, he had determined to appoint Chase they would not proceed to suggest other men. Lincoln replied, Judge Hoar wrote: "Mr. Chase is a very able man. He is a very ambitious man and I think on the subject of the presidency a little insane. He has not always behaved very well lately and people say to me, 'Now is the time to *crush him out*.' Well, I'm not in favor of crushing anybody out! If there is anything that a man can do and do it well, I say let him do it. Give him a chance."

Chase personally seemed to have high hopes at first. Later he was not so sure what the President would do. Days passed into weeks. The deliberation of the President seemed ominous to Chase. Behind the scenes it seemed that Lincoln had only one distinct doubt and this he spoke to one after another of those who came to the front for Chase. He considered sending for Chase to see whether he would dismiss at once and forever the Presidency from his mind. But when Lincoln broached this to Sumner, noted Nicolay and Hay, "he saw in a moment's conversation how liable to misapprehension such action would be . . . the construction which Mr. Chase would inevitably place upon such a proposition coming from his twice successful rival."

When one day Nicolay brought a letter from Chase, Lincoln asked, "What is it about?" "Simply a kind and friendly letter." Lincoln, without reading it and with a shrewd smile: "File it with his other recommendations."

From active enemies of Chase in Ohio came spoken and written protests against his appointment. From Treasury Department officials, from the Blair and other groups, came many descriptions of Chase as too partisan, too ignorant of men, too much of a grumbler and a marplot. Nicolay and Hay noted the President heard with respect any points of merit they had against Chase but when they tried to remind him of how and when Chase had sought to undermine him, "he sternly checked them." The secretaries believed Lincoln intended from the first to appoint Chase. To Nicolay he said, using boyhood Kentucky lingo, "I shall be very 'shut pan' about this matter."

The young Illinois Congressman Shelby M. Cullom heard of Chase letters with mean insinuations about Lincoln being offered for the President's reading and of his comment, "If Mr. Chase has said some hard things about me, I in turn have said some hard things about him, which, I guess, squares the account." And on another occasion, "I know meaner things about Mr. Chase than any of these men can tell me."

Congress had assembled. On December 6, at whatever risk and not unaware there were risks, guided by joined motives of statecraft and political balances, the President named Chase for Chief Justice.

"He communicated his intention to no one," noted his secretaries, and wrote out the nomination with his own hand. Without reference to a committee and with no discussion the Senate at once unanimously confirmed the appointment. Chase wrote to the President: "Before I sleep I must thank you for this mark of your confidence, and especially for the manner in which the nomination was made."

Congressman John B. Alley, so he wrote, had entered the President's library to hear Lincoln: "Although I may have appeared to you and to Mr. Sumner to have been opposed to Chase's appointment, there never has been a moment since the breath left old Taney's body that I did not conceive it to be the best thing to do to appoint Mr. Chase . . ." Alley repeated that the action was magnanimous and patriotic. Lincoln: "As to his talk about me, I do not mind that. Chase is, on the whole, a pretty good fellow and a very able man. His only trouble is that he has 'the White House fever' a little too bad, but I hope this may cure him and that he will be satisfied."

Nicolay and Hay saw Chase take his place on the bench with a conscientious desire to do his whole duty in his great office, and yet, "He still considered himself called upon to counteract the mischievous tendencies of the President towards conciliation and hasty reconstruction. His slighting references to him [the President] in his [Chase's] letters and diaries continued from the hour he took his place on the bench." Chase had been especially pressed upon the President by the radical antislavery wing of their party. Lincoln for his own political reasons was giving them what they wanted. He was hoping for more harmony toward his own plans for reconstruction in the South.

As the author of the National Bank Act, as an acquaintance of August Belmont who proposed in the summer of '64 the conditions under which he [Chase] would join the Democratic party, as a man of "a certain solid weight of character," Chase was not offensive to a large section of conservatives. The appointment, once made, met with little opposition, and, noted Nicolay and Hay, was "received with the greatest satisfaction throughout the Union."

Were the lines being more sharply drawn for a more continuous challenge by Congress of the executive power? It seemed so when in latter November Attorney General Bates resigned because of age and long service and the President sent to the Senate the appointment of James Speed of Kentucky. This brother of Joshua Speed, Lincoln's old bosom friend, had been an outspoken Union loyalist from the first, raised troops, and served to keep Kentucky in the Union. As an able attorney his record was unspotted.

The Senate Judiciary Committee held up the President's nomination several days, according to Noah Brooks, not because they hesitated at confirming Speed, but, as one of that committee said, "to convey a mild insinuation to the President that they did not know who James Speed of Kentucky was."

The somber and dignified old Supreme Court was filled to its limits December 15 with people who came to see Chase sworn in. The new Chief Justice read the oath of office in a clear but tremulous voice. Then, laying down the paper, he lifted his right hand, looked upward to the noble dome, and with deep feeling, "So help me God." Over the room was a breathless hush. The Chief Justice took his seat.

In the Buckeye State some who had long known Salmon P. Chase politically were unkind enough to recall a saying they had heard from him—"Be satisfied with skim milk when you can't get cream."

Chapter 39

The "Lost Army" — The South in Fire and Blood — War Prisons

In late '64, observers in America and Europe hung breathless and wondering over the audacity and fate of a general and an army that had vanished. To his wife the head of this adventure wrote that he would come out of it reputed a great general or just plain crazy. Sherman had not seen the newborn baby who had arrived at his home in June. The baby would die while he was gone, while millions were wondering where he was, and he would accept this as war.

"If you can whip Lee," Sherman had written in September to Grant as between family men, "and I can march to the Atlantic, I think Uncle Abe will give us a twenty days' leave of absence to see the young folks." This he was writing in Georgia, where he had taken Atlanta. Nearby was Hood's army, which Jefferson Davis was saying had every advantage of being on home ground, so that it would yet cut Sherman's communications and destroy Sherman. To Grant, Sherman offered his plan. He would divide his army, give Thomas 60,000 with which to take care of Hood's 41,000, and then himself start on a thousand-mile march which was to end by joining Grant in Virginia, pausing at Savannah-by-the-Sea.

Thousands of people abroad and in the South would reason, wrote Sherman, "If the North can march an army right through the South it is proof positive that the North can prevail in this contest . . . Mr. Lincoln's election, which is assured, coupled with the conclusion thus reached, makes a logical whole."

Grant wired Lincoln: "Sherman's proposition is the best that can be adopted . . . Such an army as Sherman has, and with such a commander, is hard to corner or capture." This seemed to be a day of acid test for Lincoln on whether he would get behind his two best proven generals. Within three hours after Grant's telegram arrived, Stanton telegraphed Sherman complete approval.

It seemed as though Grant trusted Sherman completely, except for a day or two of wavering on the point of Sherman's faith that Thomas could take care of Hood. In the end Grant decided he would accept Sherman's judgment of what Thomas could do. And Lincoln, with his natural caution enforced by the bitter opposition of Grant's chief of staff, Rawlins, and by Halleck's placid routine disapproval, had nevertheless thrown himself into complete trust of Grant and Sherman. This trio of Lincoln, Grant and Sherman now worked in a co-operation as smooth as that which had long existed between Lee and Davis.

When Grant had heard of steps Lincoln was taking in

Georgia in September toward beginnings of reconstruction, he had wired Stanton, "Please advise the President not to attempt to doctor up a State government for Georgia by the appointment of citizens in any capacity whatever. Leave Sherman to treat all questions in his own way, the President reserving his power to approve or disapprove of his actions." And Lincoln had accepted Grant's wish for him to go slow in any "doctoring" of state governments where Union armies were operating.

Sherman had not intended to burn as much of Atlanta as did burn. His chief engineer under orders wrecked all railroads in and about Atlanta, heated the rails red hot and twisted them around trees. Then smokestacks were pulled down, furnace arches broken, steam machinery smashed, holes punched in all boilers, all devices of industrial production wrecked against possible use. Before this work had begun, firebugs had set in flame a score of buildings, General Slocum offering a reward of $500 for the detection of any soldier involved. Atlanta buildings, 1,800, went up in smoke.

Sherman rode into the city with an aide near sunset November 15. Roses still bloomed in a few gardens of fine houses and Atlanta was a quiet city, not soothed but calm with a hint of heavy fate. The night held little quiet as an engineer corps fired more fallen buildings, as flames spread to a wrecked arsenal and shell explosions rattled the windows of hundreds of homes where no sleepers lay to be awakened. A fire department of soldiers struggled several hours of the night, managing to hold the fire mainly to the downtown and industrial districts, as intended. When Sherman rode out of the city at seven the next morning, a third, perhaps more, of Atlanta lay in ashes.

Toward the east and southward, toward Savannah and the Atlantic Ocean, toward a path that was to twist upward in the Carolinas, Sherman turned his horse. He knew this country. He had crossed many parts of it and lived in it several years of the 1840's. The ways of its people had been under his eye in part when he was superintendent of the Louisiana State Military Academy. The Macon *Telegraph* called him Judas Iscariot, a betrayer, a creature of depravity, a demon "of a thousand fiends."

Toward the east by the Decatur road Sherman paused on a hill and took a last look at smoking Atlanta. On the horizons around him a bright sun slanted down on the shining rifles of 55,000 picked men, veterans of proved capacity for action, for marching, for legwork, for many disease immunities, survivors of hard campaigns. Each man carried 40 rounds of cartridges, and in wagons were enough more to make 200 rounds per man. The sun slanted too on 65 cannon, each drawn by four teams of horses. Six-mule wagons, 2,500 of them, hauled supplies and forage. And 600 ambulances, two horses to each, were prepared for battle service. Between Sherman and his friend Grant at Richmond lay a thousand miles of cities and towns, lands, swamps and rivers, alive with a bitterly hostile people hating with a deepening despair.

To his wife Sherman had written less than a month before that in revolutions men fall and rise, are praised and then insulted. He was in a dark mood, writing: "Grant, Sheridan and I are now the popular favorites, but neither of us will survive this war. Some other must rise greater than either of us, and he has not yet manifested himself." Of the cheery soldiers singing in sun-bright weather on the start from Atlanta he was to write her: "I never saw a more confident army. The soldiers think I know everything and that they can do anything." In late October he had written her he was on a hazardous feat. "And you will not hear from me for months. The War Department will know my whereabouts, and the Rebels, and you will be able to guess."

This army had 218 regiments, all but 33 from Western States, 52 from Ohio, 50 from Illinois, 27 from Indiana, 13 from Wisconsin, 10 from Michigan, 15 from Iowa, 3 from Minnesota, 10 from Missouri, 4 from Kentucky. From New York were 16 regiments, from Pennsylvania 10, from New Jersey 3, from Massachusetts and Connecticut 2 each. They would be heard from—sometime. The word of Sherman to Grant, to the War Department and the President, was that communications were cut off from central Georgia and his next message he hoped to send from somewhere on the Atlantic Coast.

Starting November 15, marching in four columns sweeping a path 20 to 40 or more miles wide, this army began a systematic campaign of destruction. "The State of Georgia alone," Jefferson Davis had said in a recent speech in Augusta, "produces food enough not only for her own people and the army within but feeds too the Army of Virginia." On this storehouse and granary of the Confederacy worked the destroyers. What the army could not eat or carry away it burned, spoiled, ruined.

Now they had their war, was Sherman's thought, the war they had asked for. Until now the Border States had taken the punishment. Now it had come to the doorsills of the Deep South. Now sometimes you couldn't see the roses and the magnolia trees for the depot and warehouse smoke, for the dust of marching columns and rumbling wagons.

An argument began, to last long. Was Sherman a modern impersonation of Attila the Hun, a manner of sadist, a wanton and a monster who took pleasure in seeing an enemy people suffer? Or was he a soldier doing a necessary job, a kindhearted family man who wanted to end the war and saw no other way but the tactics he was using? Both sides made out a case. Wrote Sherman, ". . . the rebels . . . had forced us into the war, and . . . deserved all they got and *more*."

His conscience worried Sherman less than his sense of timing. He and Grant would join their armies some day, if their timing was right. Then the war would end. He traveled light. The saddlebags which his orderly carried held "a change of underclothing, my maps, a flask of whiskey, and a bunch of cigars." He could live as plainly as rank-and-file soldiers; they had seen him sleep in his blanket on cold ground. He watched over details till midnight and past, was out early in the morning, made up lost sleep sometimes with 10- and 15-minute naps on the ground during the day. When his troops had orders to do things that at first seemed impossible they said, "Well, *he* can't make a mistake."

A line of bridges on fire toward the rear one day, a private grunted comfortably, "Guess, Charley, Sherman has set the river on fire," Charley answering, "Well, if he has, I reckon it's all right." A stock anecdote had it that two Confederates on outpost duty were overheard trading rumors. "The Yanks can't get any more rations by railroad, for Wheeler has blown up the tunnel at Dalton." "Oh, hell, don't you know Sherman carries along a duplicate tunnel?"

Of the railroad-wrecking, wrote Sherman, "I gave it my personal attention." Bonfires were made of crossties, the iron rails laid on and when red hot carried to telegraph poles or trees and twisted around to make what were nicknamed "Sherman hairpins," though sometimes called "Lincoln gimlets." Or again they were "Jeff Davis neckties." A month of this and 265 miles of railway were *un*built.

Each brigade commander had authority to detail a forage company, usually about 50 men headed by one or two commissioned officers. Before daylight this party would leave, knowing where to rejoin their command on the march later in the day. On foot five or six miles from the brigade route, they visited every plantation and farm within range. On a farm wagon or a family carriage they loaded bacon, corn meal, turkeys, ducks, chickens, "everything that could be used as food or forage," to use Sherman's words. They regained the main road, usually in advance of their wagon train, and delivered to the brigade commissary the day's supplies gathered.

Candidly Sherman admitted, "No doubt, many acts of pillage, robbery and violence, were committed by these parties of foragers, usually called 'bummers.' " Stories came to him of jewelry taken from women, of family silverware dug up from hiding places, and of plunder of value that never reached the commissary. "But these acts were exceptional and incidental. I never heard of any cases of murder or rape." The unruly and the malicious would get out of hand, and in his official report to the War Department Sherman wrote of this hoodlum element, "A little loose in foraging they 'did some things they ought not to have done.' "

Yet no careful reading was required of the criticisms voiced by Governor Brown and General Beauregard the previous August to see they meant to say that the Confederate cavalry under General Wheeler had its own bummers. Robert Toombs then was writing to Stephens that Wheeler's band "consumes more than the whole army," was helping "accelerate the evil day," and as to their Confederate commander, Wheeler, "I hope to God he will never get back to Georgia." A letter to Secretary Seddon published in the Charleston *Mercury* went into many particulars of this Confederate unit having plunderers who took carpets, blankets, furniture in private houses, "by force in the presence of the owners."

Kilpatrick's cavalry did more than any other unit to earn a bad name for Sherman's army. They did lay hands on old men and choke them till the secret hiding places of coin, silver or jewelry were divulged. They did put their dirty boots on white bed linen, dance on polished floors to the piano music of howling comrades, smash the piano with gun butts. They did drag feather beds outdoors and scatter the feathers like a small snowstorm. They did scare women, though the incidence of rape was not conclusive in more than one or two cases. They did make free with Negro women and set special value on shapely mulattoes. But they were veteran troopers, hard fighters. Sherman tolerated them, partly because of his own belief that as tough soldiers for loyal active service they were among the best the earth had ever seen, partly because to set up a military police to watch and discipline his own men would delay when delay might be at heavy cost.

How many hundreds or thousands of stragglers, skulkers and deserters from the Confederate Army there were at this time in Georgia could not get into official records; in Georgia and all the Southern and Border States were roving bands of bushwhackers and guerrillas, lawless, desperate, living on the country. General Lee, seeing his losses by desertion on the increase in latter '64, suggested to President Davis it might be advisable to serve notice that deserters would have their rights to citizenship and property taken away. Governor Vance of North Carolina had the same year given out a long and fierce malediction on "the vile wretch who skulked in the woods, or the still viler coward who aided him, while his bleeding country was calling in vain for his help," telling them they must consider what their brave comrades would do to them when peace and independence were secured. "Ye that shelter, conceal, and feed these miserable depredators, think you that you will be spared? Nay! Never-failing eyes have marked you, every one." Misdeeds near to atrocities had been committed, according to Vance's proclamation.

In more than one case deserters said they had heard that if Lincoln was elected in November the war would be over, that it was common talk that with Lincoln President again the South would quit fighting. Many rumors of the Confederacy being on its last legs encouraged desertion. Union commanders circulated Lincoln's proclamation offering amnesty. Across picket posts, through printed circulars, by means open and secret, the report spread that deserters into the Union lines would meet good treatment. That the earlier Confederate unity was breaking, that cracks and seams had come in their governmental structure, was known to the Georgians, who saw their state legislature joined with those of Mississippi and North Carolina in refusals to take as constitutional the act of their Congress at Richmond in suspending the writ of habeas corpus. And timed with Sherman's march from Atlanta toward the sea ran the rumor that President Davis was to be impeached. It was not a harmonious Confederate Georgia over which Sherman was laying devastation. Daily as Sherman's troops swung along on the march came remarks from sidewalks, from roadsides. Most often there was silence. But General Hazen noted that the most typical expression from the Georgians was: "Why don't you go over to South Carolina and serve them this way? They started it."

One of Sherman's staff men wrote of seeing a black woman, holding a mulatto baby, point at Sherman with the cry, "Dar's de man dat rules de world!" At many a crossroads the Negroes came singing and cavorting in a faith that now their masters were overcome and the long-promised emancipation was at hand. Sherman however continued his former policy of telling them that in the right and proper hour to come they would have freedom to work for themselves instead of their masters, that they must not now harm their masters. "We don't want that." To Grant's advice that he should acquire Negroes and arm and organize them as best he could, Sherman paid no attention. In a plantation house at the crossing of the Ulcofauhatchee River he explained to an old, gray-haired Negro, "of as fine a head as I ever saw," that "we wanted the slaves to remain where they were, and not to load us down with useless mouths, which would eat up the food for our fighting men; that our success was their assured freedom; that we could receive a few of their young, hearty men as pioneers; but that if they followed us in swarms of old and young, feeble and helpless, it would simply cripple us in our great task." Sherman believed that this old man spread this message far, got it carried from mouth to mouth to an extent that saved the army from taking on a host of refugees that might have spelled famine. Some 25,000 Negroes in all, it was estimated, from time to time joined the army and were fed by it, three-fourths of them perhaps turning back homesick or unwilling or unable to stand the pace.

One raw, cold night Sherman found himself in a double-hewed log house, saw a box marked "Howell Cobb," learned from Negroes he was in the home of a Confederate brigadier general, onetime U.S. Senator from Georgia, Secretary of the U.S. Treasury under Buchanan. "Of course, we confiscated his property, and found it rich in corn, beans, peanuts, and sorghum-molasses." Sherman sent word to a staff general "to spare nothing," and that night on the Cobb plantation huge bonfires blazed.

Arriving next day at the state capital, Milledgeville, they found Governor Joseph Brown, the state officials, and the members of the legislature gone, the Governor's mansion stripped of carpets, curtains, furniture, food. Here Federal troops used stacks of Confederate paper money for a break-fast fire. Here Federal officers held a mock session in the state legislative chamber, repealed the Ordinance of Secession, voted the state back into the Union, made sarcastic speeches, and appointed a committee officially to kick the buttocks of Governor Brown and President Davis. Here were late newspapers from over the South, one having an appeal from General Beauregard to the people of Georgia to arise, obstruct, be confident, be resolute, and "Sherman's army will soon starve in your midst." Also a proclamation from Senator B. H. Hill, cosigned at Richmond by Secretary of War Seddon, that with firm and prompt action, "You have now the best opportunity ever presented to destroy the enemy." And while Sherman in Milledgeville read these and other items, thousand of bales of cotton got the torch, many cotton gins and presses were wrecked, and as Sherman reported, "I burned the railroad buildings and the arsenals; the statehouse and Governor's Mansion I left unharmed." That Governor Brown had transported the cabbages from his cellar and left the state archives for the invaders was taken by Sherman as a sign of a hurried departure, if nothing more.

The marching army moved on, no pauses, no days of rest, feeding on the fat of the land with a more savory bill of fare than any army during the war thus far. "It was gravy every day." Juicy steaks, pork chops, fried chicken, ham and eggs, yams rolled in Indian meal, sorghum syrup—at moments the war was a picnic and a frolic. Not so of course when the route shifted from east southward toward Savannah, when ground under the feet of one column heaved in explosion and several men were torn by shells and torpedoes, whereupon Sherman ordered Confederate prisoners to be marched ahead. They accommodated and dug up a line of buried torpedoes.

Sherman's army feinted toward the cities of Augusta and Macon, made no real move at them, slipped smoothly past them. No time now for the taking of cities. Confederate cavalry detached from Hood's army skirmished a little with Sherman's advance but undertook no real clash with the

Union horse troops under Kilpatrick. The convicts, on Sherman's approach let loose from the state prison at Milledgeville for military service, were no help to further good order in Georgia that month. Some of them, joined up with deserters, drifters, bushwhackers, posed as Wheeler's cavalry and raided here and there for loot. "People show little spirit," wired a defending general from Augusta to Richmond. There and at Macon were the only signs of any organized resistance to Sherman, and at these spots Sherman refused to pause. At Macon "every man was in the trenches," said the Augusta *Constitutionalist*, adding that when members of the state legislature passed through the city they were arrested and an attempt made to put them in military service. "But they were exempt by law and refused to serve."

Sherman's men as seasoned soldiers more often gave misleading than correct information when they were asked what would be the route of the army. As less and less could be gleaned from Southern newspapers, the Union army marching in Georgia, the "lost army," became a world mystery, for speculation and surmise in the North and in Europe. "If Sherman has really left his army in the air and started off without a base to march from Georgia to South Carolina," said the experts of the *Army and Navy Gazette* in England, "he has done either one of the most brilliant or one of the most foolish things ever performed by a military leader." Sherman would either come out decorated for "the success of sublime audacity" or ridiculed for "the most tremendous disaster that ever befell an armed host," believed the London *Herald*, adding that he might become "the scoff of mankind and the humiliation of the United States." The London *Times* found itself fascinated by a piece of drama: "military history has recorded no stranger marvel than the mysterious expedition of General Sherman, on an unknown route against an undiscoverable enemy."

Henry Adams wrote in early December from London to his brother with the Army of the Potomac, "Popular opinion here declares louder than ever that Sherman is lost . . .

The interest felt in his march is enormous, however, and if he arrives as successfully as I expect, at the sea, you may rely upon it that the moral effect of his demonstration on Europe will be greater than that of any other event of the war. It will finish the rebs on this side."

Grant said to a visiting committee: "Sherman is acting by order and I am waiting on him. Just as soon as I hear he is at some one of the points designated on the seacoast I will take Richmond. Were I to move now without advices from Sherman, Lee would evacuate Richmond, taking his army somewhere South and I would have to follow him to keep him from jumping on Sherman."

To a serenading party on the night of December 6 the President was brief and intimate: "I believe I shall never be old enough to speak without embarrassment when I have [nothing] to talk about. I have no good news to tell you, and yet I have no bad news to tell. We have talked of elections until there is nothing more to say about them. The most interesting news we now have is from Sherman. We all know where he went in at, but I can't tell where he will come out at. I will now close by proposing three cheers for Gen. Sherman and his army."

Sherman's brother, the Ohio Senator, came in anxiety over published Southern reports of his brother in retreat and disaster. Could anyone tell him the facts? Lincoln said: "Oh, no, I know the hole he went in at, but I can't tell you what hole he will come out of." Some two weeks after Sherman disappeared A. K. McClure in Lincoln's office was leaving when he heard, "McClure, wouldn't you like to hear something about Sherman?" McClure turned eagerly and Lincoln laughed. "Well, I'll be hanged if I wouldn't myself."

Carpenter noted Lincoln during a White House reception shaking hands with a continuous stream of people. And along came an old friend, whose name and face should be perfectly familiar to Lincoln. But Lincoln gave him only the same handshake and abstract greeting as any unknown. The old friend stood still and spoke again to Lincoln, who roused, shook himself out of a dark-brown study, again took his old friend's hand, and, "Excuse me for not noticing you. I was thinking of a man down South."

Richmond papers had no stories of attacks or effective actions against Sherman. Lincoln worried. "I assured him," wrote Grant to Sherman later, "with the army you had and you in command of it, there was no danger." Grant heard of Lincoln comforting inquirers: "Grant says they are safe with such a general, and that if they cannot get out where they want to, they can crawl back by the hole they went in at."

The same point in a less blunt style went into Lincoln's message to Congress December 6: "The most remarkable feature in the military operations of the year is General Sherman's attempted march of three hundred miles directly through the insurgent region. It tends to show a great increase of our relative strength that our General-in-Chief should feel able to confront and hold in check every active force of the enemy, and yet to detach a well-appointed large army to move on such an expedition. The result not yet being known, conjecture in regard to it is not here indulged."

That was all. Brooks puzzled; here was nothing about the direction of march or the point from which news of Sherman was expected. Laying the sheet of paper down and taking off his spectacles, Lincoln laughed at Brooks' disappointment, and added kindly, "Well, my dear fellow, that's all that Congress will know about it, anyhow."

A curious sentence which could serve several purposes was written into the first draft of the message to Congress. Then later Lincoln ran his pen through this sentence: "We must conclude that he [the General in Chief] feels our cause could, if need be, survive the loss of the whole detached force; while, by the risk, he takes a chance for the great advantages which would follow success." It could be taken to mean that Lincoln was not sharing the "risk" with Grant and Sherman.

In early December Colonel A. H. Markland of Grant's staff was leaving with mail for Sherman's army. He didn't know where he would deliver it, not knowing where he would find Sherman. Grant had told Markland to step in and see whether Lincoln had some message for Sherman. Lincoln was in a conference, but on seeing Markland's card had him shown in at once. He arose, crossed the room, meeting Markland halfway, and with a handshake: "Well, Colonel, I got word from General Grant that you were going to find Sherman, and that you would take him any message I might have. I know you will find him, because we always get good news from you. Say to General Sherman, for me, whenever and wherever you see him, 'God bless him and God bless his army.' That is as much as I can say, and more than I can write." He held Markland's hand and looked him in the eye all the time he was saying this. Tears gathered in his eyes, his lips trembled, and his voice shook, according to Markland, who noted: "He shook my hand, bade me good-by, and I proceeded toward the door, when he called to me. When I looked back he was standing like a statue where I had left him. 'Now, remember what I say,' and then he repeated the message."

An army for 32 days to the outside world "lost sight of," as Sherman phrased it, now had behind it 300 miles of naked smokestacks, burned culverts, shattered trestleworks, wailing humanity. Of the railroads every rail was twisted beyond use, every tie, bridge, tank, woodshed and depot building burned. Thirty miles ran the devastation on either side of the line from Atlanta, estimated Sherman. Kilpatrick's 5,000 horsemen had ravaged beyond the reach of foot troops. For the economy of powder they had sabered hogs, knocked horses between the ears with axes, killing more than a hundred horses on one plantation with a fine mansion, and shooting every bloodhound, mastiff or other dog that looked as though it could track runaway Negroes in swamps and forest. Over many square miles of this area now was left not a chicken, not a pig, not a horse nor cow nor sheep, not a smokehouse ham nor side of bacon, not a standing corncrib with a forgotten bushel, not a mule to plow land with, not a piece of railroad track, nor cars nor locomotives nor a bunker of coal.

On December 10 General Howard's right wing stood ten

miles from Savannah. To Washington Howard sent a telegram notifying the Government that the march had won
through. By scouts overland to Port Royal, South Carolina,
and wire relays, this good-news message reached Washington the evening of December 14. Next day Halleck passed
on to Lincoln Howard's dispatch: "We have met with perfect success thus far, troops in fine spirit and General Sherman near by."

Over the North flashed this news. Across streets in town,
over roads and fields in the country, went the jubilant cry
that Sherman had got to Savannah. From Boston to Council
Bluffs and points west there were cheers and prayers of
thanks.

On December 13 Sherman with staff officers climbed to
the top of a rice mill, looked toward the sea for the fleet,
looked toward a forest edge where the 15th corps was
ready to move on Fort McAllister. The fort overlooked a
river needed for supply transport between Sherman and the
fleet—if the fleet had arrived as planned. For hours Sherman and his aides kept their lookout. It was near sundown
when a smokestack took clearer form, at last could be seen,
and later a flag wigwagged the words, "Who are you?"
"General Sherman," said the rice-mill flag. "Is Fort Mc-
Allister taken yet?" asked the ship. "Not yet, but it will be
in a minute."

As though this was a signal, Sherman's old Shiloh division under General William B. Hazen broke from cover,
sharpshooters running out to fling themselves flat on the
ground and pick off enemy gunners, the whole line soon
charging through a hail of shot, shell and rifle bullets, rushing the defenses, soon dancing on the parapets of Fort Mc-
Allister.

By the light of a pale moon this December 13 Sherman
rode a fast yawl downstream, boarded the Union ship, the
Dandelion, and before midnight was writing dispatches to be
read five days later by Stanton, Halleck and Lincoln—and
parts of them passed on to a world starving for news and
sure fact.

Back with his army again, Sherman saw Colonel A. H.

Markland with sacks of mail. Men and officers whooped with glee over the first letters from home in many weeks. Sherman's eyes danced when Colonel Markland spoke the message from Lincoln.

Savannah fell, its garrison of 9,000 under General Hardee moving out and away toward the north the night of December 20. Sherman wrote Lincoln a message: "I beg to present you as a Christmas gift, the city of Savannah, with one hundred and fifty guns and plenty of ammunition, also about twenty-five thousand bales of cotton." The day after Christmas Lincoln wrote a letter to Sherman and sent it South: "When you were about leaving Atlanta for the Atlantic coast, I was *anxious*, if not fearful; but feeling that you were the better judge, and remembering that 'nothing risked, nothing gained' I did not interfere. Now, the undertaking being a success, the honor is all yours; for I believe none of us went farther than to acquiesce . . . Please make my grateful acknowledgments to your whole army, officers and men."

Lingering hesitations that Sherman had about Lincoln were wearing away, and the degree of trust that Lincoln held for him and Grant was deepening. The three were now closer than ever. Later Sherman was to write that the acclaim over the march to the sea pleased him, but "I experienced more satisfaction in giving to his [Lincoln's] overburdened and weary soul one gleam of satisfaction and happiness."

Stanton refused at this time to join the others in a Merry Christmas mood. To Grant he wrote: "It is a sore disappointment that Hardee was able to get off his 15,000 from Sherman's 60,000. It looks like protracting the war while their armies continue to escape."

The campaigning in Tennessee was strange and involved, with none of the dramatic simplicity of Sherman's march, General Schofield writing Sherman that they in Tennessee had the work while he in Georgia had the fun. Schofield on leaving Sherman and trying to connect his force of 29,000 with Thomas at Nashville had to fight a battle with Hood's

41,000 Confederate troops at Franklin, Hood in desperate frontal attacks thrown back with losses of 6,000 as against 2,300 on the Union side. Schofield drew off. Hood followed. Schofield joined Thomas at Nashville. There Hood camped with his army, now reduced to 26,000, intending as he said in a report of December 11 "to force the enemy to take the initiative."

Washington worried. Stanton December 2 had telegraphed Grant: "The President feels solicitous about the disposition of General Thomas to lay in fortifications for an indefinite period . . . This looks like the McClellan and Rosecrans strategy of do nothing and let the rebels raid the country. The President wishes you to consider the matter." The phrasing was Stanton's. On this same December 2 Grant had sent two dispatches to Thomas urging him to take the offensive, Thomas replying that in two or three days he would probably be ready.

Thomas, as Sherman saw him, had on occasion a granite-and-glacier certainty of movement. As West Point classmates, as young lieutenants in the same Regular Army regiment for ten years, they became "precious" to each other, Sherman feeling that "never since the world began did such absolute confidence exist between commander and commanded, and among the many mistakes I made I trace some of his earnest and vehement advice."

On December 8 Grant had wired Halleck: "If Thomas has not struck yet, he ought to be ordered to hand over his command to Schofield. There is no better man to repel an attack than Thomas but I fear he is too cautious to ever take the initiative."

To Grant from Halleck came a telegram, in all probability on so grave a matter having had scrutiny or perhaps revision by the President, reading: "If you wish General Thomas relieved, give the order. No one here will interfere. The responsibility, however, will be yours, as no one here, so far as I am informed, wishes General Thomas removed."

Grant on this December 8 tried a further telegram to Thomas: "Why not attack at once? By all means avoid the contingency of a foot-race to see which, you or Hood, can beat to the Ohio." Thomas still delayed. In cavalry Hood outnumbered him four to one; he was getting remounts and hoped to have a force of 6,000. He wired Grant that in troop concentration and transport "I have made every effort possible." Grant, receiving this December 9, wired Halleck that as Thomas had not yet attacked, "Please telegraph orders relieving him at once, and placing Schofield in command." The order was made out. Before telegraphing it to Nashville Halleck asked Grant if he still wished it to be forwarded. Grant replied, "You will suspend the order until it is seen whether he will do anything."

Thomas called his corps commanders, told them of the orders to attack Hood. The generals agreed that their commander should not fight on the slippery hills around Nashville till he was ready. No news of an attack reaching Grant, he wired December 11, "Let there be no further delay," Thomas replying, "I will obey the order as promptly as possible. The whole country is covered with a perfect sheet of ice and sleet." He would have attacked "yesterday had it not been for the storm."

Grant on December 13 ordered Logan to Nashville to replace Thomas in command. Logan started. Then Grant for the first time since he had become lieutenant general himself started on a trip back west, for Tennessee, to take personal charge there. Grant had reached Washington. Logan was at Louisville, Kentucky, less than a day's travel from Nashville. To both of them came news that Thomas had launched his troops at Hood's army.

Thomas telegraphed December 15: "I attacked the enemy's left this morning, and drove it from the river below the city very nearly to the Franklin pike, a distance of about eight miles . . . The troops behaved splendidly, all taking their share in assaulting and carrying the enemy's breast works." That night the whole army slept on its guns in line of battle and next day pushed a broken and retreating enemy at all points. "I beheld," later wrote Hood, "for the first and only time a Confederate army abandon the field in confusion." No rout of the war had been so complete. One factor was the cavalry for which Thomas had delayed action. Hood's army as a unit vanished. Parts of it, to the number of 15,000 men, held intact through the generalship of Forrest, who saved them for other Confederate commands. The Confederate losses in killed and wounded at least equaled the Union casualties of 3,000— and 4,462 Confederate prisoners were taken.

Sherman took pride in his friend "Old Tom" and was to write of this battle that it was the only one of the war "which annihilated an army." A famous metaphor was coined: the Rock of Chickamauga became the Sledge of Nashville. Congratulations came from many, including Grant, Sherman, Stanton, Sheridan, Lincoln's of December 16 reading: "Please accept for yourself, officers, and men, the nation's thanks for your good work of yesterday. You made a magnificent beginning. A grand consummation is within your easy reach. Do not let it slip." To a commission naming Thomas for the vacant major generalship in the Regular Army Grant and Lincoln joined their signatures.

For Grant the week had been, according to Colonel Horace Porter, "the most anxious period of his entire military career," and before the victory came "he suffered mental torture." To Grant, Thomas was one piece in a big game involving other pieces and Grant was trying to time and co-ordinate them toward destroying the three Confederate armies left. When Thomas won, there were only two. The extent of Lincoln's hand in the affair did not appear. He seemed to have watched every phase of it keenly, "solicitous" that by no one's mistake should there be more "McClellan and Rosecrans strategy," yet when Grant put it up to him to relieve Thomas he insisted that must be Grant's act. One of the three remaining Confederate armies having been destroyed, Grant went from Washington to Burlington, New Jersey, and spent a day of rejoicing with his wife and family.

Grant's anxiety to play no favorites, to keep clear of the politics always seething in the army, showed one day in Washington when Sherman's army was "lost" in Georgia. He then gave the President and Secretary of War a list of eight major generals and 33 brigadiers whose services the Government "could dispense with to advantage." In the matter of letting out "these useless officers," noted Colonel Porter, Grant was entirely impartial, the list having some of his warm personal friends. The President said: "Why, I find that lots of officers on this list are very close friends of yours. Do you want them all dropped?" General Grant: "That's very true, Mr. President. But my personal friends are not always good generals, and I think it but just to adhere to my recommendations."

Lee's distressing need for men ran back in part to an order of Grant in April that not another Confederate prisoner of war should be paroled or exchanged until certain conditions were met that Grant probably knew would never be met. Cruel it was, he admitted, but necessary. "Every man we hold, when released on parole or otherwise, becomes an active soldier against us at once either directly or indirectly . . . If we hold those caught they amount to no more than dead men." At the particular time in late summer when the Confederate Government proposed to exchange prisoners man for man, said Grant, it "would insure Sherman's defeat" and "compromise safety" at Richmond.

Many were the influences brought to bear on Lincoln to reverse or modify this policy of Grant. Arguments based on political power and made in the name of reason, cries and prayers for the sake of humanity, rang in his ears. But Lincoln stood by his general. He let Grant have his way. And at this time there raged over the North a propaganda of horror with proposals of vengeance for the inhuman handling of Union soldiers in Southern prisons. They were starved. And they died of starvation. This was fact. They festered in rags and became living skeletons, chilled and shivering. This, for many, was fact. Atrocities monstrous and almost beyond belief were told of in northern newspapers and pulpits and on political platforms. These too had some basis of fact. But the South had its answers. And these too held facts. Where in the South were any such parades of pleasure and riots of luxury as could be seen in the metropolitan centers of the North? A shelf of competent testimony would reduce to a verdict of both sides making war as war had always been made and meaning brought to the word "agony." The so-called laws of war were being violated, as in former wars, as an incident of humanity in the mass being violated—on both sides. Over this Lincoln troubled his mind and heart and was to refer to it in his second inaugural address.

A 27-acre piece of marshland in southwestern Georgia, fenced and stockaded for Union prisoners, bare of trees, and hiding places, was Andersonville. A man going there died a dirty and lingering death; or killed himself by stepping over a line where guards at once put a bullet through him for attempted escape; or lost his mind; or by slim chance issued forth to freedom somehow with a woebegone look and a wild-animal stare in his eyes. When a few of these hunted ones had crept into Sherman's camp one night at Milledgeville, the sight of them brought mutterings of revenge.

The place named Andersonville won distinction as the one spot on the North American map where war was more hideous to look at than any other spot that could be named. In its close-packed and swarming population was less food and more scurvy and starvation; less soap and more filth, scabs and lice; less medicine and more gangrene, fever, diarrhea, ulcers, sores, hemorrhages, bleeding gums and swollen lips symptomatic of scurvy, than anywhere else in America.

The bloodiest battle of the war had not taken such a toll of death as Andersonville from June to September 1864, with its record of 8,589 dying. This reduced the peak population of 32,000 and enlarged the average space of six square feet per man. Vice-President Stephens suggested that Jefferson Davis visit Andersonville, that the Confederate President make a solemn speech to the prisoners and let them go home and tell the North the South was fighting only for independence.

Where lay the blame? On both sides. So wrote a Confederate prisoner, Henry M. Stanley, later an African explorer,

of what he saw in a human "cattle-yard" named Camp
Douglas at Chicago. On the way to the latrines Stanley
saw "crowds of sick men who had fallen prostrate from
weakness, and given themselves wholly to despair, and
while they crawled or wallowed in their filth, they cursed
or blasphemed as often as they groaned." Every morning
came wagons whereon Stanley saw the corpses rolled in
their blankets "piled one upon another, as the New Zealand
frozen mutton carcasses are carted from the docks!"

Had Lincoln been looking toward a policy of vengeance
on the South, had he joined with Thad Stevens and the
now powerful group who planned to visit retribution on the
ruling class of the South, he could not have wished for a
better issue than Andersonville. He could have set in motion such whirlwinds of hate as the war had not yet seen.
A grumbling and muttering had begun that the President
took no action in this field, assertions, wrote Carpenter,
that he showed "a criminal indifference to the sufferings of
our prisoners at Libby, Andersonville, and other places."
There was the record, said these critics: nowhere in any
public address or message of the President could you find
any allusion to the Union soldiers murdered by foul treatment in Southern prisons. Purposely Lincoln avoided discussion of it. The issue had not become sharp till this fourth
year of the war. For maddening the Northern people into
war effort the issue could have been useful earlier in the
war. But now it could do no good toward the ends of reconciliation and rebuilding which Lincoln hoped for beyond the war's end. So he was saying nothing. Partly
the animus in the matter was political.

"When the reports, in an authentic form, first reached
Washington of the sufferings of the Union prisoners,"
wrote Carpenter, "I know he [the President] was greatly
excited and overcome by them." He was told that justice demanded a stern retaliation, that like treatment should be
given Confederate prisoners, and according to Carpenter,
he said to Congressman M. F. Odell with deep feeling, "I
can never, never starve men like that!" and again, "Whatever others may say or do, I never can, and I never will,

be accessory to such treatment of human beings."

The Southern summer heat was bad for men from the North, and the Northern zero winter weather not so good for those from the South. Official statistics ran that 12 out of every 100 Confederate prisoners died in the North, and 15 of every 100 Union captives in the South. Medical men agreed that the Southern troops were undernourished because of their own armies' inferior food supply, and therefore less resistant to disease.

Want and hunger threatened the life arteries of the Confederacy less than its own internal strife. The November message of President Davis to the Confederate Congress spoke desperately of conspiracies, of traitors and spies inside their own house. What any state capital announced was more important and authoritative to the people of that state than any proclamations from the Richmond Government. This faith in states' rights as much as want or military defeat was a gnawing and devitalizing factor in the Confederacy.

The Richmond *Whig* had spoken for an element with deep-rooted instincts about states' rights when it suggested dropping the name of Confederate States and substituting The Allied Nations or The Allied Republics. "We are sorry to see the word 'national' sometimes used with reference to Confederate affairs. We think it should be henceforth a forbidden word. This Confederacy is not a nation, but a league of nations."

Mrs. Chesnut, now in Columbia, South Carolina, wrote when Sherman was two days out from Atlanta moving toward the seacoast, "Fire and the sword are for us here; that is the word." A letter came to her from Mrs. Jefferson Davis saying she was tired of hoping and being disappointed. Her news from Richmond was that some people expected another attack soon, "but I think the avalanche will not slide until the spring." For Mrs. Davis, wrote Mrs. Chesnut, "my heart aches."

Into Mrs. Chesnut's Columbia house came a Connecticut-born woman with Northern relatives who spoke of Sherman opening a way at last so that she could go to Europe or to the North and live in comfort and ease. "I dare say she takes me for a fool," ran the diary entry that day. "I sat there dumb, although she was in my own house. I have heard of a woman so enraged that she struck some one over the head with a shovel. To-day, for the first time in my life, I know how that mad woman felt. I could have given Mrs. S. the benefit of shovel and tongs both."

Now came news of Hood's army broken and scattered, and, wrote Mrs. Chesnut, "maybe I am benumbed." A Miss Rhett was visiting her, "a brilliant woman and very agreeable," who had a saying, "The world, you know, is composed of men, women, and Rhetts." Now, said the diary, "we feel that if we are to lose our negroes, we would as soon see Sherman free them as the Confederate Government; freeing negroes is the last Confederate Government craze. We are a little too slow about it; that is all." Mournful and Biblical was her mood of December 19: "The deep waters are closing over us and we are in this house, like the outsiders at the time of the flood."

Chapter 40

The Bitter Year of '64 Comes to a Close

In New York City November 25, 1864, with phosphorus and turpentine as starters, 11 New York hotels began blazing at about the same time. The flames were caught in time and put out by quick-witted hotel workers. At Barnum's Museum, at Niblo's Garden where an audience of 3,000 was seeing a play, at the Winter Garden Theatre, the terrorizing cry of "Fire!" was raised. Cool heads slowed down the near-panics while fires were snuffed out. In this episode the same Federal secret-service operative who had carried dispatches between the Richmond Government and the Confederate commissioners in Canada brought Stanton, Dana and Lincoln information that enabled them to have the arson bugs arrested. One of the guilty was hanged, others sent to prison.

It may have been that Jacob Thompson, operating from Canada with a fund of $300,000 supplied from Richmond, expected a job at Chicago to be his masterpiece. The plot there was that at Camp Douglas, on election night, November 8, Sons of Liberty should throw in their forces, release and arm the 8,000 Confederate prisoners, "cut the telegraph wires, burn the railroad depots, seize the banks and stores containing arms and ammunition, take possession of the city and commence the release of other Confederate prisoners in Illinois and Indiana." The commandant at Camp Douglas, however, early got word of the plot, and two nights before the break was to come he arrested an English soldier, four Confederates, two Sons of Liberty. Later he arrested seven more Sons of Liberty. A military commission dealt out prison sentences to several and decreed death for one.

Was the South in heartbreak and despair now using tactics it would not have considered when the war opened? Suffering had come to Charleston, seared by a fire loss of $7,000,000, raked by shells, bombs, the awe of single incidents such as the killing of Miss Pickens, daughter of ex-Governor Pickens. One May morning she was married to Lieutenant de Rochelle, ran the *Mercury* account. "The wedding party had assembled at the house of General Bonham, when a shell from the Union forces penetrated the house and wounded the bride so that she died soon afterward. The marriage ceremony was completed as she lay dying on the floor."

At Camden Mrs. Chesnut was haunted by her memory of little Joe Davis, son of the Confederate President, killed by falling from a high porch to a brick pavement. And in the drawing room of the executive mansion at midnight she could hear the tramp of Mr. Davis' step as he walked back and forth in the room above, not another sound, the whole house silent as death. Next day thousands of children at little Joe's grave each had a green bough or a bunch of flowers to throw on a pile of crosses and evergreens.

The fighting men of South Carolina had all gone to the front, wrote Mrs. Chesnut. "Only old men and little boys are at home now." She read a column list of South Carolina dead and wounded in clashes with Grant's men, shuddering at news of Grant receiving 25,000 fresh troops in one relay. "Old Lincoln says in his quaint backwoods way, 'Keep a-peggin.' Now we can only peg out." A harsh play on words. The peg legs were too many.

"It is impossible to sleep here," wrote Mrs. Chesnut, "because it is so solemn and still. The moonlight shines in my window sad and white." She was as grave and vivid now as when in April '61, the first guns booming to bring down the parapets of Fort Sumter, she had leaped from her bed and knelt in prayer over what was to come.

In her Richmond stay she had gone shopping, "and paid $30.00 for a pair of gloves; $50.00 for a pair of slippers; $24.00 for six spools of thread; $32.00 for five miserable, shabby little pocket handkerchiefs." Soon they would be saying in Richmond, "You take your money to market in a market basket and bring home what you buy in your pocketbook." Money—it was getting ridiculous. As Confederate money sank in value from month to month pathos and pity touched deeper the Confederate cause.

Now in the North and in Europe it was taken as full of portent that President Davis recommended to his Congress that slaves be drafted for the Confederate armies. This plan would throw 400,000 able-bodied and armed black men against the Northern armies. Slavery would not be abolished, but the enlisted Negroes would be given freedom. Factions in the Confederate Congress with polite contempt offered other plans to fill the thinning armies.

As with each year the South had dwindled in man power, in money and economic resources, in commerce and industry, in the comforts or necessities of life, the North had gained. In steel, oil, railroads, munitions, textiles and other industries, scores of large fortunes were already made, many others on their way. The fast and luxurious living in most of the large cities still contrasted with sacrifices on the march, in camp and on the battlefields. Travelers from Europe commented in surprise at seeing seaboard cities of a North at war with so few signs of war and such throngs of spenders and pleasure hunters as in no European cities. From Great Britain, especially Ireland, and from Germany and the Scandinavian countries, fresh populations poured in.

Westward across the plains and to the West Coast poured an endless migration, some of it to escape the draft. From March 1 to August 10, 1864, 9,300 teams and wagons passed Fort Kearney, Nebraska. One fast traveler on the road from St. Joseph, Missouri, to Fort Kearney passed 400 wagons in one day. At Council Bluffs in April and May a line of teams three miles long waited their turn to cross a ferry whose capacity was 200 in its operation day and night. By the middle of June it was estimated 75,000 men, 30,000 horses and mules, 75,000 cattle, had made the crossing. With each year farmers of the Midwest and Northwest bought more planters, reapers, threshers for putting in crops and harvesting; these labor-saving farm machines made more men available for Grant and Sherman.

America had these lights and contradictions in 1864. Any historian of them in their vast and moving variety needed a gift for showing chaos in the current scene and a weave of paradox leading to the future. A mystic dream of a majestic republic holding to human freedom and equal opportunity ran parallel to motives of hard cash and pay dirt. These were to shape a future already begun, swaying indistinctly in many a speech or saying of Lincoln.

In the fourth December of the war, Lincoln sent his message to Congress. The tone continuously traveled with high assumption that the United States was a going concern, that the Union of States was fated to become a great World Power.

The President read the message to his Cabinet December 3. The briefs of several Cabinet members were kept in the message "pretty much in their own words," noted Welles. One unusual matter came up, indicating the favor

in which church leaders were held by Lincoln and an inno-
vation to which, it seemed, he would have consented had
the Cabinet agreed. "One paragraph," wrote Welles, "proposing an Amendment to the Constitution recognizing the
Deity in that instrument met with no favorable response
from any one member of the Cabinet. The President, before reading it, expressed his own doubts in regard to it,
but it had been urged by certain religionists."

Foreign affairs were in a "reasonably satisfactory" condition. The Republic of Liberia should be given a gunboat at
moderate cost, paying the United States for it in install-
ments. Such a beginning of a navy would "stimulate a generous ambition" in this young Negro nation. An international telegraph system, the Atlantic cable, and co-operation toward "world-encircling communication" were approved. A rebellion "long flagrant" in China "has at last
been suppressed," with "the co-operating good offices of
this government and of the other western commercial
States." Emphasis was laid on the "extension of our commerce" and a "more intimate intercourse" with China.
Japan in performing treaty stipulations "is inconstant and
capricious," though good progress had been effected by the
Western Powers "moving with enlightened concert." Money
claims of the United States had been allowed by the Japa-
nese or put in course of settlement. One Virginia port, Norfolk, and two Florida ports, Fernandina and Pensacola,
were now open, and foreign merchants might consider
whether it was not "safer and more profitable" to use those
ports than to risk blockade-running.

Thus far the message was chiefly Seward. Lincoln's hand
became evident in a paragraph on the slave trade and those
who did a business of shipping and selling black folk. "For
myself, I have no doubt of the power and duty of the Executive, under the law of nations, to exclude enemies of
the human race from an asylum in the United States."

The Treasury Department had taken in over $1,000,000,-
000 in cash and disbursed nearly as much for the Army
and Navy. "Taxation should be still further increased."
The paragraph completely endorsing the national bank-

ing system probably represented the views of Secretary Fessenden, with Lincoln in agreement.

The Navy now could show 671 vessels. Across the past year its actual increases over and above all losses by shipwreck and battle were 83 vessels, 167 guns and 42,427 tons. During the year 324 ships had been captured, making a total of 1,379 since the war commenced. Sales of condemned prize property had brought more than $14,000,000.

The Army and Navy could read of "liberal provisions" made by Congress for pensions. During the year ending June 30, 16,770 invalid soldiers and 271 invalid seamen had been added to the rolls. Of widows, orphans and dependent mothers, a total of 22,198 were on the army pension rolls and 248 on the navy rolls. Homesteaders had entered more than 4,000,000 acres of public land. Open to settlement were 133,000,000 acres of surveyed land. The Union Pacific railway had "assurance of success."

The President pointed to "the most important branch of national resources—that of living men." The North in spite of war losses had 145,551 more voters at the polls in November '64 than four years before. The fact stood out "that we have *more* men *now* than we had when the war *began;* that we are not exhausted, nor in process of exhaustion; that we are *gaining* strength, and may, if need be, maintain the contest indefinitely."

Of the word "reconstruction" Lincoln steered clear. Already it had become tinged with suspicion. Important movements had occurred during the year, wrote the President, "to the effect of moulding society for durability in the Union." Short of complete success, he admitted, but much in the right direction was it that 12,000 citizens in each of the States of Arkansas and Louisiana "have organized loyal State governments with free constitutions, and are earnestly struggling to maintain and administer them." Similar movements more extensive, though less definite, in Missouri, Kentucky and Tennessee "should not be overlooked."

The President now dealt with the crowded rumors and flying reports that peace was to be had through negotiation.

"On careful consideration of all the evidence accessible it seems to me that no attempt at negotiation with the insurgent leader could result in any good. He would accept nothing short of severance of the Union—precisely what we will not and cannot give. His declarations to this effect are explicit and oft-repeated. He does not attempt to deceive us . . . What is true, however, of him who heads the insurgent cause, is not necessarily true of those who follow. Although he cannot reaccept the Union, they can. Some of them, we know, already desire peace and reunion. The number of such may increase . . ."

He seemed to leave a quite direct inference that for himself he would be found, if and when the war closed, using his authority for the help and sustenance of men in the South who might have to consider vindictive enemies in Washington. "Pardons and remissions of forfeitures, however, would still be within Executive control. In what spirit and temper his control would be exercised can be fairly judged of by the past." Pardon and amnesty had been offered a year ago "to all, except certain designated classes." These latter, it was made known then, were "still within contemplation of special clemency."

As to slavery, the President was brief but more decisive than in any other part of the message: "I repeat the declaration made a year ago that 'while I remain in my present position I shall not attempt to retract or modify the emancipation proclamation, nor shall I return to slavery any person who is free by the terms of that proclamation, or by any of the Acts of Congress.' If the people should, by whatever mode or means, make it an Executive duty to re-enslave such persons, another, and not I, must be their instrument to perform it."

Dry with a cool Lincolnian finality, touched with a faint preposterous irony, was the closing one-sentence paragraph: "In stating a single condition of peace, I mean simply to say that the war will cease on the part of the government, whenever it shall have ceased on the part of those who began it."

Far and wide went this document. By Union armies it was spread into Confederate areas where Confederate newspapers had not reprinted it from Northern journals. In Europe it was studied and discussed in state chambers and on the streets. Over the Northern States it was examined for every shading of fear and hope and promise.

Opposition journals in the North agreed in various ways with the London *Times,* which said: "For ourselves, we never read a public document less calculated to inspire hope," adding the gratuitous comment that it was "the most uncomfortable President's address ever read to the American House of Representatives."

Harper's Weekly judged it a "calm, simple, concise statement of public affairs," and could understand a Northern opposition, "in common with the rebels," finding the message very "unconciliatory." Its tranquil tone of faith in the people, its dignity toward other Powers, its lofty confidence in peace and union "make the Message, now familiar to the country, one of the . . . most truly American papers in our political history."

Lincoln's anonymous friend in the *Spectator* of London found his latest message "drier, shrewder, and more tenacious than ever." The peace terms offered by Mr. Lincoln were "precisely the terms every monarchy in Europe always offers to rebels." His war policy held to that of the Roman patrician who would "spare the submissive, but war out the proud." His amnesty was free to everybody. His proud roll call of national resources, "of which Americans never weary," none the less had great meaning. "Faith is the source of strength."

Dry, informative, again casual as a locomotive, came the President's proclamation of December 19 calling for 300,000 more troops.

Now into only one port of the South could blockade-runners bring supplies. This port of Wilmington, North Carolina, would be lost if its defending Fort Fisher should fall. General Butler worked out a scheme to run a powder-loaded steamer near the shore under the fort, have a clock-work blow up the boat, and in the ensuing havoc and confusion move in troops to take the fort.

Admiral Porter with a naval squadron, General Butler with troop transports, joined their efforts. After Butler sailed from Fortress Monroe "three days of fine weather were squandered," according to Grant. Then heavy storms delayed action. At last on the night of December 23 the powder steamer was towed in near the fort, the clockwork set and everybody left. "At two o'clock in the morning," wrote Grant, "the explosion took place—and produced no more effect on the fort, or anything else on land, than the bursting of a boiler anywhere on the Atlantic Ocean." Porter shelled the fort with no damaging results. Butler landed troops, won footings, then drew away, put his troops back on the transports and told Porter he was through.

Grant telegraphed the President December 28 that the Wilmington expedition had proved "a gross and culpable failure," that he hoped it would be known who was to blame. Grant, however, on hearing from Admiral Porter that the army had quit when they nearly had Fort Fisher, sent word to Porter to hold on, to stay near Wilmington, that they would soon close that last Confederate port through which came medicine, food, metals, clothing, salt, arms, blankets, from Europe.

The President would soon name another man to replace Stanton, had run persistent reports since the November election. "This subject was brought up by the President in his conversation with the general-in-chief," wrote Grant's aide, Colonel Porter, "and he was considerate enough to say that in case such a change should occur, he would not appoint another secretary without giving the general an opportunity to express his views as to the selection." Grant's reply to Lincoln, as Porter noted it: "I doubt very much whether you could select as efficient a Secretary of War as the present incumbent. He is not only a man of untiring energy and devotion to duty, but even his worst enemies never for a moment doubt his personal integrity and the purity of his motives . . ." Grant privately continued to believe Stanton "timid" as a warrior, too freely arrogant in the handling of Grant's telegrams when it suited him, but Grant had no one else in mind now who better fitted the needs of the hour.

And Stanton, though in breaking health, regarded himself as an image of war and a hurler of thunderbolts. At the doorway of the war telegraph office one evening he stood, without coming in. At a table sat Lincoln writing. In the doorway Stanton postured volcanic and warlike to look at. The operator Chandler wrote of the tableau: "Mr. Lincoln did not notice him at first. As he looked up from his writing and perceived Stanton standing there, he bowed low and said with much gravity, 'Good-evening, Mars.'"

A Cabinet shake-up coming, ran rumors—a house cleaning. But it was idle talk. In neither major nor minor offices did Lincoln intend to use a broom. "I have made up my mind to make very few changes in the offices in my gift for my second term," he told one caller. "I think, now, that I shall not move a single man, except for delinquency. To remove a man is very easy, but when I go to fill his place, there are twenty applicants, and of these I must make nineteen enemies."

To Seward the Paris Consul Bigelow more than once sent word, "Burn this Mss when you have read it." Seward once replied that a note was duly "received, read, and burned," as suggested, and "The contents are known only to the President here." This latter concerned the death December 1 of Minister William L. Dayton in Paris, in the hotel apartment of a woman not his wife, the body being immediately removed to Dayton's house. This was done, according to Bigelow, "before the police could interfere, for should they become aware of what had happened they would insist upon holding an inquest upon the premises, which would involve many inconveniences, all of which would be avoided by placing the body within the precincts of the legation." Bigelow recited the insistence of the unfortunate hostess upon riding up to the legation with the body to explain how it happened. They wished to discourage her, but she insisted. "What will Mrs. Dayton think?" she exclaimed. "My reputation is involved. I must go at once." And so she went. According to the doctor's report, wrote Bigelow in a later unofficial account, Dayton "after some pleasantry on entering the apartment, called upon his hostess to give three cheers for Abraham Lincoln, the news of whose re-election had just recently reached Paris. He soon complained of feeling unwell," and died from apoplexy before the doctor's arrival. Thus a matter kept secret by the Paris Legation in Europe, and by Seward and Lincoln in America, did not reach a press which would have reveled in the details.

Had the November election given a mandate to Congress or to the President? Was it the duty of Congress now to challenge the Executive and cut down his powers? A test vote came in mid-December. Henry Winter Davis demanded a vote on his resolution that Congress had "a constitutional right to an authoritative voice" in foreign affairs, and, "it is the constitutional duty of the President to respect that policy . . . in diplomatic negotiations." Without debate or inquiry the House voted on a motion of Representative Farnsworth to lay the Winter Davis resolution on the table. This passed with 69 Yeas, 63 Nays, not voting 50.

Thus in mid-December of '64 the respect and adherence of Congress to Lincoln seemed to hang in a balance of about 69 with him, 63 against him, and 50 undecided, wavering, sick or not interested. Those with him were nearly all his own party men. Those against him were the opposition party, allied with nearly as many of his own party. Those not voting were mostly of his own party.

In stature and sagacity the President now stood on a different footing with Congress. The campaign and the election had brought an impression that Lincoln was a politician of keener touch, an Executive of more designing statecraft, than they had given him credit for. Fair words and lavish estimates spoke Thad Stevens on the President's message. "It is brief (a great virtue in public documents), it treats of subjects of great importance, not only to the nation but to the whole family of man. I do not think I am extravagant when I say that it is the most important and best message that has been communicated to Congress for the last sixty years."

Stevens saw an opposition trying to save from destruction "the darling institution of the Democratic party, the institution of human bondage." Compromise on this was sought. They condemned the "President's determination to insist on the abandonment of slavery." When the President's own leading friends besought him to compromise, he refused to sue for peace. "There never was a day since Abraham Lincoln was elected President that he stood so high . . . in the estimation of the people as at this moment." The guiding fear of Stevens was that the war by compromise evasions might end without slavery uprooted.

John M. Palmer, the Union Democrat of Illinois, waited in a White House anteroom one morning till he was told to enter the President's room. As Palmer told it, he found Lincoln in the hands of the barber, and Lincoln called: "Come in, Palmer, come in. You're home folks. I can shave before you. I couldn't before those others, and I have to do it sometime." They chatted about this and that, Palmer finally speaking in a frank and jovial mood. "Mr. Lincoln, if anybody had told me that in a great crisis like this the people were going out to a little one-horse town and pick a one-horse lawyer for President I wouldn't have believed it." Lincoln whirled in his chair, his face white with lather, a towel under his chin. Palmer at first thought the President was angry. Sweeping the barber away, Lincoln leaned forward, put a hand on Palmer's knee and said: "Neither would I. But it was a time when a man with a policy would have been fatal to the country. I have never had a policy. I have simply tried to do what seemed best as each day came."

The degree of Doctor of Laws, awarded by Knox College, at Galesburg, Illinois, an abolitionist and solidly Republican community, was less a surprise to Lincoln than a like degree conferred by the trustees of the College of New Jersey.

To Lincoln's desk in September had come a request from Governor Andrew in behalf of a widow living at 15 Dover Street, Boston. She had sent her five sons into the Union armies and all had been killed in action, according to Andrew's information from his state adjutant general, William Schouler.

On request of the War Department the adjutant general of Massachusetts made an investigation and officially certified the names, regiments and dates of death of Mrs. Bixby's five sons. This document came to Lincoln in mid-October. He could have then written a letter to Mrs. Bixby and made it public for campaign purposes. Instead, he waited. As on occasion with certain speeches or letters, he probably wrote a first draft of the letter and later changed the phrasing. On November 21 he dated the letter and sent it through the War Department to Adjutant General Schouler of Massachusetts. He addressed it to "Mrs. Bixby, Boston, Massachusetts." Her first name, Lydia, and her address in Boston, were not given. Adjutant General Schouler received the letter in an envelope addressed to himself and copied the letter. On Thanksgiving Day the General took a holiday dinner and a present of money raised among good people of Boston and delivered them at 15 Dover Street to Mrs. Bixby—along with Lincoln's letter to her. She read on that Thanksgiving Day:

> I have been shown in the files of the War Department a statement of the Adjutant General of Massachusetts, that you are the mother of five sons who have died gloriously on the field of battle.
>
> I feel how weak and fruitless must be any words of mine which should attempt to beguile you from the grief of a loss so overwhelming. But I cannot refrain from tendering to you the consolation that may be found in the thanks of the Republic they died to save.
>
> I pray that our Heavenly Father may assuage the anguish of your bereavement, and leave you only the cherished memory of the loved and lost, and the solemn pride that must be yours, to have laid so costly a

sacrifice upon the altar of Freedom. Yours, very sincerely and respectfully, A. LINCOLN.

This was the text as Schouler had copied it and as he gave it to the Boston newspapers.

Later research was to show that of the five Bixby boys Charles died in action at Fredericksburg and Oliver met death at Petersburg. Henry was reported killed at Gettysburg, was in reality taken prisoner, exchanged, returned to his mother in good health. George too was taken prisoner, secured his release by enlistment as a Confederate soldier, and was of record as having "deserted to the enemy." Edward Bixby, on the muster rolls as 18 years of age, became homesick, and his mother swore that he was only 16, had enlisted against her will, that he had periods of insanity. The order for his discharge was issued, but the worrying boy had deserted the Army and gone to sea as a sailor.

In substance, then, had the actual facts been known, what was the extent of Mrs. Bixby's sacrifice? Whether all five died on the field of battle, or only two, four of her sons had been poured away into the river of war—the two who had deserted were as lost to her as the two who had died. The one who had returned alive had fought at Gettysburg. If sacrifice could be transmuted into cold figures, she deserved the distinction and fame Lincoln gave her name. From her womb had gone blood to the altars of the Union cause. Lincoln was not deceived nor John Andrew fooled nor the War Department taken unaware.

The response to the Bixby letter, the love of its words and music that arose over the country, lay in the fact that in so many thousand of homes they did love the Union; they did hate slavery; mournfully but willingly they had sent their boys to take a chance with death on the field of battle. The war was not all waste and filth and corruption. More darkly than the Gettysburg speech the letter wove its awful implication that human freedom so often was paid for with agony.

As a living human target who daily walked with a lurking and elusive shadow of death, as a Chief Magistrate who had twice had his hat shot off by an unknown would-be

assassin, Lincoln was completely entitled to be a spokesman
for the boy phantoms who had fought his war and now no
longer answered roll call. Side by side with Governor Andrew's communication to the President about Mrs. Bixby
was presented the case of Otis Newhall of Lynn, Massachusetts, and his five vacant chairs at home. George F.
Newhall had met the steel of death at Second Bull Run.
Edward had begun marching and fighting in October '61
and had gone on with the Army of the Potomac to the battle
of the Wilderness in May '64, when he was taken prisoner.
Henry and Herman Newhall were two sharpshooters who
enlisted in October '61, had stayed on through, and were
now with Grant at Petersburg. This left James O. Newhall,
who enlisted in January '62, fought through to Spotsylvania Court House in May '64, when he received wounds
and went to hospital. Now James had recovered, and his
father, not wanting all the chairs at home vacant, had proposed Governor Andrew's recommendation to Lincoln
that James be discharged "as a graceful recognition of the
claim of a patriotic family." To the Newhall family Lincoln
gave the discharge asked for, and to Mrs. Bixby a letter
the world read.

As the months passed after Lincoln's first inaugural address, his sense of the comic, his occasional role of come-
dian, stayed with him, while significantly on the other hand
he came to know more keenly and fittingly what could be
done with the authoritative mantle of President. He
learned how better to wear it publicly, to adjust it as the
garment of a solemn spokesman. He believed the majesty of
the office backed him in telling Congress that "the fiery
trial" through which they were all passing would be written
as history and the players weighed and the balances cast up.
At Gettysburg he stood in a ceremonial role. Across many
months of '64 his authority hung by such threads that he
knew his cue was silence; no statements could be wrung
from him. Again in the Bixby letter he performed a rite,
managing language as though he might be a ship captain
at midnight by lantern light dropping black roses into the

immemorial sea for mystic remembrance and consecration.

A speech of the President in December reached the public in an unusual way. He sent for Noah Brooks "to hear a story." He had the story partly written. With a sheet five or six inches wide on one knee, his legs crossed, sunk comfortably in his armchair, he asked Brooks to wait till he finished. Soon he gave it to Brooks, who saw at the top of the sheet an underscored heading, followed by a paragraph. It read:

THE PRESIDENT'S LAST, SHORTEST, AND BEST SPEECH.

On thursday of last week two ladies from Tennessee came before the President asking the release of their husbands held as prisoners of war at Johnson's Island. They were put off till friday, when they came again; and were again put off to saturday. At each of the interviews one of the ladies urged that her husband was a religious man. On saturday the President ordered the release of the prisoners, and then said to this lady "You say your husband is a religious man; tell him when you meet him, that I say I am not much of a judge of religion, but that, in my opinion, the religion that sets men to rebel and fight against their government, because, as they think, that government does not sufficiently help *some* men to eat their bread on the sweat of *other* men's faces, is not the sort of religion upon which people can get to heaven!"

He remarked to Brooks that he wanted it copied and printed in the Washington *Chronicle,* adding, "Don't wait to send it to California in your correspondence. I've a childish desire to see it in print right away." So Brooks took it to the *Chronicle* and it was widely reprinted. "Lincoln," noted Brooks, "showed a surprising amount of gratification over this trifle."

The day before Christmas of '64 after one favor, the commutation of a death sentence, Welles pressed for another from the President. Miss Laura Jones of Richmond was engaged to be married to a man in Richmond, three years back. In Washington, having nursed her mother back to health, she wanted to return to Richmond and see her betrothed. In a letter to an old friend, Mrs. Gideon Welles, she prayed for help in getting a pass through Union lines. Noted Welles, "The poor girl . . . says truly the years of her youth are passing away. I knew if the President read the letter, Laura would get the pass."

Without reading the letter the President at once said he would give Miss Laura Jones her pass. Welles made it plain that "her sympathies were with the Secessionists, and it would be better he should read her own statement." But Lincoln wouldn't read her letter to Mrs. Welles. "He . . . said he would let her go; the war had depopulated the country and prevented marriages enough."

New Year's Eve came, the fourth for Lincoln in the White House. On the first one McClellan, with a magnificently prepared army, had gone into winter quarters without fighting, the shame of Bull Run not redeemed and the North yet to try its faith in itself. The second New Year's Eve could look back on a year highlighted by the weary Peninsula campaign, the jubilant capture of Fort Donelson, New Orleans taken, bloody Shiloh, the Second Bull Run shame, McClellan and Lee at Antietam, the preliminary Emancipation Proclamation, the delays of McClellan and his dismissal, the needless butchery at Fredericksburg. The third New Year's Eve had brought the final Emancipation Proclamation, the rout of Chancellorsville, New York draft and race riots, the turning point of the war at Gettysburg and Vicksburg, the shouting at narrowly shaded Chickamauga fighting, the cries from men in blue at the top of Lookout Mountain, the speech at Gettysburg, the beginning of the sunset of the Confederacy.

Now here was the fourth New Year's Eve looking back on Grant named to head all the Union armies, plunging into the Wilderness and on through Spotsylvania, Cold Harbor, Petersburg, with overwhelming troops and resources battering Lee pitilessly while Early's gray horsemen reached the gates of Washington with their smoke to be seen from White House windows, while Sherman took Atlanta and marched to the sea and took Savannah, while Sheridan scattered Early's army from the Shenandoah and Thomas became the sledge that broke Hood's army into the first Confederate rout of the war, while the Navy sank the *Alabama*, took Mobile and tightened its throttling grip on all Southern ports—a fateful year that had seen the President of the United States win a party renomination against the almost unanimous disapproval of his party members in the House and Senate, winning a national election in November that looked dark and all lost in August, winning in a fairly conducted contest, amid good order, so that the longer one gazed at the November ballots, the more they seemed to say momentously that the Union would be held together and the underlying cause of the war, the propertied institution of slavery, outlawed forever. Not so bitter as the other three was the taste of this New Year's Eve. Across the horizons of the New Year of 1865, however, were signs of the storm to take new phases. Heavy labors lay head, and much mist of human confusion.

The diplomatic corps in sashes and epaulets promenaded over the reception rooms of the White House. Members of the Senate and House, the Cabinet, and in larger numbers than ever before the Public were there to shake hands with the President New Year's Day.

Had Miss Betsey Canedy of Fall River, Massachusetts, been in line that day and paused for conversation with Lincoln, she could have told him of what she heard while teaching a school of Negro pupils at Norfolk, Virginia. To Negro carpenters at work on the school building one day she showed a plaster bust of Abraham Lincoln. What they said impressed Miss Canedy and some of it she wrote down: "He's brought us safe through the Red Sea." "He looks as deep as the sea himself." "He's king of the United States." "He ought to be king of all the world." "We must all pray to the Lord to carry him safe through, for it 'pears like he's got everything hitched to him." "There has been a right smart praying for him, and it mustn't stop now."

Among onlookers outside the White House, seemingly innocent bystanders enjoying a show worth while, were groups of Negroes. Nearly two hours they hung around gazing at those coming and going. Nearly two hours they waited, some of them wearing fine clothes, others in pickings from various discards ready for the rag bag.

At last they agreed the time had come for them to go in. Why not? Who would throw them out? Surely not the one man in the house they wanted to see. And an observer for the New York *Independent* wrote: "For two long hours Mr. Lincoln had been shaking the hands of the 'sovereigns,' and had become excessively weary, and his grasp languid; but here his nerves rallied at the unwonted sight, and he welcomed this motley crowd with a heartiness that made them wild with exceeding joy. They laughed and wept, and wept and laughed—exclaiming, through their blinding tears: 'God bless you!' 'God bless Abraham Lincoln!' 'God bress Marse Linkum!' Those who witnessed this scene will not soon forget it. For a long distance down the Avenue, on my way home, I heard fast young men cursing the President for this act; but all the way the refrain rang in my ears,—'God bless Abraham Lincoln!' "

Chapter 41

"Forever Free" — *The Thirteenth Amendment*

More than 1,300,000 slaves had been freed "by the Lincoln Administration or by the events of the war," indicated a statistical table in the Philadelphia *North American* in November '64. Of slaves when the war began one out of three now was free—under the Emancipation Proclamation of "military necessity." The Federal Constitution, however, still held these slaves to be property, except in Missouri and Maryland, two states which had legalized emancipation.

In many published incidents figured a changed Negro. *Leslie's Weekly* reported a Negro who took a hand in a guerrilla fight: "We fit 'em, we whopt 'em, and we kotched ten uv 'em." *Harper's Monthly* told of Confederate prisoners at Rock Island, Illinois, under Negro guards—and one guard, suddenly seeing the man who once owned him, crying out, "Hullo, massa! *bottom rail top!*"

To make all Negroes free under the law and the Constitution, Lincoln in his December message pointed to the last session of Congress. Then "a proposed amendment of the Constitution abolishing slavery throughout the United States, passed the Senate, but failed for lack of the requisite two-thirds vote in the House of Representatives."

The Senate was safe; 13 Democrats there had joined the four who voted with the Republicans the year before. But the House looked doubtful. For more than a year Lincoln had foreseen a narrow margin. Toward this day he planned when he instigated the admission into the Union of Nevada with her added votes, when he called in Charles A. Dana and arranged for patronage gifts that would have raised a high and noisy scandal if known to the opposition. Again toward this crisis Lincoln had looked when one day only two votes were needed to make a two-thirds majority in the House. Representative John B. Alley wrote: "Two members of the House were sent for and Mr. Lincoln said that those two votes must be procured. When asked, 'How?' he remarked: 'I am President of the United States, clothed with great power. The abolition of slavery by constitutional provision settles the fate, for all coming time, not only of the millions now in bondage, but of unborn millions to come—a measure of such importance that *those two votes must be procured*. I leave it to you to determine how it shall be done; but remember that I am President of the United States, clothed with immense power, and I expect you to procure those votes.' These gentlemen understood the significance of the remark. The votes were procured."

Alley's reserve indicated he had further particulars of a sort he did not care to mention. A practical man was Alley, his hide and leather trade in Lynn, Massachusetts, and his other business interests not suffering through his political dealings.

One of the largest slaveholders in Missouri, James S. Rollins, several times consulted with the President about the proposed Constitutional amendment. Rollins heard Lincoln in early January: "This is my chief hope and main reliance to bring the war to a speedy close, and I have sent for you as an old Whig friend to come and see me, that I might make an appeal for you to vote for this amendment. It is going to be very close. A few votes one way or the other will decide it."

Rollins' response was quick. The President didn't need to send for him on this matter. "Although I . . . have the misfortune to be one of the largest slave-owners in the county where I reside, I had already determined to vote for the thirteenth amendment." Then, as Rollins told it, "He arose from his chair, and grasping me by the hand, gave it a hearty shake, and said, 'I am most delighted to hear that.' " The President then asked how various Missouri Representatives stood. Rollins named those he knew to be for or against the bill. And on Rollins saying he was "on easy terms" with the entire Missouri delegation, Lincoln asked if he wouldn't "talk with those who might be persuaded to vote for the amendment," and to report soon what was the prospect. Congressman Rollins agreed.

Sumner had introduced bills to curb what he termed a usurped power of taxation in New Jersey. Railroad interests affected were seeking to get Sumner to drop these bills, for the time, in exchange for Democratic Representatives of New Jersey voting for the Constitutional amendment to abolish slavery. Nicolay's memorandum indicated the desperate tactics being used to gather a few more needed votes.

This was January 18. On the 31st at noon the galleries of the House are filled to overflowing, in the air a subdued hum of excitement. After formal preliminaries, the joint resolution for a Constitutional amendment to outlaw "slavery or involuntary servitude," except for crimes, is up for final decision.

Ashley yields the floor to a Democrat, Archibald McAllister of Pennsylvania, who announces he will change his vote of Nay last June to Yea. "In voting for the present measure I cast my vote against the cornerstone of the southern confederacy." Applause from the Republican side. Ashley again yields the floor to a Democrat, Alexander H. Coffroth of Pennsylvania, who says the Constitution has been amended before and he favors amending it now by removing slavery as a cause of future strife. Applause from the Republican side. Ashley now yields the remainder of his time to Herrick of New York, whereupon Johnson of Pennsylvania protests the proceeding is getting arbitrary. "One gentleman occupies the floor and farms it out to whoever he pleases." Speaker Colfax upholds Ashley and reads the rules.

A Kentucky Democrat, Aaron Harding, rises to rebuke two Kentucky colleagues who have changed their minds since the vote of June '64, after which he proceeds to justify slavery by familiar and conventional arguments.

Martin Kalbfleisch, a Democrat from Brooklyn, stands up and reads 22 sheets of heavy words meaning nothing much except that he has the words. The clock says three. Speaker Colfax announces the hour for voting·has arrived. Kalbfleisch says he has only six more pages to read. Speaker Colfax lets him drone on. The proposed amendment, "as if it were in truth an amendment," proceeds Kalbfleisch, "I regard as subversive of the spirit of that instrument [the Constitution]." Now as ever before he must vote against gentlemen "seeking to lay sacrilegious hands upon that venerated and almost sacred instrument, our glorious Constitution." Kalbfleisch finishes. The speeches are over. Not a Republican has made an argument. They are there to vote. The Democrats for and against have had their say on this day when only roll calls count.

On two roll calls the House refuses to table, refuses to reconsider. The hour of the final vote comes nearer. The galleries fill till standing room is gone. Crowded to the doors are the corridors and lobbies, faces beyond faces wondering if the two-thirds vote will be there. Into the reporters' gallery sweeps "a mob of well-dressed women," as Noah

Brooks describes them. With "good grace" the press writers give up their seats to the crinoline girls. The Senate seems to have come over in a body. Grave spectators are four Associate Justices of the Supreme Court and the highly tensed Chief Justice Chase.

The Yeas and Nays are ordered. Alley, Allison, Ames, Anderson and so on. These are all Republicans, their Yeas expected. Comes the name of James E. English, a Connecticut Democrat. He shouts "Aye!" A long roll of applause bursts from the gallery and Republican House members. The Speaker hammers with his gavel. The tumult goes down. Again the voice of the clerk can be heard. For the Republican Ayes as the roll call goes on there is quiet. But with each Democrat shooting his vocal Aye at the calling of his name there is a tumult of handclapping, cheers, laughter, the noisemaking of pent-up emotion let loose. Eleven Democrats answer Aye.

The roll call reaches the W's and Y's; the Wood brothers, Ben and Fernando of New York City, vote for slavery and Yeamen of Kentucky for freedom.

Swift pencils add up the lists. The clerk whispers to the Speaker who announces that the question is decided in the affirmative—Yeas 119, Nays 56, not voting 8. And, said the *Congressional Globe*: ". . . the two thirds required by the Constitution of the United States having voted in favor thereof, the joint resolution was passed."

A mass of still faces break shining and lighting. Emotions explode into a storm of cheers. Men in tears throw their arms around each other. The crowds stand up, many mounting their seats, to shout their glee. Man after man goes handshaking and backslapping. A cloud of women's handkerchiefs wave and float. Ten minutes go by before this hurricane of feeling lets down.

Outside is thunder. The air is torn. Someone has ordered three batteries of regular artillery on Capitol Hill to cry joy with a salute of 100 guns.

Victory came by the margin of three men voting Yea. Eight Democrats stayed away from this House session.

Something was due these eight Democrats, absent, noted Nicolay and Hay, "not altogether by accident."

News coming next day that Illinois had ratified the amendment, starting the line-up of three-fourths of the states necessary to amend the Constitution, Lincoln smiled. "This ends the job. I feel proud that Illinois is a little ahead." To the White House that night came a crowd with a brass band, serenaders shouting for the President. At a window they saw standing in half-lights and shadows the solemn central figure of the drama of emancipation. He remarked, "There is a task yet before us—to go forward and consummate by the votes of the States that which Congress so nobly began yesterday. (Applause and cries—'They will do it.')"

The solemn figure at the shadowy window could also have mentioned that this latest and formidable act of Congress was only an empty mouthing of phrases unless the bayonets of Grant and Sherman would give an awful meaning to the seizure without compensation of property sanctioned by the Constitution and once valued at $3,000,000,-000. A popular cartoon portrayed a Negro laughing—"Now I'm nobody's nigger but my own."

William Lloyd Garrison made his acknowledgments in the *Liberator:* "To whom is the country more immediately indebted for this vital and saving amendment of the Constitution than, perhaps, to any other man? I believe I may confidently answer—to the humble railsplitter of Illinois—to the Presidential chainbreaker for millions of the oppressed—to Abraham Lincoln!"

Chapter 42

Heavy Smoke — Dark Smoke

A social revolution moved toward its final collapses and shadows. The Southern planter class read a handwriting on the wall of fate. Not yet did the letters spell out the shape of their doom—but doom enough had already come to make it a dark story.

To Davis and Lee there seemed this winter a last hope of holding out against the North by giving freedom to blacks who would fight. The hour seemed at hand when the Confederacy had conscripted its last white man—and the efforts of Davis and Lee to put black men in fighting service were blocked by the extremist element.

Those blaming Jefferson Davis for Southern failure were in part hunting a scapegoat. He personified the Southern planter class in its pride, its aristocratic feudal outlook, its lack of touch with an almost world-wide abhorrence of slavery as distinguished from what was called "nigger-loving." The war years rolled on and Davis failed to become either an idol or a name and a figure of faith—like Robert E. Lee. Yet Lee had never been such a spokesman of the Confederate cause as Davis. On the death of his wife's mother in 1862 Lee emancipated the slaves to which his family fell heir. Privately Lee spoke of slavery as a sinister, insidious, menacing institution—the view of his high exemplar George Washington. As a voice of states' rights and secession Lee had no reputation at all. In his very silence about why the war was being fought, in the wide and deep love for him for keeping silence while he fought so magnificently, there was some clue to the human dignity of a certain remnant of the Confederacy ready for sacrifice rather than submission to those they termed invaders.

As the pressure became fiercer in early '65 Lee consented, in perfect accord with Davis, to take chief command of all the Confederate armies. As a first move he appointed General Joseph E. Johnston to head an army, made from various fragments, to block the path of Sherman from Savannah up across the Carolinas. This reflected Lee's judgment that Davis had been mistaken in his abrupt dismissal of Johnston.

The Charleston *Mercury* changed its mind about Lincoln and said in January '65: "When Abraham Lincoln took the chair of the Presidency of the United States, he promised in his flat-boat lingo, to 'run the machine as he found it' . . . he has run it with a stern, inflexible purpose, a bold, steady hand, a vigilant, active eye, a sleepless energy, a fanatic spirit, and an eye single to his end—conquest—emancipation . . . Blackguard and buffoon as he is, he has pursued his end with an energy as untiring as an Indian, and a singleness of purpose that might almost be called patriotic. If he were not an unscrupulous knave in his end, and a fanatic in his political views, he would undoubtedly command our respect as a ruler . . . Abroad and at home, he has exercised alike the same ceaseless energy and circumspection."

Late on the night of January 15, after three days' bombardment, Fort Fisher fell. Wilmington, the last open port of the Confederacy, was closed to incoming supplies and outgoing cotton. To no one was it more galling news than to Major General Benjamin F. Butler. Political and military circles were amazed at the news from Washington January 13; it was "now specifically stated that on January 6 Lieutenant General Grant indicated to President Lincoln his earnest wish that Major General Butler be forthwith relieved of his command," and next day the President directed the Adjutant General to issue the order deposing Butler and ordering him to report at Lowell, Massachusetts, his home.

Amid hue and cry and guess and gossip, Grant and Lincoln got rid of the one man in the Union armies who stood foremost as a potential dictator. He was the one commander who, under conceivable circumstances, which Hay had in mind, would not have hesitated at marching an army to Washington, taking over the Government, and issuing regulations to the country.

In the summer of '64 Grant and Lincoln could have told the country during those gloom months that Richmond stood untaken because Butler had miserably blundered. Such an explanation, however true, would have brought scorn and blame on Grant and Lincoln for letting Butler blunder, for keeping in command of the Army of the James a politician "who could strut sitting down." Pertinent was the question of why Grant did not let Butler out in the summer of '64. The reason was plain, tacitly understood between Grant and Lincoln. Butler had a national political following. Shifting, as the war rolled on, from his former loyalty to the proslavery wing of the Democratic party, he turned radical on the slavery issue, radical enough so that Wendell Phillips publicly and repeatedly wished Butler were President instead of Lincoln.

Disputes over how to run the war rose less often now. The war machine ran with fewer blowups. To Lincoln's desk came fewer tangled military matters for his final decision. During many sessions of House and Senate the war was scarcely mentioned. Discussions ran as though the call now was to build the Pacific railway, improve rivers and harbors, dig canals, make land grants to railroads and homesteaders, perfect coastal surveys, ease commerce between the states, resettle Indian tribes. The Secretary of the Interior reported on some 4,250,000 acres of public land sold and granted, railroads and homesteaders moving toward a future of expected booms.

The draft had stiffer enforcement, less resistance and evasion. Deserters met less mercy. On Governor's Island a large crowd saw the hanging of a bounty-jumper who had three times pocketed his money and three times deserted. Near City Point with elaborate military ritual thousands of troops formed in a square and saw a firing squad shoot a soldier who had deserted, received pardon, returned to his regiment and deserted again. Over the country went the story of it, with crayon sketches by artists who caught its horror.

In late January the outcry about Northern men languishing in Southern prisons reached the point where Grant decided to relent. In October '64 he had asked Lee whether the Confederate Government would deliver in exchange colored troops "the same as white soldiers," Lee rejoining that "negroes belonging to our citizens are not considered subjects of exchange." On January 24, 1865, however, when the Confederate Government again offered to exchange man for man, Grant accepted the offer without mention of color.

The information service of Grant gave him the advantage of Lee. Deserters each month by thousands, tired of short rations and hard fare in the Confederate Army, crossed the picket lines, nightly expected and welcomed by the Union forces. Always some of them would talk.

Three days after Savannah fell Old Man Blair was on hand and Lincoln wrote one sentence on a card: "Allow the bearer, F. P. Blair, Senr. to pass our lines, go South and return." Blair took a naval boat from City Point to Richmond. At the Confederate White House Blair dined with Davis, fraternized with old cronies of days agone in the Democratic party, noticed with surprise how many able-bodied men were walking the streets, men he would have expected to be in Lee's army.

On January 12, closeted with the Confederate President for a secret interview, Blair spilled his various proposals, kept from the outside world till long afterward. Blair wrote for Lincoln a report of this interview, of how he told Davis of his relations with Lincoln, that Lincoln "shunned an interview with me, until I perceived that he did not wish to hear me, but desired I should go without any explanation of my object."

Out of their suave and guarded confabulations came one thin result; Davis suggested he was willing to send men to some conference and the men he would appoint could be relied on by Mr. Lincoln. A letter written by Davis for Blair to carry back to Lincoln read in closing: ". . . notwithstanding the rejection of our former offers, I would, if you could promise that a commissioner, minister, or other agent would be received, appoint one immediately, and renew the effort to enter into conference, with a view to secure peace to the two countries."

For Blair at the White House Lincoln wrote a one-sentence letter to Davis via Blair: "Your having shown me Mr. Davis' letter to you of the 12th. Inst., you may say to him that I have constantly been, am now, and shall continue, ready to receive any agent whom he, or any other influential person now resisting the national authority, may informally send to me, with the view of securing peace to the people of our one common country."

Thus the Davis letter ending with the words "the two countries" had Lincoln's letter in reply ending with the phrase "our one common country." And where Davis had referred to Lincoln as President of "etc." Lincoln now alluded to "Mr." Davis as though whatever Davis might be President of he was definitely a "Mr." The score was about even.

Now for the first time since the Confederate capital had been moved to Richmond, Davis asked his Vice-President to meet him in conference. Stephens suggested the names of three commissioners. Davis agreed with one of the names, John A. Campbell, Assistant Secretary of War and former U.S. Supreme Court Justice, added R. M. T. Hunter, Senator and ex-Secretary of State, and Stephens himself. These were all three "peace men" or "submissionists" rather than uncompromising last-ditchers. Their instruction by Davis read: "In conformity with the letter of Mr. Lincoln, of which the foregoing is a copy, you are requested to proceed to Washington City for informal conference with him upon the issues involved in the existing war, and for the purpose of securing peace to the two countries."

With his fellow commissioners Stephens came to the Union Army lines the evening of January 29, claiming an understanding with General Grant to pass them on their way to Washington. On this being telegraphed to Washington, Lincoln at once sent Major Eckert of the war telegraph office with written directions to let the commissioners in with safe-conduct if they would say in writing they were ready to talk peace on the basis of the President's note of January 18, peace for "our one common country." Before Eckert arrived with this message the commissioners applied by a written note to General Grant for permission "to proceed to Washington to hold a conference with President Lincoln upon the subject of the existing war, and with a view of ascertaining upon what terms it may be terminated."

On receiving their note Grant at once telegraphed it to Stanton and Lincoln. Lincoln sent Seward to meet the commissioners at Fortress Monroe with written instructions that he was to make known to them three things as indispensable to peace: "1. The restoration of the national authority throughout all the States. 2. No receding, by the Executive of the United States on the Slavery question, from the position assumed thereon, in the late Annual Message to Congress, and in preceding documents. 3. No cessation of hostilities short of an end of the war, and the disbanding of all forces hostile to the government."

Seward started February 1, while Lincoln telegraphed Grant to let the war go on while peace was talked. "Let nothing which is transpiring, change, hinder, or delay your Military movements, or plans." Grant promised in reply there would be no armistice, that troops were "kept in readiness to move at the shortest notice."

General Meade wrote to his wife that when the Confederate commissioners came within the Union lines "our men cheered loudly, and the soldiers on both sides cried out lustily, 'Peace! Peace!' " This was meant as "a compliment" to the Confederate agents, and, believed Meade, "was so taken by them."

The three commissioners had been considering the very explicit instructions from the President of the United States, brought to them by Eckert, that they must agree in writing to no peace talk except on the basis of the President's note to Blair of January 18, peace for "our one common country." Their answer was a refusal. Their mission seemed at an end. Eckert telegraphed Lincoln their reply was "not satisfactory" and notified the commissioners they could not proceed.

About an hour after their refusal to meet Lincoln's terms, Grant sent a long telegram to the Secretary of War, stating "confidentially, but not officially—to become a matter of record" that he was convinced on conversation with Messrs. Hunter and Stephens "that their intentions are good and their desire sincere to restore peace and union." Grant admitted he was in "an awkward position," fearing a bad influence from the commissioners going away with no results. He saw the difficulties of receiving them and did not know what to recommend. Grant put the high point of his letter: "I am sorry, however, that Mr. Lincoln cannot have an interview with the two names in this despatch [Stephens and Hunter], if not all three now within our lines."

Lincoln next morning walked over to the War Office, read Major Eckert's report, was framing a telegram to call Seward back, when Grant's long telegram was put in his hands. "This despatch," wrote Lincoln later, "changed my purpose." He at once wired Grant: "Say to the gentlemen I will meet them personally at Fortress Monroe, as soon as I can get there."

The President went in a hurry and with secrecy. Even the trustworthy Nicolay was not told. The news leaked from several sources. Welles in his diary grumbled over it. "None of the Cabinet were advised of this move, and without exception, I think, it struck them unfavorably." Meantime down the Potomac on a naval vessel Lincoln journeyed.

"On the night of the 2nd. [of February]," ran Lincoln's account, "I reached Hampton Roads . . . On the morning of the 3rd., the three gentlemen, Messrs Stephens, Hunter and Campbell, came aboard of our Steamer and had an interview with the Secretary of State and myself of several hours duration. No question of preliminaries to the meeting was then and there made or mentioned. No other person was present; no papers were exchanged, or produced; and it was, in advance, agreed that the conversation was to be informal, and verbal merely." The instructions the President had written for Seward were insisted on. Five astute men of politics and law talked four hours in a steamboat saloon. What went on in the minds of the five men, the tangled cross-purposes underlying their words, no onlooker could have caught and reported.

As between drinking men Seward on his arrival had sent the commissioners three bottles of whisky, though aware that Stephens never took more than a teaspoon of it at a time. Hunter, who had spent most of his life in Washington, genially asked Seward: "Governor, how is the Capitol? Is it finished?" Whereupon Seward described the new dome and the great brass door.

There might be a "continental question" on which they could adjust the strife, Stephens once led off, Lincoln rejoining that Mr. Blair in Richmond on matters in Mexico had spoken with no authority from him. The people of the North were as responsible for slavery as the people of the South (as Stephens heard Lincoln say) and "He knew some [in the North] who were in favor of an appropriation as high as four hundred millions of dollars for this purpose [paying owners for the loss of slaves]. 'I could mention persons,' said he, 'whose names would astonish you, who are willing to do this if the war shall now cease.' "

On Hunter's saying it seemed that Lincoln's terms forced the Confederate people to choose nothing else than unconditional surrender and submission, Seward with quiet dignity insisted that "no words like unconditional submission had been used" nor any harsh phrases meaning degradation or humiliation. With peace, said Seward, the Southern people would again be under the Constitution "with all their rights secured thereby."

The opening query of the conference had come from Stephens to Lincoln: "Well, Mr. President, is there no way of putting an end to the present trouble . . . existing between the different States and sections of *the country?*" In this Stephens did not go so far as Lincoln's term "our one common country," but he did with intention and meaning, as his first stroke at the conference, abandon the Davis phrase "two countries."

It was news to the Confederate commissioners that the

U.S. Congress on January 31 had passed the 13th Amendment to the Constitution and when this should also pass three-fourths of the state legislatures, it would outlaw and abolish slavery.

Lincoln stressed the point that even if the Confederate States should consider coming back into the Union, he could not make any bargains with armed forces making war on his Government. At this Hunter pointed to King Charles I of England and how that monarch bargained with people in arms against his Government. Hunter's argument was long and elaborate, insisting that peace could come through Lincoln's recognizing the right of Davis to make a treaty. "Mr. Lincoln's face," ran a later newspaper account by Stephens, "then wore that indescribable expression which generally preceded his hardest hits, and he remarked: 'Upon questions of history I must refer you to Mr. Seward, for he is posted in such things, and I don't pretend to be bright. My only distinct recollection of the matter is that Charles lost his head.' That settled Mr. Hunter for a while."

A hush fell over the conference when Lincoln felt required to contradict gravely and directly remarks made by the Confederate commissioners. His words were measured and sounded like doom: the conduct of certain rebel leaders had been such that they had plainly forfeited all right to immunity from punishment for the highest crime known to law. He had come to the brink of saying they should be strung up for treason, should hang high and lonesome as traitors.

After a quiet pause Hunter gave Lincoln a steady, searching look, and then very deliberately: "Mr. President, if we understand you correctly, you think that we of the Confederacy have committed treason; that we are traitors to your government; that we have forfeited our rights, and are proper subjects for the hangman. Is not that about what your words imply?" "Yes," rejoined Lincoln. "You have stated the proposition better than I did. That is about the size of it!" Another somewhat painful pause, then Hunter with a pleasant smile: "Well, Mr. Lincoln, we have about concluded that we shall not be hanged as long as you are

President—if we behave ourselves."

An Augusta, Georgia, *Chronicle* interview with Stephens later related: "Hunter declared that he had never entertained any fears for his person or life from so mild a government as that of the United States. To which Mr. Lincoln retorted that he, also, had felt easy as to the Rebels, but not always so easy about the lampposts around Washington City,—a hint that he had already done more favors for the Rebels than was exactly popular with the radical men of his own party. Mr. Lincoln's manner had now grown more positive. He suggested that it would be better for the Rebel States to return at once than to risk the chances of continuing the war, and the increasing bitterness of feeling in Congress. The time might come, he said, when they would not be considered as an erring people invited back to citizenship, but would be looked upon as enemies to be exterminated or ruined."

A fellowship resting on thin fire, in a far cavern of gloom, seemed to have renewal between Lincoln and Stephens. Stephens came aboard the steamer wearing a coarse gray woolen overcoat that came down nearly to his feet. He looked almost like an average-sized man, though his weight was only 90 pounds. Lincoln had come into the steamer saloon and stood watching the dwarfish Georgian shake loose and step out of his huge overcoat, unwinding a long wool muffler and several shawls. Lincoln moved toward Little Aleck, whom he had not seen in 16 years, and with a smile and handshake: "Never have I seen so small a nubbin come out of so much husk." Thus Stephens remembered and told it.

Now came the friendly handshakings ending the Hampton Roads conference, a world of nations and people watching, a horde of journalists and politicians puzzling. Stephens again asked Lincoln to reconsider Blair's stalking horse, the plan of an armistice on the basis of a Mexican expedition commanded by Jeff Davis. Lincoln: ". . . I will reconsider it; but I do not think my mind will change." And further: "Well, Stephens, there has been nothing we could do for our country. Is there anything I can do for you personally?"

"Nothing." Then Little Aleck's pale face brightened. "Unless you can send me my nephew who has been for twenty months a prisoner on Johnson's Island." Lincoln's face too brightened. "I shall be glad to do it. Let me have his name."

The Confederate commissioners were put in a rowboat and taken to their steamer. Then a rowboat with a Negro at the oars headed for their steamer; he reached their deck with a basket of champagne and a note with the compliments of Mr. Seward. The commissioners waved their handkerchiefs in acknowledgment. Then they saw Mr. Seward, and speaking through a boatswain's trumpet, his words came clear: *"Keep the champagne, but return the negro!"* Thus ran the final informal words of the Hampton Roads conference.

In Washington were curiosity and fury. In New York the stock market was nervous and wavering. The gold speculators were crazy to go but couldn't figure which way. Lincoln and Seward rode a steamer up Chesapeake Bay for Annapolis where a crowd was on hand to see the President; newspapermen failed to wring anything definite from Lincoln or Seward.

Next day, February 4, the Cabinet heard from Lincoln and Seward that the conference had no results. A peculiar array of counselors it was, all against him the following day when at an evening session the President laid before them one of the boldest constructive proposals he had ever made. All were Christian churchmen, though each one withheld himself from joining Lincoln in an act for which an argument could be made that it was laden and shining with the spirit of the Sermon on the Mount.

Lincoln this day of February 5 had spent most of his time on a message and proclamation to go to the Senate and House, asking those "honorable bodies" to resolve that the President of the United States be empowered, in his discretion, to pay $400,000,000 to various Southern States, which were named. Six per cent Government bonds would form the payment, "to be distributed among said States *pro rata* on their respective slave populations, as shown by the census of 1860; and no part of said sum to be paid unless all resistance to the national authority shall be abandoned and cease, on or before the first day of April next." The adoption of such a resolution was sought "with a view to embody it, with other propositions, in a proclamation looking to peace and re-union." The proclamation would say ". . . that war will cease, and armies be reduced to a basis of peace; that all political offences will be pardoned; that all property, except slaves, liable to confiscation or forfeiture, will be released therefrom, except in cases of intervening interests of third parties; and that liberality will be recommended to congress upon all points not lying within executive control."

This document Lincoln had confidentially laid before his Cabinet. Wrote Nicolay and Hay: "There was but little discussion of the proposition. The President's evident earnestness on the one side, and the unanimous dissent of the Cabinet on the other, probably created an awkward situation which could be best relieved by silence on each hand." Usher wrote of the President somewhat surprised at all the Cabinet being opposed, and asking, "How long will the war last?" No one answered, so the President took it on himself: "A hundred days. We are spending now in carrying on the war three millions a day, which will amount to all this money, besides all the lives." With a deep sigh, noted Usher, he added, "But you are all opposed to me, and I will not send the message."

On the back of the manuscript of this proposed message, under date of February 5, 1865, Lincoln wrote: "To-day these papers, which explain themselves, were drawn up and submitted to the Cabinet & unanamously disapproved by them." He signed his name as though it was history and should be of record.

Welles with his colleagues saw the President in this a schemer rather than a solid statesman. "The Rebels would misconstrue it if the offer were made. If attempted and defeated it would do harm " Welles, whose judgment probably reflected that of most of the Cabinet, believed his guess was better than that of Lincoln on how the South would take the proposal. Also Welles looked toward Congress and the Lincoln opposition there rather than toward the country and the people, the forces by which Lincoln the year before had overcome the almost unanimous array of politicians in Congress opposed to him.

So the war would go on. The majestic and incalculably dynamic gesture Lincoln asked for, was out. A policy of nonretaliation, of "molding society for durability in the Union," as he hoped in the December message, would have to come slowly. His confidential advisers were thinking of Washington and Congress and politics; he was thinking of the great everyday masses of people North and South. The Cabinet was correct in feeling that the present controlling Southern politicians would hoot his proposed proclamation. But beyond might be a mass of Southern people moving and acting when those politicians were discredited as prophets and bankrupt as statesmen.

When the Confederate commissioners came back with their report, Richmond was turned upside down humanly. Jefferson Davis spoke; death or humiliation he would prefer "sooner than we should ever be united again." With curled lips of scorn he referred to the archantagonist "His Majesty Abraham the First" and prophesied that the Confederacy would yet "compel the Yankees, in less than twelve months, to petition us for peace on our own terms."

Little Aleck Stephens heard it as oratory bold, lofty, undaunted, but he was reminded of the Light Brigade at Balaklava and the Frenchman who summarized its useless sacrifice: "It is brilliant; it is grand; but it is not war."

Stephens reached his home at Crawfordsville, Georgia, February 20, where, as he wrote later, "I remained in perfect retirement." Stephens was too far committed to the states' rights theory to go as far as Lincoln advised. On the other hand his conscience did allow him to go home, stay there, keep silence and watch the movement of a tragic drama where his voice lacked authority.

Lincoln in Washington sent a telegram to the Johnson's Island prison. Lieutenant Stephens was pleased to hear at headquarters that the President wanted to see him. They put him on a sleigh to ride 20 miles across the ice on Lake

Erie to Sandusky. He rode the railroad cars to Washington, and at the White House found the President half sitting and half slouched on a table, talking with Seward. Lincoln rose, and with a smile: "I saw your uncle, the Honorable Alexander H. Stephens, recently at Hampton Roads. I told your uncle I would send you to him." The Lieutenant was deeply moved and just a little dizzy over the next words from the President: "You have the freedom of the city as long as you please to remain here. When you want to go home, let me know, and I will pass you through the lines." Two weeks the Lieutenant stayed in Washington, finding old friends of his own and his uncle's who entertained him. He put on weight, gained strength.

When ready to go to Richmond, Mr. Lincoln gave him a letter to carry to his uncle: "Your nephew, Lieut. Stephens, goes to you, bearing this note. Please, in return, to select and send to me, that officer of the same rank, imprisoned at Richmond, whose physical condition most urgently requires his release." He signed a pass through the Union Army and then did a sentimental thing. He handed the Confederate lieutenant a photograph of himself: "You had better take that along. It is considered quite a curiosity down your way, I believe." Did Mr. Lincoln want to help Mr. Stephens remember what an old laughing friend looked like?

In the Senate Wilson of Massachusetts was saying that Grant would have won the war by now if three months ago he could have had a reinforcement of 50,000 or 75,000 men to which he was entitled. On the basis of "a report in circulation" Wilson would like to convict the President of failing to get Grant troops needed to end the war. Wilson was taking part in a concerted move to drag down the executive and raise up the legislative end of the Government.

In the same week Ben Wade tore into the President's "pretensions" in Louisiana, saying of Lincoln's ten-per-cent plan that it was "the most absurd and impracticable that ever haunted the imagination of a statesman." Wade could hit hard, if not always clean. Perfect courtesy got mixed with a smooth-flowing insolence in short words. Doolittle of Wisconsin undertook a defense of the President and came off a bad second.

In the House session February 8, Stevens put through a resolution, much like one of Sumner's in the Senate, requesting the President to report on Hampton Roads. Many Senate and House members nursed a sullen mistrust of Lincoln's latest errand. With more than a few it was a baffled and inarticulate hate of the President. When Lincoln had followed Seward to Hampton Roads and the completely unexpected news of it went forth over Washington, undercurrents of excitement and frustration raged and whirled, wrote Noah Brooks. "The Peace Democrats went about the corridors of the hotels and the Capitol, saying that Lincoln had at last come to their way of thinking, and had gone to Hampton Roads to open peace negotiations. The radicals were in a fury of rage. They bitterly complained that the President was about to give up the political fruits which had been already gathered from the long and exhausting military struggle." The moderate Republicans of unshaken faith in Lincoln were in a minority; they failed to convince the radicals that Lincoln would not give ground on emancipation.

Thad Stevens among the bitterest, according to Brooks, was saying "that if the country were to vote over again for President of the United States, Benjamin F. Butler, and not Abraham Lincoln, would be their choice." And for the first time since Lincoln had been President a faction of his own political party, ruthless men of no hesitations about extreme methods, mentioned the final and desperate weapon they might use against him. "Others," wrote Brooks, "of the same uncompromising and unreasonable stripe [as Stevens] actually hinted at impeachment and trial."

Certainly the February 7 speech of radical Representative George W. Julian set the frame and laid the scene for a possible impeachment of Lincoln. In case the radicals should find that his report on Hampton Roads was considered by them a betrayal of their cause, Julian had opened the course with a first blast. In some 10,000 words Julian reviewed the war as a procession of mistakes, chiefly by the administration and its head. The negative, sickly and awkward policies of the administration, hoped Julian, would not be resumed.

On this day Welles found Lincoln waiting for the Cabinet to come in, "reading with much enjoyment certain portions of Petroleum V. Nasby": "Cussid be Sherman, for he took Atlanta. And he marcht thro the Confedrisy, and respected not the feelins of ennybody. And the people of the South lift up their voisis and weep, becoz their niggers are not. And he took Savanner, and cotton enuff 2 hev satisfide Bookannon's cabbynet. And he turns his eyes toward Charleston, and is serusly thinkin uv Richmond. The wind bloweth where it listeth—he listeth where he goeth."

One rumor now gaining headway and credence was that Lincoln at Hampton Roads had taken a sheet of paper, written at the top the one word "Union," and shoving it across the table toward Stephens, had said, "Let me have that one condition and you can write below it whatever peace terms you choose." This reported repudiation of the Emancipation Proclamation was to the radicals a hair-raising piece of news.

On February 10 the tension began to let down. The House had been dealing with a variety of bills when the clerk announced a message from the President. All other business was suspended. The clerk began reading. Documents, letters, dispatches, poured forth in a long stream. It seemed almost as though Lincoln had awaited this hour. The pass written for Blair to Richmond, the letter of Davis to Blair which Blair carried to Lincoln, the reply of Lincoln to Blair meant for Blair to carry to Richmond and show to Davis, the rise of the phrases "our one common country" and "the two countries," the documents passing between the Confederate commissioners showing up at Grant's army lines and what passed between them and Grant, the further transactions between Eckert and the commissioners, the Lincoln letter of instructions to Seward with its three "indispensable" points, the dispatch to Grant to keep the war going no matter what he heard about peace, Grant's reply that he would sure keep the war going, the Eckert telegram in cipher to Lincoln which for the moment wrecked all chance of a conference, the long telegram of Grant to Stan-

ton with Lincoln's brief comment that "this despatch . . .
changed my purpose," the meeting at Hampton Roads and
the reading of the commissioners' instruction from Davis
that they were there "for the purpose of securing peace to
the two countries," the negotiations ending with no result.
The foregoing, "containing as is believed all the information sought," was respectfully submitted.

Pressmen from their gallery noted "absolute silence from
first to last during the reading of this message. Looking
over the hall at the hundreds seated or standing, one might
say, wrote Noah Brooks, they "had been suddenly turned to
stone." Soon House members began exchanging smiles and
glances of meaning. The President had never for a moment
lost footing, had gone into a winding labyrinth where
anything could happen and had come out without a flaw.
"When the reading was over," and the full name of "Abraham Lincoln" signed to the communication was read by
the clerk with a certain grandiloquence, Brooks heard "an
instant and irrepressible storm of applause, begun by members on the floor, and taken up by the people in the gallery."

Washburne moved that 20,000 extra copies of the message be printed. "The entire loyal people of this country"
would approve the "wisdom and discretion in the President
of the United States" shown in this matter. Thad Stevens
spoke. "The President has thought it was best to make the
effort . . . I believe even those who thought his mission
was unwise will accord to him sagacity and patriotism, and
applaud his action."

To the Senate the President sent no such marshaled array of documents as he gave the House. To that graver and
more sedate body, empowered to ratify treaties and conduct foreign affairs, went a copy of a long note written by
the Secretary of State to Minister Adams at London, reciting the Hampton Roads negotiations.

An old order was passing. Now in the Supreme Court
chambers for the first time a Negro was admitted to practice before that high tribunal: John S. Rock, an attorney of
ability and good name in the city of Boston. The race issue

writhed and snarled again in debates over the proposed Bureau for the Relief of Freedmen and Refugees. The bill gave the President power to appoint commissioners to control the bureau, with authority to distribute "abandoned lands" among the Negroes, to pay out money and supplies.

Overshadowing all other discussions across February were those on bills for recognizing as "legitimate" the government set up in Louisiana a year earlier under the guidance of Lincoln and the military commander of the department, General Banks. The election of state officers ordered by Banks for February 22, 1864, covered an area of about one-third of the state. The voters were 11,411 white men, each having taken the oath required by the President, and they made a total of more than one-fifth of the entire vote of the State of Louisiana in 1860. They had elected three Congressmen and a governor, Michael Hahn. At a later election they had chosen delegates to a constitutional convention which met in New Orleans in April. This convention abolished slavery in Louisiana "forever" by a vote of 72 to 13. It gave the ballot to white males only, yet it empowered the legislature to give the ballot to Negro soldiers of service in the Union Army and to Negroes who could read and write, meeting the qualifications Lincoln had suggested in his letter to Governor Hahn.

The new state governments the President had guided were "shadows" and not "realities," according to the opposition. For himself he wished to regard them as "important," as "earnestly struggling," as admittedly "short of complete success."

Not to the public of this hour could Lincoln have given the painful details and sorry embarrassments he confessed in peremptory letters to Union generals who were wrecking his work. On November 14, 1864, he had begun a letter to General S. A. Hurlbut, successor to Banks in command at New Orleans: "Few things, since I have been here, have impressed me more painfully than what, for four or five months past, has appeared as bitter military opposition to the new State Government of Louisiana." He had hoped he was mistaken as to the facts, but having seen copies of letters exchanged between Generals Hurlbut and E. R. S. Canby, the hope was gone. That two of his generals should join with secessionists in trying to undo his work was "incomprehensible"—and if continued would not be overlooked.

Banks was "very sore" at Sumner over his opposition to the Louisiana plan, so Sumner wrote to Franz Lieber. Also it was near fantasy that Mrs. Lincoln at this time was writing notes to Sumner asking him to use his influence to prevent Banks' appointment to the Cabinet, which she feared might take place.

On December 18 the President had met Monty Blair and General Banks in a White House hall and called them into his office. "They immediately began to talk about Ashley's bill," wrote Hay. The bill included recognition of the new state government of Louisiana. "The President had been reading it carefully & said that he liked it with the exception of one or two things which he thought rather calculated to conceal a feature which might be objectionable to some. The first was that under the provisions of that bill negroes would be made jurors & voters under the temporary governments." Banks observed: "Yes, that is to be stricken out . . . It would simply throw the Government into the hands of the blacks, as the white people under that arrangement would refuse to vote." This was in substance the same view Banks the year before had written to Lincoln.

For weeks across January and February Ashley's bill was debated and taken back to committee for revisions and modifications. Five times it was redrafted, always fixing cast-iron requirements to be followed in letting the seceded states come back into the Union. On the final vote it failed by 80 to 65, with 37 members not voting.

In the Senate, reconstruction acts ran a different course. There Trumbull of Illinois reported from the Judiciary Committee a joint resolution declaring that the United States recognized the Louisiana government "inaugurated under and by the convention which assembled on the 6th day of April, A.D., 1864, at the city of New Orleans, as the legitimate government of the said State, entitled to the guarantees and all other rights of a State government, under the Constitution of the United States." Senators Sumner, Wade and Howard spoke amazement and scorn that their former associate in opposition to the President now acted in behalf of the President's most earnest wishes. Serene and without a flicker of resentment, Trumbull led a parliamentary fight that had his old allies sore and desperate.

In late February it was seen that most of the Democrats would vote against recognizing the new Louisiana state government. It was again the familiar Lincoln "military despotism," said Garrett Davis of Kentucky, a horse thief Government which had illegally run off with some of the best horseflesh in Kentucky, impressed for Union Army cavalry. The outspoken fear of other Democrats was that a military rule directed by a Republican administration in Washington would favor the Negroes. On the other hand the outspoken fear of the five Republican Senators who joined the Democratic opposition was that under the new state government of Louisiana, if it should be recognized, the whites would control and refuse the ballot to the Negroes. Therefore these five Republicans sought to put a rider on the bill which would insure the Negro the right to vote in Louisiana, this to be a precedent imperative on all other reorganized states. Of Lincoln's "ten-per-cent principle" Wade would say, "A more absurd, monarchical, and anti-American principle was never announced on God's earth."

Trumbull had offered the figures on the Louisiana case. He gave the first complete details, the statistics and computations, showing that in the Louisiana polls the so-called "Lincoln's ten per cent" was nearer 20 per cent or more.

Leading all others in speeches of condemnation, in amendments, in motions to delay voting, was Sumner. In the Senate gallery from day to day sat one listener, one spectator, who charmed Sumner, fascinated him. She was to him the one woman in the world. He had fallen in love with her, Alice Mason Hooper, a niece of Jeremiah Mason of Boston. "His devotion had been marked and somewhat opposite to his usual stately ways," wrote Anna Laurens

Dawes. "Among all the fascinating women of Washington she stood pre-eminent. Beauty, grace, a slender and stately form, a high-bred manner, and aristocratic reserve were all hers, and withal a special fascination, coming perhaps from the uncertain moods of an extremely variable temper—a temper which would pay its debts in the small coin of teasing or in the grand style, as fitted the mood of the hour." The match, the engagement to marry, came, wrote Miss Dawes, through "fascination and hope on the one side, fascination and ambition on the other." He was 57, a lifelong bachelor, and she at 27 sat in the gallery watching him, she with "the habits at once of a belle and a spoiled child, looking forward eagerly to the new gayeties of a senator's wife, and contemplating a near future when she should be mistress of the White House."

For her now, besides his regular public, Sumner performed, not knowing that soon after their marriage, soon after moving into a house of their own, his pride and will would come into collision with hers, they would part, he to meditate suicide and never after refer to her except as "that person." Now in February '65 he enjoyed it that his betrothed was in the gallery watching him in a parliamentary fight that called to his blood.

On the Senate floor Sumner rose to heights of stubborn granite and grandeur; also he sprawled in puddles of the ridiculous and the asinine. To brother Henry wrote Charles Francis Adams, Jr., "Sumner has run more than ever to seed, and now out-Sumners himself." Sumner argued that before he would recognize the new government of Louisiana, the right of Negroes to citizenship must be therewith guaranteed. The difference of view between Sumner and the President in this was much the same as it had been with the 13th Amendment, when Ashley had urged the President to send for Sumner and the President had replied: "I can do nothing with Mr. Sumner in these matters. While Mr. Sumner is very cordial with me, he is making his history in an issue with me on this very point. He hopes to succeed in beating the President so as to change this Government from its original form and make it a strong centralized power." Oddly enough, according to this, it was states' rights rather than Negro suffrage on which Sumner and Lincoln parted ways—and parted cordially, for Sumner never struck at Lincoln's motives.

There was laughter when Henderson inquired what had become of Sumner's "state suicide" theory. Was Louisiana in or out of the Union? Sumner: "It is in and it is not."

Sumner pressed toward the close of the debate: "The pretended State government in Louisiana is utterly indefensible . . . a mere seven-months' abortion, begotten by the bayonet in criminal conjunction with the spirit of caste."

The Senate February 27 postponed the measure by a vote of 34 to 12 "to to-morrow." This "to-morrow" never came. The session closed March 4 without a vote. Trumbull spoke his belief that there would have been a clear majority for the resolution had it not been fought by Sumner. In the last days of the session Sumner piled his desk high with documents, books, papers, notes, gave the word he was going to filibuster. He would stand and speak and read till the session officially ended. Thus he would kill three bills—a tax, a tariff and an appropriation bill. The Senate gave in. Sumner had his way. Louisiana was out. Lincoln's foremost immediate project was lost, for the time. Another Congress, further events, would pass on Louisiana.

The tangled episode of Louisiana's political fate came to its climax and diminuendo. Heavy folios of narrative would be required to tell the entire story in all its chaotic and troubled lights. Passions—the same passions that had made the war—ran through all the breath of it. Yet Sumner in all his stubborn course of procedure had cast no aspersion on the President. And Lincoln in his turn had kept a perfect serenity toward Sumner. Each had stood by his sincere convictions as spoken to the other in early winter discussions.

About this time, according to an incident later related by Joseph G. Cannon of Danville, Illinois, several Northern Congressmen in Lincoln's office were calling for retaliation. They wanted hangings of "rebel" leaders. Representative James K. Moorhead was making a second and more vitriolic attack than his first when Lincoln leaned across his table, shot out an arm and pointed a long finger: "Mr. Moorhead, haven't you lived long enough to know that two men may honestly differ about a question and both be right?"

Out of Savannah February 1 Sherman had moved, his plan of campaign a secret. A dispatch had come to Stanton and Lincoln that his route was inland. Before starting Sherman had said this march would be ten times as difficult, ten times more important, than the one from Atlanta to the sea.

In two columns with outriding cavalry Sherman's 60,000 men moved over the soil of the state that had led off in secession. Continuous winter rains had swollen all streams. Country not under water was mud and quagmire. They marched day on day with rain about two days out of three. They crossed five large navigable rivers, swollen torrents. At times every private in the army served as a pioneer, split saplings and carried fence rails for corduroy roads, laid pontoons, cleared entanglements. They waded streams, no time to bridge. Some forces worked for hours waist-deep in icy floodwaters. One captured Confederate trooper, seeing these exploits, told the 104th Illinois, "If your army goes to hell, it will corduroy the road." General Joseph E. Johnston said later, "I made up my mind there had been no such army since the days of Julius Caesar."

Confederate forces of about 15,000, chiefly under General Wade Hampton, made no headway in stopping the Northern invaders, who seemed to have saved their fury for South Carolina. Troops of the 15th corps were heard to say, "Here is where treason began and, by God, here is where it shall end." Officially Sherman's orders, as in Georgia, were against wanton violence and destruction, but Sherman did not repeat them now. In his own later words: "My aim then was to whip the rebels, to humble their pride, to follow them to their inmost recesses, and make them fear and dread us." Over the South arose a tradition that Sherman had raved in wrath, "I'm going to bring every Southern woman to the washtub."

Undoubtedly his men went farther in robbery, violence and vicious capers than he cared to have them, but their toils and marches, their readiness for hardship and fighting, were such that Sherman could not bring himself to penalize them. For himself he slept in a tree one night of flood, another night on a hard board church pew, living mostly as plain as any private.

Foragers stripped the country of many farm buildings, farm animals, fences, much property, and food of all kinds. The railroads were torn up, and weather permitting, bridges burned, cotton bales set blazing, vacant dwellings and barns fired. Looters and bummers stole jewelry, watches and silverware, smashed pianos and shattered mirrors, though the extent and the manner of these outrages became an issue of veracity as between Northern and Southern witnesses.

It was heartbreak time in South Carolina. The final dooms were weaving, Mrs. Chesnut writing February 22: "Charleston and Wilmington have surrendered. I have no further use for a newspaper. I never want to see another one as long as I live . . . Shame, disgrace, beggary, all have come at once, and are hard to bear—the grand smash! Rain, rain, outside, and naught but drowning floods of tears inside." She couldn't bear it, and rushed downstairs and out through the rainstorm to the home of the Reverend Mr. Martin, who said, "Madam, Columbia is burned to the ground." Mrs. Chesnut bowed her head and sobbed aloud.

In bloody actions of February 5, 6 and 7 Grant had so struck at Lee that by no chance could Lee send any men toward Sherman. In Washington February 22 by order of the President there was a night illumination of the high domed building on the top of Capitol Hill—lights and singing bright windows in celebration of victories resulting in Columbia, Charleston, Wilmington, and a fresh wide area coming again under the U.S. flag.

Chapter 43

The Second Inaugural

Of little help toward Lincoln's second inaugural address in a few days was the widely circulated *Leslie's Weekly* which on its front page February 25, 1865, said Lincoln showed "pigheadedness in retaining McClellan" so long, and that his retention of "worthless" Cabinet members had earned him "the strongly expressed contempt of Congress." In fact, "There is no man of less consequence in these United States than Abraham Lincoln of Illinois. A school-boy would deserve flogging for sending out documents of such prodigious moment as come from his pen in phrases so mean and unbecoming."

On March 4, 1865, hours before noon, Lincoln in a Senate wing room considered and signed bills. A parade on Pennsylvania Avenue from the White House to the Capitol moved in a light drizzle of rain and cold, gusty winds. A muddy paste coated the sidewalks lined with spectators. On one wagon platform printers from the Typographical Society, a labor union, ran a hand press and scattered programs of the day's events. A battalion of Negro troops in Union Army blue marched, and the Negro Grand Lodge of Odd Fellows.

Toward noon flocks of women streamed around the Capitol, "crinoline smashed, skirts bedaubed, velvet and laces streaked with mud." And the women, noted Brooks, kept unfailing good nature though "such another dirty crowd probably never was seen." In the galleries women in wide crinoline "filled the seats like a cloud," not a man finding a seat. "Diamonds flashed, feathers nodded (damply), bright faces gleamed, and the noise of feminine tongues was like a swarm of bees." Senator Foot of Vermont rapped his gavel for order but "a rippling storm of small talk in the galleries went on."

Invited notables trod to their reserved seats. Noah Brooks wrote of Mrs. Lincoln, attended by Senator Anthony, seated in the Diplomatic Gallery, and a buzz when the Justices of the Supreme Court entered in their black robes. A few stray governors came in, then the Diplomatic Corps, in gold lace, feathers and white pantaloons. One ambassador had to unbutton himself to get his feet on the floor. Members of the House moved in at noon, then the Cabinet.

In the middle of the front row sat Lincoln; as the clock struck twelve his eyes turned with those of others to the entrance of Andrew Johnson, Vice-President-elect, escorted by Senator Doolittle. Johnson after introduction rose with no papers, saying impromptu to the Senators, to the Supreme Court, that their power came from the mass of the people, and further, "You, Mr. Secretary Seward, Mr. Secretary Stanton, the Secretary of the Navy [he couldn't quite dig up the name of Welles], and the others who are your associates—you know that you have my respect and my confidence—derive not your greatness and your power alone from President Lincoln." He was in a mood. "Humble as I am, plebeian as I may be deemed, permit me in the presence of this brilliant assemblage to enunciate the truth that courts and cabinets, the President and his advisers, derive their power and their greatness from the people."

Part of this, of course, was Andrew Johnson's traditional stump speech. "I, though a plebeian boy, am authorized by the principles of the Government under which I live to feel proudly conscious that I am a man, and grave dignitaries are but men." He was overdoing the business of being a plebeian.

By now Hamlin had pulled at Johnson's coattails while the Senate clerk, John W. Forney, with whom Johnson had been drinking the evening before, whispered loud, hoping to catch Johnson's eye and flag him down. Johnson swept on into thanking God that Tennessee had never been out of the Union, and declaring flatly, "No State can go out of this Union; and moreover, Congress cannot eject a State from the Union."

Far more sorry than funny was this performance—the sour note of the day. His face flushed, his voice hoarse, Johnson looked worn and sick. For weeks that winter he had been in bed with typhoid fever and general exhaustion from heavy labors amid terrific excitement. He had written to Lincoln inquiring whether by any precedents he could stay in Nashville and take his oath of office. Lincoln had wired: "It is our unanimous conclusion that it is unsafe for you not to be here on the fourth of March. Be sure to reach here by that time." In Hamlin's room in the Senate building he poured one tumbler of whisky and drank it down, and according to Hamlin, just before going into the overheated Senate chamber, drank another, saying, "I need all the strength for the occasion I can have."

As Johnson got well into his speech several Republican Senators bent their heads, unable to look at him. Sumner covered his face with his hands. Seward, wrote Noah Brooks, was "bland and serene as a summer day" and Stanton seemed "petrified." Speed "sat with eyes closed." Senators "turned and twisted" in their chairs. When Johnson had repeated inaudibly the oath of office, he turned, took the Bible in his hand, "and facing the audience, said, with a loud, theatrical voice and gesture, 'I kiss this Book in the face of my nation of the United States.'"

At Lincoln's side sat Senator Henderson of Missouri, who noticed Lincoln's head drooping in humiliation. As Senator Henderson offered his arm to Lincoln for taking their place in the march to the inaugural platform outside, Henderson heard Lincoln say to a marshal, "Do not let Johnson speak outside."

A day or two later Hugh McCulloch spoke to Lincoln about alarm in some quarters. What would happen to the country if Lincoln should be suddenly removed and Johnson replaced him? Lincoln after a moment's hesitation and with unusual seriousness: "I have known Andy for many years. He made a bad slip the other day, but you need not be scared. Andy ain't a drunkard."

The procession to the Capitol portico formed and moved. The drizzle of rain had stopped. "A tremendous shout, prolonged and loud, arose from the surging ocean of humanity," wrote Noah Brooks. The President with invited notables took the platform. Then the sergeant at arms of the Senate arose and with raised hands got the crowd still. And Abraham Lincoln, rising tall, gaunt and outstanding, stepped forward to read his inaugural address. Applause roared, again and again was repeated, and finally died far away on the outer fringe of the throng.

In a silence almost profound the audience now listened. Seldom had a President been so short-spoken about the issues of so grave an hour. He read his carefully and deliberately prepared address:

[Fellow Countrymen:] At this second appearing to take the oath of the presidential office, there is less occasion for an extended address than there was at the first. Then a statement, somewhat in detail, of a course to be pursued, seemed fitting and proper. Now, at the expiration of four years, during which public declarations have been constantly called forth on every point and phase of the great contest which still absorbs the attention, and engrosses the energies of the nation, little that is new could be presented. The progress of our arms, upon which all else chiefly depends, is as well known to the public as to myself; and it is, I trust, reasonably satisfactory and encouraging to all. With high hope for the future, no prediction in regard to it is ventured.

On the occasion corresponding to this four years ago, all thoughts were anxiously directed to an impending civil-war. All dreaded it—all sought to avert it. While the inaugeral address was being delivered from this place, devoted altogether to *saving* the Union without war, insurgent agents were in the city seeking to *destroy* it without war—seeking to dissol[v]e the Union, and divide effects, by negotiation. Both parties deprecated war; but one of them would *make* war rather than let the nation survive; and the other would *accept* war rather than let it perish. And the war came.

One eighth of the whole population were colored slaves, not distributed generally over the Union, but localized in the Southern part of it. These slaves constituted a peculiar and powerful interest. All knew that this interest was, somehow, the cause of the war. To strengthen, perpetuate, and extend this interest was the object for which the insurgents would rend the Union, even by war; while the government claimed no right to do more than to restrict the territorial enlargement of it. Neither party expected for the war, the magnitude, or the duration, which it has already attained. Neither anticipated that the *cause* of the conflict might cease with, or even before, the conflict itself should cease. Each looked for an easier triumph, and a result less fundamental and astounding. Both read the same Bible, and pray to the same God; and each invokes His aid against the other. It may seem strange that any men should dare to ask a just God's assistance in wringing their bread from the sweat of other men's faces; but let us judge not that we be not judged. The prayers of both could not be answered; that of neither had been answered fully. The Almighty has His own purposes. "Woe unto the world because of offences! for it must needs be that offences come; but woe to that man by whom the offence cometh!" If we shall suppose that American Slavery is one of those offences which, in the providence of God, must needs come, but which, having continued through His appointed time, He now wills to remove, and that He gives to both North and South, this terrible war, as the woe due to those by whom the offence came, shall we discern therein any departure from those divine attributes which the believers in a Living God always ascribe to Him? Fondly do we hope—fervently do we pray—that this mighty scourge of war may speedily pass away. Yet, if God wills that it continue, until all the wealth piled by the bond-man's two hundred and fifty years of unrequited toil shall be sunk, and until every drop of blood drawn with the lash shall be paid by another drawn with the sword, as was said three thousand years ago, so still it must be said "the judgments of the Lord, are true and righteous altogether."

With malice toward none; with charity for all; with firmness in the right, as God gives us to see the right, let us strive on to finish the work we are in; to bind up the nation's wounds; to care for him who shall have borne the battle, and for his widow, and his orphan— to do all which may achieve and cherish a just, and a lasting peace, among ourselves, and with all nations.

A subdued handclapping and occasional cheers punctuated the address. Reporters noticed at the final paragraph many moist eyes and here and there tears coursing down faces unashamed.

The clerk of the Supreme Court brought the Bible. Then Lincoln, laying his right hand on an open page of the Book, repeated the oath of office after Chief Justice Chase, bent forward, kissed the Book and arose to full height again.

Presenting the Book to Mrs. Lincoln afterward, the Chief Justice pointed to the pencil-marked verses kissed by the President, in the fifth chapter of Isaiah:

> None shall be weary nor stumble among them; none shall slumber nor sleep; neither shall the girdle of their loins be loosed, nor the latchet of their shoes be broken:
> Whose arrows are sharp, and all their bows bent, their horses' hoofs shall be counted like flint, their wheels like a whirlwind.

Like the Gettysburg Address, and more particularly the House Divided speech, the second inaugural took on varied meanings. To some it was a howl for vengeance, to others a benediction and a plea—with deep music.

"Everyone likes a compliment," wrote Lincoln to Thurlow Weed with thanks for good words, and giving his own

estimate of his address. He expected it "to wear as well as
—perhaps better than—any thing I have produced; but I
believe it is not immediately popular. Men are not flattered
by being shown that there has been a difference of purpose
between the Almighty and them."

In the evening the White House was open for a reception. "The platform in front of the entrance, the walks and
drives back of the Avenue, were packed with people,"
noted Lieutenant Ashmun of the guards. Occasionally a
lady fainted or became terrified and would have to be
taken out over the heads of the close-packed crowd. From
8 until 11 Lincoln spent in almost continuous handshaking.
Newsmen wrote that he shook hands with more than 6,000
persons.

The crowds vanished and in the still midnight the White
House looked to the guard Crook, "as if a regiment of rebel
troops had been quartered there, with permission to forage." Mementoes were wanted. "A great piece of red bro-
cade, a yard square almost, was cut from the window-hang-
ings of the East Room. Flowers from the floral designs in
the lace curtains were cut out. Some arrests were made,
after the reception, of persons concerned in the disgrace-
ful business." The President, noted Crook, was "distressed
greatly." Usually he was so calm about things. Crook noted
his saying, "Why should they do it? How can they?"

An American crowd, "a motley democratic crowd, such
as could be seen in no royal country, and of which we are
justly proud," ran the version of Adelaide W. Smith, an
army nurse. She had met one Lieutenant Gosper, their
friendship not ordinary. In a skirmish before Petersburg his
right leg had been shot away and Miss Smith had been his
nurse. She wrote, "We fell into the long procession of
couples approaching the President." Swept along, Miss
Smith and Lieutenant Gosper on his crutch finally saw
Lincoln. To their surprise he stepped out before the two of
them, took the hand of Lieutenant Gosper, and in a voice
unforgettable, was saying, "God bless you, my boy!"

The two of them moved on, the lieutenant happy and saying to Ada Smith, "Oh! I'd lose another leg for a man like that!"

Mary Abigail Dodge, a trim little 109-pound woman, widely known for her sparkling magazine and newspaper writings, had on March 7, 1861, in a White House crowd put out her hand saying, "Mr. Lincoln, I am very sorry for you, but indeed I must shake hands with you," hearing him, "Ah! *your* hand doesn't hurt me." Now on March 4, 1865, in her little village of Hamilton, Massachusetts, she wrote him a letter he may have read more than once:

> I only wish to thank you for being so good—and to say how sorry we all are that you must have four years more of this terrible toil. But remember what a triumph it is for the right, what a blessing to the country—and then your rest shall be glorious when it does come!
>
> You can't tell anything about it in Washington where they make a noise on the slightest provocation— But if you had been in this little speck of a village this morning and heard the soft, sweet music of unseen bells rippling through the morning silence from every quarter of the far-off horizon, you would have better known what your name is to this nation.
>
> May God help you in the future as he has helped you in the past and a people's love and gratitude will be but a small portion of your exceeding great reward.

Chapter 44

Endless Executive Routine

Where others had made little or no headway at calming Missouri, General Grenville M. Dodge as military commander was to try his hand. More than any other state Missouri was seeing civil war, neighbors arrayed against neighbors, with roving guerrillas and bushwhackers, barn-burners, midnight shootings, Lincoln writing to Dodge January 15 of "so much irregular violence in Northern Missouri as to be . . . almost depopulating it." He suggested that Dodge consider "an appeal to the people there to go to their homes, and let one another alone," possible withdrawal of troops where they seemed an irritation. In suggesting steps he believed practical, Lincoln voiced a faith in humanity not easy to apply in Missouri at that hour.

In the weeks following inauguration, according to one of Sumner's secretaries, "Mr. Lincoln bestowed more tokens of good-will on Sumner than on any other senator." It seemed that for any Senators or Congressmen whose co-operation Lincoln sought, he would go out of his way to grant them offices or favors. During four years and one month of presidential appointive powers, Lincoln, according to a later estimate, removed 1,457 out of a possible 1,639 officials. In many responsible wartime positions the strictest of loyalty was a requirement; all under doubt had to go. In the building of a loyalist Government Lincoln carried a heavy load.

The old and tried friend of true steel loyalty, Isaac N. Arnold, while giving all he had for Lincoln in Washington, had lost his seat in Congress, but was staying on in Washington to write a biography of Lincoln and a history of the overthrow of slavery. Lincoln offered him a choice of two good offices and Arnold was thinking it over.

Fessenden had resigned as Secretary of the Treasury and begun his third term as Senator from Maine. Leading bankers and many Western politicians favored Maine-born Hugh McCulloch, who in 1833 had settled in Fort Wayne, Indiana, and won his way to the top circles of banking. Lincoln asked McCulloch to call and, as they shook hands, "I have sent for you, Mr. McCulloch, to let you know that I want you to be Secretary of the Treasury." McCulloch accepted with "distrust" of his ability; the Senate unanimously confirmed his appointment.

To replace the resigned John P. Usher Lincoln sent the

name of James Harlan, U.S. Senator from Iowa, to be Secretary of the Interior, which the Senate also confirmed. Harlan was a frontier educator who had been superintendent of public instruction in Iowa in 1847 and president of Iowa Wesleyan University in 1863. Welles wrote that the President told the Cabinet he had talked with Usher about the necessity for his resigning because two in the Cabinet from Indiana were one too many.

In some British political and journalistic circles a war scare was on. Lincoln and Seward had their conferences over how to convey assurances to Britain that the United States was not preparing for violence overseas.

The President heard Seward, Speed and Welles one day discuss the rights of courts or of Congress to go beyond public records and demand any papers whatsoever from any department of the Government. Seward pointed to the private, locked shelves of the President, saying, "They will demand those papers." "But those," said the President, according to Welles, "are private and confidential, a very different affair." "Call them what you please," said Seward, "you cannot retain them from Congress or the court if you concede the principle in this case [involving records of court-martial trials] . . . the Secretary of the Navy . . . must not furnish them copies nor must he testify." Without being convinced of Seward's points, the President was an attentive listener, and, wrote Welles, "I think his faith was somewhat shaken." The President said: "We will look into this matter fully and carefully. If the Secretary of State is right, we shall all of us be of his opinion, for this is a big thing, and this question must have been up and passed on before this day." He decided a legal opinion should come from the Attorney General with questions framed for him to answer. "The matter closed for the present," wrote Welles, "by the President instructing me not to give my evidence or copies till this question is decided."

Seward during this conference had been not merely annoyed but angry. "He denied," wrote Welles, "that the public papers of any Department were to be subjected to private examination, and most emphatically denounced any idea of furnishing copies on the claim or demand of any State court or any court in a private suit. If it was conceded in a single instance, it must be in all."

In a period of less than seven weeks Lincoln had guided the delicate legislative passage of the 13th Amendment; had conducted the elaborate finesse of the Hampton Roads conference; had gone through the broils of the failure to secure recognition for Louisiana; had kept in touch with Grant and Sherman, naval affairs, the draft sending fresh replacements to the armies; had attended to a regular grist of courts-martial, arbitrary arrests, habeas corpus, pardons; had chosen two new Cabinet members; had written his second inaugural and taken oath for a second term; had passed on hundreds of applications for office. And on Tuesday, March 14, for the first time he held a Cabinet meeting as he lay in bed, worn and haggard from emotional stress and overwork.

Seward brought up "a paper for excluding blockade-runners and persons in complicity with the Rebels from the country." The appointment of John P. Hale as Minister to Spain came up. Hale had been merciless and slashing in criticisms of the Navy Department. "Seward tried to gloss it over. Wanted Hale to call and see me," wrote Welles, "and make friends with Fox." Horizontal in bed the President, in a way, rested.

Eighteen days after reinauguration Brooks' news letter noted the President's health as "worn down by the constant pressure of office-seekers and legitimate business, so that for a few days he was obliged to deny himself to all comers." Since a new rule held to strictly, of closing the office doors at three in the afternoon, "receiving only those whom he prefers during the evening hours," the President was looking better.

Once after handling a grist of callers that included a Senator seeking to honor the Monroe Doctrine by a war with France, and a poor scrub woman who wished merely the privilege of daily earning wages by shining the Treasury Building floors, Lincoln said to Brooks, "When I get through with such a day's work there is only one word that

can express my condition, and that is—*flabbiness.*" Again
to Brooks he referred to "the tired spot which can't be
got at."

The patience of the American people the President
thought something matchless and touching; he was never
weary of commending it, noted Brooks, "I have seen him
shed tears when speaking of the cheerful sacrifice of the
light and strength of so many happy homes throughout the
land."

For so long a time now in one crisis after another the
President had seen the judgments of supposedly good
minds, some rated among "the best minds," so utterly
wrong, so completely mistaken, so ready with advice that
would have brought wreck and ruin beyond retrieving,
that he had a deeper and surer feeling about his own reason and vision in the face of chaos. This feeling in some
moods bordered on arrogance. Or if not arrogance a cold
self-assurance, a refusal to say Yes to the proposals of even
the so-called best minds until he had tested those proposals
in the fire and the ice of his own mind and heart in long
deliberations.

During four years the President had spoken many con-
fidences and eased his mind freely to Brooks; their friendship had deepened. At no time in delicate moments of
tangled affairs had Brooks mistaken his place. So the
quiet understanding was that probably the following summer he was to be appointed private secretary to the President, Nicolay and Hay taking places in the Paris legation.
Brooks had the required gravity—and humor—with loyalty,
affection and sympathy, even though he had no special
admiration for Nicolay and Hay.

That the White House couple were an oddly mated pair
seemed to be generally assumed. When in January Mrs.
Lincoln dismissed a doorkeeper who had held the post since
the Jackson administration, it was chronicled briefly in the
newspapers. With more Union victories in sight and with
her husband elected to four more years in the White House,
there was less of malicious rumor published about her—

though gossip still ran on, some of it not idle or ill-meant.

At the inaugural ball, March 6, the President with Speaker Colfax entered the long marble hall of the Patent Office. The leading lady of the grand march was Mrs. Lincoln, and her escort Senator Sumner. It meant at least they were on speaking terms, that the President and his parliamentary foe, divided on principles, had not parted as personal friends. Mrs. Lincoln had a warm personal regard for Sumner. She sent him little notes, flowers from the White House conservatory and seemed to admire him in about the degree she hated Seward.

Indications were that Mrs. Lincoln chiefly shaped the military status of young Robert. In the White House Mrs. Lincoln's sister, Emilie Todd Helm, in her diary in November '63 wrote: "She [Mrs. Lincoln] is frightened about Robert going into the army. She said today to Brother Lincoln (I was reading in another part of the room but could not help overhearing the conversation): 'Of course, Mr. Lincoln, I know that Robert's plea to go into the army is manly and noble and I want him to go, but oh! I am so frightened he may never come back to us!'" From the father came the plea, as Mrs. Helm heard it, "Many a poor mother, Mary, has had to make this sacrifice and has given up every son she had and lost them all."

Mrs. Helm recorded a call from General Sickles and Senator Harris at the White House: "Senator Harris turned to Mrs. Lincoln abruptly and said: 'Why isn't Robert in the army? He is old enough and strong enough to serve his country. He should have gone to the front some time ago.' Sister Mary's face turned white as death and I saw that she was making a desperate effort at self-control. She bit her lip, but answered quietly, 'Robert is making his preparations now to enter the Army, Senator Harris; he is not a shirker as you seem to imply for he has been anxious to go for a long time. If fault there be, it is mine, I have insisted that he should stay in college a little longer as I think an educated man can serve his country with more intelligent purpose than an ignoramus.'"

The mother had had her wish. Her boy had stayed on at

Harvard and graduated. It was probably by agreement with Mrs. Lincoln, that Lincoln on January 19, 1865, wrote to Grant: "Please read and answer this letter as though I was not President, but only a friend. My son, now in his twenty second year, having graduated at Harvard, wishes to see something of the war before it ends. I do not wish to put him in the ranks, nor yet to give him a commission, to which those who have already served long, are better entitled, and better qualified to hold. Could he, without embarrassment to you, or detriment to the service, go into your Military family with some nominal rank, I, and not the public, furnishing his necessary means? If no, say so without the least hesitation, because I am as anxious, and as deeply interested, that you shall not be encumbered as you can be yourself."

Grant replied that he would be glad to have the son "in my military family in the manner you propose." What then followed in this delicate arrangement was reported by Grant's staff member Colonel Horace Porter: "The President replied that he would consent to this upon one condition: that his son should serve as a volunteer aide without pay or emoluments; but Grant dissuaded him from adhering to that determination, saying that it was due to the young man that he should be regularly commissioned, and put on an equal footing with other officers of the same grade. So it was finally settled that Robert should receive the rank of captain and assistant adjutant-general; on February 23 he was attached to the staff of the general-in-chief. The new acquisition to the company at headquarters soon became exceedingly popular. He had inherited many of the genial traits of his father, and entered heartily into all the social pastimes at headquarters. He was always ready to perform his share of hard work, and never expected to be treated differently from any other officer on account of his being the son of the Chief Executive of the nation."

Press reports of February gave the President's income tax payment for the year at $1,279.13. Around the query "How much is Mr. Lincoln worth in money?" there seemed to be little curiosity. His salary of $25,000 a year was the largest steady income he had ever had. It was paid each month in Treasury Department warrants, with the income tax deducted. These payments Lincoln had invested in more than $75,000 worth of U.S. securities, of which more than $50,000 were "registered bonds bearing 6 per cent interest, payable in coin."   ,

In mid-March came Senator John B. Henderson of Missouri with two lists of men and boys held in military prisons in his state or nearby. All sorts of appeals had been coming to the Senator, and before leaving for home he wanted to clear up as many of these cases as he could. He laid before Lincoln first a list of those he considered fairly innocent. Lincoln looked it over. "Do you mean to tell me, Henderson, that you wish me to let loose all these people at once?" Henderson said Yes; the war was nearly over; the time had come to try generosity and kindness. "Do you really think so?" asked Lincoln. Henderson was sure he thought so; he was trying to slow down the guerrilla warfare of his torn and weary state. "I hope you are right," said Lincoln, "but I have no time to examine this evidence. If I sign this list as a whole, will you be responsible for the future good behavior of the men?" Henderson would. "Then I will take the risk and sign it," said Lincoln as he began writing the word "Pardoned" after each name of some man convicted by a military commission, finally writing a general order of release.

Henderson thanked the President and then pulled out his second list, names of men maybe not so very innocent but maybe safe to take a chance on. "I hope," said Lincoln, according to Henderson's account, "you are not going to make me let loose another lot." Yes, Henderson thought it good policy, safer and better than holding them in jails. "Yes," said Lincoln, "but you know I am charged with making too many mistakes on the side of mercy." Henderson was sure he was right and said the President ought to sign out the whole batch. "Well, I'll be durned if I don't," said the President, this being, noted Henderson, "the only time I ever heard Mr. Lincoln use a word which approached profanity." As he handed the list back, Lincoln said: "Now, Henderson, remember you are responsible to me for those men. If they do not behave, I shall have to put you in prison for their sins."

Solidarity was wanted. For the Jewish chiropodist Zacharie, Stanton must arrange a pass to Savannah and let Zacharie bring back his father and sisters, if he so wished. Blumenberg, a Baltimore Jew, Lincoln wrote Stanton in the same letter, should have a hearing. Blumenberg had "raised troops—fought, and been wounded. He should not be dismissed in a way that disgraces and ruins him without a hearing." At Bardstown, Kentucky, ran a telegraphed order, "Let no depredation be committed upon the property or possessions of the Sisters of Charity of Nazareth Academy." And two orders addressed "To whom it may concern" specified that Sisters of Mercy in charge of military hospitals in Chicago or Washington should be furnished such provisions as they desired to purchase, "and charge same to the War Department."

The man-hunter approach as often as possible was to be avoided. Some such point of view seemed more and more to animate Lincoln in the latest war flares and shadows. Against Stanton's express wishes, and knowing well that Stanton would be furious should he hear of it, Lincoln took his own whimsical course and released three secession leaders, one a brigadier general.

In the case of John Y. Beall, however, Lincoln decided the evidence proved Beall a spy, a pirate and a privateersman, leading a band which had captured vessels on the Great Lakes, seized cargoes and money, scuttled one steamer, and failed in a plan to release the Confederate prisoners on Johnson's Island. A mass of formidable influence came forward seeking from the President a commutation of death sentence to life imprisonment. Money was poured out and a vast personal influence enlisted. Over and again Lincoln and Major General John A. Dix, commanding the Department of the East, gave the same answers, Lincoln saying, "General Dix may dispose of the case as he pleases—I will not interfere!" General Dix saying, "All now rests with the President—as far as my action rests there is not a gleam of hope." And no word having come from Lincoln or Dix, Captain John Y. Beall of the Confederate Army on February 24, 1865, was hanged.

"I've had more questions of life and death to settle in four years than all the other men who ever sat in this chair put together," said Lincoln to Bromwell of Illinois, with Seward and others present. "No man knows the distress of my mind. The case of Beall on the Lakes—there had to be an example. They tried me every way. They wouldn't give up. But I had to stand firm. I even had to turn away his poor sister when she came and begged for his life, and let him be executed, and he was executed, and I can't get the distress out of my mind yet." Bromwell noticed Lincoln's eyes moisten, and turned and saw other eyes in the room the same.

On March 11 went forth the President's proclamation that any and all deserters, wherever they might be and no matter what had happened to carry their feet away from the army, on return to their regiments or companies "shall be pardoned."

On some matter of no moment Greeley had a brief interview in early March and had a feeling Lincoln was worn down to his last physical reserves. "His face was haggard with care and seamed with thought and trouble. It looked care-ploughed, tempest-tossed and weather-beaten." On March 21, however, the editor of the Baltimore *American and Commercial Advertiser* watched him an hour in the morning and an hour in the afternoon receiving many difficult visitors, and, "The President looked extremely well, seemed in excellent spirits, and bore none of those evidences of debility or failing health which the New York *Tribune* daily talks about." On one office envelope Charles A. Dana took notice of the word "Assassination" in Lincoln's handwriting. Of death threat letters Dana had taken to the President, Dana wrote, "He looked at them but made no special remark, and, in fact, seemed to attach very little importance to them. I left them with him."

Harriet Beecher Stowe one winter evening had asked if

he did not feel a great relief over the prospect of the war soon coming to a close. And Lincoln had answered, she said, in a sad way: "No, Mrs. Stowe, I shall never live to see peace. This war is killing me."

Chapter 45

Lincoln Visits Grant's Army —
Grant Breaks Lee's Line

Down Pennsylvania Avenue one day, wrote Noah Brooks, moved "a Confederate regimental band which had deserted in a body with its instruments, and was allowed to march through the streets of the national capital playing Union airs."

Congressman Ashley, just from Grant's headquarters, reported to Lincoln of Grant saying, "For every three men of ours dead, five of theirs; for every three of our cattle dead, five of theirs." And picking up some paper from a table and crushing it in his hand, "Tell the President I have got them like that!" Ashley said, "It made the cold chills run over me."

Sheridan had driven Early's army out of the Shenandoah Valley and reported in late March 780 barns burned, 420,000 bushels of wheat taken, also 700,000 rounds of ammunition, 2,557 horses, 7,152 head of beef cattle. So often now the wagons of Lee went out for food and came back empty. In comparison the Union army had nearly all needs in supplies running over.

After long bickering, with the Confederate Senate reversing itself and by a majority of one voting to arm the slaves for defense, President Davis signed the bill. At last the Negro slave was to be put in the Confederate Army to fight for his master. This was their one final hope for more soldiers.

As from Lee had come to Mrs. Chesnut an impressive

saying: "This is the people's war; when they tire, I stop."
She wrote as though she believed in this hour Lee had said
it. When a certain order of passion, faith and endurance
goes down, its final extinction is miraculously swift, Mrs.
Chestnut mused. It was like the snuffing out of a candle:
"One moment white, then gone forever."

To one White House caller Lincoln gave his picture of
the major strategy of recent weeks. "Grant has the bear by
the hind leg while Sherman takes off the hide." Pointing on
a map, he said that Sherman when last heard of had his
cavalry, vanguard and infantry columns here, there and
there, "expecting to bring them all together *here.*" Then
after a pause: "Now when he does that, he'll—but that
reminds *me* of the horsedealer in Kentucky who got bap-
tized in the river. The ceremony once over he insisted on
it a second time. The preacher hesitated but the horse-
trader had his way. And when he came up from the second
ducking he gasped, 'There now! Now I can tell the devil
to go to hell!' "

Up across North Carolina marched Sherman to Fayette-
ville, then to Goldsboro, where he paused for rest. Behind
them toward Savannah lay 425 miles of foraged and ravaged country. Since July '63 his men had come on their
feet no less than 2,500 miles, fording ordinary streams
and flooded rivers, through rains and hot sun. Many were
ragged, their trousers half gone from tussling through un-
derbrush. More than half had thrown away their worn-out
shoes, some walking barefoot, others with feet wrapped in
blanket pieces. They leaped and shouted as they slid into
new issues of shoes, uniforms, overcoats, at Goldsboro.
The troops were mainly from the West, the Midwest and
the Northwest.

Lincoln was to leave Washington to see Grant and have
a breakaway from many pressures at Washington. And he
might go over with Grant what terms should end the war.
Early in March he had written an order through Stanton
indicating Grant was to have no conference with General
Lee unless on purely military affairs: ". . . you are not to
decide, discuss, or confer upon any political questions.

Such questions the President holds in his own hands, and will submit them to no military conferences or conventions."

The President was to sail from Washington on the *Bat*, a fast, comfortable, well-armed dispatch boat. Then came later orders for Captain Barnes to report at the White House, where, noted the Captain, "Mr. Lincoln received me with great cordiality, but with a certain kind of embarrassment, and a look of sadness which rather embarrassed me. After a few casual remarks he said that Mrs. Lincoln had decided that she would accompany him to City Point—could the *Bat* accommodate her and her maidservant?"

Barnes was ushered into Mrs. Lincoln's presence, noting that "she received me very graciously, standing with arms folded." Her wishes: "I am going with the President to City Point, and I want you to arrange your ship to take me, my maid and my officer [or guard], as well as the President." Barnes was bothered. He went to Fox. They agreed the *Bat* couldn't be fixed over. Together they went to the White House. There "in very funny terms the President translated our difficulties." Fox promised another and better boat. On the unarmed and less safe though more spacious *River Queen*, with the *Bat* as convoy, the Lincoln family made the trip, Tad sleeping in a stateroom with the guard Crook.

Grant came aboard at City Point. Any hour he expected the enemy, because of their forces dwindling through desertion, to make a desperate attempt to crash the Union lines and force a path toward joining Johnston in North Carolina.

In a jolting coach over the military railroad from City Point toward the front Lincoln rode past scenery where in the first daylight hours that morning men had been mowed down by fort guns and men had fought hand to hand with bayonet and clubbed musket. Confederate troops under General John B. Gordon had taken Fort Stedman and pressed on with the aim of destroying a railroad and Union supply stores. The Union troops had rallied, had driven the enemy back and retaken Fort Stedman—and Lincoln's breakfast hour, as he wired Stanton, saw the fight "ending about where it began." Lincoln saw close up the results of desperate combat on more than a small scale. Reports gave Union losses at 500 killed and wounded, 500 captured; Confederate losses 800 killed and wounded, 1,800 captured.

While the President journeyed to the front via railway, Mrs. Lincoln was joined by Mrs. Grant, who was living with her family on the ship *Mary Martin*. The two women rode in an ambulance over a muddy, rough corduroy road. They were to join the President and Meade's staff in reviewing Crawford's division. As the wagon rolled along, Adam Badeau, Grant's secretary, seated with his back to the horses and facing the ladies, did his best at conversation, mentioning that all the wives of officers at the army front had been ordered to the rear, a sure sign of big action soon to come. Not a lady had been allowed to stay at the front, continued Badeau, unaware of what he was getting into, not a lady except Mrs. Griffin, the wife of General Charles Griffin, she having a special permit from the President.

Swift as a cat leap, Mrs. Lincoln: "What do you mean by that, sir? Do you mean to say that she saw the President alone? Do you know that I never allow the President to see any woman alone?" Badeau saw the face of a woman boiling with rage. He tried smiling toward this face, to show there was no malice. Badeau's smile was timed wrong. "That's a very equivocal smile, sir," he now heard. "Let me out of this carriage at once. I will ask the President if he saw that woman alone."

Badeau and Mrs. Grant tried to smooth and quiet her but failed. Mrs. Lincoln ordered Badeau to have the driver stop, and Badeau hesitating, she thrust her arms past him and took hold of the driver. By now however Mrs. Grant was able to coax Mrs. Lincoln to be still and to wait. As they alighted at the reviewing ground General Meade walked up, paid his respects to Mrs. Lincoln, escorted her away, later returning her with diplomatic skill, Mrs. Lincoln informing Badeau, "General Meade is a gentleman, sir. He says it was not the President who gave Mrs. Griffin the permit, but the Secretary of War." Thus ran Badeau's account.

Badeau and Mrs. Grant agreed "the whole affair was so distressing and mortifying that neither of us must ever mention it again." No inkling of it seemed to reach Meade, who wrote to his wife of her own visit to his headquarters that week "it seems so like a dream I can hardly realize you have been here." The President had spoken of Mrs. Meade, "expressed regret that your visit should have been so abruptly terminated," while "Mrs. Lincoln spoke very handsomely of you and referred in feeling terms to our sad bereavement [the recent death of a child]."

On the soil where Union countercharges began Lincoln saw the dead in blue and gray and butternut lying huddled and silent, here and there the wounded gasping and groaning. He saw a collection of prisoners taken that morning, a ragged and dusty crew, and remarked "on their sad condition," noted Barnes. "They had fought desperately and were glad to be at rest. Mr. Lincoln was quiet and observant, making few comments." On the train a "worn and haggard" Lincoln saw the loading of the Union wounded. "He remarked that he had seen enough of the horrors of war, that he hoped this was the beginning of the end." Wrote the guard Crook of this day, "I saw him [Lincoln] ride over the battlefields at Petersburg, the man with the hole in his forehead and the man with both arms shot away lying, accusing, before his eyes."

Beyond the immediate scene Lincoln gazed on that day other fighting had gone on. The Union troops advanced along the whole of Lee's right, taking entrenched picket lines. The Union estimate put their own losses at 2,080 as against 4,800 to 5,000 Confederate. Lee next day was writing Davis, "I fear now it will be impossible to prevent a junction between Grant and Sherman."

Lincoln sat for a while at the headquarters campfire, according to Colonel Horace Porter, "and as the smoke curled about his head during certain shiftings of the wind he brushed it away from time to time by waving his right hand in front of his face." To Grant and staff men gathered around he spoke of "appalling difficulties" the administration had met, field losses, troubles in finance and foreign affairs, how they had been overcome by the unswerving patriotism of the people, the devotion of the loyal North, and the superb fighting qualities of the troops. He drifted into a more cheerful vein and got into his storytelling stride by way of the Trent Affair, reeling off an elaborate version of the barber and his worried customer: "He began by lathering face, nose, eyes and ears, stropped his razor on his boot, and then made a drive at the man's countenance as if he had practised mowing in a stubblefield. He cut a bold swath across the right cheek, carrying away the beard, a pimple, and two warts. The man in the chair ventured to remark: 'You appear to make everything level as you go.' 'Yes,' said the barber; 'and if this handle don't break, I guess I'll get away with most of what's there.' The man's cheeks were so hollow that the barber couldn't get down into the valleys with the razor, and the ingenious idea occurred to him to stick his finger in the man's mouth and press out the cheeks. Finally he cut clear through the cheek and into his own finger. He pulled the finger out of the man's mouth, snapped the blood off it, glared at him, and cried: 'There, you lantern-jawed cuss, you've made me cut my finger!' And so England will discover that she has got the South into a pretty bad scrape by trying to administer to her, and in the end she will find that she has only cut her own finger."

The laugh following this subsided, and Grant asked, "Mr. President, did you at any time doubt the final success of the cause?" And Lincoln, leaning forward in his camp chair, with an emphatic right-hand gesture: "Never for a moment."

Next day Barnes "found Mr. Lincoln quite recovered," lamenting the loss of life, confident the war was ending, pleased at news that Sheridan from the Shenandoah Valley had moved in a big swing around Lee's army to the north and arrived safe at Harrison's Landing to join Grant that day.

The President's eyes caught on three tiny kittens, wandering, mewing as if lost. He picked up one and asked it, "Where is your mother?" Someone answered, "The mother is dead." And as he petted the little one: "Then she can't grieve as many a poor mother is grieving for a son lost in battle." Gathering the two others in his hands, he put them on his lap, stroked their fur, and according to Admiral Porter, meditated, "Kitties, thank God you are cats, and can't understand this terrible strife that is going on."

The *River Queen* moved down the James River and from her deck Lincoln saw the bank lined with men shouting, laughing, swimming, watering their horses—Sheridan's men washing off the dust and grit of the Shenandoah Valley. They spotted the President and sent him cheers. The *River Queen* passed through a naval flotilla. The crews cheered the Commander in Chief, saw his tall frame in a long-tailed black frock coat, a cravat of black silk carelessly tied, a black silk hat. Barnes noted, "As he passed each vessel he waved his high hat, as if saluting friends in his native town, and seemed as happy as a school boy."

Up the James steamed the *River Queen* to Aiken's Landing for a field review of part of the Army of the James. Sheridan came aboard. The President ended his long-held handshake. "General Sheridan, when this peculiar war began I thought a cavalryman should be at least six feet four high, but"—still gazing down on the short General—"I have changed my mind—five feet four will do in a pinch."

Ord on one side, Grant on the other, escorted the President over a rough corduroy road two miles to the reviewing ground. An ambulance followed bringing Mrs. Lincoln and Mrs. Grant in care of Colonel Horace Porter and Adam Badeau. Improved springs on the ambulance only served to toss the occupants higher, but Mrs. Lincoln in fear that they would miss the review asked Porter for more speed. The driver accommodated till the mud flew from the horses' heels, and the ladies' hats were jammed and heads bumped against the top of the wagon. "Mrs. Lincoln now insisted on getting out and walking," wrote Porter, "but as the mud was nearly hub-deep, Mrs. Grant and I persuaded her that we had better stick to the wagon as our only ark of refuge."

Meantime the President, with a squadron of 20 or more officers and orderlies, rode through woods and swamp. Standing at "parade rest" the division had waited for hours. The troops cheered the Commander in Chief. The review over, shellfire began on the enemy picket line in sight, heavy skirmishing lines moved forward, took the picket-line trenches, swelled the day's total of prisoners to 2,700, repulsed two fierce counterattacks, ending the day with Union losses of about 2,000 to 4,000 Confederate.

Colonel Theodore Lyman of Meade's staff at this review had his first look at Lincoln and wrote to his wife: "The President is, I think, the ugliest man I ever put my eyes on; there is also an expression of plebeian vulgarity in his face that is offensive (you recognize the recounter of coarse stories). On the other hand, he has the look of sense and wonderful shrewdness, while the heavy eyelids give him a mark of almost genius. He strikes me, too, as a very honest and kindly man; and, with all his vulgarity, I see no trace of low passions in his face. On the whole, he is such a mixture of all sorts, as only America brings forth. He is as much like a highly intellectual and benevolent Satyr as anything I can think of. I never wish to see him again, but, as humanity runs, I am well content to have him at the head of affairs."

Mrs. Lincoln and Mrs. Grant had arrived late for the review but in time for Mrs. Lincoln to see Mrs. Ord riding near the President in the reviewing column, though equally near her husband, who was the immediate commander of the troops under review. Seeing the ambulance drive in on the parade line, Mrs. Ord excused herself with, "There comes Mrs. Lincoln and Mrs. Grant—I think I had better join them." The accounts of Barnes, Porter and Badeau as to what then happened agreed that there were embarrassing moments and bitterly pathetic exhibitions, Badeau's later recollections being more complete in detail, though having slight discrepancies. It seemed, however, that as Mrs. Ord joined them, Mrs. Lincoln furiously exclaimed: "What does this woman mean by riding by the side of the President and ahead of me? Does she suppose that *he* wants *her* by the side of *him?*" She went into a frenzy that mingled extravagant rage and drab petulance. "All that Porter and I could do," wrote Badeau, "was to see that nothing worse than words occurred." They feared some wild scene of violence enacted before the troops so calmly standing at "present arms." One outburst flung itself at Mrs. Grant: "I suppose you think you'll get to the White House yourself, don't you?" Mrs. Grant kept cool, saying she was quite satisfied with her present position, that it was far greater than she had ever expected to attain. Mrs. Lincoln: "Oh! you had better take it if you can get it. 'Tis very nice." Then the slings of reproach were sent at Mrs. Ord, with Mrs. Grant quietly and at some risk defending her friend.

A nephew of Secretary Seward, a young major and a member of General Ord's staff, a joker, rode alongside and blurted out with a rich grin: "The President's horse is very gallant, Mrs. Lincoln. He insists on riding by the side of Mrs. Ord." This of course helped no one. Mrs. Lincoln cried, "What do you mean by that?" and young Major Seward shied away in a crazy gallop.

When the review had ended—and the troops were moving toward the enemy picket lines and death and wounds— Mrs. Lincoln in the presence of a group of officers, according to Badeau, hurled vile names at Mrs. Ord and again asked what Mrs. Ord meant by following the President. Enough of this sent Mrs. Ord into tears, into asking what in the world she had done. Mrs. Lincoln stormed till she spent her strength A manner of silence ensued. Porter believed "Mrs. Lincoln had suffered so much from the fatigue and annoyances of her overland trip that she was not in a mood to derive much pleasure from the occasion." Badeau saw "everybody shocked and horrified." Barnes found Mrs. Grant silent and embarrassed. "It was a painful situation, from which the only escape was to retire. Mrs.

Ord and myself with a few officers rode back to City Point."

On the return trip of the *River Queen*, "the President seemed to recover his spirits," according to Horace Porter, who thought perhaps the strength and fighting quality he witnessed that afternoon in the Army of the James "had served to cheer him up." Whatever his mood, whatever the trouble he might be disguising, he told Colonel Porter one of his favorite funny stories, repeating the same story later to Grant.

Of what happened that evening of March 26 when the *River Queen* returned to her moorings at City Point Badeau wrote: "That night the President and Mrs. Lincoln entertained General and Mrs. Grant and the General's staff at dinner on the steamer, and before us all Mrs. Lincoln berated General Ord to the President, and urged that he should be removed. He was unfit for his place, she said, to say nothing of his wife. General Grant sat next and defended his officer bravely."

Lincoln and Grant said good night. With the war and more on his hands the President was not at ease. Out in the dark night along a 40-mile front 100,000 men and more lived hugging the dirt of the earth, some in tents but more in huts and shelters. Soon they might go into the wildest, bloodiest battle of the whole war. Beyond lay the solemn matter of what kind of a peace should be signed. Yet along with these problems was a personal grief.

He sent off the ship an orderly who about 11 o'clock awakened Captain Barnes with a message that the President would like to see him. Barnes stepped into his clothes in a hurry, boarded the *River Queen*, and found Mr. and Mrs. Lincoln awaiting him in the upper saloon. A few essentials Captain Barnes would disclose· "Mr. Lincoln took little part in the conversation which ensued, which evidently followed some previous discussion with Mrs. Lincoln, who had objected very strenuously to the presence of other ladies at the review, and had thought that Mrs. Ord had been too prominent in it; that the troops were led to think she was the wife of the President, who had distinguished her with too much attention. Mr. Lincoln very gently suggested that he had hardly remarked her presence; but Mrs. Lincoln was not to be pacified, and appealed to me to support her views. Of course I could not umpire such a question, and could only state why Mrs. Ord and myself found ourselves in the reviewing column, and how immediately we withdrew from it upon the appearance of the ambulance with Mrs. Lincoln and Mrs. Grant. I extricated myself as well as I could, but with difficulty, and asked permission to retire, the President bidding me good-night sadly and gently."

Amid the scenes created by the disordered brain of a tragically afflicted woman, young Captain Barnes felt himself drawn to the one person he saw as writhing inwardly more than any other, writing, "I came to feel an affection for him that none other inspired." The melancholy of Lincoln he believed related in part to the torments Mrs. Lincoln was under. "I had the greatest sympathy for her and for Mr. Lincoln, who I am sure felt deep anxiety for her," Barnes noted. "His manner towards her was always that of the most affectionate solicitude, so marked, so gentle and unaffected that no one could see them together without being impressed by it." Though a common undertone phrase for her was "crazy woman," Barnes' more humanly decent description ran: "She was at no time well; the mental strain upon her was great, betrayed by extreme nervousness approaching hysteria, causing misapprehensions, extreme sensitiveness as to slights or want of politeness or consideration."

At intervals during this City Point visit, however, several credible observers without particular prejudice agreed in the main with Badeau's account that "Mrs. Lincoln repeatedly attacked her husband in the presence of officers because of Mrs. Griffin and Mrs. Ord." As for the head of the state, wrote Badeau, "He bore it as Christ might have done, with supreme calmness and dignity; he called her 'mother', pleaded with eyes and tones, endeavored to explain or palliate the offenses of others, till she turned on him like a tigress; and then he walked away," hiding his face that others might not see it. Toward Mrs. Grant, Mary Todd Lincoln showed no relenting, according to Badeau once rebuking the General's wife, "How dare you be seated until I invite you?"

Barnes reported as usual to the President, received "marked kindness," and in a small stateroom converted into an office heard Lincoln read dispatches from Stanton and from the front, while Tad ran in and out, sometimes "clinging to his father and caressed affectionately by him." Barnes inquired about Mrs. Lincoln, hoping she had recovered from the fatigue of the previous day. "Mr. Lincoln said she was not well at all, and expressed the fear that the excitement of the surroundings was too great for her or for any woman."

In the roomy log cabin of Grant, Lincoln spent the forenoon mainly in talk with Admiral David D. Porter, Grant a listener "in grim silence, or only answering direct questions from Mr. Lincoln" in monosyllables. In very good spirits that morning was Lincoln, thought Barnes. "Running his hands with an upward movement through his rumpled hair he would stretch himself out, and look at the listeners in turn as though for sympathy and appreciation." Grant, however, "seldom smiled." He was thinking about his armies. If Lee escaped the net now spread, the war might go another year or two—or longer.

Four years now since Fort Sumter at Charleston had crumbled. Now that captured fort was under repair, and Stanton, Admiral Dahlgren, William Lloyd Garrison, Henry Ward Beecher and Nicolay to represent the President, were preparing to go down and hold a flag-raising ceremony of speeches and prayers, with the Union banner again floating from that citadel where the war had begun.

A steamer put Sherman ashore at City Point late in the afternoon of March 27. Grant was there waiting. They walked to Grant's cabin. Sherman had talked nearly an hour when Grant interrupted. "I'm sorry but the President is aboard the *River Queen.*" They took Admiral Porter and soon the three found Lincoln alone in the after cabin.

Sherman and Lincoln after nearly four years again faced each other. The conversation ranged from laughter to solemnity.

Next morning, March 28, on the *River Queen* came a conference of the three pivotal Northern men of the war, with Admiral Porter present. Both Grant and Sherman supposed that one or the other of them would have to fight one more bloody battle, and that it would be the *last*. "Mr. Lincoln exclaimed, more than once," wrote Sherman, "that there had been blood enough shed, and asked us if another battle could not be avoided." The generals told Lincon they could not control that event.

Sherman came now to a momentous point. He wrote of it later: "I inquired of the President if he was all ready for the end of the war. What was to be done with the rebel armies when defeated? And what should be done with the political leaders, such as Jeff. Davis, etc? Should we allow them to escape, etc.? He said he was all ready; all he wanted of us was to defeat the opposing armies, and to get the men composing the Confederate armies back to their homes, at work on their farms and in their shops. As to Jeff. Davis, he was hardly at liberty to speak his mind fully, but intimated that he ought to clear out, 'escape the country,' only it would not do for him to say so openly."

Lincoln was this day talking with two men like himself terribly intimate with awful authority. They were hammering out a national fate. Before them hazards and intricacies lay too vast to put on paper. Lincoln hesitated at outlining for his generals any peace terms or reconstruction policies beyond the few simple conditions he had named at Hampton Roads.

In Europe at that hour could be heard the prediction that Sherman would take over the Washington Government and run it. Delane of the London *Times* spoke fears of that event. For two years Lincoln and these two generals had been welding a strange partnership that worked. Amid malice, conspiracy, jealousies, amid crooked and crazy entanglements of human impulse and motive that made the war a dismal swamp-jungle affair, the three held together. Of each

of them it had been graphically said that he was intensely
American and could have been born and made nowhere but
in the "U.S.A." They read each other now by signals, intentions and hopes.

Sherman was eager to hear any specific recommendations
that might have occurred to the mind of the President. Of
the answers Sherman later wrote: "Mr. Lincoln was full and
frank in his conversation, assuring me that in his mind he
was all ready for the civil reorganization of affairs at the
South as soon as the war was over; and he distinctly authorized me to assure Governor Vance and the people of North
Carolina that, as soon as the rebel armies laid down their
arms, and resumed their civil pursuits, they would at once
be guaranteed all their rights as citizens of a common country; and that to avoid anarchy the State governments then
in existence, with their civil functionaries, would be recognized by him as the government *de facto* till Congress
could provide others . . . His earnest desire seemed to be to
end the war speedily, without more bloodshed or devastation, and to restore all the men of both sections to their
homes . . . When at rest or listening, his legs and arms
seemed to hang almost lifeless, and his face was care-worn
and haggard; but, the moment he began to talk, his face
lighted up, his tall form, as it were, unfolded, and he was
the very impersonation of good-humor and fellowship."

The three Northern pivotal men were parting, Sherman
to remember Lincoln in a most simple manner: "Sherman,
do you know why I took a shine to Grant and you?" "I don't
know, Mr. Lincoln, you have been extremely kind to me,
far more than my deserts." "Well, you never found fault
with me."

Lincoln and Sherman had done most of the talking, Grant
not mentioning a matter he later brought before Lincoln.
"I told him that I had been very anxious to have the Eastern
armies vanquish their old enemy. If the Western armies
should be even upon the field, operating against Richmond
and Lee, the credit would be given to them for the capture,
by politicians and noncombatants from the section of the
country which those troops hailed from. Western members

[of Congress] might be throwing it up to the members of the East that they were not able to capture an army, or to accomplish much but had to wait until the Western armies had conquered all the territory south and west of them, and then come on to help them capture the only army they had been engaged with. Mr. Lincoln said he saw that now, but had never thought of it before, because his anxiety was so great that he did not care where the aid came from so the work was done."

Back at City Point Lincoln kept close to Grant, whose company he would lose in a day or two, when a big push was to begin and Grant would live at the fighting front with his troops in motion.

That sword of Robert E. Lee—how it had vanished and come back and held its ground beyond prophecies! With those valiant bayonets on which the Confederate Government had been carried for three years, could Lee again swing round and baffle pursuit, perhaps win to the mountains, fight guerrilla style till he could recruit a new army?

What did the night's darkness hold? Would Grant take Lee? If he did, then both the structure and the dream of a Confederate States of America were sunk with the fabrics of all shadows and dust. A republican Union of States cemented and welded with blood and iron would stand for a long time among World Power nations, committed to government of, by, and for the people. Only for the assurance of that reality had Lincoln cared to toil and groan these last four years of burdens and bitterness.

Beyond the screen and mist of the night lay what? Peach blooms and apricot blossoms had risen in the air the last few days in rare spots. April was near. What of this April?

At 8:30 the morning of March 29, 1865, Lincoln went ashore from the *River Queen* to Grant's shanty. They were putting the horses aboard the railroad train that was to take Grant and his staff to the Petersburg front.

Mrs. Grant stood by, her face pale and sorrowful. At the door Grant kissed her, over and again, joined Lincoln; the two walked down to the railroad platform. "Mr. Lincoln looked more serious than at any other time since he had visited headquarters," noted Horace Porter. "The lines in his face seemed deeper, and the rings under his eyes were of a darker hue. It was plain that the weight of responsibility was oppressing him." At the train the President gave a warm handshake to the General and to each member of the staff, and then stood near the rear end of the car while they went aboard. The train was ready to start. They all raised their hats in respect to the President. His hat went off to them and his voice was broken and he couldn't hide it as he called to them: "Good-by, gentlemen. God bless you all! Remember, your success is my success." The whistle sounded. The train moved. Grant was off to a campaign all hoped would be his last and the last of the war.

Lighting a cigar Grant went over plans with staff officers, once saying: "The President is one of the few who has not attempted to extract from me a knowledge of my movements, although he is the only one who has right to know them. He will be the most anxious man in the country to hear from us. I think we can send him some good news in a day or two."

Fair weather of several days on the evening of March 29 gave way to torrents from the sky. Fields became beds of quicksand. Troops waded in mud above their ankles. Horses sank to their bellies and had to be pulled out with halters. Wagon wheels sank to the hubs and in some cases above the axles to the wagon box. Roads became sheets of water. Marching on such terrain was only worse than trying to sleep in wet blankets on soaked ground. On March 30 men's tempers showed. Rawlins gloomed and Grant held that soon as the weather cleared up the roads the men would be gay again.

Having studied his map, as he relayed telegrams to Stanton, Lincoln commented: "Judging by the two points from which General Grant telegraphs, I infer that he moved his headquarters about one mile since he sent the first of the two dispatches." Also to Stanton, Lincoln wired the personal item that Mrs. Lincoln had started for Washington, and he would thank Stanton "to see that our coachman is at the Arsenal wharf at Eight (8) o'clock to-morrow morning, there wait until she arrives."

Sheridan went on dashing where the fire was most furious, waving his battle flag, praying, swearing, shaking his fist, yelling threats and blessings. With fixed bayonets and a final rousing cheer, the Union columns under General Ayres overran the enemy earthworks, swept everything before them, killed or captured in their immediate front every man whose legs had not saved him.

Lincoln while this battle raged did his best at picturing it from a dispatch sent by Grant. He wired Seward that "Sheridan, aided by Warren, had at 2 P.M. pushed the enemy back so as to retake the five forks, and bring his own Head Quarters up . . ." The next two days Lincoln sent to Stanton a series of Grant's dispatches, relayed as Grant wrote them, and these the Secretary of War gave to the press. Thus millions of readers in the North had what they took as authentic information about the crumbling of Lee's lines foreshadowing the fall of Richmond.

Anxious Northern readers, including a horde of speculators and gamblers, saw in the public prints that Sheridan with his cavalry and the 5th corps had captured three brigades of infantry, several thousand prisoners—that Grant had telegraphed at 4:30 P.M. April 2: "The whole captures since the army started out will not amount to less than 12,000 men, and probably fifty pieces of artillery . . . All seems well with us, and everything is quiet just now." And Lincoln had telegraphed Grant: "Allow me to tender to you, and all with you, the nations grateful thanks . . . At your kind suggestion, I think I will visit you to-morrow."

At a lesser price than predicted Lee's army was cut off from Richmond, and on the night of April 2 his troops, ordered out of Petersburg and other points on the line, were reconcentrating to march west. Lincoln boarded a railroad car at City Point and rode to Petersburg, where Grant and his staff were waiting, ready to go. Grant wrote of their meeting, "About the first thing that Mr. Lincoln said to me was: 'Do you know, general, that I have had a sort of sneaking idea for some days that you intended to do something like this.' " At City Point Lincoln wired Stanton at 5 P.M. this April 3: ". . . staid with Gen. Grant an hour & a half and returned here. It is certain now that Richmond is in our hands, and I think I will go there to-morrow."

As Lincoln visited the sick and wounded among avenues of hospital tents at City Point that week, Adelaide Smith, the nurse, heard the camp talk that when the President's party came to one set of tents young Dr. Jerome Walker of the Sanitary Commission pointing at them said, "Mr. President, you do not want to go in there." "Why not, my boy?" "They are sick rebel prisoners." "That is just where I do want to go," and he strode in and shook hands from cot to cot.

Shot-torn in both hips, lay Colonel Harry L. Benbow, who had commanded three regiments at Five Forks. And according to Colonel Benbow: "He halted beside my bed and held out his hand. I was lying on my back, my hands folded across my breast. Looking him in the face, 'Mr. President,' I said, 'do you know to whom you offer your hand?' 'I do not,' he replied. 'Well,' said I, 'you offer it to a Confederate colonel who has fought you as hard as he could for four years.' 'Well,' said he, 'I hope a Confederate colonel will not refuse me his hand.' 'No, sir,' I replied, 'I will not,' and I clasped his hand in both of mine."

Over 5,000 men of both sides were in City Point hospitals. Lincoln tried to visit every last man of them but couldn't find time to make the complete rounds. His right arm lame from handshaking, the head surgeon said it certainly must ache. Lincoln smiled, mentioned "strong muscles," stepped out the door of the surgeon's shanty, took an ax, sent chips of logs flying, then paused and slowly with his right arm raised the ax till he was holding it at full horizontal without a quiver. Before leaving he was offered what he might like by way of a drink. He took a glass of lemonade.

Chapter 46

Richmond Falls — Appomattox

On the Sabbath day of April 2, 1865, in the Davis family pew of St. Paul's Episcopal Church, seated erect and calm under the chancel, was Jefferson Davis. An adjutant, mud on his boots, a hard-riding man, came up the aisle in a swift military stride and handed a paper to Davis, who read the words Lee had long delayed: "I advise that all preparation be made for leaving Richmond tonight. I will advise you later, according to circumstances." Davis arose, walked to the War Department, telegraphed to Lee that a move from Richmond that night would "involve the loss of many valuables, both for the want of time to pack and of transportation." Lee in the field on receiving this message, according to one of his staff men, tore it into bits, saying, "I am sure I gave him sufficient notice," and replied calmly by telegraph to Davis that it was "absolutely necessary" to abandon the position that night.

By railroad at 11 that Sabbath night, Davis with his Cabinet and other officials left their capital city, their Executive Mansion, their arsenals and stores, arriving safely in Danville the next afternoon. Word spread in Richmond that Lee's army had taken its last man and gun out of Petersburg —and Richmond would fall next. On railroad trains, on wagons, carts, buggies, gigs, on horses piled with bundles and belongings, the Government and many citizens in flight had a moving day.

Burning and dynamiting of bridges, arsenals and warehouses went on through the night. Heavy smoke clouds rose from cotton warehouses. Just after daylight April 3 a crowd of thousands of men, women and children swarmed at the doors of a commissary depot. Many of them had not tasted a full, nourishing meal in months. Behind those depot doors they had heard—and heard correctly—were barrels of ham, bacon, whisky, flour, sugar, coffee. Why these had not gone to General Lee's half-starved army weeks before was for responsible officials to answer. Rampaging humans broke through those depot doors, so long guarded. Raging, laughing, snarling, the crowd surged in.

General Godfrey Weitzel received the surrender of Richmond that morning of April 3 at the city hall. By midafternoon his troops had stopped the rioting and main disorders.

In Washington, wrote David Homer Bates, "Lincoln's despatch from City Point gave us in the War Department the first news of the capture of Petersburg and Richmond." Shortly after that message, came the first one in four years wired from Richmond, General Weitzel saying: "We took Richmond at 8:15 this morning." The news spread fast. Press extras sent the excitement higher. Thousands crowded around the War Office; Stanton spoke gratitude to Almighty God for deliverance.

Record-breaking crowds lined the saloon bars. From the Capitol on to the White House and executive buildings, Pennsylvania Avenue took on bunting and banners. The sky was shaken by a salute of 800 guns. In the streets people hugged each other, men made up old quarrels, marched singing and prankish.

From City Point the *Malvern* with Lincoln aboard steamed toward Richmond. Dead horses floated by, broken ordnance, wrecked boats. Nearing Richmond, the *Malvern* went aground. Admiral Porter ordered a 12-oared barge to carry the President ashore, Tad and Crook sat amid the oarsmen. A gig holding Barnes and a few others acted as escort. Lincoln was reminded of a fellow who failed at getting high or low offices and finally "he asked me for an old pair of trousers. It is well to be humble."

At a place called Rockett's the little barge landed the President. The receiving crowd ashore was, according to Porter and Crook, entirely Negro. By the grapevine some had heard here was Lincoln. One old-timer of 60 sprang forward: "Bress de Lawd, dere is de great Messiah!" He fell on his knees and bowed at the President's feet, other Negroes doing the same. The President: "Don't kneel to me. You must kneel to God only and thank him for your freedom." From corners that had seemed deserted suddenly sprang black folk, some silent and awe-struck, others turning somersaults and yelling with joy. With some Lincoln shook hands.

Twelve armed sailors formed an escort. At his left the President had Porter and Captain Penrose, at his right Crook holding Tad by the hand. This procession began its march. Barnes saw a lone cavalryman at a street corner and sent him galloping to Weitzel's headquarters with the news of who was coming. Wrote Crook: "Every window was crowded with heads. But it was a silent crowd. There was something oppressive in those thousands of watchers without a sound, either of welcome or hatred. I think he would have welcomed a yell of defiance. I stole a look sideways at Mr. Lincoln. His face . . . had the calm . . . of a brave man . . . ready for whatever may come."

Nearly two miles along dusty streets on a warm April day this little presidential party marched to the center of Richmond. Not a soldier, citizen, horse or wagon had met them. The President had stopped a moment to gaze at Libby Prison, according to Porter, and on someone calling, "Pull it down," he replied, "No, leave it as a monument."

The cavalry escort arrived and led them to the Confederate Executive Mansion, a two-story house fronted with tall Colonial pillars, now the headquarters of General Weitzel and the temporary government. Dusty and sweating from his walk amid sights of burned buildings, wreckage on the streets and terror in the air, Lincoln sank into a chair at a long table, "pale and haggard, utterly worn out," noted Barnes, his first words, "I wonder if I could get a glass of water." It interested him to know this was the chair in which Jefferson Davis had sat and over this table had handled high documents.

With a cavalry escort and with Weitzel, Porter and others, Lincoln rode in a carriage over the city, seeing some of the 700 burned dwellings and stores, Libby Prison, Castle Thunder, thousands of homeless whites and Negroes. Into the disordered building where the now fugitive Confederate Congress had held its sessions, Lincoln was ushered. And if he was reminded of any anecdote no one made a record of it—though it was said his eyes often had a dreaminess.

Weitzel's aide Graves went along on this ride, and of it wrote that he heard General Weitzel ask one very important question: What should he, Weitzel, do in regard to this conquered people? "President Lincoln replied," wrote Graves, "that he did not wish to give any orders on that subject, but as he expressed it, 'If I were in your place, I'd let 'em up easy, let 'em up easy.'"

Porter and Crook heaved sighs of relief on getting the President aboard the *Malvern*, which had now been brought upriver. Any one of many kinds of fools could have taken a pot shot at Lincoln that day.

At noon April 6 Mrs. Lincoln arrived at City Point in a party of important persons, including Senator Sumner. And on this day Lincoln telegraphed Grant that Seward had been thrown from his carriage, seriously injured, and this with other matters would take him to Washington soon. At Richmond, he wished Grant to know, he had met Judge Campbell and put in Campbell's hands "an informal paper" repeating the Hampton Roads peace conditions, "and adding that if the war be now further persisted in by the rebels, confiscated property shall, at the least, bear the additional cost; and that confiscations shall be remitted to the people of any State which will now promptly, and in good faith, withdraw its troops and other support, from resistance to the government. Judge Campbell thought it not impossible that the rebel Legislature of Virginia would do the latter, if permitted; and accordingly, I addressed a private letter to Gen. Weitzel (with permission for Judge Campbell to see it)."

The matter was delicate—but Lincoln was taking a chance. He was meeting fully and squarely any leanings toward the Union, any changed attitude that might have developed among the Virginia legislative members. Having once officially seceded their state from the Union now they could officially return if they chose. They could construe for themselves the extent of dignity and authority accorded them by the President's telegram to Weitzel dated April 6 at City Point: "It has been intimated to me that the gentlemen who have acted as the legislature of Virginia, in support of the rebellion, may now desire to assemble at Richmond, and take measures to withdraw the Virginia troops, and other support from resistance to the General government. If they attempt it, give them permission and protection, until, if at all, they attempt some action hostile to the United States, in which case you will notify them and give them reasonable time to leave; & at the end of which time, arrest any who may remain. Allow Judge Campbell to see this, but do not make it public."

Of this attempt at results by legal device Lincoln wrote Grant he did not think it probable anything would come, "but I have thought best to notify you, so that if you should see signs, you may understand them."

Grant wired Lincoln a message from Sheridan reporting captures of several thousand prisoners, including Custis Lee, the son of General Robert E. Lee, and Generals Ewell, Kershaw, Button, Corse and Debray, Sheridan closing his dispatch, "If the thing is pressed I think that Lee will surrender." Lincoln wired Grant: "Gen. Sheridan says 'If the thing is pressed I think that Lee will surrender.' Let the *thing* be pressed."

An estimate of Lincoln, partly as General Lee failed to see him, came from a later commentator, an intimate of the documented Lee, a four-volume biographer of Lee. This set forth Lincoln in the role of a spokesman, a sayer. "Lee's balancing of the ponderables on the military scales was accurate," ran this picture. "He could not realize, and few even in Washington could see, that an imponderable was tipping the beam. That imponderable was the influence of President Lincoln. The Richmond government had discounted his every moderate utterance and had capitalized his emancipation proclamation in order to stiffen Southern resistance. The Confederate people had mocked him, had despised him, and had hated him. Lee himself, though he had avoided unworthy personal animosities and doubtless had included Mr. Lincoln in his prayers for all his enemies, had made the most of the President's military blunders and fears . . . He was much more interested in the Federal field-commanders than in the commander-in-chief. After the late winter of 1863-64, had Lee known all the facts, he would have given as much care to the study of the mind of the Federal President as to the analysis of the strategical methods of his immediate adversaries. For that remarkable man, who had never wavered in his purpose to preserve the Union, had now mustered all his resources of patience and of determination. Those who had sought cunningly to lead him, slowly found that he was leading them. His unconquerable spirit, in some mysterious manner, was being infused into the North as spring approached."

Lincoln in Virginia relaxed a little, eased off the Washington burdens. It was the nearest approach to a vacation he had had since the war began. It wasn't much of a holiday to look at the ruins of Richmond, nor an interval of sport to shake hands in tent hospitals with men fever-smitten and bullet-mutilated. But Washington with its intrigue and smug satisfactions was worse. Grant and others thought they saw Lincoln's anxiety diminish in the City Point stay of 15 days.

On Saturday, April 8, the *River Queen* was leaving for Washington. A military band came on board, and after several pieces, Lincoln called for "Dixie," saying, "That tune is now Federal property." The musicians were surprised. Lincoln wanted it to be a good-will song of the reunited states.

On Sunday, April 9, steaming up the Potomac, Mrs. Lincoln, noted Sumner, spoke of Jefferson Davis: "Do not allow him to escape the law—he must be hanged!" The President replied calmly, "Judge not, that ye be not judged." And by Sumner's account, when pressed again by the remark that the sight of Libby Prison made it impossible to pardon the Confederate chief, Lincoln repeated twice over the words, "Judge not, that ye be not judged."

The roofs of Washington came into view. Sumner in a carriage with the President and Mrs. Lincoln, drove to the White House. Then straight to the home of Seward the

President drove. Four days before on a sunny spring afternoon Seward in his customary daily drive, in company with his son and daughter, had watched his fast young horses prance and go, had enjoyed it. Suddenly the horses took fright and plunged into a wild runaway. Seward stood up, tried for a leap to the pavement, was thrown in the air, and when a crowd gathered he was unconscious. Taken home, physicians found the right shoulder badly dislocated, the jaw broken on both sides, his slow and partial return to consciousness coming with agonizing pain. His wife had journeyed from Auburn, New York, with heartache saw his face so bruised, swollen, discolored, his voice so changed and hoarse, that he seemed a man she had never before seen. At first he wandered in delirium, but on the third day was again in his right mind.

The gaslights in the house were turned low as Lincoln entered, the rooms quiet, everyone moving softly and speaking in whispers. On a bed in the center of his second-floor room lay the Secretary of State, swathed in bandages. Young Frederick Seward guided the President, who sat down on the side of the bed near the left arm of the sick and broken man. The wounded right arm was at times crazy with pain. The face looked out from a steel frame that held the jaw for healing. Lincoln spoke softly, solemnly, his greetings and sympathy. From the swollen tongue came with pain and effort the hoarse whisper, "You are back from Richmond?"

Lincoln leaned across the bed, rested on an elbow so as to bring his face nearer to the face of his friend, and told of many things he had seen and heard on the trip to City Point. Seward listened, his mind eager. "They were left together for a half hour or more," wrote the son Frederick. "Then the door opened softly, and Mr. Lincoln came out gently, intimating by a silent look and gesture that Seward had fallen into a feverish slumber and must not be disturbed."

In ten days of latter March and early April Lee had lost 19,000 men to Grant as prisoners. In a series of desperate fights the total of Lee's killed and wounded ran high—and of effective troops he had none to spare. The race westward on parallel lines was clocked with running battles. The one day's stop at Amelia Court House instead of expected food supplies for Lee's men saw nothing at all. The rank and file of the army must march on slim rations, mainly of parched corn. At Sayler's Creek enough of the Union army had over-taken Lee to force a combat that resulted in Lee's saying to one of his officers, "General, that half of our army is de-stroyed." The cannon of Lee were on short rations as well as the foot soldiers and cavalry horses. The artillerists knew that in a straight frontal battle they wouldn't have shells to last through.

Grant knew probably better than anyone that he could beat this army, smash pieces of it and send it recoiling in retreat. But he wouldn't swear he could capture it. To bag such an army of proved wit and flair—to take the whole of it and end the war—that was something else. Anything could happen.

While Lincoln journeyed toward Washington the night of April 8, Grant in the rear of the Army of the Potomac pressing Lee's rear guard, stopped at a farmhouse with a sick headache. He spent the night bathing his feet in hot water and mustard, putting mustard plasters on his wrists and the back of his neck, moving restlessly on a sitting-room sofa trying to snatch a little sleep. His mind had concen-trated intensely on notes he had written to Lee and Lee's answers. Each of these great and adroit commanders was making deep guesses about what was going on in the mind of the other. Grant however believed he knew the mind and feeling of Lincoln beyond instructions. Their many talks at City Point made him sure of what he could offer Lee that would be as though from the President. He sent Lee another note to the effect that while he had "no authority to treat on the subject of peace," he would however state "that I am equally anxious for peace with yourself, and the whole North entertains the same feeling." Lee read the note as an invitation for him to meet Grant and discuss terms of sur-render, this in line with Grant's hope "that all our difficulties may be settled without the loss of another life."

On Palm Sunday morning, April 9, 1865, across the path of Lee's army and blocking its way stood the cavalry of Phil Sheridan. At five o'clock that morning General Lee on high ground studied the landscape and what it held. Eight o'clock came. Also came word that Sheridan's cavalry had fallen slowly back and widened out. Behind the cavalry, and screened by woodland, waited heavy bodies of infantry in blue, the troops of Ord and Griffin, who had made an almost incredible march of 30 miles the night and day before, coming up at daybreak to support Sheridan and invite battle. To the left, to the rear, were other Union lines.

Lee's staff officers heard him say, "There is nothing left me to do but to go and see General Grant, and I would rather die a thousand deaths." "Oh, General," protested one, "what will history say of the surrender of the army in the field?" "Yes, I know they will say hard things of us! They will not understand how we were overwhelmed by numbers. But that is not the question, Colonel. The question is, is it right to surrender this army. If it is right, then I will take all the responsibility."

Lee sent a note asking Grant for an interview "with reference to the surrender of this army." Grant at once wrote Lee to name the place for their meeting. Grant riding toward the front said to Colonel Horace Porter, "The pain in my head seemed to leave me the moment I got Lee's letter."

At the McLean house on the edge of Appomattox village, 95 miles west of Richmond, the two great captains of men faced each other in a little room and Lee gave over his army to Grant—Lee tall and erect, Grant short and stoop-shouldered; Lee 58 years old with silver hair, near the evening of life, Grant 42 with black hair and unspent strength of youth yet in him; Lee in a clean and dazzling military outfit, Grant in a rough-worn and dusty blouse telling his high rank only by the three stars on the shoulders, apologizing to Lee that he had come direct from the field and hadn't had time to change his uniform.

Lee inside was writhing over the bitter ordeal, and Grant later admitted he was embarrassed—though both wore grave, inscrutable faces and no one could have read the mixed feelings masked by the two commanders. "I met you once before, General Lee," began Grant in even voice, "while we were serving in Mexico . . . I have always remembered your appearance, and I think I should have recognized you anywhere." "Yes, I know I met you on that occasion, and I have often thought of it and tried to recollect how you looked, but I have never been able to recall a single feature."

Talk about Mexico ran into memories of that war when they both wore blue. Grant just about forgot why they were there, it seemed. Lee brought him to the point. "I suppose, General Grant, that the object of our present meeting is fully understood. I asked to see you to ascertain upon what terms you would receive the surrender of my army."

Grant went on as between two good neighbors. "The terms I propose are those stated substantially in my letter of yesterday—that is, the officers and men surrendered to be paroled and disqualified from taking up arms again until properly exchanged, and all arms, ammunition and supplies to be delivered up as captured property." "Those," said Lee, "are about the conditions I expected would be proposed."

Grant, seated at a table, put it in writing, his staff aides and corps commanders standing by; Lee was seated with his aide Colonel Charles Marshall standing behind his chair. Grant rose, stepped over to Lee and handed him the paper scrawled in pencil. Lee took out spectacles, pulled a handkerchief and wiped the glasses, crossed his legs, read slowly and carefully the strangest and most consequential paper that had ever met his eyes. And with his first touch of warmth he said to Grant, "This will have a very happy effect on my army."

Grant asked for any further suggestions. Lee had one. In his army the cavalrymen and artillerists owned their horses; he wanted these men to have their mounts for spring plowing on their farms. Grant said: "I take it that most of the men in the ranks are small farmers, and as the country has been so raided by the two armies, it is doubtful whether they will be able to put in a crop to carry themselves and their families through the next winter without the aid of the horses they are now riding." So without changing the written terms he would instruct officers receiving paroles "to let all the men who claim to own a horse or mule take the animals home with them to work their little farms." Lee showed relief. "This will have the best possible effect upon the men. It will be very gratifying and will do much toward conciliating our people."

Lee shook hands with some of Grant's generals who offered theirs, bowed, then turned to Grant saying that a thousand Union prisoners had been living the last few days on parched corn only; they required attention, and of provisions "I have, indeed, nothing for my own men." This was discussed briefly and Grant directed that 25,000 rations be sent to Lee's men.

Lee wrote an acceptance of Grant's terms, signed it, and the documents of surrendering an army were completed. There remained only such formalities as roll call and stacking of arms. Union gunners made ready to fire a salute of grand national triumph, but Grant forbade any signs of rejoicing over a broken enemy he hoped hereafter would no longer be an enemy.

Lee rode among his men—who crowded around him crying, "We'll fight 'em yet"—and explained, with tears and in a choked voice, that they had fought the war together, he had done his best, and it was over. Many were dazed. Some wept. Others cursed and babbled. The army could die but never surrender, they had hoped. Yet they still worshiped Lee. They touched his hands, his uniform; they petted his horse Traveller, smoothing his flanks with their hands. One man, throwing down his musket, cried to the blue heaven: "Blow, Gabriel, blow! My God, let him blow, I am ready to die!"

For Grant it was one more odd day. Three times now he had bagged a whole army, at Fort Donelson, at Vicksburg, at Appomattox. He had kept his pledge to Lincoln that he would do his best to avoid a final bloody battle.

Next day it rained. The paroles numbered 28,231. Grant

and Lee sat their horses between lines for a farewell talk. Grant said that not a man in the South had so great an influence with soldiers and people as General Lee, that if Lee would now advise the surrender of the other armies his advice would be followed. Lee said he could not do this without first consulting Davis. And with no misunderstandings Grant and Lee said good-by.

One of the great Confederate combat leaders, General John B. Gordon, had sat his horse and spoken farewell to his men. Some he had seen weeping as they folded burnt and shot-pierced battle flags and laid them on the stacked arms of surrender. As he told his troops of his own grief he tried to give them hope to rebuild out of the poverty and ashes to which many would return. Gordon could never forget a Kentucky father who lost two sons, one dying for the North, the other for the South. Over the two graves of his soldier boys the father set up a joint monument inscribed "God knows which was right."

From Appomattox Grant telegraphed Stanton at 4:30 P.M. April 9: "General Lee surrendered the Army of Northern Virginia this afternoon on terms proposed by myself."

The war was over. It would have various dying flares in a sunset sky. The costs and sacrifices could never be forgotten. There would be hates and rankling memories. The war nevertheless had spent itself and had gone now into a realm of memory and hallucination, a national ordeal and fever over and past.

Newsmen wrote their stories, put on wires the glad tidings, and then went out and got drunk, or as Noah Brooks said, "unbent themselves." Cannon boomed over Washington at dawn. Over muddy streets surged people singing and cheering. Government departments gave their clerks another holiday.

The area in front of the White House filled with an enormous crowd. Brass bands had their music interrupted by guns. Tad showed at the well-known window from which the President always spoke; the crowd roared as he waved a captured Confederate flag. Hats went in the air with volleys of yells as the President came out to look at a throng where hatless men were now throwing into the air other men's hats and wild emotion poured out in screams that rose and curved in rockets. As the heaving surface of hats, faces and arms quieted down, the President spoke brief congratulations on the occasion, said arrangements were made for a formal celebration. "I propose closing up this interview by the band performing a particular tune . . . I have always thought 'Dixie' one of the best tunes I have ever heard."

Over the North that day of April 10 everything done before in victory celebrations was done again—but longer, oftener and with complete and final enthusiasm. To the prowar celebrants were joined the antiwar people, peace men and women who had always said the war was a cruel and costly failure; they too were glad now. So many, even many of the loyal ones, had been heartsick about the way it dragged for four years beyond all first expectations. Great God, but Lincoln must be thankful today. Hurrah for the Union! Hurrah for Lincoln! Hurrah for Grant and Sherman, the grand right and left arms of Lincoln! Get out the flags. Hang out every rag in the house that looks like a flag. Hang out red, white and blue bunting. Make a show. Great Jehovah, but we're glad the war's over! Men on horseback rode up and down swinging cowbells and tooting horns. Men tied tin cans to sticks, to ropes, and stood on street corners rattling their noisemakers.

The night saw torches and transparencies, bonfires, songs and howling. Nobody could be too foolish this day. Men climbed lampposts, stood upright on bareback horses. Laughing men rode sober-faced mules, riding backward and brandishing the mule's tail at onlookers. For many there was nothing to do but get drunk. Shake hands once, shake hands again, put your arms around anybody, today we love everybody, the war is over, throw your hat on the windmill, throw your hat over the moon.

In Willard's an elderly gentleman having had a few drinks, but not too many for the day, leaped up on the bar and led the crowd in singing "Praise God from whom all blessings flow."

Motley wrote of 20,000 businessmen in New York City uncovering their heads and singing in unison the psalm of thanksgiving: "Praise God."

Chapter 47

"Not in Sorrow, but in Gladness of Heart"

April 11 the President issued a proclamation closing Southern ports. Any ship or vessel from beyond the United States trying to enter these ports with articles subject to duties, "the same, together with its tackle, apparel, furniture and cargo, shall be forfeited to the United States."

Also of this date was a proclamation barring from all U.S. ports the war vessels of any foreign country whose ports refused equal privileges and immunities to U.S. war vessels. The home war fading, the Union could risk challenging other countries.

The President spent his best working hours this day on his speech for the evening. He was seizing the initiative to set in motion his own reconstruction program. Not until next December would Congress meet, not unless he called a special session. He intended to speak to the country so plainly that before Congress met, he could hope the majority of the people would be with him.

A loose, informal, nameless aggregate of political power was responsive to him, with common understandings; he was their voice for remolding Southern society and politics toward peaceful resumption of their place as states in the old Union. He knew his American people. Panic, want, fanaticism, race hatred, cries for retribution, lust for big money and fortunes, these were spread over the country. Lincoln had his choice of going with those who, to win a complete and abstract justice for the Negro, would not hesitate about making the South a vast graveyard of slaughtered whites, with Negro state governments established and upheld by Northern white bayonets. The caldron of war hate still boiled under the surface rejoicing of April 10 over Appomattox. The passions of Sumner, Wade and others had become a habit with them and their followers.

A "carefully written paper" rather than a speech the President held in waiting for the crowd. With bands of music and banners of freedom, with shouting and hoorah, an immense throng poured into the area in front of the White House. Many were the surging calls and cries for the President. "There was something terrible," thought Noah Brooks, "in the enthusiasm with which the beloved Chief Magistrate was received. Cheers upon cheers, wave after wave of applause, rolled up, the President patiently standing quiet until it was all over."

He began to read his speech holding a candle in his left hand and the manuscript in the right. "Speedily becoming embarrassed with the difficulty of managing the candle and the speech," wrote Brooks, "he made a comical motion with his left foot and elbow, which I construed to mean that I should hold his candle for him, which I did." Then, "We meet this evening, not in sorrow, but in gladness of heart . . . A call for a national thanksgiving is being prepared, and will be duly promulgated . . . To Gen. Grant, his skilful officers, and brave men, all belongs. The gallant Navy stood ready, but was not in reach to take active part."

This to the crowd was in somewhat the expected tone. Then the key changed. The crowd was "perhaps surprised," thought Brooks. The President read on, dropped to the floor each written page when read, and became aware that Tad was picking them up as they dropped. He could hear Tad, unseen to the crowd, calling for "another" and "another" of the fluttering sheets. He read on: "By these recent successes the re-inauguration of the national authority—reconstruction—which has had a large share of thought from the first, is pressed much more closely upon our attention. It is fraught with great difficulty. Unlike the case of a war between independent nations, there is no authorized organ for us to treat with. No one man has authority to give up the rebellion for any other man. We must simply begin with, and mould from, disorganized and discordant elements."

Those of the crowd who had come for hoorah wondered how much more of it there would be. It was a little heavy, it seemed. Others knew he was talking not to the thousands on the White House lawn but to the whole American and European world.

Three years he had been studying what to do about getting Louisiana properly back into the Union. "From about July 1862, I had corresponded with different persons, supposed to be interested, in seeking a reconstruction of a State government for Louisiana. When the Message of 1863, with the plan before mentioned, reached New-Orleans, Gen. Banks wrote me that he was confident the people, with his military co-operation, would reconstruct, substantially on that plan. I wrote him, and some of them to try it; they tried it, and the result is known. Such only has been my agency in getting up the Louisiana government. As to sustaining it, my promise is out, as before stated. But, as bad promises are better broken than kept, I shall treat this as a bad promise, and break it, whenever I shall be convinced that keeping it is adverse to the public interest. But I have not yet been so convinced."

Off to the discard he was throwing those labored legal arguments in Congress that the seceded states through the act of secession had "committed suicide" and thereby were no longer states. "Good for nothing at all," he held this question. "A merely pernicious abstraction." He would offer this reasoning: "We all agree that the seceded States, so called, are out of their proper practical relation with the Union; and that the sole object of the government, civil and military, in regard to those States is to again get them into that proper practical relation . . .

"The amount of constituency, so to speak, on which the new Louisiana government rests, would be more satisfactory to all, if it contained fifty, thirty, or even twenty thousand, instead of only about twelve thousand, as it does. It is also unsatisfactory to some that the elective franchise is not given to the colored man. I would myself prefer that it were now conferred on the very intelligent, and on those who serve our cause as soldiers. Still the question is not whether the Louisiana government, as it stands, is quite all that is desirable. The question is 'Will it be wiser to take it as it is, and help to improve it; or to reject, and disperse it?' 'Can Louisiana be brought into proper practical relation with the Union *sooner* by *sustaining,* or by *discarding* her new State Government?'

"Some twelve thousand voters in the heretofore slave-state of Louisiana have sworn allegiance to the Union, assumed to be the rightful political power of the State, held elections, organized a State government, adopted a free-state constitution, giving the benefit of public schools equally to black and white, and empowering the Legislature to confer the elective franchise upon the colored man. Their Legislature has already voted to ratify the constitutional amendment recently passed by Congress, abolishing slavery throughout the nation. These twelve thousand persons are thus fully committed to the Union, and to perpetuate freedom in the state—committed to the very things, and nearly all the things the nation wants—and they ask the nations recognition, and it's assistance to make good their committal. Now, if we reject, and spurn them, we do our utmost to disorganize and disperse them."

He gave his forecast, spoke as a sad prophet: "We in effect say to the white men 'You are worthless, or worse—we will neither help you, nor be helped by you.' To the blacks we say 'This cup of liberty which these, your old masters, hold to your lips, we will dash from you, and leave you to the chances of gathering the spilled and scattered contênts in some vague and undefined when, where, and how.' If this course, discouraging and paralyzing both white and black, has any tendency to bring Louisiana into proper practical relations with the Union, I have so far, been unable to perceive it."

He would turn from these dark visions. "If, on the contrary, we recognize, and sustain the new government of Louisiana the converse of all this is made true. We encourage the hearts, and nerve the arms of the twelve thousand to adhere to their work, and argue for it, and proselyte for it, and fight for it, and feed it, and grow it, and ripen it to a complete success. The colored man too, in seeing all united for him, is inspired with vigilance, and energy, and daring, to the same end. Grant that he desires the elective franchise, will he not attain it sooner by saving the already advanced steps toward it, than by running backward over them? Concede that the new government of Louisiana is only to what it should be as the egg is to the fowl, we shall sooner have the fowl by hatching the egg than by smashing it."

He came to his closing words. "Important principles may, and must, be inflexible. In the present '*situation*' as the phrase goes, it may be my duty to make some new announcement to the people of the South. I am considering, and shall not fail to act, when satisfied that action will be proper."

As he stood for a moment taking the plaudits of the crowd, he smiled to the candle-bearer Brooks. "That was a pretty fair speech, I think, but you threw some light on it."

There were applause and cheers, with no such uproar as had begun the evening. The speech had been too long, too closely reasoned, to please a big crowd. He would hear from the country about the speech. What he heard would help guide him further. His powers were vast. Before Congress met in December he might put through a series of decisions and actions that would channel and canal future policy for years, in accord with his outspoken designs of this evening.

The New York *Tribune* reported the speech "fell dead, wholly without effect on the audience," and furthermore, "it caused a great disappointment and left a painful impression." Other newspapers noted frequent applause and "silent attention" between the punctuations of applause.

On the calendars the day of April 11 was marked off. Midnight came. The lighted windows of the White House had darkened. The curves of light shining from the Capitol dome were gone. The moist air stayed on. Washington slept in the possession of a mist that crept everywhere, finespun, intangible, elusive.

Chapter 48

Negotiations — An Ominous Dream

Stanton and others were in a fury over what they feared had been open recognition of the seceded Virginia Legislature by the Federal Executive. Before the incident could come to a boiling point, Lincoln swept away all preparations with a telegram to Weitzel. From the operator Albert Chandler he borrowed a Gillott's small-barrel pen—No. 404—and, while standing, wrote:

> I have just seen Judge Campbell's letter to you of the 7th. He assumes as appears to me that I have called the insurgent Legislature of Virginia together, as the rightful Legislature of the State, to settle all differences with the United States. I have done no such thing. I spoke of them not as a Legislature, but as "the gentlemen who have *acted* as the Legislature of Virginia in support of the rebellion" . . . as Judge Campbell misconstrues this . . . let my letter to you, and the paper to Judge Campbell both be withdrawn or, countermanded, and he be notified of it. Do not now allow them to assemble; but if any have come, allow them safe-return to their homes.

A careful diary entry of Welles indicated that the President strongly inclined to let the insurgent Virginia Legislature have wide powers, that he peremptorily stopped that legislature from convening because once more his Cabinet of select advisers was against him—and it was one of the cases where it was better to go along with them—and wait. The "so-called legislature," Welles told the President, "would be likely to propose terms which might seem reasonable, but which we could not accept."

Seward was among those who mainly favored the President's policy of good will, of being generous and taking chances on double-dealing. Through different processes of thought, "we frequently arrived at the same conclusion," Seward described their joint operations; on the large questions "no knife sharp enough to divide us."

Among those high in the Government persistently vocal for punishing the defeated Confederates was Vice-President Johnson. To Dana in Richmond he insisted "their sins had been enormous," and if they were let back into the Union without punishment the effect would be bad, raising dangers in the future.

To Grant it came that Vice-President Johnson in Washington, in Richmond, had an "ever-ready" remark: "Treason is a crime and must be made odious." To Southern men who went to Johnson for assurances that they might begin some sort of rebuilding, he offered vehement denunciations. To Grant this was a sorry performance, Grant believing that the Lincoln view had behind it "the great majority of the Northern people, and the soldiers unanimously," the Lincoln view favoring "a speedy reconstruction on terms that would be the least humiliating to the people who had rebelled against their government." Grant also believed with Lincoln that a majority of the Northern people were not in favor of votes for the Negro. "They supposed that it would naturally follow the freedom of the negro, but that there would be a time of probation, in which the ex-slaves could prepare themselves for the privileges of citizenship before the full right would be conferred."

Sherman's ideas about peace terms and reconstruction, it would be too easy to say, were identical with those of Grant. The union general who more than any other favored a war strategy of punishment and destruction of the South decidedly favored a mild and kindly peace policy. Between

Sherman and Joe Johnston was not merely respect but a curious affection. They always fought fair and clean, each having admiration for the style of the other. Not often does it happen in war, but a fellowship had grown up between the two commanders. Neither Sherman nor Johnston had ever owned slaves. Both disliked Jefferson Davis. Grant knew Sherman would drive no hard bargain.

In the balances of early April the three high commanders and a million soldiers were, to use Grant's word, "unanimous" for ending the war on practically any terms that would bring a restored Union with slavery gone.

To Carpenter, Dana, Brooks and others, came an anecdote used by Lincoln when he was asked what to do with Jefferson Davis. Lamon had his version of Lincoln saying: "When I was a boy in Indiana, I went to a neighbor's house one morning and found a boy of my own size holding a coon by a string. I asked him what he had and what he was doing. He says, 'It's a coon. Dad cotched six last night, and killed all but this poor little cuss. Dad told me to hold him until he came back, and I'm afraid he's going to kill this one too; and oh, Abe, I do wish he would get away!' 'Well, why don't you let him loose?' 'That wouldn't be right; and if I let him go, Dad would give me hell. But if he would get away himself, it would be all right.' Now," said Mr. Lincoln, "if Jeff Davis and those other fellows will only get away, it will be all right. But if we should catch them, and I should let them go, 'Dad would give me hell.'" It was not unpleasant for Lincoln to look back and consider that in all his speeches and papers no one could find a phrase of hate or personal evil wish against the head of the Confederate Government.

The two men who most often warned Lincoln about his personal safety were Stanton and Lamon. To Lamon he had laughing retorts. The envelope on which he had written "Assassination," wherein he filed threat letters, numbered 80 items in latter March. He told Seward, "I know I am in danger; but I am not going to worry over threats like these."

Lamon took no ease about this matter because of a dream

Lincoln told him. To Lamon he spoke more than once of
his failure to produce again the double image of himself in
a looking glass, which he saw in 1860 lying on a lounge in
his home in Springfield. One face held glow of life and
breath, the other shone ghostly pale white. "It had worried
him not a little . . . the mystery had its meaning, which was
clear enough to him . . . the lifelike image betokening a safe
passage through his first term as President; the ghostly one,
that death would overtake him before the close of the
second."

Sternly practical and strictly logical man that Lincoln
was, using relentless scrutiny of facts and spare derivations
of absolutes from those facts, he nevertheless believed in
dreams having validity for himself and for others. According to Lamon's study, Lincoln held that any dream had a
meaning if you could be wise enough to find it. When a
dream came Lincoln sought clues from it. Once when Mrs.
Lincoln and Tad were away he telegraphed her to put away
a pistol Tad was carrying. "I had an ugly dream about him."

To Lamon it was appropriate that Lincoln held the best
dream interpreters were the common people. "This accounts
in large measure for the profound respect he always had for
the collective wisdom of the plain people,—'the children of
Nature,' he called them." The very superstitions of the
people had roots of reality in natural occurrences. "He
esteemed himself one of their number, having passed the
greater part of his life among them."

Of the dream that came to Lincoln this second week of
April '65, Lamon wrote that it was "the most startling incident" that had ever come to the man, of "deadly import,"
"amazingly real." Lincoln kept it to himself for a few days;
then one evening at the White House, with Mrs. Lincoln,
Lamon and one or two others present, he began talking
about dreams and led himself into telling the late one that
haunted him. Of his written account of the evening, Lamon
said, "I give it as nearly in his own words as I can, from
notes which I made immediately after its recital."

Mrs. Lincoln remarked, "Why, you look dreadfully solemn; do *you* believe in dreams?" "I can't say that I do," re-

turned Mr. Lincoln; "but I had one the other night which has haunted me ever since. After it occurred, the first time I opened the Bible, strange as it may appear, it was at the twenty-eighth chapter of Genesis, which relates the wonderful dream Jacob had. I turned to other passages, and seemed to encounter a dream or a vision wherever I looked. I kept on turning the leaves of the old book, and everywhere my eye fell upon passages recording matters strangely in keeping with my own thoughts,—supernatural visitations, dreams, visions, etc."

He now looked so serious and disturbed that Mrs. Lincoln exclaimed: "You frighten me! What is the matter?" "I am afraid," said Mr. Lincoln, seeing the effect his words had upon his wife, "that I have done wrong to mention the subject at all; but somehow the thing has got possession of me, and, like Banquo's ghost, it will not down."

This set on fire Mrs. Lincoln's curiosity. Though saying she didn't believe in dreams, she kept at him to tell what it was he had seen in his sleep that now had such a hold on him. He hesitated, waited a little, slowly began, his face in shadows of melancholy:

"About ten days ago I retired very late. I had been up waiting for important dispatches from the front. I could not have been long in bed when I fell into a slumber, for I was weary. I soon began to dream. There seemed to be a death-like stillness about me. Then I heard subdued sobs, as if a number of people were weeping. I thought I left my bed and wandered downstairs. There the silence was broken by the same pitiful sobbing, but the mourners were invisible. I went from room to room; no living person was in sight, but the same mournful sounds of distress met me as I passed along. It was light in all the rooms; every object was familiar to me; but where were all the people who were grieving as if their hearts would break? I was puzzled and alarmed. What could be the meaning of all this? Determined to find the cause of a state of things so mysterious and so shocking, I kept on until I arrived at the East Room, which I entered. There I met with a sickening surprise. Before me was a catafalque, on which rested a corpse wrapped in funeral vestments. Around it were stationed soldiers who were acting as guards; and there was a throng of people, some gazing mournfully upon the corpse, whose face was covered, others weeping pitifully. 'Who is dead in the White House?' I demanded of one of the soldiers. 'The President,' was his answer; 'he was killed by an assassin!' Then came a loud burst of grief from the crowd, which awoke me from my dream. I slept no more that night; and although it was only a dream, I have been strangely annoyed by it ever since."

"That is horrid!" said Mrs. Lincoln. "I wish you had not told it. I am glad I don't believe in dreams, or I should be in terror from this time forth." "Well," responded Mr. Lincoln, thoughtfully, "it is only a dream, Mary. Let us say no more about it, and try to forget it."

The dream had shaken its dreamer to the depths, noted Lamon. As he had given the secret of it to others he was "grave, gloomy, and at times visibly pale, but perfectly calm." To Lamon afterward, in a reference to it Lincoln quoted from *Hamlet*, "To sleep; perchance to dream! ay, *there's the rub!*"—stressing the last three words.

Once again and with playful touches, bringing his sense of humor into use as though he might laugh off the dream, he said to Lamon: "Hill, your apprehension of harm to me from some hidden enemy is downright foolishness. For a long time you have been trying to keep somebody—the Lord knows who—from killing me. Don't you see how it will turn out? In this dream it was not me, but some other fellow, that was killed. It seems that this ghostly assassin tried his hand on someone else. And this reminds me of an old farmer in Illinois whose family were made sick by eating greens. Some poisonous herb had got into the mess, and members of the family were in danger of dying. There was a half-witted boy in the family called Jake; and always afterward when they had greens the old man would say, 'Now, afore we risk these greens, *let's try 'em on Jake. If he stands 'em,* we're all right.' Just so with me. As long as this imaginary assassin continues to exercise himself on others I can stand it." He then became serious and said: "Well, let it go.

I think the Lord in His own good time and way will work this out all right. God knows what is best."

This last he gave with a sigh, and in a way as if talking to himself with no friend Lamon standing by.

Chapter 49

The Calendar Says Good Friday

From mid-April '61 to mid-April '65 some 3,000,000 men North and South had seen war service—the young, the strong, the physically fit, carrying the heavy load and taking the agony. The fallen of them had seen Antietam, Murfreesboro, Fredericksburg, Chancellorsville, the Wilderness, Spotsylvania, Cold Harbor, each a shambles, a human slaughterhouse. In the burned and blackened Shenandoah Valley were enough embers of barns and men to satisfy any prophet of doom. From Malvern Hill and Gettysburg down to Chickamauga, Chattanooga, Island Number 10, Vicksburg, the Red River and beyond, the burying grounds deep and shallow held the consecrated dead.

They were a host proven in valor and sacrifice—swept to the Great Beyond. No man who actually and passionately loved the cause of either flag could evade moments when he reproached himself for being alive. Robert E. Lee had those moments, well attested. So did Abraham Lincoln. His Gettysburg speech and his letter to Mrs. Bixby had an undeniable undertone of this reproach.

Killed in action or dead from wounds and disease were some 620,000 Americans, 360,000 from the North, 260,000 from the South—planted in the tomb of the earth, spectral and shadowy. They were phantoms never absent from Lincoln's thoughts. Possibly from that vanished host, rather than from the visible and living, Lincoln took his main direction and moved as though the word "reconciliation" could have supreme beauty if he could put it to work.

In Greensboro, North Carolina, at a rather ordinary house, in an upstairs room having a bed, a few small chairs, a table with pen and ink, Jefferson Davis, with four remaining Cabinet members and two veteran generals, held a final meeting over the affairs of the Confederate States of America, its government, its armies and prospects. They agreed a letter should be written to Sherman asking for terms. Johnston asked Davis to write it—which he did. They parted.

The sunset of the Confederacy had shaded over into evening stars, into lasting memories of a Lost Cause. Some would find welfare and kindness in the old Union. Two sections of the country fought a duel and came out with honors enough for both—this was the philosophy of some who really loved two flags—and why was a mystery, their personal secret. Some who had starved and suffered and taken wounds in the rain and lived on the food of rats and lost everything except a name for valor and endurance—some of these could never repent or be sorry.

As Davis packed his kit for moving farther south he knew there were not a few in the North who wished to see him hang on a sour-apple tree. One report credited Lincoln with saying: "This talk about Mr. Davis tires me. I hope he will mount a fleet horse, reach the shores of the Gulf of Mexico, and ride so far into its waters that we shall never see him again."

Lincoln sat for a photograph by Alexander Gardner—and for the first time when facing a camera in the four years of his administration permitted a smile to wreath his face. Until this camera register in the second week of April '65, he had most often been grave and somber. Now he smiled. The hurricane was spent, the high winds gone down. Rough weather and choppy seas were ahead—but the worst was over and could not come again. He hoped for good will and mutual trust and let that hope shine on his face.

Slimmer than a single cobweb thread was the hope that the President would call an extra session of Congress and let the legislative end of the Government dictate the reconstruction. When Speaker Colfax saw Lincoln about it he heard the President say he should "put it off as long as possible."

Crusader opposition to the President saw a long hard fight ahead. They would have to break Lincoln's control of his party. They would have to pry loose from him several powerful Northern economic factors that had not suffered loss at his hands and expected favors to come. They had not yet been able to solve the political genius by which he had so repeatedly foiled those seeking to unhorse him. Phillips, Sumner, Wade, Stevens, were not sure what strategy would overcome the odds against them. But they were sure the fight must be made; the Executive must somehow be shorn of his power. On the calendar it was Holy Week and April 14th was Good Friday. Some were to say they had never before this week seen such a shine of beneficence, such a kindling glow, on Lincoln's face. He was down to lean flesh and bone, 30 pounds underweight, his cheeks haggard, yet the inside of him moved to a music of peace on earth and good will to men. He let it come out in the photograph Gardner made this Holy Week.

The schedule for this day as outlined beforehand was: office business till eight; breakfast and then interviews till the Cabinet meeting at 11; luncheon, more interviews, a late afternoon drive with Mrs. Lincoln; an informal meeting with old Illinois friends; during the day and evening one or more trips to the War Department; another interview, then to the theater with Mrs. Lincoln and a small party. Such was the prepared docket for this Good Friday.

The city of Washington outside the White House kept on being gay. Flags and bunting still flew across streets. Churchgoers in large numbers heard Good Friday sermons of the Prince of Peace having brought unutterable blessings to the country.

In Washington General Grant had arrived from the front, heard shouts of welcome, and in trying to walk from his hotel to the War Department had to call on the police to help make a path through the curious, cheering throngs. The

Secretary of War had announced that after "consultation with the lieutenant-general," it was decided to stop all drafting and recruiting.

At breakfast with Robert the President heard his son tell of life at the front, and he probably did, as one story ran, take up a portrait of Robert E. Lee his son had brought him, and after placing it on the table scan it long, saying: "It is a good face. I am glad the war is over at last."

After breakfast came Speaker Colfax. Other callers included Congressman Cornelius Cole of California, a Grand Rapids, Michigan, lawyer, W. A. Howard, and the "lame-duck" Senator John P. Hale of New Hampshire. The President emphasized restoration of good will between the two sections whose war had ended.

Senator John A. J. Creswell came, one of the Union men who kept Maryland from secession. Creswell said that an old friend had drifted South, got into the Confederate Army, fallen into Federal hands, and was now a prisoner. "I know the man acted like a fool, but he is my friend and a good fellow. Let him out, give him to me, and I will be responsible for him."

"Creswell," said Lincoln, "you make me think of a lot of young folks who once started out Maying. To reach their destination they had to cross a shallow stream, and did so by means of an old flat boat. When they came to return, they found to their dismay that the old scow had disappeared. They were in sore trouble, and thought over all manner of devices for getting over the water, but without avail. After a time one of the boys proposed that each fellow should pick up the girl he liked the best and wade over with her. The masterly proposition was carried out, until all that were left upon the island was a little short chap and a great, long, gothic-built elderly lady. Now, Creswell, you are trying to leave me in the same predicament. You fellows are all getting your own friends out of this scrape, and you will succeed in carrying off one after another until nobody but Jeff Davis and myself will be left on the island, and then I won't know what to do. How should I feel? How should I look lugging him over? I guess the way to avoid such an embarrassing situation is to let them all out at once."

Others came seeking pardons, releases, discharges, which Lincoln wrote with an easier hand than he could while the war was on. A fever of bright new time coming possessed many this day. "Washington was a little delirious," wrote Crook. Everybody was celebrating. The kind of celebration depended on the kind of person. It was merely a question of whether the intoxication was mental or physical. A stream of callers came to congratulate the President.

Lincoln was disinclined to go to the theater party planned by Mrs. Lincoln. A third-rate drama, *Our American Cousin,* which the star Laura Keene had carried to popularity, was showing at Ford's Theatre. But Mrs. Lincoln had set her heart on it, and on his suggestion she invited General and Mrs. Grant. And General Grant accepted, the newspapers were announcing.

Grant however had changed his mind. Mrs. Grant, in all probability, had told the General that the more she thought about it, the more it seemed impossible that she could endure an evening with the unfortunate woman she had last seen in such outbursts of temper and rages of jealousy at City Point. The General himself, anyone who knew him would testify, could see no fun in such a social evening.

Grant sat that morning in his first session with a President and a Cabinet. Welles wrote in his diary the President's comment on re-establishing law and order and new state governments in the South. Changing Welles' report from the third person to the first, Lincoln said:

"I think it providential that this great rebellion is crushed just as Congress has adjourned and there are none of the disturbing elements of that body to hinder and embarrass us. If we are wise and discreet we shall reanimate the States and get their governments in successful operation, with order prevailing and the Union reestablished before Congress comes together in December . . . I hope there will be no persecution, no bloody work after the war is over. No one need expect me to take any part in hanging or killing those men, even the worst of them. Frighten them out of the country, open the gates, let down the bars, scare them off"—throwing up his hands as if scaring sheep. "Enough lives have been sacrificed."

Early in this Good Friday session of the Cabinet curiosity was sharp about army news. Stanton had not arrived. Grant said he was hourly expecting to hear from Sherman. Wrote Welles: "The President remarked it would, he had no doubt, come soon, and come favorable, for he had last night the usual dream which he had preceding nearly every great and important event of the War. Generally the news had been favorable which succeeded this dream, and the dream itself was always the same. I inquired what this remarkable dream could be. He said it related to your (my) element, the water; that he seemed to be in some singular, indescribable vessel, and that he was moving with great rapidity towards an indefinite shore; that he had this dream preceding Sumter, Bull Run, Antietam, Gettysburg, Stone River, Vicksburg, Wilmington, etc. General Grant said Stone River was certainly no victory, and he knew of no great results which followed from it. The President said however that might be, his dream preceded that fight. 'I had,' the President remarked, 'this strange dream again last night, and we shall, judging from the past, have great news very soon. I think it must be from Sherman. My thoughts are in that direction, as are most of yours.' "

Young Frederick Seward attended this Cabinet meeting as Acting Secretary of State in place of his father, who still lay abed with a broken jaw. Young Seward's account of the session added details that escaped Welles. Curiosity was spoken about the "rebel" leaders. Would they escape? Would they be caught and tried, and if so, what would be the penalties? "All those present thought that, for the sake of general amity and good will, it was desirable to have as few judicial proceedings as possible." "I suppose, Mr. President," said Postmaster General Dennison, "you would not be sorry to have them escape out of the country?" "Well," came a slow answer, "I should not be sorry to have them out of the country; but I should be for following them up pretty close, to make sure of their going."

As to various details of any new state government, Seward heard the President: "We can't undertake to run State governments in all these Southern States. Their people must do that—though I reckon that at first some of them may do it badly."

So the Cabinet session of Friday, April 14, came to an end with the expectation that on Tuesday, April 18, they would again meet and resume discussion of how to bind up the nation's wounds.

A new British Minister, Sir Frederick Bruce, had arrived in Washington and was awaiting presentation to the President. Young Seward asked at what time the next day would it be convenient? Lincoln paused a moment, then: "Tomorrow at two o'clock?" Seward supposed it would be in the Blue Room. "Yes, in the Blue Room," said Lincoln.

Chaplain Neill came to Lincoln's office with a Vermont colonel seeking a brigadier general's commission Lincoln had signed. The President had not returned from lunch. Neill was looking among papers on the President's desk. Lincoln came in eating an apple. "I told him for what I was looking," wrote Neill of this, "and as I talked he placed his hand on the bell-pull, when I said, 'For whom are you going to ring?' Placing his hand upon my coat, he spoke but two words,—'Andrew Johnson.' Then I said, 'I will come in again.' As I was leaving the room the Vice-President had been ushered in, and the President advanced and took him by the hand." Seldom had Lincoln and Johnson met. Definitely Lincoln had on several occasions avoided a conference sought by Johnson. Before Johnson left Lincoln would have sounded and fathomed him on immediate issues.

A black woman faint from hunger and a five-mile walk arrived at the White House gate, where the guards queried, "Business with the President?" and heard her grimly: "Befo' Gawd, yes." "Let her pass—they'll stop her further on," she heard one guard say as she took a deep breath and went on. The main entrance guard stopped her: "No further, madam. Against orders." In a flash she darted under his arm and went straight to the guard at the farther door. "Fo' Gawd's sake, please lemme see Mistah Lincoln."

"Madam, the President is busy. He can not see you."

Either a cry she gave or the little tumult of her coming had reached inside, because, as she afterward related: "All of a sudden de do' open, and Mistah Lincoln hissef stood lookin' at me. I knowed him, fo' dar wuz a whimsy smile on his blessed face, an' he wuz sayin' deep and sof'-like, 'There is time for all who need me. Let the good woman come in.' "

He heard Nancy Bushrod tell of her life with her husband Tom, how they were slaves on the old Harwood plantation near Richmond till the Emancipation Proclamation brought them to Washington. Tom joined a regiment with the Army of the Potomac, leaving Nancy with twin boys and a baby girl. At first his pay kept coming every month. Then it stopped. The soldiers were behind in pay from the Government. She had tramped seeking work but Washington was overrun with Negro help. Could the President help her get Tom's pay?

He heard her through and, according to Nancy, told her: "You are entitled to your soldier-husband's pay. Come this time tomorrow and the papers will be signed and ready for you." And as Nancy told it, "I couldn't open my mouf to tell him how I'se gwine 'membah him fo'evah for dem words, an' I couldn't see him kase de tears wuz fallin'." He called her back. "My good woman, perhaps you'll see many a day when all the food in the house is a single loaf of bread. Even so, give every child a slice and send your children off to school." With that, the President bowed "lak I wuz a natchral bawn lady."

Assistant Secretary of War Dana had a report that Jacob Thompson, the Confederate commissioner in Canada who had fomented raids, explosions and various disorders in the Great Lakes region, was to arrive in Portland this night of April 14 to take a steamer for Liverpool. Stanton said promptly, "Arrest him!" and changed to: "No, wait; better go over and see the President." Dana found Lincoln with his coat off in a closet attached to the office, washing his hands. "Halloo, Dana!" said the President. "What is it now?" "Well, sir, here is the Provost Marshal of Portland, who reports that Jacob Thompson is to be in that town to-night, and inquires what orders we have to give." "What does Stanton say?" "Arrest him." "Well," continued Lin-coln, drawling the words, "no, I rather think not. When you have an elephant by the hind leg, and he's trying to run away, it's best to let him run."

This answer Dana carried back to the War Department, which on Stanton's wish sent no reply to the Provost Mar-shal's anxious inquiry. If the Marshal on his own initiative should make the arrest, Stanton would have Thompson where he wanted him—without having ordered the arrest.

A long afternoon carriage drive made an interlude. Mrs. Lincoln told Crook and others later of her query whether some friends should be invited for this drive, Lincoln say-ing No, he wanted "just ourselves." As the carriage rolled along he talked about the next four years in Washington, how he hoped afterward perhaps for a trip abroad, then a return to Springfield, perhaps law practice and a prairie farm on the banks of the Sangamon. Mrs. Lincoln spoke too of a happiness moving him, a happiness so strange and un-usual that she could not read it, and it troubled her. She quoted him as saying, "I never felt so happy in my life," and a fear crossed her as she replied, "Don't you remember feeling just so before our little boy died?"

Walking over to the War Department late this afternoon of April 14, Lincoln did one thing perhaps for the first time. Always others had brought up the matter of possible harm to come to him—and he had laughed them off or promised to take care. In this instance it was Lincoln who first men-tioned it, according to Crook's account. They passed some drunken men, profane, violent, irresponsible. And Lincoln turned, saying, "Crook, do you know, I believe there are men who want to take my life?" And after a pause, half to himself, "And I have no doubt they will do it."

Lincoln's tone was so calm and sure that Crook found himself saying, "Why do you think so, Mr. President?" "Other men have been assassinated"—this still in the man-ner of half talking to himself. "I hope you are mistaken, Mr. President," offered Crook. And after a few paces in silence, Lincoln in a more ordinary tone: "I have perfect confidence in those who are around me—in every one of you men. I know no one could do it and escape alive. But if it is to be done, it is impossible to prevent it."

Of this visit to the telegraph office, the Cipher-Operator Charles A. Tinker wrote, "Lincoln . . . came . . . while I was transmitting a cipher dispatch that was couched in very laconic terms. Lincoln read the dispatch, and after taking in the meaning of the terse phrases, he turned to me and with his accustomed smile said, 'Mr. Tinker, that reminds me of the old story of the Scotch lassie on her way to market with a basket of eggs for sale. She had just forded a small stream with her skirts well drawn up, when a wagoner on the opposite side of the stream called out, "Good morning, my lassie; how deep's the brook and what's the price of eggs?" She answered, "Knee deep and a sixpence." ' Mr. Lincoln, still with a smile, lifted his coat tails in imitation of the maiden and passed into Secretary Stanton's room adjoining."

After a short conference in Stanton's office Lincoln came out, Crook noticing that the "depression" or "intense seriousness" had passed. "He talked to me as usual." Of the theater party planned for the evening he said: "It has been advertised that we will be there, and I cannot disappoint the people. Otherwise I would not go. I do not want to go." This surprised Crook, who knew well the ease and enjoyment Lincoln usually found at the theater. So Crook meditated, "It seems unusual to hear him say he does not want to go tonight." At the White House door he stood facing his guard a moment and then, "Good-bye, Crook." This puzzled Crook somewhat. Until then it had always been "Good-night, Crook."

At the White House Congressman Samuel Shellabarger of Ohio pleasantly asked that one of his constituents be appointed to a staff position in the Army. Lincoln pleasantly said he was reminded of when he was a young man in Illinois and a woman in the neighborhood made shirts. "An Irishman went to her and ordered a white shirt for some special function. The woman made it, and laundered it and sent it to her customer. When he got it the Irishman found the shirt had been starched all the way around, instead of only in the bosom, and he returned it with the remark that he didn't want a shirt that was all collar. The trouble with you, Shellabarger, is that you want the army all staff and no army." Thus Shellabarger told it to his Buckeye friend J. Warren Keifer.

Dick Oglesby, the new Governor of Illinois, and Dick Yates, the new U.S. Senator from Illinois, had an evening hour at the White House with Lincoln. They were home folks. Oglesby was salty and Yates convivial. Lincoln read to them horseplay humor from the latest outpouring of Petroleum Vesuvius Nasby, said Oglesby, perhaps including a letter dated April 10 wherein the satirist took his fling as follows: "I survived the defeet uv Micklellan (who wuz, trooly, the nashen's hope and pride likewise), becoz I felt assoored that the rane uv the Goriller Linkin wood be a short wun; that in a few months, at furthest, Ginral Lee wood capcher Washington, depose the ape, and set up there a constooshnal guverment, based upon the great and immutable trooth that a white man is better than a nigger." The Confederates had "consentratid" and lost their capital. "Linkin rides into Richmond! A Illinois rale-splitter, a buffoon, a ape, a goriller, a smutty joker, set hisself down in President Davis's cheer, and rites dispatchis! . . . This ends the chapter. The Confederasy hez at last consentratid its last consentrate. It's ded. It's gathered up its feet, sed its last words, and deceest . . . Linkin will serve his term out— the tax on whisky won't be repeeled—our leaders will die off uv chagrin, and delirium tremens and inability to live so long out uv offis, and the sheep will be skattered. Farewell, vane world." This extravaganza rested Lincoln. It had the flavor Oglesby liked. And Yates could take it.

After dinner Speaker Colfax called by appointment. He asked whether the President intended to call an extra session of Congress during the summer. The President assured him he had no such intention. This left Colfax free for a trip to the West Coast. Lincoln gave him a message to the mountain regions that their gold and silver mines must count in a coming peace prosperity. Colfax spoke of how uneasy all had been over his going to Richmond and taking risks amid the tumult there. "He replied," noted Colfax, "pleasantly and with a smile (I quote his exact words), 'Why, if anyone else had been President and gone to Richmond, I would have been alarmed too; but I was not scared about myself a bit.'"

Congressman George Ashmun of Massachusetts waited below, said a card brought in. A loyal party man, presiding chairman of the 1860 convention that had nominated Lincoln for President, he was entitled to a hearing. One published report assumed to give concretely the gist of their interview. Ashmun spoke for a client of his who had a cotton claim against the Government and he desired a "commission" appointed to examine and decide on the merits of the case. Lincoln was quoted as replying rather warmly: "I have done with 'commissions.' I believe they are contrivances to cheat the Government out of every pound of cotton they can lay their hands on." Ashmun's face flushed. He answered that he hoped the President meant no personal imputation. Lincoln saw that his sudden and sharp comment on such "commissions" had been taken as personal and he had wounded a good friend, instantly saying: "You did not understand me, Ashmun. I did not mean what you inferred. I take it all back." He would see Ashmun first of all callers on the docket next morning, and taking a card, wrote:

> April 14, 1865.
> Allow Mr. Ashmun
> & friend to come in
> at 9 A.M. tomor-
> row—
>   A. Lincoln

They joined Colfax, Mrs. Lincoln and Noah Brooks. The President was unusually cheerful, thought Brooks, "never more hopeful and buoyant concerning the condition of the country, full of fun and anecdotes," though he had no enthusiasm about the play for the evening, felt "inclined to give up the whole thing." The party stepped out on the White House portico, Lincoln going toward the carriage, saying, "Grant thinks we can reduce the cost of the army establishment at least a half million a day, which, with the reduction of expenditures of the navy, will soon bring down our national debt to something like decent proportions, and bring our national paper up to a par, or nearly so, with gold —at least so they think."

Good old Isaac N. Arnold of Chicago came along, mentioned his errand as Lincoln was stepping into the carriage, and was answered, "Excuse me now. I am going to the theater. Come and see me in the morning."

Chapter 50

Blood on the Moon

In the carriage into which the President and his wife stepped were Henry Reed Rathbone, assigned by Stanton to accompany the President, and his fiancée, Miss Clara Harris. He was 28 years old, of a well-to-do clan of Rathbones in Albany, New York, a major of volunteers since November '62, a trusted War Office attaché. His sweetheart was the daughter of Judge Ira Harris of Albany, since 1861 U.S. Senator from New York.

The guard with Lincoln this evening was John F. Parker, one of the four officers detailed from the Metropolitan Police Force of the city for White House duty in staying close to the President and keeping a sharp eye on anyone who might have designs on the life and person of the President. Of these four guards only one, it afterward appeared, had a questionable record—and he was John F. Parker. On this evening he was 35 years old lacking one month; born in Frederick County, Virginia, he had worked at the carpenter's trade in Washington, enlisted in the Army as a three-month man, in '61 joining the Metropolitan Police as a patrolman. At his home on 750 L Street he had a wife and three children.

In March and April of '63 Parker was on trial on various charges: of being found asleep on a streetcar when he should have been patrolling his beat; of conduct unbecoming an officer through five weeks of residence in a house of prostitution, where it was alleged he had been drunk, had been put to bed, had fired a revolver through a window; the board found he was "at a house of ill fame with no other excuse than that he was sent for by the Keeper (Miss Annie Wilson)," although there was "no evidence that there was any robbery there or disturbance of the peace or quiet of that neighborhood." The list of trials, the repeated similar charges against Parker, the board's findings in the evidence showed conclusively that he was of loose habits rather than a steady reliable man.

How Parker found his way into the White House to begin with was not clear in the records. On April 3, however, when he was drafted for army service, Mrs. Lincoln on Executive Mansion stationery had written to the District of Columbia Provost Marshal, James R. O'Beirne, a certificate "that John F. Parker . . . has been detailed for duty at the Executive Mansion by order of [signed] Mrs. Lincoln."

The carriage left the White House with its four occupants, coachman Francis Burns holding the reins, and alongside him the footman and valet Charles Forbes. At Ford's Theatre, Burns pulled up his horses. Forbes swung down to the sidewalk and opened the carriage door. The President and his wife stepped out, followed by Major Rathbone and Miss Harris. The guard Parker was at hand. The party walked into the theater at about nine o'clock. An usher led them to their box. The audience in their 1,000 seats saw or heard that the President had arrived. They applauded; many rose from their seats; some cheered. The President paused and nodded his acknowledgment of their welcome to him.

On the stage proceeds a play written 14 years before by the English dramatist Tom Taylor; on rehearsal he decided it was not for the British public and later had sent it to the New York producer Lester Wallack, who had told Laura Keene it would fit her. She had put it on, but after a fairly good run it has about reached its limit.

The play proceeds, not unpleasant, often stupid, sprinkled with silly puns, forced humor. The story centers around the Yankee lighting his cigar with an old will, burning the document to ashes and thereby throwing a fortune of $400,000 away from himself into the hands of an English cousin. The audience agrees it is not bad. The applause and laughter say the audience is having a good time.

From the upholstered rocking armchair in which Lincoln sits he can see only the persons in the box with him, the players on the stage and any persons off stage on the left. The box has two doors. The door forward is locked. The President's party has the roominess and convenience of double space, extra armchairs, side chairs, a small sofa. In the privacy achieved he is in sight only of his chosen companions, the actors he has come to see render a play, and the few people who may be off stage to the left.

This privacy however is not as complete as it seems. A few feet behind the President is the box door, the only entry to the box unless by a climb from the stage. In this door is a small hole, bored that afternoon to serve as a peephole —from the outside. Through this peephole it is the intention of the Outsider who made it with a gimlet to stand and watch the President, then at a chosen moment to enter the box. This door opens from the box on a narrow hallway that leads to another door opening on the balcony of the theater.

Through these two doors the Outsider must pass in order to enter the President's box. Close to the door connecting with the balcony two inches of plaster have been cut from the brick wall of the narrow hallway. The intention of the Outsider is that a bar placed in this cut-away wall niche and then braced against the panel of the door will hold that door against intruders, will serve to stop anyone from interference with the Outsider while making his observations of the President through the gimleted hole in the box door.

At either of these doors, the one to the box or the one from the balcony to the hallway, it is the assigned duty and expected responsibility of John F. Parker to stand or sit constantly, with unfailing vigil. A Ward Lamon or an Eckert on this duty would probably have noticed the gimleted hole, the newly made wall niche, and been doubly watchful.

"The guard . . . acting as my substitute," wrote the faithful Crook later, "took his position at the rear of the box, close to an entrance leading into the box . . . His orders were to stand there, fully armed, and to permit no unauthorized person to pass into the box. His orders were to stand there and protect the President at all hazards. From the spot where he was thus stationed, this guard could not see the stage or the actors; but he could hear the words the actors spoke, and he became so interested in them that, incredible as it may seem, he quietly deserted his post of duty, and walking down the dimly-lighted side aisle, deliberately took a seat."

The custom was for a chair to be placed in the narrow hallway for the guard to sit in. The doorkeeper Buckingham told Crook that such a chair was provided this evening for the accommodation of the guard. "Whether Parker occupied it at all, I do not know," wrote Crook. "Mr. Buckingham is of the impression that he did. If he did, he left it almost immediately, for he confessed to me the next day that he went to a seat, so that he could see the play." The door to the President's box is shut. It is not kept open so that the box occupants can see the guard on duty.

Either between acts or at some time when the play was not lively enough to suit him or because of an urge for a pony of whisky under his belt, John F. Parker leaves his seat in the balcony and goes down to the street and joins companions in a little whiff of liquor—this on the basis of a statement of the coachman Burns, who declared he stayed outside on the street with his carriage and horses, except for one interlude when "the special police officer [meaning John F. Parker] and the footman of the President [Forbes] came up to him and asked him to take a drink with them;

which he did." Thus circumstances favor the lurking and vigilant Outsider.

The play goes on. The evening and the drama are much like many other evenings when the acting is pleasant enough, the play mediocre, the audience having no thrills of great performance but enjoying itself.

Out in a main-floor seat is one Julia Adelaide Shephard, writing a letter to her father about this Good Friday evening at the theater. "Cousin Julia has just told me," she reports, "that the President is in yonder upper right hand private box so handsomely decked with silken flags festooned over a picture of George Washington. The young and lovely daughter of Senator Harris is the only one of his party we see as the flags hide the rest. But we know Father Abraham is there like a Father watching what interests his children. The American cousin has just been making love to a young lady who says she'll never marry but for love but when her mother and herself find out that he has lost his property they retreat in disgust at the left hand of the stage while the American cousin goes out at the right. We are waiting for the next scene."

And the next scene? The next scene is to crash and blare and flare as one of the wildest, one of the most inconceivable, fateful and chaotic that ever stunned and shocked a world that heard the story.

The moment of high fate is not seen by the theater audience. Only one man sees that moment. He is the Outsider, the one who waited and lurked and made his preparations. He comes through the outer door into the little hallway, fastens the strong though slender bar into the two-inch niche in the brick wall, and braces it against the door panel. He moves softly to the box door and through the little hole studies the box occupants and his Human Target seated in an upholstered rocking armchair. Softly he opens the door and steps toward his prey, in his right hand a one-shot brass derringer pistol, a little eight-ounce vest-pocket weapon winged for death, in his left hand a steel dagger. He is cool and precise and times his every move. He raises the derringer, lengthens his right arm, runs his eye along the barrel

in a line with the head of his victim less than five feet away
—and pulls the trigger.

A lead ball somewhat less than a half-inch in diameter
crashes into the left side of the head of the Human Target,
into the back of the head, in a line with and three inches
from the left ear. "The course of the ball was obliquely forward toward the right eye, crossing the brain in an oblique
manner and lodging a few inches behind that eye. In the
track of the wound were found fragments of bone, which
had been driven forward by the ball, which was embedded
in the anterior lobe of the left hemisphere of the brain."

For Abraham Lincoln it is lights out, good night, farewell—and a long farewell to the good earth and its trees, its
enjoyable companions, and the Union of States and the
world Family of Man he has loved. He is not dead yet. He is
to linger in dying. But the living man can never again speak,
see, hear or awaken into conscious being.

Near the prompt-desk off stage stands W. J. Ferguson,
an actor. He looks in the direction of the shot he hears, and
sees "Mr. Lincoln lean back in his rocking chair, his head
coming to rest against the wall which stood between him
and the audience . . . well inside the curtains"—no struggle
or move "save in the slight backward sway." Of this the
audience knows nothing.

Major Rathbone leaps from his chair. Rushing at him
with a knife is a strange human creature, terribly alive, a
lithe wild animal, a tiger for speed, a wildcat of a man
bareheaded, raven-haired—a smooth sinister face with glar-
ing eyeballs. He wears a dark sack suit. He stabs straight at
the heart of Rathbone, a fast and ugly lunge. Rathbone par-
ries it with his upper right arm, which gets a deep slash of
the dagger. Rathbone is staggered, reels back. The tigerish
stranger mounts the box railing. Rathbone recovers, leaps
again for the stranger, who feels the hand of Rathbone holding him back, slashes again at Rathbone, then leaps for the
stage.

This is the moment the audience wonders whether something unusual is happening—or is it part of the play? From
the box railing the Strange Man's leap for the stage is

slightly interrupted. The draped Union flag of silk reaches out and tangles itself in the spur of one riding boot, throwing him out of control. He falls perhaps ten feet to the stage, landing on his left leg, breaking the shinbone a little above the instep.

Of what he has done the audience as yet knows nothing. They wonder what this swift, raven-haired, wild-eyed Strange Man portends. They see him rush across the stage, three feet to a stride, and vanish. Some have heard Rathbone's cry "Stop that man!" Many have seen a man leap from a front seat up on the stage and chase after the weird Stranger, crying "Stop that man!" It is less than half a minute since the Strange Man mounted the box railing, made the stage and strode off.

Off stage between Laura Keene and W. J. Ferguson he dashes at breakneck speed, out of an entrance, 40 feet to a little door opening on an alley. There stands a fast bay horse, a slow-witted chore boy named John Peanuts holding the reins. He kicks the boy, mounts the mare; hoofs on the cobblestones are heard but a few moments. In all it is maybe 60 or 70 seconds since he loosed the one shot of his eight-ounce brass derringer.

Did the Strange Man now riding away on a fast bay horse pause a moment on the stage and shout a dramatic line of speech? Some said he ran off as though every second of time counted and his one purpose was escape. Others said he faced the audience a moment, brandished a dagger still bloody from slashing Rathbone, and shouted the state motto of Virginia, the slogan of Brutus as he drove the assassin's knife into imperial Caesar: *"Sic semper tyrannis"*—"Thus be it ever to tyrants."

The audience is up and out of its 1,000 seats, standing, moving. Panic is in the air, fear over what may happen next. Many merely stand up from their seats, fixed and motionless, waiting to hear what has happened. The question is spoken quietly or is murmured anxiously—"What is it? What has happened?" The question is yelled with anguish— "For God's sake, what is it—what has happened?"

A woman's scream pierces the air. Some say afterward it

was Mrs. Lincoln. The scream carries a shock and a creeping shiver to many hearing it. "He has shot the President!" Men swarm up to the edge of the stage, over the gas-jet footlights onto the stage. The aisles fill with people not sure where to go.

Some 200 soldiers arrive to clear the theater. The wailing and the crazy chaos let down in the emptying playhouse—and flare up again in the street outside, where some man is accused of saying he is glad it happened, a sudden little mob dragging him to a lamppost with a ready rope to hang him when six policemen with clubs and drawn revolvers manage to get him away and jail him for safekeeping.

Mrs. Lincoln in the box sees her husband seated in the rocking chair, his head slumped forward. With little moaning cries she springs toward him and with her hands keeps him from tumbling to the floor. Major Rathbone has shouted for a surgeon, has run out of the box into the narrow hallway, and with one arm bleeding and burning with pain he fumbles to unfasten the bar between wall and door panel. An usher from the outside tries to help him. They get the bar loose. Back of the usher is a jam of people. He holds them back, allowing only one man to enter, a young-looking man with mustache and sideburns, 23-year-old Charles A. Leale, assistant surgeon, U.S. Volunteers.

Dr. Leale holds Mrs. Lincoln's outstretched hand while she cries "Oh, Doctor! Is he dead? Can he recover? Will you take charge of him? Do what you can for him. Oh, my dear husband! my dear husband!" He soothes her a little; he will do all that can possibly be done.

The man in the chair at first scrutiny seems to be dead, eyes closed, no certainty he is breathing. Dr. Leale with help from others lifts the man from the chair and moves him to a lying position on the floor. Dr. Leale lifts the eyelids and sees evidence of a brain injury. He rapidly passes the separated fingers of both hands through the blood-matted hair of the head, finding a wound and removing a clot of blood, which relieves pressure on the brain and brings shallow breathing and a weak pulse.

Dr. Leale bends over, puts a knee at each side of the body, and tries to start the breathing apparatus, attempts to stimulate respiration by putting his two fingers into the throat and pressing down and out on the base of the tongue to free the larynx of secretion. Dr. Charles Sabin Taft, an army surgeon lifted from the stage into the box, now arrives. Another physician, Dr. Albert F. A. King, arrives. Leale asks them each to manipulate an arm while he presses upward on the diaphragm and elsewhere to stimulate heart action. The body responds with an improvement in the pulse and the irregular breathing.

Dr. Leale is sure, however, that with the shock and prostration the body has undergone, more must now be done to keep life going. And as he told it later: "I leaned forcibly forward directly over his body, thorax to thorax, face to face, and several times drew in a long breath, then forcibly breathed directly into his mouth and nostrils, which expanded his lungs and improved his respirations. After waiting a moment I placed my ear over his thorax and found the action of the heart improving. I arose to the erect kneeling posture, then watched for a short time and saw that the President could continue independent breathing and that instant death would not occur. I then pronounced my diagnosis and prognosis: 'His wound is mortal; it is impossible for him to recover.' "

Brandy and water arrive. Dr. Leale slowly pours a small quantity into the President's mouth. It is swallowed and retained. While they are waiting for the President to gain strength, wrote Leale later, Laura Keene "appealed to me to allow her to hold the President's head. I granted this request, and she sat on the floor of the box and held his head in her lap. We decided that the President could now be moved to a house where we might place him on a bed in safety."

Four soldiers from Thompson's Independent Battery C, Pennsylvania Light Artillery, lift the President by the trunk and legs, Dr. Taft carrying the right shoulder, Dr. King the left shoulder, Dr. Leale the head. They come to the door of the box. Dr. Leale sees the passageway packed with people. He calls out twice, "Guards, clear the passage!" A captain goes into action with troopers. They show muskets, bayonets, sabers. "Clear out!" rings the repeated order. "Clear out!" they cry to the curiosity seekers, and to some who hesitate and still insist on blocking passage. "Clear out, you sons of bitches!"

Then the solemn little group with their precious freight carried headfirst moves slowly through a space lined by protecting soldiers. At the stair head they shift so the feet are carried first. Two more soldiers join the original four in holding the President and moving him. As they go out of the door of the theater Dr. Leale is again asked if the President can be taken to the White House and answers, "No, the President would die on the way."

Overhead is night sky. Clouds of dark gray unfold and unroll and show a blazing white moon and fold and roll and cover it again. On Tenth Street between E Street and F humanity swirls and wonders and wants to know. "Is that the President they are carrying?" "Is it true that he was shot and will live?" "Oh, God, it can't be true!" "Where are they taking him?" "Who shot him?" "Was he stabbed or shot? I heard he was stabbed." "Was he shot bad or will he live?" "For God's sake, is there no chance for him?"

Packing Tenth Street straight across from the front door of Ford's Theater is a crowd so massed that there is no hope of a path for those carrying the President unless something is done. The same captain who had managed clearance inside the theater comes to Leale: "Surgeon, give me your commands and I will see that they are obeyed." Leale asks the captain to clear a passage to the nearest house opposite. The captain draws a sword, commands the people to make an opening; they move back, and the procession begins its slow crossing. Several times they stop while Dr. Leale removes the newly gathered blood clots on the head wound. A barrier of men forms to keep back the crowds on each side of an open space leading to the house. Now comes the report that this house is closed. At the next house, Mr. Peterson's, No. 453 Tenth Street, Dr. Leale sees a man standing at the door with a lighted candle, beckoning them to come in. "This we did," ran Leale's account, "not having been interrupted in the slightest by the throngs in the street; but a number of the excited populace followed us into the house."

There they lay their stricken Friend of Man in the rented room of William Clark, a boarder in the house of William Peterson—on a plain wooden bed—at about 10:45 o'clock, somewhat less perhaps than a half-hour after the moment the trigger of the little eight-ounce derringer was pulled.

The President lies on his back in the center of the humble walnut bed. Now Dr. Leale holds the face upward to keep the head from rolling to either side. The long knee elevation troubles Leale. He orders the foot of the bed removed. Dr. Taft and Dr. King report it is a fixture. Leale requests it be broken. This it seems cannot be done with any satisfaction. Leale then has Lincoln moved so he lies diagonally across the bed and, propped with extra pillows, is gently slanted with a rest for head and shoulders, finally in a position of repose.

On white sheets lies the unconscious patient still in frock coat and long boots. Under the white sheets is a cornhusk mattress resting on rope lacings. The room fills with anxious people. Leale calls an officer, directs him to open a window, and to order all except the doctors and friends to leave.

After a short rest for the patient Leale decides to make a thorough physical examination to see if there are other wounds. He requests all except surgeons to leave the room. The captain reports all have left but Mrs. Lincoln, with whom he does not feel authorized to speak. Leale makes his wish known to Mrs. Lincoln and she leaves at once. They undress the patient, search the body from head to foot, finding no other wound. The lower extremities are cold; Leale sends a hospital steward for hot water and hot blankets. He sends for a large mustard plaster; this is applied over the solar plexus and to every inch of the entire anterior surface of the body.

The breath comes hard; pulse 44, feeble; the left pupil much contracted, the right widely dilated; both eyes totally insensible to light. The President is completely unconscious, an occasional sigh escaping with the labored breath.

In a nearby room Mrs. Lincoln has the company of Miss Harris, of several women who have arrived, and of the Reverend Dr. Gurley. Major Rathbone has fainted from loss of blood and is taken home. At intervals Mrs. Lincoln is notified she may visit her husband. Once she cries to him, "Live! you must live!" and again, "Bring Tad—he will speak to Tad—he loves him so."

Dr. Robert K. Stone, the Lincoln family physician, arrives, followed soon by Surgeon General Joseph K. Barnes and his assistant Dr. Charles H. Crane, who take charge. Dr. Leale reports to his chief what he has done. At 2 A.M. Dr. Barnes tries to locate the bullet and after a time further exploration for the bullet is considered of no avail.

The room is 15 feet long by 9 wide, entered from the hallway by a door having a large pane of glass covered with a curtain on the inside. A Brussels carpet is on the floor. The wallpaper is brown figured with white. Around are a few chairs, a plain bureau, a small wood stove, a washstand with pitcher and bowl. Here there is waiting for the end to come.

Outdoors a vagrant white moon, over which dark clouds had earlier rolled and unrolled their smokelike shadows, is now long hidden and lost behind a cold gray sky, an even monotone of a sky.

In the White House Robert Lincoln and John Hay sit gossiping pleasantly, Nicolay away at the Fort Sumter flag-raising. The doors burst open and several voices at once tell them the news. They run downstairs, take a carriage, cannot quite believe what they have heard. Slowly their carriage plows a path through the gathering thousands of people around Tenth Street. Dr. Stone gravely and tenderly tells Robert the worst: there is no hope. He chokes. The tears run down his face. After a time he recovers and does his best during hours of the night at comforting his mother.

At about the same hour and minute of the clock that the President is shot in Ford's Theatre a giant of a young man rides on a big one-eyed bay horse to the door of the Seward house on Lafayette Square, gets off his horse, rings the doorbell, says he is a messenger from the attending physician and has a package of medicine that must be personally delivered to the sickroom of the Secretary of State. The servant at the door tries to stop the young man, who enters and goes up the stairs, suddenly to turn in a furious rush on Fred Seward, beating him on the head with the pistol, tearing the scalp, fracturing the skull and battering the pistol to pieces.

Young Seward grapples with the intruder, and in their scuffling the two of them come to the Secretary's room and fall together through the door. There Fred Seward fades out and for days knows nothing, in a stupor of unconsciousness. The Secretary's daughter and a soldier-nurse, Sergeant George T. Robinson, spring from their chairs. The murderbent young giant knocks them right and left, gives Robinson a knife thrust, then rushes to the bed where the Secretary of State has lain nearly two weeks with a steel frame about the head and face. He stabs over and again at the throat of the sick man, delivers three ugly gashes in the cheek and neck. The steel frame foils a death gash. And the quick wit or odd luck of the victim still further foils him; the Secretary of State rolls off between the bed and the wall.

Now the stranger in the house hurls himself down the stairs, lashes an attendant on the way, is out of the front door unhurt, leaps into saddle and rides out Vermont Avenue toward an eastern suburb. Behind him he has left a quiet home transformed into a battlefield hospital, five persons bleeding from ghastly wounds, failing of death for any of them. Behind him too he has left a bloodstained knife, the battered pistol and his slouch felt hat.

This horror affair is the basis for the wildfire rumor that nearly all the Cabinet members have been assassinated. Senator Sumner finds a hack, is driven to Tenth Street above E, makes inquiries, is stopped by guards at the door of the Peterson house, says, "I *will* go in"—and his face and manner pass him. He quietly watches and waits, occasionally with moist eyes.

Two friends of Chase drop in to tell the Chief Justice the President has been shot. "My first impulse," Chase writes in his diary for April 14, "was to rise immediately and go to the President, but reflecting that I could not possibly be of any service, I resolved to wait for morning and further intelligence."

Secretary Welles is just falling asleep about 10:30 when his wife calls him. His messenger James Smith has arrived, excited, saying the President has been shot. In the Peterson house at the bedside of "the giant sufferer" Welles' outstanding impressions were: "He had been stripped of his clothes. His large arms, which were occasionally exposed, were of a size which one would scarce have expected from his spare appearance. His slow, full respiration lifted the clothes with each breath that he took. His features were calm and striking. I had never seen them appear to better advantage than for the first hour, perhaps, that I was there. After that, his right eye began to swell and that part of his face became discolored."

One by one the other Cabinet members arrive till all are in the Peterson house except Seward and McCulloch. Vice-President Andrew Johnson comes early for a brief visit.

At one in the morning, wrote the New York *Herald* man, "Senator Sumner was seated on the right of the President's couch, near the head, holding the right hand of the President in his own. He was sobbing like a woman, with his head bowed down almost on the pillow of the bed on which the President was lying."

Nerves are wearing away, faces haggard. Dr. Leale continues the one expedient of keeping the wound opening free from blood clot. The surgeons direct or perform every necessary act that comes to mind. They are supposed to be coldly practical, with no emotion to interfere with clear thinking, yet Surgeon Taft noted moments when "there was scarcely a dry eye in the room." To Dr. Leale it is vastly more than one more surgical case. From a distance he had loved the President. He had gone to Ford's Theatre chiefly to have a look at a public man he admired as a heroic character. So he is softly moved to a procedure he later described: "Knowledge that frequently just before departure recognition and reason return to those who have been unconscious caused me for several hours to hold his right hand firmly within my grasp to let him in his blindness know, if possible, that he was in touch with humanity and had a friend."

The one man dominant in the house is Edwin McMasters Stanton. He seems to have lived for this night, for the exercise of the faculties on which he prided himself. Over Washington wild rumors were running that a new uprising of the Confederacy was breaking, a city guerrilla warfare— that secretly armed secessionists were to swarm from their hiding places, take strategic points, and make a last desperate stand for the Confederate cause. "Stanton," wrote one of his friends, "instantly assumed charge of everything near and remote, civil and military." He ordered troops to keep clear the spaces around the house, to let no one enter the house except high Government officers and persons on special business. He sent for the District of Columbia Chief Justice David K. Cartter, who arrived soon and in an adjoining room began taking testimony, with a shorthand reporter present, of persons who might have evidence bearing on the high crime. To Charles A. Dana, Assistant Secretary of War, who could write shorthand, Stanton dictated telegrams to all parts of the country.

Stanton sent for several army officers to act as aides; directed General Thomas M. Vincent to take charge of affairs in the Peterson house; telegraphed to General Grant at Philadelphia that Lincoln had been shot and to return at once to Washington; telegraphed to Chief Kennedy of New York to send on his best detectives immediately; wrote and dispatched a note to Chief Justice Chase, saying the President could not live and to be ready to administer the oath of office to Vice-President Johnson; notified the Vice-President that the President was dying; and sent to the country and the people bulletin after bulletin concerning the tragedy and the President's condition. Thus, wrote a friend of Stanton, "he continued throughout the night, acting as president, secretary of war, secretary of state, commander-in-chief, comforter, and dictator."

As daylight began to slant through the windows, with its white clarity making the yellow gas jets and lamplights look

garish and outdone, it became evident the President was
sinking. Surgeon General Barnes, seated near the head of
the bed, occasionally held his finger over the carotid artery
to note its pulsation. Dr. Stone sat on the edge of the foot
of the bed. Dr. Leale held the President's right hand, with
an extended forefinger on the pulse.

At 5 A.M. the oozing from the wound ceased entirely and
the breathing became stertorous and labored. On the haggard faces of the silent ones circled about, it was written
more than once they thought the end had come.

From 11 at night until six in the morning Welles had "remained in the room . . . without sitting or leaving it." At six
o'clock he went out of the house, tasted a deep breath of
fresh air, looked up at a gloomy sky, and took a 15-minute
walk. Every few rods were huddles and bunches of people,
all anxious, all wanting to know what of the night, some of
them having stood waiting all night and into the morning.
One or more would step out from each of these groups and
ask Welles, bearded and fatherly-looking, about the President. "Is there no hope?" He was impressed, reading "intense grief" on every face at his answer that the President
could survive but a short time. "The colored people especially—and there were at this time more of them, perhaps,
than of whites—were overwhelmed with grief."

A cold rain began falling. Out of a montonous sky inex-
orably gray a cold rain began falling.

A little before seven Welles went into the room where a
warm Friend of Man was going cold, moving into the final
chill that all men at the last must know. "His wife soon after
made her last visit to him. The death-struggle had begun.
Robert, his son, stood with several others at the head of the
bed. He bore himself well, but on two occasions gave way to
overpowering grief and sobbed aloud, turning his head and
leaning on the shoulder of Senator Sumner."

The last breath was drawn at 21 minutes and 55 seconds
past 7 A.M. and the last heart beat flickered at 22 minutes
and 10 seconds past the hour on Saturday, April 15, 1865.
Dr. Barnes' finger was over the carotid artery, Dr. Leale's
finger was on the right wrist pulse, and Dr. Taft's hand was

over the cardium when the great heart made its final contraction.

The Pale Horse had come. To a deep river, to a far country, to a by-and-by whence no man returns, had gone the child of Nancy Hanks and Tom Lincoln, the wilderness boy who found far lights and tall rainbows to live by, whose name even before he died had become a legend inwoven with men's struggle for freedom the world over.

The voice of Phineas D. Gurley: "Let us pray." Kneeling at the bedside, his sonorous tones shook with submission to the Everlasting, to the Heavenly Father, with pleading that the dead man's country and family be comforted.

The widow was told. She came in and threw herself with uncontrollable moaning on the body. When later she went away the cry broke from her, "O my God, and I have given my husband to die!"

Over the drawn face muscles Dr. Leale moved a smoothing hand, took two coins from his pocket, placed them over the eyelids, and drew a white sheet over the face. Over the worn features had come, wrote John Hay, "a look of unspeakable peace." Stanton, it was said afterward, pronounced the words: "Now he belongs to the ages." By his wish this became legend.

The Cabinet, with Seward and McCulloch absent, met in the back parlor, arranged to notify the Vice-President and the Chief Justice of the Supreme Court, and to meet again at noon in the room of the Secretary of the Treasury and take action with the newly sworn-in President toward "preserving and promoting the public tranquillity."

The young surgeon, the good Dr. Leale, who all through the night had stood to his armpits in a vortex and a pit of desolation, had done all that could be done and was leaving the fated house where Mr. Peterson with a lighted candle had beckoned him in nine hours ago—it seemed nine years—nine hundred years.

"I left the house in deep meditation," ran his story. "In my lonely walk I was aroused from my reveries by the cold drizzling rain dropping on my bare head, my hat I had left in my seat in the theater. My clothing was stained with blood. I had not once been seated since I first sprang to the President's aid; I was cold, weary and sad." His eyes happened to fall on his wrists and the detachable cuffs. They had been laundered stiff and immaculately white. Now they were limp, wet, blood-soaked. He decided he would keep the cuffs as long as he lived. To him they were "stained with the martyr's blood."

Now there was a tincture of deep violet given to the Gettysburg phrases: "We cannot consecrate—we cannot hallow—this ground." Now there was a snow-white fabric crossed with sunset vermilion around the words written to the Boston widow woman: "The solemn pride that must be yours to have laid so costly a sacrifice upon the altar of freedom."

Chapter 51

Shock — The Assassin — A Stricken People

The tolling of the bells began in Washington. Likewise in New York, Boston, Chicago, Springfield, Peoria, metropolitan centers and crossroads villages, the day had tolling bells hour on hour, flags at half-mast, the gay bunting, red, white and blue festoons brought down and crape or any fold of black put out and hung up for sign of sorrow.

Out on the Illinois prairie of Coles County they went to a farmhouse and told the news to an old woman who answered: "I knowed when he went away he'd never come back alive." This was Sally Bush Lincoln, prepared for her sorrow which came that day.

Edwin Booth, the world's foremost Shakespearian actor, lay abed in Boston the morning of April 15 when a servant came in and told him that his brother, John Wilkes Booth, had shot and killed the President. And as Edwin Booth related it to Joseph Jefferson, his mind "accepted the fact at once," for he thought to himself that his brother "was capable of just such a wild and foolish action." Edwin Booth added: "It was just as if I was struck on the forehead by a hammer." To General Grant's secretary, his old friend Adam Badeau, Edwin Booth on Sunday, April 16, wrote, "Abraham Lincoln was my President for, in pure admiration of his noble career and his Christian principles, I did what I never did before—I *voted* and *for* him!"

The man hunters and the fugitive John Wilkes Booth were second in national interest only to the death of Lincoln. Who was this Booth? Out of a mediocre fame he had now wrapped the letters of his name with a weird infamy. His own Southern heroes almost universally repudiated him as a madman, one who fought foul. And he was that—a lunatic—a diabolically cunning athlete, swordsman, dead shot, horseman, actor. Now his face and name were published with a War Department promise of $50,000 for his capture dead or alive.

John Wilkes Booth was one of ten children born to Mr. and Mrs. Junius Brutus Booth on a big wooded farm 25 miles from Baltimore. Junius Brutus Booth seemed to be a man filled with a compassion that often shook his controls and ran over into the pathetic, the ridiculous, even the comic. When he died in 1852 his feet had wandered before all shrines and altars and paid homage. He was brought up an Episcopalian; he made it a custom to keep some of the sacred days of the Koran; Catholic priests claimed him for one of their own because of his familiarity with their faith; and in synagogues he had been taken for a Jew when he joined fluently in their worship in their own tongue; Masons buried him in a Baptist vault. He was widely accepted as a figure in American cultural life, the supreme Shakespeare player.

He drank hard and often, and in moods and periods was definitely insane. In time Junius Brutus Booth came to sense the oncoming seizures of insanity and would make for home, where a rare and faithful wife nursed him through dark tortures. The daughter Asia wrote of these attacks being looked on in their home "with awe and reverence."

The son, John Wilkes Booth, had room to play, a 200-acre wooded farm, an oak-floored bedroom facing the east and the sunrise, on the walls deer antlers, swords, pistols, daggers, a bookcase holding Bulwer, Marryat, Byron, Shakespeare. Over the father's dark spells and grand whims, over Edwin's impenetrable melancholy, over the failings of others of the family, the mother and loyal Asia had no such brooding near to anguish as they gave the boy and youth Wilkes. They knew it was said "women spoiled him," that he did what he pleased and took what he wanted and kept his secrets. They saw vanity grow in him—vague, dark personal motives beyond reading and to be feared, projects and purposes vast with sick desire, dizzy with ego.

To the hanging of John Brown went J. Wilkes Booth as a lieutenant in the Richmond Grays. Though he hated John Brown's cause, he was fascinated and spellbound by the dramatic, lone-handed audacity of Old Ossawatomie.

His first stage successes came in Southern cities. As the Southern States moved into secession he moved North as a player. William Winter saw the young star's acting as "raw, crude and much given to boisterous declamation." He delighted in leaps and bounds while acting. The Baltimore *Sun* critic ticketed Wilkes Booth "the Gymnastic actor." There were fellow actors, such as E. L. Tilton, knocked into an orchestra pit while fencing with Wilkes Booth; some had been cut by his sword in mimic duels.

Over a piece of scenery more than five feet high, wrote W. J. Ferguson, he saw Wilkes Booth jump "with little effort." These unexpected feats were accepted as part of a "dashing buoyancy" natural to him. "I saw him, after a rehearsal," wrote Ferguson of Booth the swordsman, "take on two men at once with the foils and disarm them both within a few seconds." In a billiard-hall quarrel Ferguson saw Booth, swiftly and without anyone but Ferguson seeing him, throw a heavy book that hit a man in the back. The man turned, accused an innocent party, and started a free-for-all fight. The lights went out and Booth made his getaway, having had one more of his practical jokes.

In April '61, when Booth played with a stock company

in Albany, the leading lady, Miss Henrietta Irving, rushed into his room at Stanwix Hall and with a dirk tried to stab him, landing only a light cut on his face. Then she retired to her own room and stabbed herself, though not seriously. A trifle short for heroic roles, noted Charles Wyndham, "he made up for the lack by his extraordinary presence and magnetism . . . He was the idol of women. They would rave of him, his voice, his hair, his eyes."

From '61 continuously as he traveled the North he spoke as openly as was convenient for the Confederate cause. In Albany the theater treasurer found him at breakfast one morning and explained that he would ruin his engagement there and put himself in personal danger if he went on talking secession. "Is not this a democratic city?" asked Booth. The reply: "Democratic? yes—but disunion, no!" After which Booth quieted in his talk, though sullen and sour about being gagged.

In '64 when he was filling fewer engagements because of a failing voice, Booth seemed to have a deepening sense of guilt over keeping himself in safety and comfort while the war raged and the Southern cause sank lower. His broodings took two directions. He would perform a deed saving the Southern cause while at the same time giving the world a breath-taking dramatic performance. In August '64 he won two recruits to "the enterprise," as they termed it. Samuel Arnold and Michael O'Laughlin, two former schoolmates of Booth at St. Timothy's Hall, after two years in the Confederate Army, considered themselves "engaged" with Booth as leader. The "enterprise," worked out in their talks, designed the "capture" or "abduction" of the President. Having gotten their prisoner out of Washington down to Richmond, they would exchange him for enough Confederate prisoners to win the war.

Most of the time until April 14, 1865, Booth lived in Washington, checking in and out of his National Hotel quarters, taking many trips on errands whose purpose he kept secret. He studied Lincoln's ways and habits, particularly as a theatergoer. At both Grover's Theatre and Ford's, Booth was at home, receiving his mail at Ford's. The en-

tries and exits of these theaters knew him, every door, corner, hall, lobby, passageway, familiar to him. To the stock
actors, stagehands, front-office employees, he was a distinguished figure whose nod they valued.

In November he rode a horse over Maryland and Virginia south of Washington, studied the roads, paths and
hiding places by day or night. To Asia, in whom he had
every trust, he gave an envelope later found to contain some
bonds and oil stock certificates—and a letter. This gave
the key to his scrambled brain, his vanity and self-importance, his desire to show the South that he was a Confederate hero even though they no longer loved him or cared
about him. He referred in passing to his plan for making
"a prisoner of this man, to whom she [the South] owes so
much of her misery."

The letter indicated a "master mind," of a sort, holding
sway over a little band of schemers and hopers meeting in a
boardinghouse on H Street between Sixth and Seventh in
Washington. They included a drugstore clerk, 20 years old,
David E. Herold, out of work and seeking a job when
Booth found him. Another was a hump-shouldered, scrag-
gly-bearded fellow, dark, sly, fierce of looks though a coward in a pinch; he was of German descent, a carriage-maker
at Port Tobacco, Virginia. Booth's promises of gold brought
him in—George A. Atzerodt. Then there was a tall, broad-
shouldered 20-year-old athlete joining ox and tiger in his
frame, a veteran of Antietam and Chancellorsville, wounded
at Gettysburg. In January '65 this youth after nearly four
years of hard fighting at bloody salients had despaired of
the Confederacy and deserted, happening in Baltimore
when he was homeless, penniless, in rags, without money
to buy food, to meet Booth, finding sympathy, praise, new
clothes and money. This was the man known as Lewis
Paine (Lewis Thornton Powell), whose entry into the Seward home had resulted in five persons stabbed and the Secretary of State narrowly missing a death wound. The keeper
of the boardinghouse where the plotters met was the widow
of a Confederate informer and dispatch-carrier, Mary E.
Surratt.

Daily Mrs. Surratt saw her boarders acquainting themselves with weapons, holding vague whispered conversations, telling her nothing definite, intimating they would save the sinking Southern cause. The air had a touch of terror. Daily she crossed herself and more often hurried to church to pray. Mrs. Surratt's son John H., Jr., at first opposed and then gave way to Booth's eloquence. Just old enough to vote, six feet tall, slender but powerful, blond, with eyes sunken under a bulging forehead, he knew his footing more surely than the others. He quit his job as an Adams Express Company clerk to join Booth. With him came one Louis J. Weichmann, a wavering, suspicious and careful young man who had been Surratt's chum for two years at college when Surratt studied for the priesthood. Weichmann had been a schoolteacher in Washington, later getting a clerkship in the office of the comissary general of prisoners.

Of the two former Maryland schoolmates of Booth, Samuel Arnold was a farm hand who hated farm work, rather lazy, a student of books with an unmanageable vocabulary; Michael O'Laughlin was a Baltimore livery-stable worker, fairly good at handling horses and better yet at carrying liquor. The crew filled the seven bedrooms of Mrs. Surratt's boardinghouse. Some of them subsisted on money furnished by Booth, and all except Weichmann were led and lighted by Booth's stratagems and wildfire eloquence over the glory awaiting them all for their service to the Confederacy.

On at least one day Booth prowled the White House grounds with Paine. And if later statements of Paine to Major Thomas T. Eckert were correct, Booth directly suggested to the powerful young panther from Florida that he should go into the White House, send in his card, enter Lincoln's office like any one of many petitioners—and then and there shoot the President. Booth seemed to have taunted Paine with lacking nerve in this. Yet on Booth's suggestion Paine lurked among bushes in front of the White House conservatory. After a light rain had come a freeze with a crust of ice crackling under footsteps. Lincoln

walked by in company with Eckert, and Paine heard Lincoln say, "Major, spread out, spread out, or we shall break
through the ice." Paine in the bushes heard Lincoln telling
Eckert of Illinois days once when neighbors returning from
mill with their meal bags were crossing the frozen Sangamon River and as the ice cracked when they were part
way over someone called the warning, "Spread out, spread
out, or we shall break through the ice."

April 8 Washington is ablaze with flags and the North
howling joy over the surrender of Lee's army. Paine, Atzerodt and Herold are left to Booth, awaiting his wish and
whim. The evening of April 11 Booth is with Paine on the
White House lawn near the window where the President
speaks. He is shaken with rage at the President's saying
the elective franchise, the ballot, should be given to the
colored man, "the very intelligent, and . . . those who serve
our cause as soldiers." He urges Paine to shoot the speaker,
Paine protesting the risk is too great. The two walk away,
Booth muttering, "That is the last speech he will ever
make."

Events had swept away all doubts for Booth as to his
course. He would be the whirlwind dark angel of retribution and justice—this was the fond wish. Never for a
moment in the piled and ramified materials of evidence was
there an indication that he examined his own heart and
studied himself on the question of what was driving him
on and whether he was first of all an actor. Until this week,
believed his sister Asia, who perhaps understood him
through a deeper love than he had ever had to search himself with, he was sane. "If Wilkes Booth was mad," she
wrote, "his mind lost its balance between the fall of Richmond, and the terrific end."

In an inside coat pocket he carried the photographs of
four actresses, beautiful women as the pictures rendered
their faces, Fay Brown, Effie Germon, Alice Gray, Helen
Western—and a fifth woman, half-smiling, later identified
merely as "a Washington society woman." Whether any of
them had intimacy of word and mind with him so as to
know the seething concentrated purpose that swept aside

all other passions—the later record revealed nothing.

John Deery, who kept a bar in front of Grover's Theatre, during this April week saw Booth often. Said Deery, "He sometimes drank at my bar as much as a quart of brandy in the space of less than two hours of an evening." Later Deery was to judge of this, "Booth was crazy, but he didn't show it." His theory was that any natural and inherited insanity dominating Booth this week was heightened and accentuated by liquor.

On April 12 Booth writes to a woman in New York who signs herself "Etta." She answers April 13, "Yes, Dear, I can heartily sympathize with you, for I too, have had the blues ever since the fall of Richmond, and like you, feel like doing something desperate." He has enlisted her in some phase of his projects and she lets him know: "I have not yet had a favorable opportunity to do what *you* wished, and I so solemnly promised, and what, in my own heart, I feel ought to be done. I *remember* what happiness is in store for us if we succeed in our present undertakings." She informs him that "the means you gave me when we parted" is gone. She quotes, "Money makes the mare go" and assures him, "I do as you desired and keep as secluded as a nun, which is not agreeable to me as you have found."

On April 14 Booth writes to his mother a letter dated "2 A.M." of that day. "Dearest Mother:" he begins. "I know you hardly expect a letter from me. Excuse brevity; am in haste. With best love to you all I am your affectionate son ever. John." That was all. To his mother, to his brother Edwin, to such friends as John T. Ford and John Deery, no inklings of a deed and a motive for which he is willing to pay with his life. The word "assassin," several commentators were to note, took root from the word "hashish" or "hasheesh," an East Indian drug that inflates the self-importance of the one eating it.

Between 11 and 12 o'clock of Good Friday morning, April 14, Booth comes to Ford's Theatre for his mail, hears that a messenger from the White House has engaged a box for the President that evening. He goes into action, hires a bay mare for himself to be ready at four o'clock in the afternoon. He calls on Mrs. Surratt just as she with Weichmann is leaving for Surrattsville, handing her a package holding a field glass to be delivered at a tavern there. To the empty Ford's Theatre he goes, seeing the two boxes thrown into one, the rocking chair brought for the President's corner of the box. He inspects locks, bores a hole through the box door, digs a niche in the plastered brick wall.

At seven in the evening Booth leaves his room at the National Hotel. In passing he asks the hotel clerk if he is going to Ford's Theatre this evening. The clerk hadn't thought about it. "There will be some fine acting there tonight," says Booth; he hurries to the Herndon House and sees Paine. They arrange their timing: at the same hour and minute of the clock that night Paine is to kill the Secretary of State and Booth is to kill the President. Atzerodt, run the further plans, is to kill Vice-President Johnson. Herold is to guide Paine to the Seward home and then hurry to the support of Atzerodt. On the street Booth talks with Atzerodt, who has heard of the fighting nerve of Andy Johnson and now tells Booth he enlisted for abduction but not killing. Atzerodt begs and whimpers. Booth storms at him and curses him.

Atzerodt, armed with a revolver he knows he can never use, drifts away, never to see Booth again. Early in the morning on foot headed toward his boyhood home 22 miles west of Washington, in Georgetown pawning his revolver for $10, was a muddled wanderer, one of the only three men in the world who could have told the police beforehand to the hour of Booth's intentions that night.

At a stable near Ford's and close to ten o'clock Booth, Paine and Herold get on their horses and part, Booth to go to Ford's, Herold to guide Paine to the Seward house. At the back door of Ford's Booth calls for the theater carpenter Spangler to hold his horse, enters and goes down under the stage, out of a private door into an alley and therefrom to the street in front of the theater. Spangler meantime calls the door boy John Peanuts to hold Booth's horse.

Peanuts says he has to tend his door, Spangler saying if anything goes wrong to lay the blame on him. Out front on the street Booth sees the President's carriage at the curb, a crowd of curiosity seekers on the sidewalk, some of them waiting to have a look at the presidential party when it leaves the theater. The play is more than half over and a stir of voices and laughter drifts out from the windows to the lighted and cheerful street.

Booth walks past the doorkeeper Buckingham and with a pleasant smile and "You'll not want a ticket from *me?*" asks the time, and is pointed to the clock in the lobby. He requests a chew of tobacco from Buckingham, who draws a plug from which Booth takes a bite, as customary a proceeding as gentlemen of a previous generation exchanging snuff. On the street an actor who is to sing a new patriotic song asks the time and the theater costumer steps into the lobby and, looking at a large clock on the wall, calls out, "Ten minutes past ten." Booth opens a door from the lobby into the parquet, takes note of the presidential box, whether there are any visitors. He has seen *Our American Cousin* played and has calculated to fine points the strategic moment for his deed. Soon only one actor will be out front on the stage, only a woman and a boy in the wings. A laugh from the audience usually follows the exit of two ladies, a loud enough laugh perhaps to smother any unusual noises in a box.

Booth goes up the stairs leading to the dress circle, picks his way among chairs behind an outer row of seats, reaches the door of the passageway leading to the presidential box. He leans against the wall, takes a cool survey of the house. On the stage is only one actor. Booth knows him well, Harry Hawk, playing the character of Asa Trenchard, a supposedly salty American character. Mrs. Mountchessington has just left Asa alone with a rebuke that he was not "used to the manners of good society." Asa meditates alone over this: "Well, I guess I know enough to turn you inside out, old gal—you sockdologizing old mantrap."

Booth opens the door into the narrow hallway leading to the box, steps in, closes the door, fixes the bar in the mortised niche and against the door panel. On soft tiger feet he moves toward the box door, puts an eye to the hole bored through the door, sees his victim is precisely where he wishes and as he had planned. Softly he swings the door back and with his brass derringer pistol in the right hand and a long dagger in the other, he steps into the box.

Up till that instant any one of a million ordinary conceivable circumstances of fate could have intervened and made the next moment impossible. Yet not one of those potential circumstances arrived. What happened that next moment became world history—not because of him who did what was done, but because of the name, life and works of the victim of the deed.

"Think no more of him as your brother," wrote Edwin Booth to Asia; "he is dead to us now, as soon he must be to all the world, but imagine the boy you loved to be in that better part of his spirit, in another world." And referring to a weeping nameless betrothed one, Edwin added, "I have had a heart-broken letter from the poor little girl to whom he had promised so much happiness."

And the one man whose sworn duty it was to have intercepted the assassin—John F. Parker? There were charges brought against him by Superintendent A. C. Richards of the Metropolitan Police Force, "that Said Parker was detailed to attend and protect the President Mr. Lincoln, that while the President was at Ford's Theatre on the night of the 14th of April last, Said Parker allowed a man to enter the President's private Box and Shoot the President." But there was no trial on these charges, and it was not till three years later that Parker was to be dishonorably dismissed from the police force for sleeping on his beat.

Neither Stanton nor La Fayette C. Baker nor any member of Congress nor any newspaper metropolitan or rural, nor any accustomed guardian of public welfare, took any but momentary interest in the one guard sworn to a sacred duty who distinguished himself as a marvelous cipher, a more curious derelict than any during the war shot by a firing squad for desertion, cowardice in the face of the enemy, or sleeping at the post of duty. The watchguards of public welfare all had other fish to fry, and it was to be many years before the dereliction of John F. Parker, a nonentity and as such a curiously odd number, was to be duly assessed.

How did Parker take the news of Lincoln's assassination? It woke some lethargy in his bones. Probably all night long he wandered half-dazed over the streets of Washington, stopping in saloons, gathering the news, wondering, bothering his head about what explanations he could make. At six in the morning, according to the police blotter, he brought to headquarters a woman of the streets he had arrested, her name Lizzie Williams. Parker had decided he would make it a matter of record that he was on the job as a police officer, that early in the morning he was on the job. So he brings in a forlorn, bedraggled streetwalker—against whom he proved no case, and Lizzie Williams was promptly discharged. This was his offering: instead of intercepting the killer of the President shortly after 10 P.M. he brings in to headquarters a battered and worn prostitute at 6 A.M. in a cold gray rain and the sky a noncommittal monotone.

The guard Crook awoke in his home the morning after Good Friday to hear the news, and his first thought was, "If I had been on duty at the theater, I would be dead now." His next thought was to wonder whether his fellow guard Parker was dead. Years later he was to wonder why the negligence of the guard on duty had "never been divulged," writing: "So far as I know, it was not even investigated by the police department. Yet, had he [Parker] done his duty, President Lincoln would not have been murdered by Booth." Crook reasoned that a single guard at the box entrance could have made a struggle and an outcry that would have resulted in the disarming of Booth. "It makes me feel rather bitter," wrote Crook, "when I remember that the President had said, just a few hours before, that he knew he could trust all his guards."

In company with Senator Ben Wade went Congressman Henry Laurens Dawes to greet in the Kirkwood House the newly sworn-in President Andrew Johnson. And Wade's greeting, as Congressman Dawes told it to his daughter Anna, ran: "Mr. Johnson, I thank God that you are here. Lincoln had too much of the milk of human kindness to deal with these damned rebels. Now they will be dealt with according to their deserts." This feeling ran through a caucus of the Republican party radicals meeting that day to consider, as Congressman George Julian phrased it, "a line of policy less conciliatory than that of Mr. Lincoln."

Of the new President little was known, and from the Judge Advocate's office, at headquarters of the Department of the South, Hilton Head, South Carolina, John C. Gray, Jr., wrote to John C. Ropes: "He may turn out more of a man than we hope. Henry Ward Beecher told an officer on the dock [at Charleston] a few hours after the news was announced of Lincoln's death, that Johnson's little finger was stronger than Lincoln's loins, and though I have heard nothing so bad myself, I can see that a good many think that Mr. Lincoln would have been too lenient with the rebels."

The single event of an assassination swept away a thousand foundations carefully laid and protected by the living Lincoln. A long series of delicate roots of human relationships the living Lincoln had nursed and guarded were torn up in a night.

One question was held pertinent: What from year to year during the war did Wilkes Booth meet that might generate a motive and play on it and shake it with finality? He saw and heard hundreds of men of the educated and privileged classes indulging in an almost unrestricted freedom of speech. Did they tell him anything else of import than that this one man had by his own whim and determination carried the war on through four devastating, howling, bitter years of agony? On the head of this one man Lincoln had been heaped a thousand infamies any one of which could easily inflame the mind of a vain and cunning fool. What was one more killing of a man in a land already strewn with corpses and cripples and famished skeletons in prisons?

The New York *Herald* on Easter Sunday, April 16, editorialized on the press as no factor of enlightenment, no sobering influence at all. It said directly that newspaper editors shared in the guilt of leading an assassin toward his bloody work. "It is as clear as day that the real origin of this dreadful act is to be found in the fiendish and malignant spirit developed and fostered by the rebel press North and South. That press has, in the most devilish manner, urged men to the commission of this very deed."

Party spirit and its mouthpieces, the press, the politicians and orators, came in for blame from *Harper's Weekly*. Directly and indirectly, openly and cunningly, the passions of men were set on fire by "the assertion that Mr. Lincoln was responsible for the war, that he had opened all the yawning graves and tumbled the victims in . . . Is it surprising that somebody should have believed all this, that somebody should have said, if there is a tyranny it can not be very criminal to slay the tyrant?"

Mrs. Chesnut saw a tide rolling toward her people, writing in her diary: "Lincoln, old Abe Lincoln, has been killed . . . Why? By whom? It is simply maddening. . . . I know this foul murder will bring upon us worse miseries."

Sherman on his way to a conference with the Confederate General Joseph E. Johnston had a decoded telegram handed him from Stanton: "President Lincoln was murdered about 10 o'clock last night." Sherman pledged the operator to say nothing to anyone of the telegram. When Sherman and Johnston sat alone in a small farmhouse, Sherman handed over the telegram. Johnston read. On his forehead slowly came sweat "in large drops," as Sherman watched him, Sherman remembering so clearly and for so long a time afterward how one of the greatest of Confederate captains said that "Mr. Lincoln was the best friend they had" and the assassination was "the greatest possible calamity to the South." In the surrender terms they were to sign, Sherman's motive, according to his keenest interpreter, probably ranged around a thought: "Lincoln is dead. I will make his kind of a peace." When later the dread news was given to Sherman's army, many were ready to burn the city of Raleigh to the ground. Logan made speeches against it, other officers intervened, and discipline prevailed.

Now Laura Keene and Harry Hawk and the cast of *Our American Cousin* were in jail, detained for inquiry. Now the gentle sister Asia Booth was taken from her Philadelphia home to a Washington prison. Now the brother Edwin announced he would play no more drama for the American public—not for years, if ever again. Now the pursuit of the fugitive Jefferson Davis was urged more furiously by Stanton. Now a colonel had come to Charles A. Dana's house early of a morning to say, "Mr. Lincoln is dead and Mr. Stanton directs you to arrest Jacob Thompson." Lincoln had said No to this but now Stanton and a host of officials had no hesitations about drastic policies of punishment.

The fugitive Jefferson Davis wrote later of his dominant feeling: "The news [of the assassination] was to me very sad, for I felt that Mr. Johnson was a malignant man, and without the power or generosity which I believed Mr. Lincoln possessed." *Harper's Weekly* reported: "Roger A. Pryor stated in Petersburg that he believed Mr. Lincoln indispensable to the restoration of peace, and regretted his death more than any military mishap of the South. General Lee at first refused to hear the details of the murder . . . He said that when he dispossessed himself of the command of the rebel forces he kept in mind President Lincoln's benignity, and surrendered as much to the latter's goodness as to Grant's artillery. The General said that he regretted Mr. Lincoln's death as much as any man in the North."

Yet Booth had not entirely miscalculated. A small extremist minority element North and South exulted over his deed. In front of the New York post office April 15 a man saluted someone, "Did you hear of Abe's last joke?" In a few minutes he was encircled by raging men beating his head and crying "Hang him!" "Kill him!" "Hang the bastard up!" Police rescuers took a volley of bricks and stones.

A young Englishman, Peter Britton, having had a few drinks, chronicled the New York *Herald*, walked Vandewater Street snarling oaths at Lincoln, saying, "I came a good ways to see the --- -- - ----- buried." Rescued by police from an excited crowd and taken before Justice Dowling, Britton was sentenced to six months in prison at hard labor. Police Sergeant Walsh of the 6th precinct, at the corner of Chatham and Pearl Streets threw a knockout blow to the mouth of one George Wells on hearing from that mouth: "Old Abe, the son of a bitch, is dead, and he ought to have been killed long ago." Justice Dowling sent Wells to prison for six months.

New York, the major draft-riot city, saw more of this tumult than other places. From coast to coast, however, there was a Copperhead minority to whom Booth was a hero. At Swampscott, Massachusetts, dispatches recited that one George Stone "said in public it was the best news we had received for four years, and gave three cheers." Citizens and soldiers tarred and feathered Stone. In most of these cases the offender spoke his first personal reaction to the news, without stopping to think of his community's reaction. The Lincoln-haters at first had no notion of how crushed with grief, how exquisitely sensitive, were an overwhelming number of Lincoln loyalists.

In Chicago on Madison Street and on Canal Street men and boys sent rocks crashing through the big glass windows of several places where a Copperhead saloonkeeper had hung in the front window a large portrait of J. Wilkes Booth.

The North was in grief. Everywhere the eye might turn hung the sign of this grief. The sermons, editorials, talk in streets, houses, saloons, railroad cars and streetcars, the black bunting and the crape—these were attempts to say something that could not be said. Men tried to talk about it and the words failed and they came back to silence. To say nothing was best. Lincoln was dead. Was there anything more to say? A great Friend of Man had suddenly vanished. Nothing could be done about it. Silence, grief and quiet resolves, these only were left for those who admired and loved and felt themselves close to a living presence that was one of them.

Thousands on thousands would remember as long as they lived the exact place where they had been standing or seated or lying down when the news came to them, recalling precisely in details and particulars where they were and what they were doing when the dread news arrived.

Hundreds of thousands there were who had been the foundation and groundwork of what he had done. These people—the basic Lincoln loyalist legion—had no words; they had only grief—sorrow beyond words. "A stricken people came to their altars." Whatever was sensitively and humanly aware wore crape, seen or unseen.

Far out on the rolling prairie of the Iowa frontier, a farmer rode a fast horse and shouted from the saddle, first to this neighbor and then the next, "Lincoln is shot!" or "Lincoln is dead—shot in a theater!" That was all. The rider was gone. They had heard him. They stood in their foot tracks, amazed, dumbstruck, sadly waited for further news, some saying, "What will the country do now?"

On an early morning streetcar in Philadelphia a good Quaker unrolled a morning newspaper, stared at it, and broke out: "My God! what is this? Lincoln is assassinated!" In the gray dawn on this streetcar men cupped their faces in their hands and on the straw-covered floor fell hot tears. The driver of the streetcar came in to make sure of what he heard. Then the driver went out and took the bells off his horses. And he drove on with his car filled with mourners, some silent, some sobbing.

Newsboys at their stands cried no headlines, handed the damp sheets from the press to the buyers, one boy noticed as he brushed with his dirty hand the tears from his dirty cheeks. In thousands of stores the merchants told the clerks they would close for the day; in many schools the sobbing teacher could only tell the children, "Go home, there will be no school today." The father, the children, coming home unexpected, the mother asked what was wrong and heard "Mama, they've killed the President" or

"Our President is dead." Then the family hunted up crape or black cloth for the front doorway.

In Charleston, South Carolina, one old black woman walked a street looking straight ahead, wringing her hands and crying: "O Lawd! O Lawd! Marse Sam's dead! O Lawd! Uncle Sam's dead!" In Boston a thousand or more men found themselves on the Common, marching in a silent procession, two by two, not a word spoken, just walking, just seeing each other's faces, marching an hour or so and then slowly scattering, having reached some form of consolation in being together, seeing each other in mute grief.

In a home at Huntington, Long Island, a mother and son, Walt Whitman, heard the news early in the morning, sat at breakfast and ate nothing, sat at other meals during the day and ate nothing, silently passed newspaper extras to each other during the day and said little, the son deciding that as long as he lived he would on April 14 have sprigs of lilac in his room and keep it as a holy day for the man he later characterized as "the grandest figure on the crowded canvas of the drama of the nineteenth century."

Many of those who mourned knew there were times when with nothing to say, he said nothing, slept not at all, and wept at those times in a way that made weeping appropriate, decent, majestic.

Now Father Abraham was gone. Old Abe—there would be no more stories about him, alive there in the White House in Washington. They had saved the newspapers or they had clipped from the paper such pieces as the Gettysburg speech and the letter to Mrs. Bixby and the second inaugural. Now the newspapers had black borders, night's crape darkness, on the front-page columns. Now there was a memory to keep. That was left—the life he had lived—the meanings and the lights of that life. This could not be taken away.

Farmers in southern Illinois said the brown thrush no longer sang, that in the year to come the brown thrush never once sang. One Illinois boy going to town, holding his father's hand, having heard the church and town-hall bells all day, having seen only dark sorrow on all faces, looked up at the sky and found it strange the night stars were all out. Lincoln was dead—and yet as always the stars moved alive over the night dome.

Like a vast sunset of flame and changing gold ending a day and punctuating a period of time their faraway friend at Washington had vanished into the overhead planets and the same constellations of mist that had taken that long roll call of soldiers no longer answering "Here" to the company sergeant calling the names.

In a million and more American households they sought words that might help and assuage. "The land mourneth, every family apart," ran one Easter Sunday text. Also "The steps of a good man are ordered by the Lord: and He delighteth in his way." Over doorways, in store windows, on arches spanning streets, ran the legend "And the Lord blessed Abraham in all things."

On one arch of crape and white over Broadway in New York ran the sentence "The great person, the great man, is the miracle of history."

Chapter 52

A Tree Is Best Measured when It's Down

In great stone cathedrals of the cities, in modest frame churches of small towns, in little cabin churches at country crossroads, in hospital chapels and in at least one state prison, on Navy ships and in outdoor Army camp services, there were Easter Sunday sermons memorializing the dead President.

A large minority of Protestant ministers made reference to the death in a playhouse, the Reverend Justin Dewey Fulton in Tremont Temple, Boston, saying: "He was shot in a theatre. We are sorry for that. If ever any man had an excuse to attend a theatre, he had. The cares of office were heavy upon him. His brain reeled. His frame grew weak. In conversing with a friend, he said, 'Some think I do wrong to go to the opera and the theatre; but it rests me. I love to be alone, and yet to be with the people. A hearty laugh relieves me; and I seem better able after it to bear my cross.' This was his excuse. Upon it we will not pronounce a judgment. This we will say: we are all sorry our best loved died there. But take the truth with its shadow."

The Reverend Dr. Phineas D. Gurley in the New York Avenue Presbyterian Church in Washington, facing the Lincoln pew, would reveal a deep abhorrence: "Our lamented President fell in the theatre. Had he been murdered in his bed, or in his office, or on the street, or on the steps of the Capitol, the tidings of his death would not have struck the Christian heart of the country quite so painfully; for the feeling of that heart is that the theatre is one of the last places to which a good man should go."

Parts of the loathing undoubtedly Lincoln had heard from the pulpit, Dr. Gurley saying: "I have always regarded the theatre as in the main a school of vice and corruption —the illumined and decorated gateway through which thousands are constantly passing into the embrace of gaiety and folly, intemperance and lewdness, infamy and ruin. I have always hated and avoided it, and taught my children to avoid it."

One Reverend Dr. Duffield of Detroit, however, rivaled Dr. Gurley: "Would that Mr. Lincoln had fallen elsewhere than at the very gates of Hell—in the theater to which, through persuasion, he reluctantly went." The Reverend L. M. Glover in Jacksonville, Illinois, would rather it had occurred "in the street, in the council chamber, in the national museum or even the sanctuary of God."

That Lincoln, without being an affiliated churchman, had by a natural reverence, without affectation, won his way to many hearts of the clergy was evident in pulpit tributes paid him. In Boston the Reverend Samuel K. Lothrop mourned: "Brethren, but one theme can command your attention today . . . I feel almost incompetent to direct your thoughts this morning, as I have scarcely been able for the last twenty-four hours to collect and guide my own. Language is impotent." Over and again were the parallels drawn of Lincoln and Christ in blood of atonement dying for mankind, of Lincoln having his Judas no less than Christ. "The last and costliest offering which God demanded has been taken," said the Reverend C. B. Crane of the South Baptist Church of Hartford, Connecticut. "Jesus Christ died for the world, Abraham Lincoln died for his country."

Octavius Brooks Frothingham, pastor of the Third Congregational Unitarian Society in New York City, saw Lincoln as far spent. The people were sorrowing now not because of the crime but because they had lost a friend they loved simply as a man. "His belongings were nothing; dignities would not stick to him. His personal qualities protruded from his official skin, as the angular lines of his figure did from his court dress—as the bones of his great hands did from his kid gloves. The costumer, official or other, could make nothing of him. He was a character—not a doll. The decorators tried their hands on him in vain.

"The country does not go wild over him; it silently weeps for him; it does not celebrate him as a demigod—it mourns for him as a friend. He let the people work through him; and in his own esteem held a high place enough when he acted as an organ and an instrument. Such humility almost passes understanding—it runs into self-forgetfulness; it borders even on saintliness. He hoped little, expected nothing. A man of low temperament and sad nature, he worked and waited, waited and worked, bearing all things, enduring all things, but neither believing all things nor all things happening; bearing and enduring oh how much! even from his friends. What a history was written on that care-worn and furrowed face—of suffering accepted, sorrow entertained, emotions buried, and duty done!"

In scores of sermons was sounded the note of doom for the Southern leaders, for those who incarnated what the Reverend E. B. Webb of Boston termed "the same hell-born spirit that dastardly takes the life of our beloved President." Too long had "a driveling, morbid, perverted sense of justice" been permitted under the shadow of the Capitol at Washington. "It makes me shudder." Thus Mr. Webb in his Easter Sunday sermon stood in horror at the animating spirit of Lincoln in the Louisiana speech of April 11 and the final counsels with the Cabinet on April 14.

Many sermons and editorials likened Lincoln to Moses on Mount Pisgah, each taken away after the hard desert journey—and the Promised Land in sight. The Reverend J. M. Manning of Boston when he considered that Mr. Lincoln "disliked the sight of blood," that Mr. Lincoln "was melted by tears," that Mr. Lincoln was "made soft as woman by the tones of pleading wretchedness," said he would not attempt to scan the counsels of the Most High, though he must confess: "Perhaps it is better for us that we should be orphans today, than that he whom we loved to call 'Father' should have been spared. His paternal heart, had it still throbbed in life, might have proved too tender for the stern work we are yet to do." The Reverend W. S. Studley of Boston cried for multiple hangings of Southern traitors, and declared from the pupit: "In dealing with traitors, Andrew Johnson's little finger will be thicker than Abraham Lincoln's loins. If the *old* president chastised them with whips, the *new* president will chastise them with scorpions."

In scores of sermons before large congregations of the well-to-do and influential, radicals pressed the need for trials and hangings of Southern leaders. In the Protestant churches of Boston such clergymen were in a large majority of the pulpits. In other cities and communities, however, the clergy in the main humbly held themselves to spiritual ministration and kept out of politics. The Reverend Edward Everett Hale in his Unitarian Church in Boston intimated that in the passions of the hour, including his own, it behooved good men to think twice and speak slow: "I dare not trust myself to speak a word regarding this simple, godly, good, great man . . . To speak of him I must seek some other hour." Mr. Hale saw the Republic as eternal, ready to live through successive assassinations, ending his sermon, "Fear not, little flock; it is your Father's good pleasure to give you the kingdom."

In like tone with the living Lincoln were many of the sermons in Roman Catholic churches and in Hebrew synagogues. "We pray," said Archbishop McCloskey in St. Patrick's Cathedral, New York, "that the sentiments of mercy and clemency and conciliation that so filled the heart of the beloved President whom we have just lost will still actuate and guide the breast of him who, in this critical and trying hour, is called to fill his place."

Henry Ward Beecher threw himself with a flowing vitality into the occasion. Nothing now of that remark of his in Charleston a few days earlier that Johnson's little finger was stronger than Lincoln's loins. Beecher's Easter Sunday congregation in Plymouth Church, Brooklyn, filled all pews and added chairs in the aisles. Hundreds outside had failed to get in, scores had climbed up on the window sills to stand and listen. Beecher pointed to the murderer as one suckled and nursed in the slave system and its cruel and boisterous passions. Never would men forget that the slavery institution with its "mischiefs and monsters" had martyred one American President. "Never! while time lasts, while heaven lasts, while hell rocks and groans." The most often reprinted passage from sermons of this Easter Sunday was Beecher's closing. He pictured a coffined martyr moving in triumphal march, with cities and states as pallbearers, bells and cannon beating the hours. He intoned a dead march:

"Pass on, thou that has overcome! Your sorrows, oh people, are his peace! Your bells, and bands, and muffled drums, sound triumph in his ear. Wail and weep here; God made it echo joy and triumph there. Pass on!

"Four years ago, oh Illinois, we took from your midst an untried man, and from among the people. We return him to you a mighty conqueror. Not thine anymore, but the nation's; not ours, but the world's.

"Give him place, oh, ye prairies! In the midst of this great continent his dust shall rest, a sacred treasure to myriads who shall pilgrim to that shrine to kindle anew their zeal and patriotism.

"Ye winds that move over the mighty places of the West,

chant his requiem! Ye people, behold a martyr whose blood, as so many articulate words, pleads for fidelity, for law, for liberty!"

Miss Anna Dickinson in her Academy of Music speech in Philadelphia cried for punishment of the Southern leaders. "Their crimes have rendered them unworthy of the respect of honest men." Where few or none in the North had gone beyond naming Jefferson Davis as suitable for the gallows, Miss Dickinson included General Robert E. Lee. She spoke of Lincoln's assassin and added, "Of the two, Lee is a viler murderer." In the tumult Wendell Phillips was saying nothing. He too could have moved the pools of public emotion. The event was involved. He would have one brief comment. Granted that Lincoln was a great oak. "We watered him," said Wendell Phillips, the agitator.

In black-border crape typography, in editorial comment, letters, poetical effusions, the newspapers went along with the public grief. The weekly periodicals, the monthly magazines, these too wore crape in the national mood. An issue of the New York *Herald* with its remarkable extended biographical sketch and its thorough news coverage in Washington sold out 15 minutes after its arrival. The price for an obtainable copy in Washington next day was $10. Under the heading "The Great Crime—Abraham Lincoln's Place in History" the *Herald* on April 17 published a shrewd and lavish portrayal. He was a *new* figure. All other nations of the human family would study him "as the type man of a new dynasty of nation-rulers," holding that "the best and strongest rule for every intelligent people is a government to be created by the popular will, and choosing for itself the representative instrument who is to carry out its purposes." Gravely the *Herald,* naturally conservative though responsive to both property rights and human movements, noted: "The triumph of the democratic principle over the aristocratic in our recent contest is an assurance that time has revolved this old earth on which we live into a new and perhaps happier—perhaps sadder—era."

Lincoln was baffling, found the *Herald*. The more one gazed on him, the less easy it became to reckon what would be the end of his teachings. He was democracy beyond Cromwell or Napoleon, so completely modern that his like was not to be found in the past, "a character so externally uncouth, so pathetically simple, so unfathomably penetrating, so irresolute and yet so irresistible, so bizarre, grotesque, droll, wise and perfectly beneficent . . . It will take a new school of historians to do justice to this eccentric addition to the world's gallery of heroes; for while other men as interesting and original may have held equal power previously in other countries, it is only in the present age of steam, telegraphs and prying newspaper reporters that a subject so eminent, both by genius and position, could have been placed under the eternal microscope of critical examination."

George William Curtis in *Harper's Weekly* was sure that those who knew Lincoln personally now felt "that the deep, furrowed sadness of his face seemed to forecast his fate." The nation had lost him, but it was something that he had lived to see daybreak. "He saw farther and deeper than others because he saw that in the troubled time upon which he was cast little could be wholly seen . . . he acquired a curious ascendency in the public confidence; so that if good men differed from his opinion they were inclined to doubt their own."

An old proverb known to woodsmen was fitting: "A tree is best measured when it's down." Often came the statement that over the world the whole civilized Family of Man shared in regrets or grief for the loss of a hero who belonged to humanity everywhere. The story of the living and actual Lincoln had come to an end. Now began the vast epic tale of the authentic Lincoln tradition mingled with legend, myth, folklore. Believers and atheists, those of fixed doctrine or the freethinkers—both were to argue he was theirs. Letters and pamphlets were to picture him as Freemason or Spiritualist, as Protestant or Catholic or Jew or having Negro blood in his veins. The teetotalers were to claim properly he was theirs because he never drank alcoholic liquors; the saloon crowd amid the sawdust and the spittoons were to say his stories alone put him in their class.

Some had one sweeping claim: "He was humanity."

Lost in the huge and swelling choral acclaim were the few who agreed with the imperialist and Tory organ of London, the *Standard,* saying on April 21: "He was not a hero while he lived, and therefore his cruel murder does not make him a martyr." Of more import than the continued muddling and arrogance of the *Times* was the simple confession of the *Pall Mall Gazette:* "He was our best friend. He never lent himself to the purposes of that foolish and wicked minority which tried to set enmity between America and England. He never said or wrote an unfriendly word about us." Among the people of England, the masses whose sentiment kept the government from recognizing the Southern Confederacy, the mourning was genuine.

A letter to Mrs. Lincoln signed by Victoria Regina was deeply personal, woman to woman, the Queen saying: "No one can better appreciate than I can, who am myself *utterly broken-hearted* by the loss of my own beloved husband, who was the *light* of my life, my stay—*my all*—what your suffering must be; and I earnestly pray that you may be supported by Him to whom alone the sorely stricken can look for comfort." The House of Lords joined in an official address of sympathy to the American people.

In the French Senate and Chamber of Deputies imperialists and republicans joined in formal expressions of grief. A massive gold medal, bought with two-cent subscriptions from masses of people, was brought to the American Minister by a committee of liberals. It was for Mrs. Lincoln, with their message, "Tell her the heart of France is in that little box." In Germany many *Bunds* and *Vereins,* workingmen's clubs, co-operative societies, labor journals, spoke their loss. In Austria one parliamentary deputy noted a human memory taking on "supernatural proportions," Lincoln becoming "a myth, a type of the ideal democracy."

In Sweden flags were ordered at half-mast on the ships in harbor at Göteborg and there were expressions as in the *Nya Daglig Allehanda* of Stockholm: "It is a beautiful death, and Lincoln forever will be surrounded by the rays of impeccable glory. The time for impartial judgment will not come for many years." And in the harbor of Stockholm flags hung at half-mast on all ships. Excitement and sorrow rooted partly in Swedish sentiment over the victory of the *Monitor,* designed by John Ericsson and carrying guns invented by Admiral John Adolph Dahlgren. One observer wrote: "Our men clenched their fists in vain fury and our blue-eyed women shed many tears in memory of the remarkable man." In the harbors of Norwegian cities also flags were at half-mast. Thousands in that country had blood relations in Wisconsin and Minnesota regiments. Young Henrik Ibsen in a flowing turbulent poem, "The Murder of Abraham Lincoln," challenged Europe's right to mourn over the passing of the foremost son of democracy in the Western world.

In the Orient, China, Japan and Siam framed resolutions of condolence. To the four corners of the earth began the spread of the Lincoln story and legend. What he seemed to mean was reached for, Russia's Leo Tolstoy saying Lincoln had become a world folk legend through "peculiar moral powers and greatness of character . . . He was what Beethoven was in music, Dante in poetry, Raphael in painting and Christ in the philosophy of life. If he had failed to become President, he would be no doubt just as great, but only God could appreciate it." Of all great national heroes and statesmen of history Tolstoy was to say to the journalist James Creelman, "Lincoln is the only real giant." He named heroes but they were lesser than Lincoln "in depth of feeling and in certain moral power." Mystic shadows and a bright aura gathered around Lincoln's memory for the famous Russian. "Lincoln was . . . a Christ in miniature, a saint of humanity whose name will live thousands of years in the legends of future generations. We are still too near his greatness, and so can hardly appreciate his divine power; but after a few centuries more our posterity will find him considerably bigger than we do."

Lincoln, in Emerson's analysis, grew according to need. In the whirlwind of the war he was "no holiday magistrate, no fair-weather sailor . . . He is the true history of the

American people in his time. Step by step he walked before them; slow with their slowness, quickening his march by theirs, the true representative of this continent; an entirely public man; father of his country."

The suave diplomat John Bigelow believed that in ordinary peacetime conditions Lincoln would have been a very ordinary President. In a wild crisis calling for a man deep in moral issues, the nation found Lincoln "even as the son of Kish found a crown while searching for his father's asses." His greatness was peculiar. "He was so modest by nature that he was perfectly content to walk behind any man who wished to walk before him . . . St. Paul hardly endured more indignities and buffetings without complaint."

Lincoln had stood as the national Fate, amid violence that was the shortest cut to a common Union of destiny for the states. Thus the Brazilian Minister Joaquin Nabuco who said, "I construe to myself that War as one of those illusions of life, in which men seem to move of their own free will, while they are really playing a tragedy composed by a Providence intent on saving their nation." Lincoln, as the leading player in the drama, "saw distinctly that the South was not a nationality, and that it could not think of being one, except during the hallucination of the crisis." In the velocities of modern change, the year 2000 would be governed by currents of political thought impossible to read. "But, whether the spirit of authority, or that of freedom, increases, Lincoln's legend will ever appear more luminous in the amalgamation of centuries, because he supremely incarnated both those spirits."

Walt Whitman would have blossoms and green branches piled on the coffin—armfuls of roses fresh as the morning —in loaded arms sprigs of lilac just off the bushes—brought and poured on the coffin. He would study sea-blown cities and moving harbor ships, the changing lights of the Ohio River shores and the flashing bosom of the wide Missouri, far-spreading prairies covered with grass and corn—he would in his psalm bring these to the coffin. He would consider the miracle of light so gentle and soft-born from the most excellent sun so calm and haughty—evening and the welcome of night and the stars—these too he would carry along in a threnody of praise to death—lovely and soothing death—the sure-enwinding arms of cool-enfolding death. He had listened to a hermit thrush singing in solemn shadowy cedars and still ghostly pines—under the evening star a carol of death with praise of its serene arrival and its husky whispering to "the huge and thoughtful night." This too he would bring to the coffin as his offertory and benediction, his chant of sane and sacred death. He gave it the title "When Lilacs Last in the Dooryard Bloom'd," in a closing line inscribing it "for the sweetest, wisest soul of all my days and lands—and this for his dear sake."

In thousands of commentaries Lincoln incarnated two results—Emancipation and Union. Two causes directed by Lincoln had won the war. Gone was the property status of the Negro, gone the doctrine of secession and states' rights. Black men could now move from where they were miserable to where they were equally miserable—now it was lawful for them to move. Now too for the Negro no longer was it a crime for him to be found reading a book nor was it any longer a crime to teach a Negro to read.

Now, too, as Lincoln had pledged, a whole mesh of trammels and clamps on Western migration were to be cut loose. The many homesteaders held back by political bickering could get going. And the Union Pacific railway could begin laying its rails; the jealousies suffocating it were out. With almost explosive force the industrial, financial and transportation systems of the North could be let loose, free to go. The war had done that. Now also, as a result flowing from the war, the United States was to take its place among nations counted World Powers. And as a World Power the expectation was it would be a voice of the teachings of Washington, Jefferson, Jackson—and Lincoln—speaking for republican government, for democracy.

Out of the smoke and stench, out of the music and violet dreams of the war, Lincoln stood perhaps taller than any other of the many great heroes. This was in the mind of many. None threw a longer shadow than he. And to him the great hero was The People. He could not say too often that he was merely their instrument.

Chapter 53

Vast Pageant, Then Great Quiet

In the East Room of the White House lay the body of a man, embalmed and prepared for a journey. On a platform under a canopy of folds and loops of black silk and crape rested the coffin. Tassels, shamrock leaves, silver stars and silver cords could be seen on facings and edges. A shield with a silver plate had the inscription:

Abraham Lincoln
Sixteenth President of the United States
Born Feb. 12, 1809
Died April 15, 1865

It was Tuesday, April 18, and outside surged the largest mass of people that had ever thronged the White House lawn, the estimate 25,000. In two columns they filed through the East Room, moving along the two sides of the coffin, many pale and limping soldiers out of the convalescent wards of the hospitals, many women and children sobbing and weeping aloud as they passed, pausing only the slightest moment for a look.

On Wednesday, April 19, arrived 60 clergymen, the Cabinet members, the Supreme Court Justices, important officials, foreign Ministers, General Grant with white sash across his breast, the new President Andrew Johnson—600 dignitaries in all. Mrs. Lincoln was still too distracted to be present, but Robert Lincoln came.

Bishop Matthew Simpson of the Methodist Episcopal

church offered prayer that smitten hearts might endure, might not be called upon for further sacrifices. A bitter cup from the hand of a chastening Divine Father had been given the mourning nation, said the Reverend Dr. Phineas D. Gurley in the funeral address. "His way is in the sea, and His path in the great waters; and His footsteps are not known . . . We bow, we weep, we worship . . . We will wait for His interpretation . . . He may purify us more in the furnace of trial, but He will not consume us."

The closing invocation was spoken by a Baptist clergyman, chaplain of the U.S. Senate, the Reverend Dr. E. H. Gray. The final ceremonial words spoken in the White House over the mute form of the author of the second inaugural and the Louisiana reconstruction speech of April 11 were: "O God, let treason, that has deluged our land with blood, and devastated our country, and bereaved our homes, and filled them with widows and orphans, and has at length culminated in the assassination of the nation's chosen ruler—God of justice, and avenger of the nation's wrong, let the work of treason cease, and let the guilty author of this horrible crime be arrested and brought to justice."

The services were over. The pallbearers took the silver handles. The bong of big bells on cathedrals struck and the little bells of lesser steeples chimed in, as across the spring sunshine came the tolling of all the church bells of Washington and Georgetown, and Alexandria across the river. Counting the minutes with their salutes came the hoarse boom of fort guns encircling the national capital and several batteries sent into the city.

Out of the great front door of the Executive Mansion for the last time went the mortal shape of Abraham Lincoln, 16th President of the United States. On the one-mile route to the Capitol, pavements and curbs were packed with onlookers, who also filled every roof, window, doorway, balcony and stairway. Sixty thousand spectators watched a parade of 40,000 mourners. From his sickbed, sore with his dagger wounds, Secretary Seward gazed from the window with mingled grief and thanks.

In the rotunda of the Capitol, under the great white dome that had come to its finished construction while the war raged, 12 sergeants of the Veteran Reserve Corps carried the coffin to a huge catafalque.

In silence during night watches the body of Lincoln lay with eyes never opening to see far above him the arches of the great dome that for him symbolized the Union. In the night watches while the guard mount changed, whispering, quiet on soft feet, into midnight and past into daybreak, midway between House and Senate chambers, midway between those seats and aisles of heartbreak and passion, he lay a horizontal clay tabernacle.

In the morning at ten o'clock the doors opened in special consideration for wounded soldiers from the hospitals, weak and battered men, some with empty sleeves, others on crutches, to file by. Afterward came the public, at times 3,000 to the hour, before midnight 25,000 persons.

Friday morning, April 21, saw the coffin placed aboard a special burial car at the Washington depot. Railroad-yard engine bells tolled and a far-stretching crowd stood with uncovered heads as the train of seven cars moved out of Washington for Baltimore.

This was the start of a funeral journey that was to take the lifeless body on a 1,700-mile route which included practically the same points and stops that the living form had made four years and two months before on the way to the first inauguration. Aboard the coaches were five men who had made that earlier journey: Colonel Ward Hill Lamon, Justice David Davis, General David Hunter, John G. Nicolay and John Hay. A committee of Senate and House members included Washburne, Yates and Arnold of Illinois, Harlan of Iowa and Julian of Indiana. Mrs. Lincoln, Robert and Tad were to undergo an ordeal; with them was their kinsman Ninian W. Edwards. The Illinois delegation aboard included Lincoln's first law partner John T. Stuart and such Sucker State familiars as Lyman Trumbull, William Bross, Jesse K. Dubois, Shelby M. Cullom and General John A. McClernand. Among state governors aboard were Oglesby of Illinois, Morton of Indiana, Brough of Ohio, Stone of Iowa.

Baltimore wore mourning everywhere and paid reverence; the human outpouring was unmistakable. More than surface changes had come to Maryland in the four furnace years. As the funeral train moved slowly over Pennsylvania soil, at lonely country crossroads were people and faces, horsemen, farmers with their wives and children, standing where they had stood for hours before, waiting, performing the last little possible act of ceremony and attention and love— with solemn faces and uncovered heads standing and gazing as the funeral car passed. In villages and small towns stood waiting crowds, sometimes with a little silver cornet band, often with flowers in hope the train might stop and they could leave camellias, roses, lilies-of-the-valley, wreaths of color and perfume. At York in a short stop six ladies came aboard and laid a three-foot wreath of red and white roses on the coffin.

Through heavy rains at Harrisburg came 30,000 in the night and morning to see the coffin in circles of white flowering almond. At noon on Saturday, April 22, in Philadelphia a half-million people were on hand for the funeral train. In Independence Hall stood the coffin. Outside the line of mourners ran three miles. "A young lady had her arm broken," said the New York *Herald*, "and a young child, involved in the crush, is said to have been killed. Many females fainted with exhaustion, and had to be carried off by their friends." Besides doors, through two windows in a double column a third of a million people entered and passed by the casket. A venerable Negro woman, her face indented and majestic as a relief map of the continent of Asia, laid evergreen on the coffin and with hot tears filling the dents and furrows, cried, "Oh, Abraham Lincoln, are you dead? Are you dead?" She could not be sure.

At Newark, New Jersey, on the morning of April 24 the train moved slowly amid acres of people, a square mile of them. At Jersey City was a like scene. The Empire State formally received the body from Governor Parker of New

Jersey. A hearse moved through street crowds. The ferry-boat *Jersey City* moved across the Hudson River, neared the wharf at Desbrosses Street. The Seventh Regiment National Guard formed a hollow square into which moved the funeral cortege. The procession marched to the City Hall through streets packed to capacity.

Never before, so everyone agreed, had New York put on such garb and completely changed its look so that it seemed another city. On the marble and brownstone fronts, in the ramshackle tenements of "those who live from hand to mouth," came out crape or black folds or drapery or black muslin, rosettes, sable emblems, what the news reporters termed "the habiliments of mourning."

From near noon Monday, April 24, to noon the next day the remains of Abraham Lincoln, horizontal amid white satin, lay in the City Hall. A vast outpouring of people hour by hour passed by to see this effigy and remembrance of his face and form. They came for many and varied reasons. Hundreds who had helped wreck, burn and loot this city, killing scores of policemen and Negroes in the draft and race riots of year before last, came now with curiosity, secret triumph, hate and contempt, a story traveling Manhattan that one entered a saloon hangout of their breed, saying, "I went down to the City Hall to see with my own eyes and be sure he was dead." An overwhelming many came as an act of faith and attestation; they had come to love him and follow him. The few women who sought to kiss his face were hurriedly moved on by the guards. Each might have had some sufficient reason; most of the boys at Malvern Hill and Gettysburg had mothers.

At noon on Tuesday, April 25, a procession moved from the City Hall to Ninth Avenue and the Hudson River Railroad depot. Nearly every race, nationality, religion, political faith, was represented among those who marched, near 100,000. The troops in Union Army blue alone numbered 20,000. The panoramic show took hours. It was massive, bizarre, spectacular, dazzling—yet somber. A hundred thousand strangers had come to New York to see it. The sidewalk, street, curb and window spectators ran perhaps to a million. At the procession's end came a delegation of 2,000 Negroes, some wearing the Union Army service blue. There had been mutterings from a draft- and race-riot element that they would "never let the damned niggers march." This would have interested the man in the hearse, could he have heard it. It was customary and expected. A telegram to General Dix spoke plain that the Secretary of War desired "no discrimination respecting color." And it was so ordered. At the Union Square exercises following the parade the Roman Catholic Archbishop McCloskey pronounced the benediction, Rabbi Isaacs of the Jewish Synagogue read from their scriptures, the Reverend Stephen H. Syng of St. George's Church offered a prayer, the Reverend J. P. Thompson intoned Lincoln's second inaugural. Evening had come.

An epidemic of verse seized thousands. They sent their rhymed lines to the New York *Herald,* which publicly notified them that if it were all printed there would be no space for news, wherefore none at all would be printed. The Chicago *Tribune* editorially notified them it "suffered" from this "severe attack of poetry," that three days brought 160 pieces beginning either "Toll, toll, ye mourning bells" or "Mourn, mourn, ye tolling bells."

Up the Hudson River east bank the night of April 25 chugged the train of seven cars. On every mile of the route to Albany those on the train could see bonfires and torches, could hear bells and cannon and guns, could see forms of people and white sorry faces. Past midnight of April 25 into the morning hours of April 26 the columns of mourners passed the coffin in Albany.

On this morning of April 26, hunted like a wild beast and cornered like a rat, his broken shinbone betraying him, J. Wilkes Booth met his end. Near Bowling Green, Virginia, in a burning barn set afire from the outside, a bullet drove through his neck bone "perforating both sides of the collar," and he was dragged away from reaching flames and laid under a tree. Water was given him. He revived, to murmur from parched lips, "Tell my mother—I died —for my country." He was carried to a house veranda, there muttering, "I thought I did for the best." He lingered for a time. A doctor came. Wilkes Booth asked that his hands might be raised so that he could look at them. So it was told. And as he looked on his hands, he mumbled hoarsely, "Useless! useless!" And those were his last words.

Across the Empire State that day and night it was mural monotone of mourning, the Erie Canal zone in sober grief with evergreens, flowers, sable emblems. The endless multitudinous effect became colossal. Thirty-six young ladies, gowned in white with black shoulder scarfs and the flag of their country, approached the dazzling when seen for the first time. But when seen and noted the 20th, 30th, 40th time, they took on a ritualist solemnity smoldering and portentous. Involved was the basis of the stubborn passion that had carried on four years of the bloodiest war known to mankind.

At Buffalo Millard Fillmore, one of the three living ex-Presidents of the United States, attended the funeral, which also was witnessed by the youth Grover Cleveland.

Reports had been published that the face in the coffin was shrunken and decayed to such an extent that perhaps good taste should forbid further exposure of it to public gaze. The embalmer on the train had several times by his craft wrought improvement. However this might be, there came from Toledo an old friend and a valued comforter of Lincoln, David R. Locke, who wrote under the pen name of Petroleum V. Nasby. He wrote now: "I saw him, or what was mortal of him in his coffin. The face had an expression of absolute content, of relief, at throwing off a burden such as few men have been called upon to bear—a burden which few men could have borne. I had seen the same expression on his living face only a few times, when, after a great calamity, he had come to a great victory. It was the look of a worn man suddenly relieved. Wilkes Booth did Abraham Lincoln the greatest service man could possibly do for him—he gave him peace."

At Cleveland the committee on arrangements had a pagoda put up in the city park, with open sides through which two columns could pass the coffin. Over the coffin

Bishop Charles Pettit McIlvaine read from the Episcopal burial service. At ten o'clock when the park gates were shut it was said that more than 1,000,000 pilgrims from northern Ohio had paid their homage. A lashing wind drove torrents of rain as the night procession moved escorting the hearse through crowded streets to the depot.

From Cleveland to Crestline the rain kept on in torrents. Nevertheless at all towns and crossroads were the mourners, with uncovered heads, with torches and flags crossed with black. Five miles out from Columbus stood an old woman alone as the slow train came by, tears coursing down her furrowed cheeks. In her right hand she held out a black mourning scarf. With her left hand she stretched imploringly toward the rain-and-storm-bedraggled funeral car, reaching and waving toward it her handful of wild flowers, her bouquet and token.

In the rotunda of Ohio's capitol, on a mound of green moss dotted with white flowers, rested the coffin on April 28, while 8,000 persons passed by each hour from 9:30 in the morning till four in the afternoon. In the changing red-gold of a rolling prairie sunset, to the slow exultation of brasses rendering "Old Hundred" and the muffled booming of minute guns, the coffin was carried out of the rotunda and taken to the funeral train. It was now two weeks since the evening hour that Abraham Lincoln cheery and alive had left the White House in Washington to attend a performance in Ford's Theatre, and from his carriage had taken a final casual glance at the Executive Mansion where he had lived four years and 41 days.

The slow night run from Columbus to Indianapolis saw from the car windows a countryside of people thronging to the route of the coffin. At Pleasant Valley were bonfires. Nearly every town had its arch of evergreens, flags and black drapings. At Urbana ten young women strewed roses on the coffin, one of them breaking down in uncontrollable tears. At Piqua were 10,000 at midnight; at Richmond, Indiana, 10,000 again at three o'clock in the morning.

Tolling bells and falling rain at Indianapolis saw the coffin borne into the State House for a Sabbath to be remembered. On the slow night run to Chicago it was as in Ohio, thousands in Lafayette standing mute and daybreak not yet, thousands more at Michigan City. Now over flat lands ran the slow train, between it and the blue levels of Lake Michigan the long slopes of pine-crept dunes.

The day was Monday, May 1, but in effect the Chicago obsequies had begun the day before when Speaker Colfax delivered in Bryant Hall a formal funeral oration. To his portrait of Lincoln as the most forgiving of men Colfax joined allegations of Confederate atrocities: they had at Bull Run buried Union soldiers face downward and carved their bones into trinkets; they had wickedly and systematically starved Union prisoners to death. Colfax was for his own purposes still fomenting war hate and metaphorically waving a bloody shirt of incitation.

In the changed tone of the Chicago *Times* could be read the fact that among those who would gaze into the Lincoln coffin with a sincere grief this day would be at least a remnant of Copperheads. "There are not on this day mourners more sincere than the democracy of the Northern States. Widely as they have differed with Mr. Lincoln . . . they saw in the indications of the last few days of his life that he might command their support."

By railway train, by wagon or buggy and on horseback, something like 100,000 people had come into Chicago from all points of the Northwest. The vocal attempts at solemn grief often failed and were overdone. But there was a silent grief—broken only by choked snufflings, by low wailing, by almost inaudible moans—a loss afraid of words. There was a curious dumb sorrow, perhaps deeper than any other.

Slowly at Twelfth Street and Michigan Avenue the funeral train came to a stop. A procession of 50,000 people, witnessed by double as many, escorted the hearse to the courthouse. Not hitherto, however, had any Confederate soldiers marched—though here was a regiment of Confederate prisoners of war who had taken the oath of allegiance and aligned themselves for Union service. In the line of march and looking on, sharing something common, were native-born Yankees and Mayflower descendants, Sons and Daughters of the Revolution, Jews, Negroes, Catholics, Germans, Irishmen, Dutchmen, Swedes, Norwegians, Danes —the so-called "big bugs" and the so-called "ragtag and bobtail" for once in a common front.

A drizzle of rain fell, the streets slushy with a slippery mud. Occasionally planks or supporting two-by-fours of the wooden sidewalks crashed with spectators. Women fainted and two-horse ambulances came. Barkeepers were busy. So were pickpockets. The police-station cells were filled. Considering the extent of the swarming human crush, however, the day was orderly, even sedate.

All night long Monday, and through the early morning hours and all the day hours of Tuesday, the columns moved in and out of the courthouse. An estimated 125,000 people had taken their last glance at the Man from Illinois. A thousand men with blazing torches escorted the coffin to the funeral car for the slow night run to Springfield on the Alton Railroad.

At Joliet were midnight torches, evergreen arches, 12,000 people. Every town and village, many a crossroads and lonely farm, spoke its mournful salutation. Here and there an arch or a depot doorway had the short flash "Come Home."

Then at last home to Springfield. In the state capitol where he had spoken his prophet warnings of the House Divided, stood the casket. Now passed those who had known him long, part of the 75,000 who came. They were awed, subdued, shaken, stony, strange. They came from Salem, Petersburg, Clary's Grove, Alton, Charleston, Mattoon, the old Eighth Circuit towns and villages. There were clients for whom he had won or lost, lawyers who had tried cases with him and against, neighbors who had seen him milk a cow and curry his horse, friends who had heard his stories around a hot stove and listened to his surmises on politics and religion. All day long and through the night the unbroken line moved, the home town having its farewell.

On May 4 of this year 1865 anno Domini a procession

moved with its hearse from the state capitol to Oak Ridge
Cemetery. There on green banks and hillsides flowing away
from a burial vault the crowded thousands of listeners and
watchers heard prayers and hymns, heard the second inaugural read aloud. Bishop Matthew Simpson in a moving
oration spoke as an interpreter and foreteller: "There are
moments which involve in themselves eternities. There are
instants which seem to contain germs which shall develop
and bloom forever. Such a moment came in the tide of time
to our land when a question must be settled, affecting all
the powers of the earth. The contest was for human freedom. Not for this republic merely, not for the Union
simply, but to decide whether the people, as a people, in
their entire majesty, were destined to be the Governments
or whether they were to be subject to tyrants or aristocrats,
or to class rule of any kind. This is the great question for
which we have been fighting, and its decision is at hand,
and the result of this contest will affect the ages to come.
If successful, republics will spread in spite of monarchs
all over this earth." Came then from the people, noted the
Illinois State Journal, exclamations of "Amen! thank God!"

Evergreen carpeted the stone floor of the vault. On the
coffin set in a receptacle of black walnut they arranged
flowers carefully and precisely, they poured flowers as sym-
bols, they lavished heaps of fresh flowers as though there
could never be enough to tell either their hearts or his.

And the night came with great quiet.

And there was rest.

The prairie years, the war years, were over.

SOURCES AND ACKNOWLEDGMENTS

The chief center of the research on the life of Lincoln before he became President was the Abraham Lincoln Association with its office in Springfield, Illinois, with funds subscribed by a national membership and with outside grants. From 1933 through 1941 the Association published four volumes, each giving "the day-by-day activities of Abraham Lincoln," where he was and what he was doing, so far as known by documents. Harry Pratt's two volumes, *Lincoln Day by Day 1809-1839* and *1840-1846,* are followed by Benjamin P. Thomas' for *1847-1853* and by Paul Angle's for *1854-1861*—the four books making a massive, formidable work that will be of use as long as there are sober and anxious students of Lincoln. Approaching the colossal is the nine-volume edition sponsored by the Association, published in 1953, *The Collected Works of Abraham Lincoln.* Heavy, exacting and thorough were the five-year labors of Roy P. Basler, editor, and Marion Dolores Pratt and Lloyd A. Dunlap, assistant editors. Their texts of letters, speeches, documents, are from originals or photostats of originals, except in a few instances which they report and discuss. This carefully documented assemblage of Lincoln utterance is possibly the best historical account by any one man on how and why the titanic war of 1861-1865 arose and was carried through. This utterance record of more than a million words holds the keys or clues to the subtle, wide-ranging personality of Lincoln more than any other work to be read and studied. A large one-volume compilation with an able biographical introduction is *The Life and Writings of Abraham Lincoln* (1940) by Philip Van Doren Stern. The most useful, well-annotated single volume in this field is *Abraham Lincoln: His Speeches and Writings* (1946) by Roy P. Basler.

From the Abraham Lincoln Association group and its associates came monographs revealing forgeries of four Lincoln letters printed earlier in books of reputation; they published evidence that the marble-enshrined log cabin at Hodgenville, Kentucky, is not the real and actual birth-cabin of Lincoln but rests on a tissue of traditions; they re-examined the legend of Ann Rutledge and Lincoln, made a strong case that the "romance" rested on conjecture and assumption while the often related grief and borderline insanity of Lincoln at her death were improbable. The Association reproduced in facsimile in 1938 a campaign biography, *Life of Abraham Lincoln* by W. D. Howells, with 14 corrections made by Lincoln's pencil in the summer of 1860; the value of such a book is in the corrections written in it and also in the bulk of statements that Lincoln let stand as fact.

Benjamin P. Thomas' book, *Lincoln's New Salem* (1934), brought to bear his long familiarity with that frontier community; it is the classic on Lincoln's "Alma Mater." Paul M. Angle's *Here I Have Lived: A History of Lincoln's Springfield 1821-1865* (1935) is a master report on Lincoln's home town. William E. Baringer's three volumes, *Lincoln's Vandalia* (1949), *Lincoln's Rise to Power* (1935), *A House Dividing* (1945), represent fresh research, especially on Lincoln in the Illinois Legislature and the intricacies of politics leading to Lincoln's nomination for President in 1860. A research not made thitherto appears in Donald W. Riddle's *Lincoln Runs for Congress* (1948). Harry Pratt's *Concerning Mr. Lincoln: In Which Abraham Lincoln Is Pictured as He Appeared to Letter Writers of His Time* (1944) gives swift and fleeting personal glimpses of Lincoln. Pratt's larger work, *Personal Finances of Abraham Lincoln* (1943), covers more ground than any previous studies of Lincoln's earnings and spendings and his sense about money. From the Abraham Lincoln Association, disbanded in 1953, for nearly 30 years there poured forth bulletins, books, a quarterly magazine, threshing out major and minor phases of the Lincoln story. Logan Hay, who died in 1942, is cherished as the founder and an ever-dynamic force in the Association.

All of the aforementioned books and publications came to print since I was writing *Abraham Lincoln: The Prairie Years*. Also in this period have come the important volumes of James G. Randall, *Lincoln the President: From Springfield to Gettysburg*, two volumes (1945) and *Lincoln the President: Midstream* (1952), this latter one of the most profound and charming studies of Lincoln. His *Lincoln and the South* (1945) and *Lincoln the Liberal Statesman* (1947) hold his keenly searching popular lectures and essays. And it happened that "Jim" Randall, greatly beloved, constantly an inspirational force in the field of Lincoln study, was himself taken away midstream of his great work. His widow, Ruth Painter Randall, published *Mary Lincoln: Biography of a Marriage* (1953), the most elaborately and scrupulously documented narrative of the girl who became wife and widow of Lincoln. There came from David Donald a skilled and brilliant book, *Lincoln's Herndon* (1948), the first book-length biography of Lincoln's law partner for 16 years. *Diplomat in Carpet Slippers* (1945) was Jay Monaghan's floodlight on Lincoln amid foreign affairs. *Lincoln and the Patronage* (1943) by Harry J. Carman and Reinhard H. Luthin has in extensive documented detail, in wide coverage, the appetites, connivings, whispers, howls of American politics and Lincoln at center. *Lincoln and the Press* (1951) by Robert S. Harper shows the uses of printer's ink in support, praise and defamation of an American President. *Lincoln and the War Governors* (1948) by William B. Hesseltine presents the state executives with whose co-operation or antagonism Lincoln had to deal. Margaret Leech's *Reveille in Washington: 1860-1865* (1941) is a pageant of scandal, drama, heroism, vividly written.

Lawyer Lincoln (1936) by Albert A. Woldman is an advance on former treatments of Lincoln in law practice, his *Lincoln and the Russians* (1952) presenting diplomats, letters, reports. *The First Lincoln Campaign* (1944) by Reinhard H. Luthin is an original and distinctive contribution stressing the economic factors and political personalities that clashed or interwove to make Lincoln the most "available" candidate for President in 1860. Again original and distinctive, probing deep among motives, is David M. Potter's *Lincoln and His Party in the Secession Crisis* (1942). T. Harry Williams is enlightening and worth scrutiny in *Lincoln and the Radicals* (1941) and *Lincoln and His Generals* (1952). The suave, breezy, eloquent, scrupulous Kentuckian William H. Townsend, has given us *Lincoln and Liquor* (1934) and *Lincoln in His Wife's Home Town* (1929), besides monographs of value. The objective viewpoints of a distinguished physician are in Dr. William A. Evans' *Mrs. Abraham Lincoln: A Study of Her Personality* (1932). A professor of mathematics, a veteran of two wars, Kenneth P. Williams was fully authorized to write his massive two-volume documented study, *Lincoln Finds a General* (1950). Independent and well written is Bruce Catton's *Mr. Lincoln's Army* (1951). Fletcher Pratt's *Stanton* (1953) is a military history of the war with Stanton as a central figure. John E. Washington in *They Knew Lincoln* (1942) sketches "Billy the Barber" and other Negroes in the personal life of Lincoln. George S. Bryan's *The Great American Myth* (1940) is a re-examination of facts and inventions regarding the murder of Lincoln. *The Mad Booths of Maryland* (1940) by Stanley Kimmel renders in wealth of detail the family and environment from which came Lincoln's assassin. The meditations of an idealist in poetry and philosophy are in T. V. Smith's *Abraham Lincoln and the Spiritual Life* (1951). The new biographies, Francis Brown's *Raymond of the Times* and Helen Nicolay's *Lincoln's Secretary* (1949) have their close-ups of Lincoln, as also does the five-million word *Diary of George Templeton Strong* (1952) edited by Allan Nevins. Basic as document and highly readable is *Lincoln and the Civil War in Diaries and Letters of John Hay* (1939) by Tyler Dennett. The controversial *Herndon's Lincoln: the True Story of a Great Life* (1889) in three volumes by William H. Herndon and Jesse W. Weik became available in a one-volume edition in 1930 with an introduction and notes by Paul M. Angle which make it the one Herndon edition most worth reading. Albert J. Beveridge died in 1927 before midstream of his two volumes published in 1928, *Abraham Lincoln: 1809-1858*. Emanuel Hertz died in 1940 shortly after publication of *The Hidden Lincoln* and *Lincoln Talks*. Oliver R. Barrett died seven months after my book, *Lincoln Collector,* was published in praise of his zeal and intelligence, its pages holding now some of the unity of his notable collection later auctioned. William E. Barton died in 1930, a year after the publication of *The Lineage of Lincoln,* a book two-fifths documents chiefly related to Lincoln kinfolk. The 1860-1861 New York *Herald* newsletters of Henry Villard, with deletions, are in *Lincoln on the Eve of '61* (1941). In *The American Iliad,* Otto Eisenschiml and Ralph Newman give a narrative of the Civil War by selected eyewitnesses and contemporaries. Eisenschiml's *In the Shadow of Lincoln's Death* (1940) relentlessly asks grim unanswerable questions. In *Legends that Libel Lincoln* (1946), Montgomery S. Lewis throws corrective light on three major libels. *Lincoln's War Cabinet* (1946) is a competent study by Burton J. Hendrick. George Fort Milton's *Abraham Lincoln and the Fifth Column* (1942) covers wide ground as to "Copperheads" and treasonable activities in the North. An elusive sweetheart flits through the pages of *Lincoln's Other Mary* (1946), the facts by R. Gerald McMurtry, the fiction by Olive Carruthers.

Benjamin P. Thomas, a trained historian, a resident of Springfield familiar with all the streets and roads most often traveled by Lincoln, personally acquainted with descendants of characters who figured in Lincoln's life, in 1952 published his one-volume *Abraham Lincoln.* As a narrative and close-up portrait of Lincoln it makes use of all early source materials and also the later accumulations which he often saw in manuscript before their publication; he was one of the most active workers, and at one time secretary of the Abraham Lincoln Association. Thomas is out of Midwest soil and long broodings over Lincoln. Closing his book, he soberly affirms Lincoln: "Only with the slow march of time would it be given to most of his countrymen to understand the supreme meaning of his life . . . Because to him the American people were the leaders of an awakening of plain people the world over." When he was writing his one-volume Lincoln I told him, "If or when I get written and published a one-volume Lincoln, I hope and believe the two books will stand on the Lincoln shelf as good companions supplementing each other."

None of the foregoing books had been published at the time I was writing *Abraham Lincoln: The Prairie Years*. Most of them have seen publication since I wrote *Abraham Lincoln: The War Years*. All of them, however, have been used in the preparation of this one volume, for corrections or added lights. I have also used the files of *The Journal* of the Illinois State Historical Society, the Lincoln Memorial University's *Lincoln Herald*, the periodicals *Lincoln Lore* and *The Lincoln Kinsman* written by Louis A. Warren. To the stream of Lincoln source materials was added in 1941 the Herndon-Weik papers made available by Library of Congress purchase, and in 1947 the Robert T. Lincoln collection, a bequest to the Library. From the latter collection in 1948 came from David Mearns two volumes, *The Lincoln Papers*, with selections covering 1809 to July 4, 1861. A reader of these can step back into a generation of vanished Americans and see them in speaking likenesses, a variety of fine persons and odd fools.

In the preface to *The Prairie Years* I mentioned the Daniel Fish bibliography in 1906 listing 1,080 books and pamphlets about Lincoln and that of J. B. Oakleaf in 1925 listing 1,600 items. In 1945, however, came Jay Monaghan's listing of 3,958 items. By now, in 1954, there are more than 4,000 books and pamphlets dealing principally with Abraham Lincoln, his ancestry, wife and kin, even excluding such sources as the indispensable Welles and Browning diaries which deal with Lincoln incidentally. In 13 pages of a foreword to *The War Years* are enumerated and evaluated the array of source materials used in the writing of those four volumes.

The Blue and the Gray: the Story of the Civil War as

Told by Participants, two volumes (1950), by Henry Steele Commager is a procession of witnesses and documents, Douglas Southall Freeman joining with others to attest its author as extraordinarily well equipped to present "a history of the Civil War in the words of those who fought it." The background of national events, the storms and the quiet between storms through which the American people moved from the 1847 Congress in which Lincoln had a seat to the 1861 inauguration of Lincoln, are presented as a moving panorama in Allan Nevins' *The Ordeal of the Union,* two volumes (1947), and *The Emergence of Lincoln,* two volumes (1950). These books embody vivid writing and vast research in original sources; they are important if not imperatively requisite for those who seek to know more concretely the wild onrushes of violent events along with quietly inexorable streams of invention, migration, territorial expansion, of those 14 years; they were shaping the national scene where Lincoln was fated to play the somber and leading role.

James O'Donnell Bennett's *Private Joe Fifer* (1936) quotes that Civil War soldier and governor of Illinois as having from Milton Hay the saying of Lincoln, "You can fool some of the people all of the time and all of the people some of the time but you can't fool all of the people all of the time," Fifer adding, "In 1894, after my term as governor, I made a speech in Piatt County, this state, in which I repeated what Milt Hay had told me. The speech was printed in the St. Louis *Globe-Democrat,* the Chicago *Inter-Ocean* and other papers and thus the saying was first given publicity. None of the Lincoln biographers had ever discovered it."

In 1946 came *A Shelf of Lincoln Books* by Paul M. Angle, "a critical, selective bibliography of Lincolniana." He lists and evaluates 81 basic items, reporting their now generally accepted merits and deficiencies. Ralph Newman of the Abraham Lincoln Bookshop in Chicago lists 100 titles of the books he regards as most indispensable to the Lincoln student. In 1947 came Benjamin P. Thomas' *Portrait for Posterity,* a stormy, intensely human story of the procession of Lincoln biographers, their toils, hopes and miseries, their disputes, quarrels and quandaries. Thomas quotes from hundreds of letters they wrote. The book interweaves plots and characters into one of the strangest stories in American literary history. Thomas concludes: "The realist's ruthless searching gives the necessary facts. Yet the realist is ill-advised to scorn the idealist's sensitivity to those soul-qualities of Lincoln which documentary facts alone may not disclose."

END OF VOLUME III

Index